The Author

Chris Prouty is a graduate of Antioch College,
Ohio. She began studying Ethiopian history
when her husband, Eugene Rosenfeld, was
assigned by the U.S. Information Service to
Addis Ababa, after posts in India and Tanzania.
A Chronology of Menilek II: 1844-1913 was
published by the African Studies Center,
Michigan State University, in 1976, and the
Historical Dictionary of Ethiopia, co-authored
with Eugene Rosenfeld, was published by
Scarecrow Press in 1981. She is a member of
the Society of Women Geographers, the African
Studies Association, the Ethiopian Studies
Association, Friends of Ethiopia and the Société
Francaise pour les Etudes Ethiopiennes.

Dedicated to Seble Desta
and all Ethiopian women
who are either in prison or
struggling in the prison of poverty

Empress Taytu
and Menilek II
Ethiopia 1883~1910

Chris Prouty

RAVENS EDUCATIONAL &
DEVELOPMENT SERVICES
27 Old Gloucester Street
London WC1N 3XX

THE RED SEA PRESS
Publishers & Distributors of Third World Books
556 Bellevue Avenue
Trenton, New Jersey 08618

Empress Taytu and Menilek II: Ethiopia 1883-1910
was first published by

Ravens Educational and Development Services
London

ISBN 0-947895-01-9

and by

The Red Sea Press
556 Bellevue Avenue
Trenton, New Jersey 08618

ISBN 0-932415-10-5 (Hb)
ISBN 0-932415-11-3 (Pb)

Produced by Millennia Limited
Box 20631, Hennessy Road Post Office, Hong Kong

Cover designed by Rosanne Chan
Printed and bound in Hong Kong

Contents

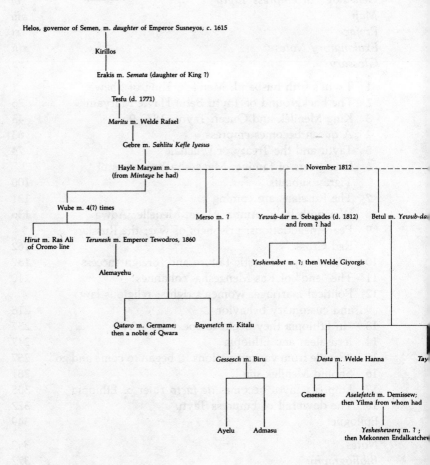

SEMEN LINE

Helos, governor of Semen, m. *daughter* of Emperor Susneyos, *c.* 1615

Kirillos

Erakis m. *Semata* (daughter of King ?)

Tesfu (d. 1771)

Maritu m. Welde Rafael

Gebre m. *Sahlitu Kefle Iyesus*

Hayle Maryam m. _ November 1812 _ _ _ _ _
(from *Mintaye* he had)

Wube m. 4(?) times   Merso m. ?   *Yewub-dar* m. Sebagades (d. 1812)   Betul m. *Yewub-da*
                                      and from ? had

Hirut m. Ras Ali   *Terunesh* m. Emperor Tewodros, 1860   *Yeshemabet* m. ?; then Welde Giyorgis
of Oromo line

Alemayehu

Qataro m. Germame;   *Bayenetch* m. Kitalu   *Desta* m. Welde Hanna   *Tay*
then a noble of Qwara

Gessesch m. Biru

Gessesse   *Aselefetch* m. Demissew;
            then Yilma from whom had

Ayelu   Admasu   *Yesheshewerq* m. ? ;
                   then Mekonnen Endalkatche

Women said to be related to *Taytu*   *sister named *Askala* who may be
but unable to be placed on chart: the mother of *Teruwerq Jale*
Dinqinesh Mercha; Altash Tedla;
Azalech; "Zandietu," Yetemegnu Wele

OROMO LINE

Omar Sheik settled in Yejju, *c.* 1529

His great grandson, Abba Seru Gwangul m. *Gelebu Fares, c.* 1735

Ali-gaz   Ali   *Kefey* m. Merso Barentu

Gugsa m. *Amata Selasse*, daughter of Emperor Tekle Giyorgis (dethroned 1800)

— — — — — — — *Hirut*   Alula m. *Menen Leben Amede* (who later m. Emperor Yohannes III)

Ras Ali m. *Hirut Wube* of Semen line; from ?

Tewabech (d. 1858) m. Emperor Tewodros (who later m. *Terunesh Wube* of Semen line)

Wele m. 4 (?) times   Alula (d. *c.* 1882) m. ?

Gugsa m. *Zewditu Menilek*   *Kefey* m. Nadew Abba Wello;   *Mentewab* m. Mekonnen;   *Yetemegnu* m. Gebre Medhin;
                              then Mengesha Yohannes from whom had   then Kebede Mengesha Atikem   then Hayle Giyorgis; then ?

Almaz   *Aster*

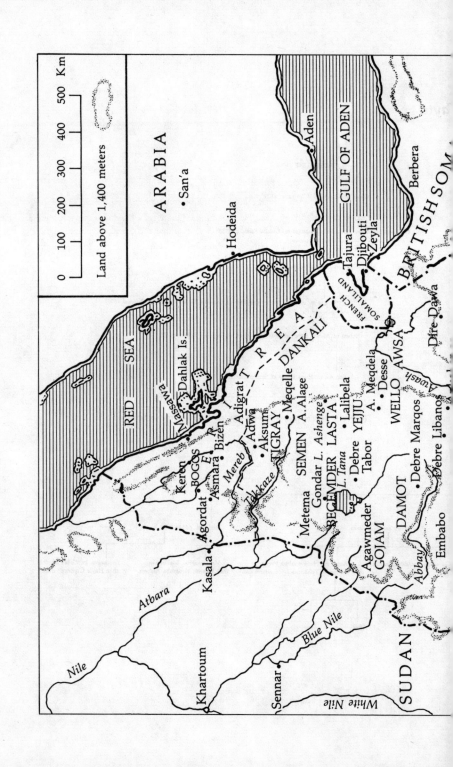

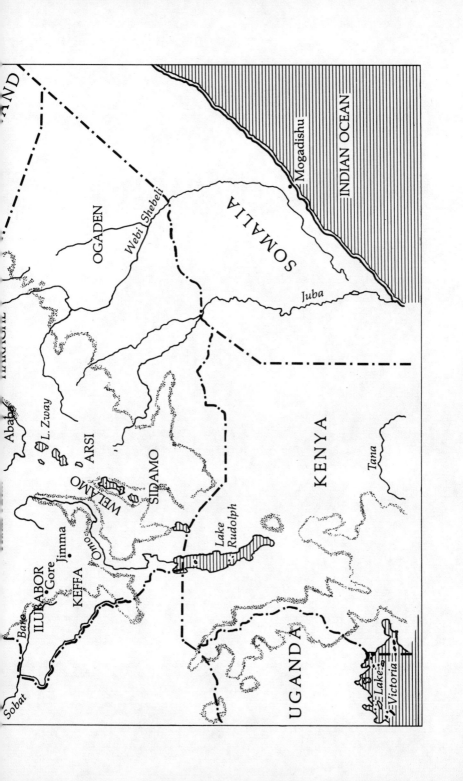

Preface

When my husband was assigned to Addis Ababa for the United States Information Service in 1965, the sum total of my knowledge about Ethiopia consisted of the biblical "Queen of Sheba," the impression that its religion was "Coptic," and a memory of newsreels showing the diminutive figure of the emperor of Ethiopia standing before the League of Nations in 1935. As a teenager I knew the slang for "goodbye" as "Ab-bys-seen-ya." People told me that the Ethiopians were beautiful, and cruel.

Now I know that King Solomon's trick seduction of the Ethiopian Queen of Sheba may have no verifiable truth. In Ethiopia her name is Makeda, and not only is she the heroine of the national epic, *Kebre Negest*, but she is also proclaimed in Ethiopia's first written constitution (1931) as the founder of the Solomonic dynasty in the 10th century B.C.

The Ethiopian emperor failed to arouse the world when Italy invaded his country in 1935 and the vague disquiet in European and North American foreign offices proved to be fully justified during the Second World War. Few people realize that the seeds of that revanchist war were sown in 1895-6 when Italy lost a war in Ethiopia to the forces of Emperor Menilek II and Empress Taytu.

Ethiopia's religion is not Coptic. "Copt" means "Egyptian," hence use of this word is equivalent to calling the Ethiopians "Egyptians." Their religion is "Ethiopian Orthodox," a monophysite branch of Christianity that includes the Coptic church of Egypt and the Syrian and Armenian Christians who broke away after the Council of Chalcedon in A.D. 431, denying any distinction between the divine and human natures of Christ. The fact that the Coptic patriarchate in Alexandria has been responsible for appointing the head of the Ethiopian church from the 5th century A.D. to the mid-20th century, when the church of Ethiopia became autocephalic, has led to the confusion.

"Abyssinia" was used so universally during the occupation by Italy from 1935 to 1941 that the emperor had to remind the world on his return to rule that his country's name was "Ethiopia." "Abyssinian" is an acceptable description of those who are Christian, speak Amharic or Tigrinya, and comprise the ruling group, both pre- and post-revolution, though they number barely 50 per cent of the population. "Are you Ethiopian?" is a question now fraught with political overtones as Oromo and Eritrean separatists fight for their identities.

Beautiful the Ethiopians are — distinct on the continent of Africa for their straight noses, thin lips, attenuated body structure and olive skin. As for cruelty, the Ethiopians are far behind those who spawned concentration camps, *gulags* and international terrorism.

Imperial Ethiopia ended in 1974 when a military junta deposed Hayle Selasse. The twists and turns of that junta are not relevant to this study, but whatever the aims of the present government, its leaders still must contend with the same historical forces, economic patterns and ethnic and religious differences faced by their predecessors.

Many academics, among them Richard Pankhurst, Sven Rubenson, Harold Marcus, Donald Crummey, Peter Garretson, and the late Dr. Richard Caulk, forgave my amateur status as an historian. Their help has ranged from encouragement to the sharing of arduously mined research treasures. Dr. Zewde Gabre-Sellassie, both an historian and a former United Nations official, gave me hours of his personal recollections and critical advice. Bairu Tafla, Belatchew Jemaneh, Mary Lou Masey, David Geyle, Lizbeth Jacobson, Edward Bennett, Joan Hubbard, Yoli Jaeckel, Anthony Poggioli, Marissa Hawes, Lisa Sergio and Max Kraus have assisted me with their knowledge of Russian, German, Amharic or Italian. Rosemary Beavers made valuable editorial suggestions, and Eugene Rosenfeld edited, photocopied and indexed with remarkable tolerance.

My constant companion has been the official chronicle of Menilek II, written by his Minister of Pen, Gebre Selasse (romanized in French as Guébrè Sellassié). The chronicle was translated into French by an Ethiopian Catholic, Tesfa Salassie, and then annotated and published by a French ambassador to Ethiopia, Maurice de Coppet, as *Chronique du règne de Ménélik II, roi des rois d'Ethiopie* in 1930 and 1931. The Amharic original was not published in Ethiopia until 1966. As Empress Taytu herself worked closely with the chronicle's author, contributing, revising, adding and deleting, I consider the chronicle the nearest thing to her autobiography. In this text, the word "chronicle" always refers to the French translation of this hagiography, and "chronicler" to its compiler.

Chris Prouty
1 January 1986

Explanatory Notes

Nomenclature

There is no family name in Ethiopia. Sons and daughters attach to their given name the "first" name of the father. Thus the son of Menilek Hayle Melekot becomes Asfaw Wesen Menilek and his son could be Merid Asfaw Wesen. Some names cannot be separated, such as those preceded by Hayle (power of), Welde (son of), and Welette (daughter of), but in general it is proper to address an individual as Ato (Mr.) Mengesha though his full name may be Mengesha Yohannes.

Women do not change their names upon marriage. They take on the title Weyzero, a title that used to be restricted to the aristocracy but is now used as the equivalent of "Mrs." The title Weyzerit for an unmarried woman is an innovation of the 20th century, as was Li'ilt for princess.

Detective work in Ethiopian genealogy is complicated by multiple names. There can be a "pet" name used within the family, a "world" name, a baptismal name, and in the case of royals, a "throne" name. Men may be referred to by their "horse" name. Emperor Menilek was often referred to as "Abba Dagnew," the name of a horse he once rode into battle.

"Who is your father?" is an insulting question implying bastardy, for almost every child will know his antecedents for seven generations removed. Yet bastardy does not connote inferior social position, nor inequality in inheritance. Acknowledgment of paternity by the father is all that is required.

Calendar and Time

The calendar year runs from 11 September to 10 September and is dated seven years earlier than the Gregorian calender: thus 3 tir 1886 is equivalent to 11 January 1894. There are 12 months of 30 days each and one month of five days (six in a leap year). The day begins at sunrise, not midnight. Each day of the month is dedicated to some holy figure, and Ethiopians often express the date of an event as "my horse ran away on St. Mikael's day;" this is confusing as there are several St. Mikael's days. Thirty-three days of the year are dedicated to the Virgin Mary. Non-Christians have other ways of defining the passage of time depending on their religious persuasion, whether it be Muslim or some other faith.

Titles

There were more than 100 civil and military titles in use and they outlasted the actual exercise of the duty. I have restricted them to what I think is necessary to show rank and importance or to distinguish two individuals with the same name. Those titles which are used in the text of the book are listed and defined in the glossary.

Transliteration of Amharic

The romanization of Amharic is burdened with a variety of diacritical marks which account for the discrepancies in the names included in the bibliography. It was decided for the sake of simplicity not to use any diacritical marks in this book. The reader is informed that the final "e" in Amharic proper nouns is pronounced, but without emphasis.

Glossary

abba	father; also used for a priest
Abba	part of an Oromo name/title
Abeto	Father of the house
abun	archbishop
Abune	Archbishop, when used as title followed by name
aderach	imperial reception room
afenegus	chief justice, literally "mouth of the king"
aleqa	chief of the priests; lay administrator
alga	throne-couch
amba	flat-topped mountain, used as treasury, jail or fortress
ar	excrement
askari	native soldier in the service of a European power; native policeman, guard or watchman
Ato	title equivalent to "Mr."
awaj	public edict
azaj	overseer of functions at court; overseer of an estate; state jailor
azmari	poetess, public singer or composer
balabat	local notable, squire, used for a man or a woman
balamberas	ruler of a fort
baldarabba	intermediary for a visitor to the court
balemwal	favorite person
basha, bashi-bazouk	customs official; artillery officer; native soldier in a foreign army; member of irregular military unit
begenna	10-string lyre
bejirond	treasurer of state money
berbere	red pepper
Bidwoded	Beloved (used as title)
blatta	executive at court

brondo	raw meat
damoz	marriage contract for fixed duration stipulating fixed salary for the wife
debtera	chorister or scribe
dejazmach	commander of the gate
desta	joy; nickname for the emperor's tent on campaign
doro dabo	stew of chicken and hard-boiled eggs
echege	highest office for an Ethiopian in the church before it became autocephalic
elfign	royal apartments whether in the capital or on the road
Emabet	title for a high-ranking woman
ferengi	foreigner
fitawrari	commander of the vanguard
Ge'ez	language of the sacred texts
gelemota	ancient term for a woman of easy virtue
gembo	container for drink
gendebel	tent carriers of the advance guard who carry weapons
gibbi	royal enclosure whether in the capital or on the road
grazmach	commander of the left
gult	land granted by the emperor to a holder who is entitled to receive income from it
Habesha	Abyssinia, Abyssinian
Haj, Haji	title for a Muslim who has been to Mecca
hakim	medical practitioner
hamle	Ethiopian calendar month, *c.* 8 July-*c.* 6 August
har	silk
hayle	power of
hedar	Ethiopian calendar month, *c.* 11 November-*c.* 10 December
hydromel	mead with honey base
indod	soap plant
injera	fermented bread

itege	empress
Jabarti	Ethiopian Muslim
Jan Hoy	Your/His Majesty
Janterar	title for the ruler of Ambasel
jus-basha	officer of native troops in the employ of foreign army
kentiba	office of mayor
kenyazmach	commander of the right
khedive	ruler of Egypt from 1867 to 1914 governing as a semi-independent viceroy of the sultan of Turkey
kosso	plant used as a purgative
lebasha	thief-finder
leul-ras	high prince
li'ilt	princess, term used in the 20th century
lij	child of noble birth
liqemekwas	official close to a king who dresses like him in battle to mislead the enemy
maheber	social dining club for men
mateb	neck cord, sometimes blue, signifying a Christian
megabit	Ethiopian calendar month, c. 10 March-c. 8 April
memher	literally "master;" usually abbot of a monastery
meridazmach	terrorizing commander
Mesqal	commemoration of the finding of the true cross
messob	woven basket table
miazia	Ethiopian calendar month, c. 9 April-c. 8 May
mize	best man at a wedding
Nebura-ed	head of St. Mary's Church at Aksum and Keeper of the Ark of the Tabot; now also head of the church at Addis Alem
neftegna	soldier-settler; literally "he who has a gun"
negadras	head of traders

negus	king
neguse negast	king of kings
noug	*Guizotia abessenica*, member of the sunflower family
orkit	pure gold in ring form
Qebat	early 17th-century schism from monophysitism which argued that the two natures of Christ were united by unction
qes	priest
qurban	communion; marriage by communion
ras	prince
Ras-Bidwoded	Beloved Prince
rist	privately owned land inherited within a family
semanya	civil marriage contract; the number "80"
sene	Ethiopian calendar month, *c.* 8 June–*c.* 7 July
senga	ox
shamma	woven cotton length used as shawl, some having colored borders
shermuta	Arabic word for prostitute
shihir	cow
shum	head of village or district
Sost Ledat	schismatic doctrine that maintained that Christ was born three times
tabot	replica of the Ark of the Covenant
tarik	history
Tawahedo	doctrine of the Ethiopian Orthodox Church
tej	alcoholic drink of fermented honey
tella	beer made from wheat
teqempt	Ethiopian calendar month, *c.* 12 October–*c.* 10 November
teskar	funeral; remembrance ceremony
Timkat	Epiphany, usually celebrated by re-baptism
tir	Ethiopian calendar month, *c.* 9 January –*c.* 7 February

tukul	thatched round hut
Wagshum	Governor of Wag district
wat	peppery stew
Welde	Son of
Welette	Daughter of
Weyzerit	title for an unmarried woman, used in the 20th century
Weyzero	title for a woman, formerly restricted to the aristocracy, now the equivalent of "Mrs."
yekatit	Ethiopian calendar month, *c.* 8 February-*c.* 9 March
zar	demon-spirit
Zemene Mesafint	Era of the Princes (1750-1855)

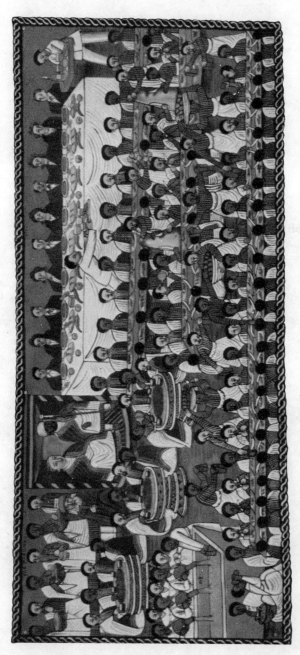

Folk painting of a banquet given by Emperor Menilek and Empress Taytu at which foreigners are seated at the top right table

Photo by George Talanos

1

Taytu's fifth husband: Menilek, King of Shewa

The marriage of the strong-willed Taytu Betul, descended from a northern princely family, to the king of the southern province of Shewa, did not take place until 1883 when both of the spouses had lived almost half their lives. For an aristocratic Christian man or woman to have been married and divorced repeatedly was unremarkable — permitted by custom and law. When Menilek became Taytu's fifth husband he was known to be ambitious for the crown of king of kings, held firmly at that time by Emperor Yohannes IV.

As the time of Menilek's birth in 1844 Ethiopia was so fragmented that his grandfather Sahle Selasse, Shewa's seventh dynastic king, acted as an independent sovereign of an independent country. He extended the borders of Shewa by conquest, paid no tribute to an emperor and welcomed the first embassy from a foreign country to Shewa.

Three years previously, in the spring of 1841, Her Majesty Queen Victoria of Great Britain had empowered a mission to set off from Bombay to look into the slave trade and offer the king of Shewa a treaty to secure "free and unrestricted commercial intercourse." It took only nine days for the steam-powered frigate to cross the Indian Ocean, but the journey inland to Shewa took the 33-man party, under the command of Captain Cornwallis Harris, four months. Three men were killed on the way as fractious chiefs made it difficult to acquire camels, mules, water, and guides to cross the desert littoral. Then, "as if by the touch of a magician's wand, the scene passed from parched and arid wastes to the green and lovely highlands of Abyssinia ... each fertile knoll crowned with its peaceful hamlet, each rural vale traversed by its crystal brook ... cool mountain zephyrs redolent of eglantine and jasmine ... the turf spangled with clover, daisies and buttercups ... the aromatic fragrance of mint and thyme ..." [1]

Sahle Selasse received the embassy, attired in a "silken vest of green brocade, shrouded in a white cotton robe ... with broad crimson stripes." He was 40 years old and "his full bushy head of hair was arranged in elaborate curls after the fashion of George I; although

he was considerably disfigured by the loss of his left eye, his
expression was open, pleasant ... and commanding."

The gifts of Kashmiri shawls, Delhi embroidered cloth, clocks,
music boxes and a carpet elicited the gracious thanks of the king,
but when the cannon was wheeled in and 300 muskets piled in front
of his divan, Sahle Selasse was visibly overcome with joy.

The Harris mission, during its two-year stay in Shewa, met the
numerous members of Sahle Selasse's family, noting in particular
Hayle Melekot, the heir apparent, and his brother Seyfu, the two
sons borne by the Shewan autocrat's legal wife, Bezebesh. A year
after the embassy had departed with a treaty of sorts* Hayle Melekot
fathered Menilek on 17 August 1844. The name of the mother was
Ejjigayehu, and the chronicler of Menilek was obligingly frank about
the precise details of his conception. Ejjigayehu, "a woman
distinguished in character and birth," had been brought to court to
be a companion to Queen Bezebesh and her two boys. One of her
duties was to ensure that the two young princes "heard no evil and
spoke no evil." They called her "sister." One day, "inspired by the
Holy Spirit, the older boy had relations with her." A less respectful
source says that the young prince was tipsy and stumbled into her
bed, but found her so ugly in the cold light of morning that he did
not care to see her again.[2]

The pregnant Ejjigayehu complained to Queen Bezebesh who
informed her husband of his son's misconduct. Sahle Selasse was
understanding: "Oh well, a mother cannot keep her eye on her son
every moment," and he placed Ejjigayehu under royal protection
during her confinement. Sahle Selasse might well have been
understanding for he claimed at least 14 children from women other
than his queen, and used them and their mothers as instruments of
a policy to administer the kingdom.† His natural sons were made
governors, and loyal warriors were rewarded with the hand of one
daughter or another. Queen Bezebesh had contributed four girls from
her former marriage. Captain Harris attended one of these political
weddings, at which the bride was Beletshachew, a "shrew possessing
a most diabolical temper whom two husbands have already
divorced." Of another daughter of the queen, Harris wrote: "she

---

*Treaty of Friendship and Commerce, 16 November 1841, between King Sahle Selasse,
King of Shewa, Efat and the Galla, and Great Britain.
†"If all of Sahle Selasse's descendants were gathered together," wrote Heruy in the
1930s, "they would number more than 1,000."

demonstrates signs of being the sole and undisputed mistress of Mafud which her hen-pecked husband governs."

Bezebesh herself was a forthright lady. "She passes for being well educated in this country and Sahle Selasse makes no decision without consulting her," wrote the French explorer and treaty-maker, Rochet d'Héricourt.* The Harris mission had been asked to leave in 1843 and Bezebesh clearly had something to do with the expulsion. She confided to Rochet, whom she liked and allowed the intimacy of treating her for a toothache, that "the English came to explore our country in order to seize it later. They brought the king rich presents, but had he listened to me, he would not have accepted them." She asked Rochet whether there were any poor people in England, and on his assurance that there were she wondered why the Harris group did not sell all their gifts in order to give money to their own poor people.[3]

In 1844, at the time of Menilek's birth, his great-grandmother, Zenebe Werq, ruled almost half the province of Shewa and was second in importance only to her son, Sahle Selasse, whom she provided with the black wool of Menz district for his tents. She was excused from all other tribute. The Menz people were loyal to her and took their oaths in her name. The old lady, as well as his wife, was probably consulted by Sahle Selasse on the legitimization and naming of Menilek,[†] that is, having him brought up as a royal child. Hayle Melekot in the meantime had become enamored of another woman of the court, Tideneqialesh, whom he married after his father gave her permission to get a divorce.

Hayle Melekot succeeded to the throne when Sahle Selasse died in October 1847, thereby enhancing Menilek's importance, for no children were born from the union with Tideneqialesh. During his father's eight-year reign Menilek learned what was traditional for the sons of nobles to learn: equestrian arts, use of shield and spear, and swimming. Despite the number of rivers to be crossed on a military campaign, only the "well-born" were taught to swim. The young prince learned to repeat by rote the Psalms of David and other

---

*A French treaty of Amity and Commerce, 7 June 1843, has been cited for many years as the basis of French-Ethiopian relations but it has been proven by Rubenson that Rochet d'Héricourt's treaty was neither signed nor sealed by the Shewan king.
[†]Tekle-Tsadik Mekouria speculated that the reason why this name had not been used by kings or emperors for 3,000 years since Menilek I, son of the "Queen of Sheba," was a reluctance to admit the relationship of the Ethiopian queen with the Jewish king, Solomon. Other Ethiopians say this is nonsense.

prayers in Ge'ez, the liturgical language, but was not taught to read or write Amharic as those chores were performed by *debtera* (choristers or scribes). One etiquette lesson that Menilek did not master was that the scion of an aristocratic house should be impassive, for "to speak one's mind or show one's feelings is done only by children and animals." Menilek, as an adult, had a lively personality, was often smiling or laughing, and his face could show stern disapproval, anger or sadness.[4]

He grew up hearing the fables, proverbs and poems of Amhara culture, a striking number of which inculcate the notion that women (except mothers) are the most unreliable creatures on earth.[5]

When the Capuchin missionary, Father Massaia, wrote that Menilek was progressive in spite of the prejudices he was born with, he was referring to the resistance of Ethiopians to new ways and strange people. The English mission of 1841 had aroused suspicion because they had tried to make *injera* (Ethiopian bread) more palatable by toasting it, and a soldier who carried a metal canteen to a stream for filling with water was accused of poisoning the stream. Telescopes frightened people. Sahle Selasse was interested in new inventions, but had been forced to have a hydraulic mill destroyed when his priests damned it as the work of the devil.[6] Menilek's guardian-tutor was a layman, Ato Nadew, whose good sense must have counterbalanced the superstitious religious environment, for Menilek's thirst for knowledge, especially for the workings of mechanical objects, was almost insatiable.

Menilek's youth ended just as soothsayers had predicted to his grandfather. "The son of your son will be remarkable and he will restore the glory of Shewa after its ruination by a terrible tyrant from the north." The "terrible tyrant" was Emperor Tewodros II, who marched on Shewa at the end of June 1855. King Hayle Melekot sickened and died as Shewan resistance to Tewodros collapsed. Officers of the defunct king gathered up Menilek and galloped south in an effort to frustrate his capture by the "tyrant" but they failed.

The chronicler records that 11-year-old Menilek wept when chains were put on him, so touching the heart of Tewodros that he had him released and never again restrained him or spoke a harsh word to him. Ejjigayehu voluntarily accompanied her son into captivity, as did Ato Nadew and a number of other Shewans. The widow of Hayle Melekot was granted permission to go to Jerusalem to live as a nun and Tewodros provided her escort to the coast. The dowager-queens, Bezebesh and Zenebe Werq, remained at Sala Dingay. Seyfu, the younger brother of Hayle Melekot, escaped Tewodros's net and carried on the Shewan resistance movement for five years until his death. Tewodros appointed a viceroy and Shewa's independence ended.[7]

In Menilek's own words, Tewodros became a second father to him, and initiated his practical education in government by making him a page at his court. "Court" was more often than not a movable military camp. The hegemony of Emperor Tewodros required the emperor's armed vigilance. In 1858 Father Massaia, summoned from his mission to the Oromo* by Tewodros, saw young Menilek at one of these camps. Years later Menilek told the priest that he had made a tremendous impression on him that day as he patiently stood up to the emperor's inquisition. Very likely Menilek saw other foreigners with Tewodros, such as John Bell, an English adventurer who was his friend and military adviser; Walter Plowden, the British consul from Massawa who often traveled with Tewodros; and possibly the Protestant missionaries, Mayer, Kienzlen, Bender and Flad. Tewodros openly revered the manual skills and scientific knowledge of these artisan-missionaries. Mayer and Kienzlen attended his mortally ill wife, Tewabech, but could not help her. Her death in August 1858 plunged Tewodros into despair, from which he diverted himself by engaging in an unusually bloody campaign in Wello.[†] Nevertheless Kienzlen wrote that Tewodros was a "model prince" and disdained all personal comforts and luxury in his concern for the good of his people.[8]

John Bell, deducing that the emperor's increasing irascibility stemmed from the celibacy he had imposed on himself after the death of Tewabech, succeeded in 1860 in persuading him to marry again. Bell was trusted to escort the bride, Terunesh Wube, to the emperor. Terunesh was a haughty young lady who looked down on the obscure origins of Tewodros, as her father had been lord of Tigray until Tewodros had captured and imprisoned him. Terunesh gave him a son, but did not give him comfort. Tewodros began taking

---

*The Oromo people were called "Galla" in every source for this period, an offensive appellation to them. Absorption of the Oromo into the polity called "Ethiopia" was the aim of every emperor from the 17th to the 20th century.

†An important buffer province between northern and southern Ethiopia, settled largely by Oromo, some of whom adopted Islam. Oromo governing traditions were modified into dynastic inheritance and seven family clans had emerged, competing with each other for dominance.

concubines on his campaigns and left Terunesh and his baby son at Meqdela.[9]

Meqdela, one of the *amba* (flat-topped mountains) so characteristic of the Ethiopian terrain, was fortress-treasury for Tewodros and then prison for Menilek, his mother and most of the other Shewans. Theophilus Waldmeier, a missionary temporarily resident at Meqdela, taught the mechanical arts to whomever he could corral, and one of his pupils was Menilek. "He was a very nice young gentleman and we were on intimate terms." "Quick, gentle and unpretending," observed another missionary who said that Menilek had propitiated the tyrant and been honored "with the hand of a royal princess [Altash], a daughter of the invincible emperor."[10]

Emperor Tewodros was far from invincible. By early 1865 he had so miscalculated the basis of his power that half the country and the entire church hierarchy whose lands he had tried to redistribute were in rebellion against him. His viceroy in Shewa had declared himself independent in 1863 and Tewodros did not have the power to put him in his place. The declaration of independence was galling as well to the Shewan aristocrats at Meqdela because the viceroy was a commoner. The Shewans engineered the escape of Menilek on 30 June 1865.

The escape was planned by Germame Welde Hawaryat, a Shewan who had feigned loyalty to Tewodros and been given the hand of Qataro Merso* at the same time that Menilek had been married to Altash Tewodros. Germame gave a large party (the captives lived in considerable freedom with their wives and servants and could prepare food and drink as their resources allowed), and saw to it that everyone got drunk, including Qataro Merso, his wife, whom he suspected was a spy for the emperor. After midnight, when everyone was in a drunken stupor, Germame led about 20 Shewans, including Menilek and his intrepid mother, through the gates of the fortress which had been left unguarded with the connivance of Tewodros's elder son, Meshesha, who had long been out of favor with his father. By dawn the fugitives, on horses purchased in advance by Germame's agents, had reached a camp in Wello some kilometers to the south.[11]

The escape was all the more daring because the emperor was in

---

*Qataro Merso, Terunesh Wube and Taytu Betul were cousins, though the father of Terunesh was only half-brother of Merso and Betul.

residence at the time at Meqdela. He was informed by his terrified servants — he had been known to execute bearers of bad news — and hurried to the edge of the precipice with his field glasses. Increased activity in the camp of the Wello queen, Werqitu, was discernible. Altash, the deserted wife, wept in her pavilion, "convulsed with shame and indignation." "I don't blame him for escaping, but why did he leave his young wife behind?" Tewodros is alleged to have asked. Tewodros then took the 25 hostages he held from Queen Werqitu's clan, including her son and heir, and had their hands and feet amputated and the bodies thrown over the precipice to die in agony.[12]

The Wello paid the terrible price for Menilek's escape. Tewodros did nothing to the Shewans still at Meqdela. Thus ended Menilek's 10 years with his "father," Emperor Tewodros. This forced opportunity to see the variety of peoples and the geography beyond Shewa modified his provincialism. Meeting the foreign men and women at Meqdela who coped so industriously with their incarceration stimulated in Menilek fresh concepts about the world outside Ethiopia.

Early in his reign, Tewodros had been considered a merciful and gentle man, with a great concern for family morals. A compassionate defender of widows, orphans and farmers, he would punish his soldiers when he caught them stealing from the helpless. Though Tewodros preferred that everyone in his empire be Christian, he objected, as would Menilek, to the cruder prejudices of his men who refused to sit at the same meal with Muslims or animists. Menilek, like Tewodros, forbade emasculation of victims of war and the selling of slaves, and like Tewodros, was unable to enforce his edicts. The negative results of the excessive barbarity of the later years of Tewodros were not lost on Menilek. He told his advisers that he would win people to his side by the generous distribution of talers, *tej* (an alcoholic drink of fermented honey) and *brondo* (raw meat).[13]

Menilek proclaims his kingship of Shewa, August 1865

The reinstatement of the Shewan dynasty was not accomplished without violence. The incumbent put up a fight but lost the battle. The desire for vengeance by Menilek's followers was so intense that Germame, to whom Menilek owed his escape, beat the royal drums and proclaimed, "Let bygones be bygones." Germame's presumption in giving this order shocked Menilek and his advisers into a council meeting. Germame defended his action eloquently and threatened that if the random cruelty was allowed to continue he would retire to a monastery. His order was confirmed by Menilek.[14]

Only 21 years old and almost completely ignorant of the Shewan political and religious scene, Menilek was closely advised during the next few years. That he chafed under this guidance was implicit in a remark Menilek made to Father Massaia about Emperor Tewodros: "He governed alone ... did not let himself be overwhelmed ... or tolerate contradiction of his intention or design." Menilek had to take counsel on the reorganization of taxation and land distribution, and on the religious disputes between clerical factions.

Menilek restored to supremacy at Shewa's principal monastery, Debre Libanos, those clerics who subscribed to the doctrine of Sost Ledat. The Sost Ledat doctrine, which taught that Christ was born three times, was considered heretical by the Orthodox who believed that Christ was the perfect union of two natures, the Tawahedo doctrine. The controversy was nearly three centuries old, and in this complex theological matter neither Tewodros nor the metropolitan Abune Selama, with whom Menilek had studied at Meqdela, influenced Menilek's judgment, except to make him impatient and irritated with religious dissension. Debates had become so heated in Shewa that Menilek forbade all Christological arguments and any priest convicted of engaging in them risked the death penalty.[15]

Building up an army was the first priority. The town of Letche was constructed and fortified as Shewa's first line of defense should Tewodros try to recapture Menilek. Two years after he reestablished the Shewan dynasty Menilek asked for arms in a letter to the French agent at Aden and requested recognition of his kingship from the British consul at Aden, signing himself presumptuously as "King of Kings."

Menilek and his council gave some thought to the prisoners still suffering from the manic-depressive whims of Tewodros; among them was his uncle, the respected Darge Sahle Selasse. False hopes were raised in the hearts of the Meqdela prisoners in July and November 1867 as news circulated that Menilek's army was near Meqdela for a rescue operation. Hearing that they had approached, and then retreated, Henry Stern, one of the missionaries, called Menilek a "fat coward who wears out three mules a day." A 20th-century analyst echoed this opinion by pointing out that "Menilek lacked neither numbers nor mobility ... he lacked daring."[16]

The British ultimatum to Tewodros in May 1867 that they would send an army unless he released his European captives was carried out when 32,000 troops from the British army of India, 44 elephants, tons of provisions, and 176 Chinese coolies (to build a supply railroad from the coast to the highlands), landed at the port of Zula in December of that year. As this huge force was debarking, three Catholic priests were crossing the Gulf of Aden to Tajura in a dhow, their objective being Shewa. One of these priests was Father Gugliemo Massaia, whom Menilek had seen at Tewodros's camp 10 years before. As he left Aden, Massaia was handed a letter by the British vice-consul to deliver to King Menilek. The letter unequivocally demanded that Menilek refuse asylum to Tewodros should he try to escape into Shewa. Massaia was not an intentional agent of the British, but he realized afterwards that his postman's hat had compromised his cassock. Father Massaia and his colleagues, Fathers Taurin de Cahagne and Ferdinand, were hospitably greeted by Menilek, but the king refused to discuss their onward trek to revive Massaia's old mission to the Oromo. Menilek had found a foreign adviser and his "third father", as he affectionately called Massaia, though he ignored his advice almost as often as he asked for it.[17]

The young man who grasped the hand of the Catholic priest was 1.78 meters tall, with a robust and muscular build. His skin was darkish, his teeth very white and slightly pronated, his eyes dark and lively, his lips fleshy. Physically, Menilek did not have the classic, slim, elegant face and figure of the typical Amhara Christian.

Massaia spoke Amharic and was able to translate the letter he had carried from the English to Menilek. Immediately, Menilek went into a meeting with his council to discuss the English war on Tewodros and what they should do.

The suicide of Emperor Tewodros, 13 April 1868

Tewodros's troubles with the British had begun with his anger at their consul, Duncan Cameron, for failing to bring an answer to the letter he had written to Queen Victoria in 1862 (received in London in February 1863) pleading for sympathy in his impending war with the Turks (an omnibus word for any Muslim enemy). When a recall order for Cameron, but no answer to his letter, arrived by courier in November 1863, an enraged Tewodros put the consul in chains.

The emperor's frustration at being unable to control the rebellions against him, his anger at the constant criticism by the head of the church, Abune Selama, whom he imprisoned at Meqdela in April 1864, and this slight from the British with whom he had had cordial relations for many years, contributed to a deterioration in his personality. He was often drunk, licentious and wantonly cruel. He not only vented his resentments on his own people, but by 1867 some 60 European men, women and children had also been placed under some form of restriction, either at Meqdela or at the European settlement at Gafat.

When a message from Cameron finally reached London that a civil reply to the emperor's letter must be sent immediately, the Foreign Office began to look for the lost letter. This particular lapse would cost the British government nine million pounds, the sum appropriated by parliament to mount the expedition under General Robert Napier to free the captives. The belated answer from Queen Victoria finally arrived, but it was unsatisfactory to Tewodros and he kept his motley collection of "whites" under guard.

It was successfully argued in the House of Commons that if a willful Abyssinian king could insult Great Britian, her prestige in Africa and Asia would be more difficult to maintain. Thus the Napier expedition was authorized.

Tewodros made no attempt to harass the Anglo-Indian army, and he withdrew as they advanced. He dragged the cannon constructed by his captive missionaries and marched his dwindling followers back towards Meqdela fortress where he waited. On 10 April 1868 his army of about 4,000 descended to attack the British advance force of about 2,000 on the plain below Meqdela. The Ethiopians were slaughtered by effective rifle fire and bayonets in hand-to-hand combat. When dusk fell, with the Ethiopians rallying again and again, 700 dead bodies were counted and the wounded were estimated at more than 1,000. The Anglo-Indian forces had 20 wounded of whom two died later.[*]

Tewodros had watched the battle through field glasses, and when he comprehended his defeat he released all the Europeans and barricaded himself behind the gates of Meqdela. The fortress was stormed on Easter Monday, 13 April. As the soldiers poured on to

---

[*]However, from diseases caught on the 25-week campaign, more than 6,000 soldiers were invalided out of the army and 512 died.

the mountain plateau, they did not immediately notice the body of the emperor lying on the ground. He had led the resistance at the gate, and then, rather than be captured, had taken the pistol sent to him by Queen Victoria in happier times, and shot himself in the mouth.[18]

The Wello queen, Werqitu, informed Menilek by courier of the emperor's death, upon which both Easter and the death of Tewodros were observed simultaneously in Shewa. Menilek did not join in the exuberant cheering as he was sincerely grieved. To Father Massaia he expressed admiration for Tewodros's courage in taking his own life and received in turn a sermon on the sin of suicide. Then Menilek expressed his main concern: "Tewodros is dead and who will succeed him? Will the English leave someone in his place? What will they think of me since I was found neither at Meqdela nor at the frontier?" He instructed the reluctant Massaia to write a letter to the English general justifying his non-appearance. This letter was never delivered, nor was his gift of cattle and grain, as the British had already razed the mountain top before turning it over to Queen Mestawet, an Oromo rival of Queen Werqitu, and departed — just as they had promised to do in a psychological warfare broadside to the Ethiopian people at the onset of the campaign.[19]

The two contenders for the vacant throne were Wagshum Gobeze of Lasta and Kasa Mercha of Tigray. Gobeze proclaimed himself "Emperor Tekle Giyorgis," but there was no bishop to anoint him as Abune Selama had died at Meqdela in 1867. As "Emperor Tekle Giyorgis" he had a short and turbulent reign that ended in 1870 when he was defeated in battle by Kasa Mercha. In Father Massaia's view, Menilek should have gone to the aid of Tekle Giyorgis but he did not do so because he was weak and lacked courage. "This poor young man is blessed with many good qualities and wants to do the right thing, but the corruption in this country ... the bad habits of society, and that woman ..."

"That woman" had become the companion of Menilek soon after his return to Shewa in 1865. Bafena was nearly twice his age and had eight sons and daughters by various husbands, among whom was a one-time viceroy for Emperor Tewodros. She was in her own right a *balabat* (squire) of Merhabete district. Menilek's relationship with her was in defiance of his counselors, many of whom left the court rather than address her as "queen;" others defected when their lands were taken and granted to her. She was beautiful, clever, and seductive. To the priest Massaia, she was sly, immoral and a trouble-maker despite her generous and frequent gifts to him. Knowing that Menilek's union with her was "irregular," Massaia had no wish to meet her, and he had heard that Menilek's mother had been obliged to move away from the court because she did not get along with this "siren."

Bafena forced the meeting with Father Massaia. She wished to consult him about the nausea and weakness she suffered every month. "I know King Menilek has great confidence in you and loves and respects you. Could you not advise him to marry me according to the rite of communion? Once that ceremony is performed, I have been assured that we would have a child."* She knew, Massaia wrote, that Menilek was under pressure to send her away and marry a younger woman who could give him sons. Diplomatically, Massaia agreed to give the advice "if the opportunity arose."

Massaia had undergone a couple of years' medical training, but he knew from his experience at his station in Keffa that the practice of medicine would result in neglect of his spiritual mission. Again, Bafena forced the issue. She brought her nephew, whose jaw festered with syphilitic sores, to the priest. The patient's mother, Bafena's cousin, was the wife of Menilek's cousin,† so Massaia could hardly refuse treatment. Soon Massaia's hut was surrounded by the sick and the dying. He did his best to catechize them during his consultations.

It became more difficult for Father Massaia to remain on polite terms with Bafena when religious questions intruded. Massaia could not resist attempting to convert two high-ranking schismatic Sost Ledat priests to Catholicism, or giving instruction to Menilek's grandmother, Bezebesh, though Menilek told him to keep these activities secret. Menilek adopted a *laissez-faire* policy towards Massaia's religious activities mainly because he admired his good works and fine character at a time when moral turpitude and simony infected the Ethiopian priesthood, rather than because he wished to uphold the principle of freedom of conscience. The priests begged Father Massaia to become bishop of Shewa, an office over which they had no control.

---

*In 1882 Bafena gave birth to a deformed child who died shortly after birth.
†Welde Giyorgis was the son of Ayahlush, a daughter of Sahle Selasse and Meridazmach Aboye. Aboye was one of Bafena's husbands. Welde Giyorgis married a cousin of Empress Taytu subsequently.

Bafena pretended that she too wished Father Massaia to become the bishop of Shewa, because "his holiness would transform Shewa into a paradise." Her own sons, she said, had become "little angels" just by being in his presence. Massaia believed that Bafena had already made a secret deal with the Abune Atinatewos and Emperor Yohannes IV to help them stamp out the Sost Ledat in Shewa in return for one of her sons being made king.

It is impossible to absolve Bafena from these allegations in the light of her subsequent behavior. Since Bafena's convictions would have been no secret to Menilek, it shows how little Menilek cared whether Jesus Christ was born twice, or three times, or how the miracle was accomplished.* The only way for Father Massaia to avoid these touchy religious-domestic tensions was to move. Menilek permitted him to go a few "mule" hours away to Gilogov, where he established his mission under the protection of Gobena and his wife, the notable Ayeletch Abarasa.[20]

Emperor Yohannes IV, Menilek and Egypt, 1872-6

Menilek declined to make formal submission to Yohannes when he came to the throne in 1872. Menilek was heard to say that he would never let "that bishop", Atinatewos, set foot in Shewa, and that he would continue to call himself "king of kings." Yohannes could not put Menilek in his place because he had more serious problems. The forces of Khedive Ismail[‡] had occupied most of the Ethiopian province of Bogos in 1872, and Egyptian control of the port of Massawa prevented merchandise and arms from reaching the emperor. Yohannes's protests to European monarchs and the Cairo government were ignored, except for a letter from Queen Victoria

---

*There was yet another schism between those who argued that the two natures of Christ were united by unction (Qebat) and the orthodox view that unction was not needed, for Christ had been born blessed.

†Massaia said that several times a week Ayeletch rose at sunrise and traveled two kilometers to arrive in time for morning prayers, and then checked the food and work in progress. After giving orders she went home under the burning rays of the sun. "You take care of our souls and educate my sons and leave to me the care of your station," she said to him. "Her zeal and piety ... and behavior were more valuable than my preaching," admitted Massaia. She had had 11 children, seven of whom had died. She wanted to become a Catholic but Massaia would not receive her into the church unless she and Gobena were married by communion, which Gobena refused to do. She was related to Menilek's mother. (Zewde Gabre-Sellassie)

‡In 1865 Ismail had obtained from the sultan of Turkey cession of the ports of Suakin and Massawa and in 1867 conferred on himself the hereditary title of Khedive.

assuring him that Egypt would never invade his country.[21]

Egypt invaded Ethiopia in October 1875. The Egyptians, commanded by an assortment of out-of-work officers from the American civil war, plus Danes, Germans and Austrians, were soundly defeated by the armies of Yohannes in November. The rout was kept secret in Egypt and a new expeditionary force sailed for Massawa. Again, in March 1876 they were trounced. Though Yohannes's armies had suffered heavy casualties, they gained enormous amounts of booty in the form of guns, ammunition and gold.

Interpretations of Menilek's failure to assist in the defeat of Egypt range from "disloyal passivity," to "outright treason," with the evidence tilting towards treason. That Menilek intended to overthrow Emperor Yohannes by attacking him in the rear as he faced the Egyptian armies comes from a pro-Menilek source who was with Menilek in 1875. Menilek knew that a second Egyptian force, coordinated with the first Massawa landing, was making its way from Tajura to link up with him. But Emperor Yohannes also knew about their landing and ordered the sultan of Awsa to annihilate them, an order which was carried out. Menilek, the realist, promptly sent congratulations to Yohannes and a token cavalry unit to help in the second encounter with Egypt. The "disloyal passivity" view asserts that Menilek's dealings with the khedive were innocent of conspiracy. It is said that he only wanted artisans, doctors and workers to come from Egypt "to help progress," and that Egypt floated the rumor that Menilek would attack in order to demoralize Yohannes. It is documented, however, that Menilek sent his stern rebuke for the khedive's aggression in the north only *after* Yohannes had defeated two Egyptian armies.[22]

The Egyptians did manage to occupy Harar* on Menilek's flank, and by the end of 1878 Menilek was complaining of Egypt's interference in his affairs to Queen Victoria, King Umberto and King Leopold II. "I am about to die from anger because I have been unable to bring in one new skill ... [Egypt] prevents me from bringing in rifles, cannons and workers."[23] Menilek had lost hope of ever

---

*Harar, an ancient walled city, had long been an independent sultanate, some of whose emirs had paid tribute to Ethiopia. Under the Egyptians it revived as a busy trading center, a major entrepôt about a week's camel journey from the coast, and another two weeks onward to Shewa. Harar became known through Richard Burton's account of his being the first "white man" (disguised) to enter it in 1854.

hearing from Pierre Arnoux whom he had commissioned two years earlier to represent him to the khedive.

Menilek and Pierre Arnoux

Since 1867, the year in which Menilek had sent his initial letters to Aden seeking European contacts, he had consistently held out his hand both to welcome foreigners and to receive their gifts. His preferred gift was a gun, which he was also ready to buy. Father Massaia and his saintly colleagues helped by writing letters, but not in procuring armaments. So when Pierre Arnoux arrived at the end of 1874 with sample rifles and revolvers and a thrilling vision of the future greatness of Ethiopia under the enlightened guidance of Menilek and with the benign assistance of France, Menilek was enchanted.

Arnoux and the two artisans he had recruited with the promise of fabulous business opportunities had had a traumatic trip across the desert during which two of their party had been murdered by nomadic tribesmen. Their ghastly safari ended with an enthusiastic welcome by King Menilek. Menilek's reception of Arnoux showed not only a sophisticated grasp of public relations, but demonstrated his capabilities as an importer of gold-embroidered silk trappings.*

I dressed in black frock coat, silk hat and polished boots. Outside our tent on the plains, 3,000 men on horseback awaited us and as we came out, dismounted as one man. Darge, the king's uncle, extended his hand ... we mounted the mules they provided and another 1,000 men ran at a trot ahead of us ... in sight of Letche, a salvo of 18 guns heralded our approach.

We dismounted at the door of the palace [a huge thatched hut], and crossed three courtyards, swept clean and carpeted with foliage. Welde Tsadiq took my hand and we went up a dozen steps into a huge room entirely covered with oriental rugs.

My escort prostrated themselves and kissed the earth before the king, who was visibly moved on seeing me, knowing all I had endured to get there. For me and Joubert, armchairs were placed on the right and left of the king. After I told of the horrible death of our compatriots, Menilek frowned, covered his lower face with his shawl and moments later spoke: "French blood shed by the Adals is my blood. Since you and your friends left your own country for the purpose of seeing me, their death was my fault. I will avenge them."

---

*Traders such as Pierre Labatut and Bogos Macarian had been active in Shewa as early as 1870 along with many Muslim buyers and sellers of slaves and ivory who bought credit for Menilek in the bazaars of Cairo.

Menilek provided the French with a house, 15 servants, and plenty of food and drink, even before Arnoux presented the gifts he had purchased with money put together by a Marseilles-based consortium on his promise of lucrative trade with Ethiopia. The gifts included engraved vermeil goblets, stationery, architectural designs, and a range of model guns. In the months that followed, Menilek approved all of Arnoux's grandiose schemes to establish a French colony in Shewa from which would stem all the benefits of advanced agriculture, industry, arts, medicine, education, freedom for slaves and morality for all. Persuaded by Arnoux that it would make a good impression in Europe, Menilek immediately proscribed slavery. "Morality for all" was somewhat beyond the capacities of Menilek, Arnoux, the Pope and the President of France.

Arnoux spent a year and a half in Shewa assembling a caravan of goods that he could trade on Menilek's behalf. During that time he taught Menilek to read invoices and packing case numbers, as well as giving him the Amharic formulas for the medicine he had brought. This was all done in secret because Menilek did not want his advisers to know that he stooped to activities generally left to minions. His mathematics homework was carried to Arnoux, after night fell, by Menilek's cousin, Mekonnen Welde Mikael.* Even though he knew he was causing grave anxiety to his misoneistic priests, Menilek watched attentively as Joubert and Pequignol (the two artisans who came with Arnoux) got to work on an hydraulic mill.

The lady Bafena, to whom Arnoux gave perfume, fabric, stockings and a mirror, was a beauty, Arnoux wrote, and a woman of remarkable good sense. The royal pair were enthralled, he said, with his descriptions of Paris, railroads, telegraphs, printing and "all the marvels of civilization." Despite all this rapport and his good intentions, nothing came of Arnoux's proposals. On his return to the coast, Arnoux formed the Franco-Ethiopian trading company at Obok,† and eventually sent a representative, Léon Chefneux, back to Shewa, who expedited arms shipments to Menilek and was transformed into an invaluable adviser and negotiator. But the French government did not commit itself to

---

*Mekonnen Welde Mikael, the future father of Emperor Hayle Selasse, was the son of Tenagne Werq, a daughter of King Sahle Selasse.
†Arnoux was murdered in Obok in 1882.

attaining privileged-nation status in Ethiopia as Italy was to do.[24]

The Italian connection

Father Massaia was appalled to learn in 1872 that Menilek intended to send a priest, Abba Mikael, to Italy to establish contacts. The Italian priest had a low opinion of the Ethiopian cleric, considering him a swindler, a liar and incompetent to boot. Abba Mikael lived up to this characterization; he was imprisoned for embezzlement when he returned from Rome. However, his exaggerations and lies (he recounted that Shewan horses were green, and that he was Menilek's older brother who had renounced the throne) so piqued the interest of the Italian Geographical Society that they appropriated funds for an expedition to Ethiopia.

Father Massaia was summoned to Letche to explain to Menilek and his council why Italian explorers were coming to Shewa. The council was disturbed that a new batch of white men, so soon after the departure of the Arnoux caravan, was coming to distract their king. Menilek's old tutor, Ato Nadew, presented the council's view to Massaia:

How is it possible for these people to leave their country, take such a long trip with hundreds of camels loaded with arms and rich things, without some political aim? The English came to Shewa [Harris mission of 1841-3]. We received them as friends, but we had to send them away. We thought our country would enter their minds no more. Now, behold! A king who lives in Rome sends these Italians. Even the word "Rome" frightens us. Our king's heart is sincere ... and when people come from over the sea, he greets them as friends without looking into their intentions. But we, trained by ancient tradition, consider it prudent to suspect strangers. Now give us your opinion.

Massaia, forewarned by Menilek, voiced his concern for the integrity of the kingdom, but he could prove to the council what a mistake it had been to expel the English. Was it not the English who came to fight Tewodros, thereby freeing the Shewans? Had the English been ambitious for territory would they have gone home after their victory? Would not Abyssinia, except for the English, still be weeping under the yoke of that ferocious tyrant and would Shewans now be free and independent? Massaia named the true enemies of Ethiopia: Muslims, particularly Arabs and Egyptians. He related how the governor of Egypt had tried to prevent him, Father Massaia, from coming to Ethiopia because "it belongs to Egypt and no priest may go there without swearing fealty to us." Massaia had struck the right note, as Egypt's recent invasion was fresh in everyone's mind. The

Europeans, Massaia promised, were coming only to bring new things, develop trade, explore, learn languages and advance science. "They, whom you scornfully call *ferengi* [foreigners] are your true friends who want to help you."[25]

The council voted to permit the Italians to proceed on their way. Those unplanned, unstructured, lurching steps that would end in the Italo-Ethiopian war of 1895-6 were taken by this "Great Expedition" led by a sweet-tempered ornithologist, the 65-year-old Marchese Orazio Antinori,* who exchanged a handsome palazzo in Florence for the exigencies of the "simple" life in Ethiopia. Menilek welcomed him and his fellows, Giovanni Chiarini and Lorenzo Landini, and their Italian servants on 7 October 1876.

Enmity between Emperor Yohannes and Menilek

Why Menilek and his generals invaded Gojam in 1877, presumably making a bid to depose Emperor Yohannes, is inexplicable since Yohannes had increased his supply of weapons by the capture of thousands of guns from the Egyptians while Menilek had acquired only hundreds, as gifts or by purchase. He left Letche protected by only a few soldiers, and set out for Gojam.

Menilek's mother, Ejjigayehu, warned Antinori that a group of Oromo were about to attack Letche in her son's absence. The Marchese, who only a few days before had accidentally shot off his right hand, was carried on a litter to a safer place. A message was sent to Menilek who was being nursed by Chiarini for fever at Were Ilu, seven days' march from Letche. When Menilek sent Chiarini back to succor the maimed Antinori and dispatched horses to strengthen Letche's defenses, the attack was aborted. It was an omen, however, of a more serious rebellion in Shewa, planned, it was said, by Bafena.[26]

Once recovered from his illness, Menilek continued on through Wello and Begemder with his army and crossed the Abbay River into Gojam in mid-March. The campaign was a fiasco, for Gojam's ruler, Ras Adal, had secured himself in an impregnable fortress to

---

*Antinori, an experienced explorer, was a founding member of the Società Geografica Italiana in Florence in 1867. His appeals that the society should back the agricultural colony founded in Bogos, Ethiopia, by Father Stella in 1867 were ignored. He went with two friends in 1870 to inspect the port of Assab and then to Bogos to find that Father Stella had died. The Società grew from its initial 70 members to 1,000 by 1870, and its journal had a circulation of 2,000.

avoid a confrontation with Menilek. Emperor Yohannes wheeled his armies from Tigray to march to Gojam. Menilek's soldiers, far from home and reluctant to invade Gojam in the first place, were demoralized from hunger. They had to forage for food in hostile territory and were frightened at the prospect of facing the well-armed men of Emperor Yohannes.

Meanwhile, back in Shewa, the old and half-paralyzed uncle of Menilek, Hayle Mikael,* declared himself king of Shewa and circulated propaganda to the effect that Menilek, at 30 years of age, was too young to govern and too much under the thumb of Germame (the man who had helped Menilek escape from Meqdela). Germame was acting as governor in Menilek's absence. Hayle Mikael burnt the town of Ankober and his followers inflicted a number of casualties† before he was captured by Germame and Afenegus Bedane (yet another ex-husband of Bafena).

A message was sent to Menilek about the attempted coup. Bafena, who was with Menilek, proposed that she be sent back to Shewa to investigate. She stole some stationery already stamped with Menilek's seal and had her scribe forge an order naming her as Menilek's regent. When she reached Letche, she proclaimed that everyone was to obey her orders. Germame was helpless in the face of Menilek's royal seal.

Bafena's first command was to transfer all the royal valuables and arms to Tamo, Shewa's most defensible fort. This site had the advantage of being near her own relations in Merhabete. She next ordered Shewa's most important political prisoner, Meshesha Seyfu,‡ to be brought to her. Meshesha Seyfu had already been mortified by Bafena. His wife, Bafena's daughter, had been forcibly divorced from him; his lands had been turned over to Bafena; and he had been in prison for five months because Bafena had convinced Menilek he was treasonous.

When Meshesha Seyfu found himself in Bafena's presence, he

---

*Hayle Mikael was one of the "claimed" sons of Sahle Selasse. He had been appointed viceroy of Shewa in 1855 by Tewodros. Aboye and Bezebeh were succeeding viceroys until Menilek returned in 1865.

†Among the casualties was Louis Pottier who had come with Arnoux and was training a group of very young Shewans in military drill. Chiarini was in Ankober when Hayle Mikael attacked, but managed to escape.

‡Meshesha Seyfu was considered by many to have a better claim to the throne of Shewa than Menilek because his father, Seyfu, brother of the deceased King Hayle Melekot, had continued fighting the appointees of Emperor Tewodros while Menilek was in his benign imprisonment.

pretended to fall in with her plans. She told him that she had
engineered this rebellion in order to make him king, and to prove
her good faith she would restore her daughter to him. Meshesha
Seyfu and Bafena rode side by side as the valuables were transferred
to Tamo. When they reached the fort, she ordered her men to put
him in chains.

The two sons of Bafena, on whose behalf this coup d'état was
designed, were with the army in Gojam, but hearing of their mother's
success, rode hard for Shewa. At the same time, Muhammad Ali,
governor of Wello,* declared he would no longer serve Menilek. As
he was the husband of another daughter of Bafena, his action was
presumed to be related to the conspiracy.

At Tamo fortress, in Father Massaia's rich prose, "this wicked vixen
saw her dreams go up in smoke. The soldiers set Meshesha Seyfu
free and declared him their leader. They unmasked the nefarious aims
of this ambitious woman ... and suggested that he throw her over
the precipice. But Meshesha Seyfu, who had been educated by the
Catholics [Massaia and Father Taurin], did not have the heart to do
this, especially to a woman." Bafena was placed under 24-hour guard.

Menilek returned to Shewa in June, not because of the machinations
of Bafena, but because he knew Emperor Yohannes was about to
attack him in Gojam and that it behooved him to get his army back
across the Abbay river before the rains would trap them. He seemed
to have perceived the problems in Shewa as an attempt by Meshesha
Seyfu to seize power, for his cousin now held considerable resources,
as well as Menilek's wife, Bafena, at Tamo. Menilek ordered an assault
on Tamo, which not only failed, but some of his own people joined
Meshesha Seyfu. Menilek called on Father Massaia to negotiate with
him. Meshesha Seyfu's answer to the priest's appeal was:

This fort was taken from a rebellious female and her soldiers then consigned
it to me. I have no ambitions and will never make war on my cousin. But
if he attacks me, I will defend myself ...
  Bafena has always persecuted me so if she regains her status, I am lost.
The army which chose me as its leader hates that woman who forced them
to betray their king. Since these soldiers unchained me ... I will not abandon
them to the vendetta of Menilek nor the hatred of Bafena.

  It took six months to work out an agreement with Meshesha Seyfu.

---

*Muhammad Ali's stepmother was Werqitu, the Oromo queen who had helped
Menilek escape from Meqdela. Menilek had verified his leadership of Wello in 1876
and again in February 1877.

In December 1877 Meshesha came down from his mountain, his soldiers were amnestied and his lands and title of Dejazmach restored. Bafena's lands were confiscated. Her sons were deemed innocent parties and remained high in Menilek's favor.

Bafena admitted her guilt to Menilek, pleading that she had been out of her mind with jealousy over his attentions to another woman, Welette Selasse.* Bafena was banished from court, but not for long. Soon Menilek was asking people to visit her and listen to her side of the story. The visitors would return, praising her resignation, her love for Shewa and for Menilek, and her religious loyalty to the Sost Ledat schism. Massaia insisted that she told the religious emissaries whatever they wanted to hear. Her friends convinced Menilek that he could not run the royal establishment without her. She was allowed to return, her treachery forgotten, and some of her lands were restored. On the eve of Emperor Yohannes's punitive march into Shewa, Menilek entrusted her with the care of his young daughter, Zewditu.†

Menilek's stubborn defense of Bafena appears foolish in a man who was reputed to be a political realist, but rather endearing in a country where opportunism usually overcame feelings of love and loyalty. Aside from his vanity in believing that the woman was insane with jealousy, Menilek knew that Bafena could not be blamed totally for the plot. He did not honor his promise to Meshesha Seyfu regarding Bafena; still there must have been more than just her lies to justify Menilek's renewed incarceration of his cousin two years later.[27]

Father Massaia believed that it was Bafena's return to court that decided Yohannes on the timing of his march on Shewa, because the emperor thought that she had undermined Menilek's prestige and because he relied on her as his religious ally and spy. Whether the belief is true or not, Emperor Yohannes crossed the border into Shewa with his army in January 1878.[28]

Political and religious incorporation of Shewa into the empire, 1878

The Shewans were prepared to fight, but Menilek told Father Massaia

---

*Welette Selasse was a Guraghe, sister of a chief named Toro, and had two sons by Menilek. She was still a favorite of the king in 1879, according to Bianchi. As Bairu Tafla pointed out, many nobles married Guraghe women because of a prophecy that a son by a Guraghe would inherit the throne, and also because they were relatively free of venereal disease.

†Zewditu was his daughter by Weyzero Benchi.

he had decided to seek peace with the emperor. It was a somber, dejected Menilek who knelt before Yohannes on 26 March 1878, though the emperor did everything he could to ensure dignity in the ritual. He placed a crown on Menilek's head and granted him officially the title he had been using, Negus of Shewa. Menilek had to relinquish hegemony over Wello, pay regular tribute, send troops when required and expel all missionaries. Then Yohannes laid down his religious policy which aimed to eliminate all schisms under the guise of a conference on the subject.

Menilek summoned the Shewan clerics to a conclave where they might defend in open debate their beliefs as espoused in Sost Ledat with the clerics of the emperor. It was foreordained, of course, that the Shewan priests would lose the debate. Three of those who refused to recant had their tongues cut out, and others fled into remote mountain hideaways.

Yohannes announced a Christianizing campaign to be pressed particularly in Wello, long a stronghold of Islam. Those who were not Christian would not be given government appointments. Those non-Christians currently in office must convert within three months; other Muslims were given three years and pagans were allowed two years to see the light; women were ignored.* The two rival Oromo leaders of Wello, Muhammad Ali and Abba Watew, met the three-month deadline. Emperor Yohannes stood as godfather at Muhammad Ali's conversion into Dejazmach Mikael, and King Menilek did the same for Abba Watew's conversion into Dejazmach Hayle Maryam.

As for the missionaries in Shewa, Yohannes gave Menilek a year's grace, though his own attitude was unequivocal. Yohannes could not understand what missionaries were doing in a country that was already Christian. There were two Protestants and five Catholics in Shewa, two of whom, Fathers Massaia and Taurin de Cahagne, were actively proselytizing. Menilek was so dilatory in banishing them that Yohannes finally did it himself in October 1879, under

---

*This lack of attention to women contrasts dramatically with the policy of the Catholic church which considered women crucial to the raising of children in the faith. The devotion of Ethiopian Christian women to the church was remarkable considering how they were treated. On the one hand the church elevated to sainthood a noblewoman of the 16th century, Welette Petros (for arousing the people against the Roman Catholic conversion of Emperor Susneyos), and on the other made life difficult for female religious communities. Women of advanced age who adopted the ascetic life might settle a discreet distance from a monastery; monks were often accused of taking advantage of them.

the pretext of asking them to undertake some diplomatic chores for him in Europe, about which he would write to them later.[29]

For four years after his parleys with Yohannes, Menilek behaved as a vassal king should. With the full knowledge, if not the urging, of Emperor Yohannes he carried out wars of conquest between 1879 and 1882 to bring the Oromo and Guraghe peoples under his jurisdiction. Arsi, Sidamo and parts of Keffa paid tribute to Menilek, a portion of which he had to pass along to the emperor.

Conflict over the riches of the southwest province of Keffa led to blood-letting between King Tekle Haymanot and King Menilek in 1882. Tekle Haymanot had been Menilek's prey in 1877, under the name of Ras Adal. Ras Adal had been renamed and crowned as King of Gojam and Keffa by Emperor Yohannes in 1881, thus depriving Menilek of the exclusivity of the kingly title as well as of his claim on Keffa. Menilek would not give up Keffa without a fight.

In the middle of 1882, Ras Gobena, Menilek's general in charge of stripping Keffa of ivory, coffee, gold and hides, was facing Tekle Haymanot's army, and was joined by Menilek. Despite repeated appeals from Emperor Yohannes to avoid civil war and submit their dispute to him, they went to war. During a day of fighting, 6 June 1882, Menilek captured the wounded Tekle Haymanot and two of his sons. "With great kindness," wrote Menilek's scribe, "he released soldiers on both sides so they could return to their ploughs before the rains came," and then brought the booty and his catch of royals back to Entotto.

Part of the booty was an Italian doctor, Raffaele Alfieri. After treating the wounds of his erstwhile employer, Tekle Haymanot, Alfieri became Menilek's physician, a prize Menilek had long sought. The doctor turned out to be Menilek's most immediate gain at a cost of some 2,000 casualties on the Shewan side alone. Menilek succumbed to hyperbole in announcing his victory: "The king of Gojam defied me. I marched against him and took his crown ... made him prisoner ... took all his lands." He backed down when Emperor Yohannes asserted his fury, first by marching from Debre Tabor to Were Ilu, where he released Meshesha Seyfu and threatened to make him Menilek's replacement, and then by ordering Menilek to bring his royal Gojamese captives to his camp, where he released them on the spot. The emperor seized the weapons Menilek had taken during the battle and annulled Menilek's suzerainty over Wello. The loss of Wello was mitigated when Yohannes confirmed Menilek's control of Keffa and made a marriage contract between his 15-year-old son, Araya, and Menilek's young daughter, Zewditu.[30]

Yohannes sent his son to Shewa with an escort of 1,800 men for the betrothal ceremony and exchange of gifts that took place on 22 October 1882. Eight-year-old Zewditu was taken back to Debre Tabor. Three months later the youngsters took communion together in the presence of three *abun* (bishops): Petros, Luqas and Matewos. Such a service of marriage was so rare between young people that it must have been the wish of Emperor Yohannes and lends credence to those who said that he commanded Menilek to do the same.[31]

Emperor and vassal king met again in February 1883 and this time Menilek returned to Shewa with one of the *abun*, Matewos. Emperor Yohannes had accomplished the most innovative change in the religious organization of the empire in centuries. He had requested, paid for, and obtained from the Alexandrian patriarchate four bishops, instead of the traditional one. They were to facilitate his clean-up of schisms in the church. Unfortunately one of the four *abun* died soon after his arrival, so after keeping one, Abune Petros, at his side, he had only two to disperse. One he sent to Gojam, and the other to Shewa.

Abune Matewos presided over the communion service uniting Menilek and Taytu Betul in an irrevocable bond on Easter Sunday, 29 April 1883, at Medhane Alem church in Ankober. It was psychologically interesting that Menilek chose a woman who was not unlike Bafena in personality and strength of character, and in the tradition of his assertive grandmother (Bezebesh) and great-grandmother (Zenebe Werq).

A couplet popular at the time of this marriage can be rendered as follows: "The sun has dissipated the fog," the "sun" being the literal meaning of *taytu*, and the "fog" alluding to the word *dafana*, hence a play on Bafena's name.

But there is a coda to the story of Bafena. Menilek did not forget the well-being of his ex-favorite and instructed one of his officers, who had once been intimate with her, to marry her. "How dare I touch a woman who once belonged to my king," said this gentleman. "You hypocrite!" shouted Menilek. "When you stole her from me you liked her, and now that I order you to marry her you don't want her." This man kissed the ground before Menilek and gave consolation to the afflicted Bafena. She died a few years later and was buried at the most holy place in Shewa, Debre Libanos.[32]

Menilek and Taytu about the time of their marriage

As Menilek was known as a womanizer his communion marriage heightened his prestige. Curiously the event was not mentioned by any of the foreigners who were in Ankober on that day, not even by Father Gonzague de Lasserre (in disguise because of Yohannes's ban on missionaries) who had seen Menilek the night before. Ankober was a small place and the movements of the king and Abune Matewos were usually accompanied by noise and panoply. One can only surmise that the service was conducted between midnight and dawn, merging into the usual Easter all-night prayers, and that it was not followed by any celebration.[33]

As Menilek entered his forties, he could look upon an enlarged kingdom, some promising European connections, good relations with Emperor Yohannes and the broadening of his power base through Taytu Betul's family connections in Semen, Yejju and Begemder. She would devote herself to the achievement of all of his ambitions and become first minister in his government.

2

The background of Taytu Betul Hayle Maryam

The chronicler ensures that posterity will know that Taytu Betul's
family was descended from a daughter of Emperor Susneyos
(1607-32), thus of the Solomonic line and the equal, if not the
superior,* in genealogical specie to Menilek.[1]

Emperor Susneyos had 25 sons and daughters by several wives,
so his descendants were scattered far and wide. The reign of Susneyos
has never been forgotten in Ethiopia because he not only converted
to Catholicism under the tutelage of the Portuguese Jesuit, Pero Paez,
but also decreed the disestablishment of Ethiopian Orthodoxy.
Susneyos began to comprehend the havoc wrought by his betrayal
of the Ethiopian church one day in 1631 when 6,000 people died of
religious fratricide. It so unnerved him that after restoring the primacy
of the national religion, he asked his son Fasilidas to take command.[2]

Nothing of the apostasy of Susneyos was included in the chronicle
as it sped through the centuries to Taytu's great-grandfather, Ras
Gebre of Semen, whose fame in the 19th century was measured by
the fact that he made the Shanqila[†] pay taxes in gold and that his
subjects gave up farming because food and drink were so copiously
provided by him. Ras Gebre ruled Semen for 44 years at the
beginning of the period known in Ethiopia as Zemene Mesafint or
the "Era of the Princes." What the phrase conceals is that during
the years from 1769 to 1855 the lords of each province and district
continuously fought each other for supremacy. An emperor was
always crowned but functioned as little more than the mayor of the
imperial city of Gondar. Accession to the throne depended on the
political whim of whichever chief controlled the region. Taytu Betul
was born as this turbulent period neared its violent end, when a
charismatic leader from Qwara district, Kasa Haylu, proclaimed
himself Emperor Tewodros II.[3]

---

*A comparison of an earlier form of the chronicle with the one used in this text revealed
that the early draft did not have the long genealogy of Taytu, nor a whole chapter
devoted to her coronation, which suggests that the empress added it herself either
after Menilek's decline, or after the death of the chronicler in 1912. (Hussein Ahmed)
[†]A derogatory term for the Hamitic-Nilotic peoples who have darker skins, thicker
lips and kinkier hair than the Amhara-Tigray group.

Even though it is engraved on Empress Taytu's tomb in Addis Ababa that she was born in E.C. 1832 (1839-40 of the Gregorian calendar), that date is not definitive. Other sources state just as absolutely that the Gregorian year 1853 was the year of her birth. The date of 1850-1 dovetails best with the known facts of her life. Marking birthdays is not an Ethiopian custom; the stonemason of the Menilek mausoleum erred on almost every date he chiseled.[4]

At the time Taytu was born the decision on who should be emperor rested with Ras Ali Alula,* seconded by his mother, Menen Leben Amede. It was Menen's third husband, the much younger Yohannes III, who was given the crown.

The central provinces of Begemder and Gojam were ruled from Debre Tabor, the military camp-city of Ras Ali. Tigray province, the northern gateway to Ethiopia from the Red Sea, was ruled by Dejazmach Wube, half-brother to Taytu's father, Betul Hayle Maryam, while Shewa in the south was governed by Menilek's father, Hayle Melekot. Shewa's geographical position enabled it to stay removed from the ruinous wars of the north.

Wube, Betul and his older brother, Merso, were all born in Semen, a mountainous district adjacent to Tigray. Semen was governed by their father, Dejazmach Hayle Maryam. Merso was his father's death-bed choice as successor in 1826, but his officers rejected Merso because "he would choose [to promote] people from his mother's part of the country." Wube, whose mother "was a woman of our country," was therefore elected. In just such sentences the historian can see not only the importance of the woman's connections, but the fear this princely family had of the Oromo dynasty in Gondar.

The mother of Merso and Betul was suspect because she was the daughter of Ras Gugsa, a leader from a Yejju ruling family (the Weresek) of Oromo origin. The Oromo were and are a major ethnic group in Ethiopia, but there exist within it tremendous variations from settlement to settlement. In Wello, Yejju and parts of Gojam and Begemder the Oromo had taken on the linguistic and cultural

---

*Ras Ali Alula (1818-66) was selected to rule when he was 13 years old, after the deaths in rapid succession of his father and three uncles. His mother dominated his actions for 10 years. Once her husband was crowned, she lived in Gondar, far removed from her son's headquarters at Debre Tabor, and her influence on him weakened. Ras Ali was known for his tolerance in religious matters (his family espoused Christianity), was friendly to foreigners and resorted to cruel punishments sparingly. His putative daughter, Tewabech, would marry Kasa Haylu (Tewodros II) and become an empress.

traditions of each area. But their past history as migrants from the 16th to the 19th century branded them in Christian-Amhara eyes as intruders. By military service and intermarriage with the Christian aristocracy, whom they obliged by converting to Christianity, the Wello and Yejju ruling families had become the dominant force, as evidenced by the fact that from 1800 to 1825 it was Ras Gugsa who appointed emperors.

Genealogy is important to Ethiopians and Taytu's enemies never allowed her to forget that her grandmother was the daughter of Ras Gugsa. "She is just a Galla [Oromo]," "She is just a Felasha [Jew]" or "She is just an Arab," they would whisper. Whispering was necessary because punishment would swiftly fall on anyone who maligned the empress. The only connection between Taytu and the Felasha was that they were at one time concentrated in Semen province. Semen itself was the object of insulting jokes by other provincials. "He who has nothing to eat is content with broccoli; he who has no country is content with Semen," was one saying. Semenites were ridiculed as soldiers whose shields were made of sheepskin. After Dejazmach Wube won a battle in the 1830s the Amhara skeptics marveled, "How can it be? Have the Semen sheep brought forth goats?" Semen women, however, were renowned for their light skin, and Taytu was a prime example of their pale, honeyed complexion.[5]

Taytu made no attempt to conceal her Oromo heritage, nor the "Arab" in her lengthy genealogy.* But her forebears' conversion to Christianity early in the 18th century is stressed and the "Era of the Princes" is falsely described as a time when "no man was in revolt, his [Gugsa's] army gave no battle and everyone lived in unity and peace." After Gugsa's death in 1825 war and conspiracy were the preoccupation of almost every petty lord. Still, avows the chronicler, "peace, joy and happiness reigned everywhere and they drank wine and arak like water ..."

Humiliated by Wube's usurpation of their inheritance, his two half-brothers and their mother emigrated to Tigray where their sister, Yewub-dar, had become the wife of Tigray's overlord, Sebagades. But Wube's Semen "sheep" became tigers, left their mountains and conquered Tigray between 1832 and 1836. Thus Merso and Betul,

*For example, her ancestor, Ras Ali (the elder), was a descendant of an Arab, Omar, who came with the armies of Ahmad ibn-Ibrahim and was responsible in 1638 for capturing Minas, a son of Emperor Lebna Dengel. (Tekle Tsadik Mekouria)

"superb young men, perfect horsemen, magnificently brave warriors," found themselves back in the service of their despised half-brother. One of them, probably Merso the older, was seen at Wube's court "dressed as a domestic and treated like one."[6]

A French doctor, Petit, met Merso in 1840. Merso was suffering from a "cruel disease" and when Dr. Petit prescribed a course of treatment (probably mercury pills for syphilis), Merso invited him to go along to his district seat. Dr. Petit was eager to go, but was advised not to as "it might excite the jealousy of Wube who resents his brothers." A few weeks later Dr. Petit heard that Merso had rebelled against Wube and fled. The doctor's sympathy for Merso vanished when he met a victim of Merso's brutality whose voice to tell the tale was about all he had left. Merso had chopped off the fingers of the right hand one by one to force this gentleman to order his soldiers to cede his fortress without a fight. When he refused, the fingers of his other hand were similarly removed, and then his feet and his ears, and finally he was blinded. "This human trunk survives," wrote Dr. Petit, "he has even fathered a child, conceived, he told me, by the thought of vengeance."[7]

Merso and Betul had switched their loyalties to the cause of their cousin, Ras Ali Alula, and were with him in February when one of the more confusing battles of the Zemene Mesafint took place.

Wube had long seen himself as the man who would liberate Ethiopia from those "Yejju Gallas," personified at this time in Ras Ali. The fact that he had married his daughter to Ras Ali a few years before did not stand in Wube's way. When the new metropolitan for Ethiopia, Abune Selama, arrived from Alexandria in late 1841, Wube determined to make use of him. It was not difficult to convince the 21-year-old, inexperienced Copt that Ras Ali was more Muslim than Christian and Wube secured his blessing for a crusade to overthrow Ali. The army of Tigray marched towards Debre Tabor.

Ras Ali placed his beloved wife, Hirut Wube, in the asylum church of Mahdere Maryam. Her sanctuary was cynically violated with the connivance of the new bishop who declared her marriage void on the grounds that her husband was a Muslim. An ally of Wube's was allowed to make off with her.

Wube's army was victorious at Debre Tabor and routed Ras Ali and his followers. The celebration began with captured honey-beer, but a remnant of Ras Ali's army, which included Merso and Betul, lay in wait. They interrupted the drunken festivities, captured Wube, and recalled Ras Ali. With his restored authority, Ras Ali rewarded Merso with the governorship of Semen. Merso first went to Gondar to pay his respects to Empress Menen. What with Merso's haughty behavior and the empress's pique at not being consulted by her son about this appointment, the meeting was not a cordial one. Arnauld d'Abbadie, who met Merso at this time, provided a description of him as short, well-formed, and fair-skinned with "feminine features." His reputation, "aside from his fighting renown and intolerable arrogance," was of a man who behaved "coarsely with women," but who was popular with his own soldiers with whom he fraternized on an equal footing.

Merso, accompanied by Betul, was half-way to Semen and in joyous anticipation of claiming the ancestral province, when a messenger arrived from Ras Ali, annulling the appointment. Abune Selama had negotiated a ransom payment for the release of Wube, rebaptized Ali and promised the return of his wife. Wube was released and Semen was returned to him. Compounding this treachery, Ras Ali agreed to help capture Merso and Betul. The brothers were chained briefly and then granted governance of small districts in Gojam.

Arnauld d'Abbadie was the only foreigner to record a face-to-face encounter with Betul, the father of Empress Taytu. "Betul ... welcomed me with disdainful familiarity ... bade me sit near him on his rug and asked if I could embroider shirts for women ..." One of the male-female role reversals in Ethiopia was that sewing was done only by men. D'Abbadie was offended because Betul used grammatical forms that were those of a superior to an inferior. Betul changed his language after one of his aides, who knew d'Abbadie, whispered in his ear. Betul confided to d'Abbadie that he was inclined towards the banner of Dejazmach Goshu of Gojam whose loyalty to Ras Ali was intermittent. Ultimately Betul betrayed his older brother, Merso, who died in the chains of Ras Ali. Betul's 1844 "inclination" towards Goshu did not last and he returned to the service of Ras Ali.[8]

Betul fathered a family of two boys and two girls, of whom Taytu was the third-born. Taytu's mother was named Yewub-dar.* In the wealth of family detail given by Empress Taytu in the chronicle there

---

*As Yewub-dar is also the name of Betul's sister who married Sebagades of Tigray, some writers have confused the two women.

is an intriguing lacuna on her mother, which suggests that she was not the daughter of anyone important. However, oral sources asserted that "she was a fine lady from Gondar."[9]

Assuming the year of Taytu's birth to be 1850-1, her father would then have been serving in the army of Ras Ali. Yewub-dar would not have accompanied her husband on military campaigns if she had been the well-born lady she was said to be. Officers of rank left their wives in safety and took along a "thigh" maid to cook, carry their gear, and serve their sexual needs. Women, of whatever status, were generally not molested prior to or as a consequence of war.* Before an attack the drums were sounded to warn women and children to remove themselves. Certain villages, such as Dima in Gojam, and Mahdere Maryam in Begemder, were designated for asylum.

Mahdere Maryam, a half-day mule ride from Debre Tabor, was called a "town of aristocratic women," and despite Taytu's remark to one writer that she had been "brought up in Were Sehin in Yejju," it was very likely to have been her birthplace. Special permission had to be given for anyone to enter this village by any means other than on foot. All the women wore Turkish slippers, possessed jewelry and took pains with their looks. Their houses were clean and tidy and their gardens of vegetables gave them a "suburban" air. It was in Mahdere Maryam that Menen, the mother of Ras Ali, received homage and heard appeals before her move to Gondar and her coronation as empress. It was in Mahdere Maryam that Ras Ali placed his wife for sanctuary in 1842 only to have her safety violated by her own father with the connivance of the head of the church.[10]

Taytu's mother was remarkable for having given birth to four children who lived into adulthood, and for having herself survived into her eighties. Mortality rates for both mother and child in the Ethiopia of the mid-19th century may not have been higher than those of Europe, where antiseptic methods in childbirth did not begin to alter statistics until after 1865. But in Ethiopia survival in the post-natal period was jeopardized by two customs: the mother was sequestered for 40 days; the child, whether male or female, was circumcised. European middle- and upper-class women were housebound, but not immobile, for a month. The Ethiopian woman had to stay in a small, unventilated, smoke-filled birth hut for 40

---

*Recorded exceptions: Welde Selasse's takeover of Tigray in 1780 included the slaughter of women; Welde Rafael slew the women of Womberta in 1816; and the period from 1800 to 1840 was described as "a bad time for women."

days without taking any exercise. The poorest women, those who were the beasts of burden on military exercises, were exempt from these rules and were probably healthier for it. "We heard a hustle and a bustle," wrote Father Massaia of one of these camp-followers, "as the poor woman feeling delivery near, wanted to stop but was forced to continue, though her companions lightened her load. On the road she became a mother and after an hour of rest, tucking her little creature into a basket, she followed along."

For difficulty in childbirth there were many prescriptions of varying repulsiveness. Horse dung diluted with honey-beer could be drunk to force the expulsion of a dead foetus; the abdomen might be sprinkled with the diluted ordure of a dog to ease birth. For severe labor pains, foul-smelling sulphur might be burned in the birth hut, or a man's trousers placed on the roof. A breech delivery was not permitted by some midwives; the foetus was forced back into the birth canal and turned around by hand. First births were usually at a precocious age, as girls married at about the age of 12, and the penalty was paid in future births by early loss of muscle tone. Gynecological infection and trauma in very young girls often led to spontaneous abortion, stillbirth and sterility. The birthrate was low, and is still low in modern Ethiopia. Many lords had large families, but their children were by different women. Whether a woman was married or not, her pregnancy was much respected. Passers-by would invoke the name of the Virgin Mary and wish her luck. When she was noticeably pregnant, her husband was expected to cease sexual relations with her. He would otherwise be committing sodomy if there were a male in the womb, or incest if there were a female.

Just before confinement, the woman might take *kosso* as a purgative, as women in other countries have been given enemas. She would also put on her filthiest clothes, offering yet another opportunity for sepsis. *Kosso* is a vilely bitter herb, but the Ethiopians were accustomed to it, taking it about once a month to expel worms ingested from eating one of their favorite dishes, raw meat.*

The midwife would rub the belly of the mother-to-be with butter, then sit her almost upright on a smooth stone smeared with butter.

---

*Dr. Petit, in 1840, tried *kosso*. "Abundant salivation, persistent bitter taste, violent headache, tendency to faint ... after two hours expelled the worm; afterwards, excessive sweating, stiffness and nausea." The *kosso* taker retires from all social life for several days. Emperor Menilek had drums beaten when he took *kosso*, to warn off all appointments. *Kosso*, in diluted form, can be bought in some French pharmacies today.

Other women held her firmly by the shoulders, knees and waist. Virgins and barren women were barred from the vicinity, and men and women passing by were told to loosen their belts to help this child into the world. If labor was lengthy, priests might be called to recite a prayer over some water which the patient then drank. Should that inducement fail to work, her husband's knees would be washed and the water saved from the ablution served to her. A final expedient might be the surprise firing of a gun, which, "if it didn't frighten her to death, would expel the stubborn heir into the world."

The infant was caught in a wicker basket filled with flour or straw, and then washed in cold water by the midwife who also molded the head and features of the baby by pressing with her fingers to make them handsome. The boy child might be carried out to his father who would stick the tip of his lance into his mouth to make him courageous. At the moment of birth, the attending women called out the sex of the baby. If the father owned a rifle he would inform the entire populace by firing it seven times for a boy, and three times for a girl; in the absence of a rifle, he and his friends would cheer the corresponding number of times.

The lesser status of a woman began from the moment of birth.

When a woman is born the demon enters her through her feet. As she grows the demon climbs up hand by hand to her neck. Thus, when grown, the demon has reached her forehead, and then her head where he takes up his abode. When a male is born, the demon attacks him in the forehead, and as he grows, the demon descends and this man becomes brave, serious and perfect. Then when the demon reaches his feet, he gives him a kick and he is gone. After that he is an honest person who gives beer to the thirsty, food to the hungry, clothes to the naked and haven to the tired.

After severing the infant from the placenta, the midwife would touch a dab of yeast to its tongue, or a piece of butter mixed with *kosso*. The latter practice courted danger, for purging a new-born could cause internal rupture. The purpose of the butter was to ensure a pleasant voice. In later life a loud-mouthed person might be asked whether he or she had tasted butter at birth. The placenta of a girl baby was buried outside and to the left of the house, symbolizing her eventual departure from her home when she married. The male child's placenta was buried inside and to the right, indicating that he would follow in his father's footsteps. When a person is dilatory in taking leave from someone's house, jokers will say that his afterbirth must be buried there.[11]

An infant's toilette consisted of daily bathing and rubbing with butter. There were no diapers. Finely ground clay or powdered burned cattle dung was placed in the armpits and between the thighs to prevent chafing. The child might be nursed for a couple of years, which was also a crude form of birth control, though aristocratic women often gave their babies over to wet nurses.

Circumcision with unsterile knives, shards of glass or sharp rocks, took place on the eighth day for boys and some time between the 15th and the 80th day for girls. There were only two sentinels against infection: prayer and urine. Circumcision of girls in most parts of the country consisted of trimming the labia minora. The more brutal forms of female mutilation, clitoridectomy, infibulation and excision, were common in areas that border on Muslim countries, Sudan in the west, Egypt in the north, and along the Red Sea littoral.

Female circumcision is still common in Ethiopia and most of the Middle East. It is believed to control a girl's sexual appetite, prevent masturbation and ensure her virginity until marriage. It is said in Ethiopia that an uncircumcised woman will not only be unfaithful to her husband, but she will also drop and break things in her home.

The circumcision wound was packed with butter or with ashes from a burned cloth and, if there was no infection, would heal quickly. The sequelae of female circumcision, such as hemorrhage, internal infection, trauma, difficulty in urination and menstruation, were not as likely when only the labia minora were trimmed. Nonetheless, any undue loss of blood in the first few weeks of life was yet another obstacle to staying alive.

Infant mortality was so commonplace that no name was given to the child in order to conceal its existence from all those lurking devils who caused death. There were a myriad of magic formulas devised by priests to thwart death. A mother who had lost children at birth might cut a tiny nick out of her newborn's ear and swallow it or she might shave half her head before delivery, but the best insurance against harm to her child was a sliver of iron worn in her hair or placed in her bed, for "Satan is afraid of iron."[12]

When the mother finally carried her child to the church for baptism (males on the 40th day, females on the 80th)* she was shaded by a parasol, for sunlight is dangerous. A male relative would walk ahead of her with a knife or sword to ward off evil spirits. The priests

---

*These days were determined by the Ethiopian belief that this was the difference in time between Adam and Eve's reception of the holy spirit.

were busy for hours with holy water, purifying the birth hut, the
mother, and anyone who had been in contact with the birth process.
Baptism itself was a rigorous event. First, there were two hours of
praying, singing and reading from the Old Testament and the
Ethiopian book of baptism, a volume so enormous that one man
could not hold it. The head cleric blew into the baby's face to drive
out evil, anointed the forehead, breast and shoulders, and turned
the child towards the east, pouring water over it as the godfather
or godmother held up the child's right thumb. Confirmation followed
immediately. The child was again anointed and the priest bestowed
the Holy Spirit by placing his hand on the head, and then wrapped
the tiny body in white cloth. A communion morsel was placed in
the mouth and a cord tied around the neck.[13]

The baptismal name of Empress Taytu was Welette Mikael
(daughter of St. Mikael), which indicated that she was baptized on
the 12th of a certain month, as that day is always dedicated to St.
Mikael. After the birth of her sister Desta, their father died on 29
June 1853 of wounds received at the battle of Ayshal, according to
folklore.[14] This was the battle that ended the rule of Ras Ali, and
led to the coronation of Emperor Tewodros in 1855.

When this event took place Taytu, her sister, her brothers and her
mother were at the monastery of Debre Mewi in Gojam, where her
mother's second husband was the *aleqa* (lay administrator). Her
brothers, Wele and Alula, must have been old enough to be soldiers,
but apparently on the losing side, as they became prisoners of
Emperor Tewodros at Meqdela about 1857. It was there that they
became acquainted with the young prince of Shewa, who was also
a captive. Menilek admired them so much that he asked them if they
had a sister; he was told she was in a monastery with her nurse.

Since marriage is a contract made for the mutual interests of the
families involved, the story that Taytu's family vetoed betrothal of
their daughter to the imprisoned Menilek "because Tewodros hates
us" has validity. The family might have a safer future if she married
one of Tewodros's generals. This officer, called a parvenu by the
chronicler, has a variety of names depending on the source.[15]

Taytu Betul made an abrupt transition, as did most Ethiopian girls,
from childhood to adulthood (marriage) at about the age of 10. She
knew she was being prepared for marriage when she was quietly
dismissed by the priests from communion, which she had attended
since infancy, when she was no longer allowed to run about in the

fields herding cattle with her playmates, and when she was more
closely supervised by her mother in her chores of chopping onions,
grinding pepper, baking bread and learning to spin. Once the
respective genealogies were checked to make sure there was no
kinship to the seventh degree and respective dowries were agreed
upon, there was a wedding.

The nuptial night was traditionally a night of conquest. To
enhance the male sense of a battleground on which he must triumph,
the girl's sex education consisted of being told she must resist
her husband's advances as fiercely as possible. Young men were
encouraged to have pre-marital experience (with married women,
divorcees or a household servant), but if they failed to penetrate
their virgin bride, or if the young wife took the instruction to
resist too seriously, the groom might call in his best man to assist
in the defloration. One of the toasts offered to a bridegroom
was that he have a penis shaped like the sharp horn of an
antelope. Victory in the bed chamber was symbolized by the blood-
stained cloth brought out and displayed for the cheering wedding
guests.[16]

Tragically, some failures by grooms on wedding nights could
be due to physical blockage caused by the wound adhering after
inept circumcision of the girl in infancy. Whether Taytu underwent
excision or the cutting away of clitoris and labia minora, or the less
damaging removal of the labia minora alone, is not known. Infection
from either of these mutilations could have damaged her fallopian
tubes and been a cause of her sterility.

After marriage, the girl became an adult and could begin to assert
herself, as Ethiopian women do in hundreds of original and clever
ways. The alteration in behavior from the "sweet, young thing" to
the "libertine" manners of the young married woman shocked many
foreigners, who wrestled with the paradoxes and contradictions in
Ethiopian society, particularly those connected with religious
devotion and sexual freedom. "We were shocked because our minds
were not so open," was the thoughtful conclusion of Combes and
Tamisier, two St. Simonians,* in 1837. "The Abyssinian woman
loves everyone for money and no one for free ... and to think that
it is morally wrong would be sheer romanticism. Only those who

---

*The society of St. Simonians was formed in 1830 of men and women dedicated not
only to sexual equality but to the concept of an androgynous God and the possibility
of discovering a female messiah.

have everything can think that. Here, misery is more to be feared than the absence of love."[17]

Their athletic initiation into woman's estate did not appear to prejudice women against the enjoyment of sex, for which they had a reputation equal to men. The compensations for the girl-woman in the married state were great. She joined the society of people who possessed things. She had her cooking pots, her dresses, shawls, headband, perhaps a mirror, a ring, an ankle bracelet, an umbrella, and soon her own house. She began to dress her hair in intricate braids and protect it from disarray by the use of a small wooden pillow. Other women taught her depilation, for both men and women removed their pubic hair and women would pluck out their entire eyebrows and substitute thin, dark lines.

Taytu Betul did not come from an area where this type of cosmetology was prevalent, and did not take to it even when she moved to Shewa.

The first sight of Shewan women is particularly striking to a foreigner, not only on account of their shaven heads but also an account of their shaven or plucked out eyebrows ... curved lines are drawn to cheek bone, where they end in circles. A still greater disfigurement is ... painting a broad stripe, blood-red in color, over their noses, cheeks and forehead by which their often handsome features are dreadfully disfigured.

This red cosmetic touch was observed in the 1840s, but had died out by the 1880s.[18]

Womanliness was complete only when a child was born. If a woman did not have a child, she could be abandoned by her husband, and unless she was well connected, like Taytu Betul, or had an exceptionally advantageous property settlement from her divorce, she would have difficulty finding another husband. A sterile woman was a pathetic outcast in Amhara society, unless she chose to become a nun, or a prostitute. In Begemder province, the disgrace of being sterile was perpetuated in death, for the woman would be buried face down.[19]

Taytu's first marriage to the officer of Emperor Tewodros ended badly, wrote Pietro Antonelli. "He [Tewodros] gave them a cruel wedding present by putting her husband in chains a few days after the ceremony and she was forced to follow the army on foot like a peasant, chained at the wrist, grinding grain and cooking for the soldiers."

The beginning of Taytu's marital history was embellished by another source, Mekonnen Endalkatchew,* who had the best possible credentials to know the truth. Mekonnen, the nephew of Tessema Nadew (son of Menilek's tutor) and the husband of Taytu's great-niece, was brought up at the palace under the supervision of Empress Taytu. He told a bizarre story with the mild apologia that he had "sweetened" history just a little.

Emperor Tewodros was told about a beautiful woman in Gondar and had her brought in for inspection. He offered her gifts and his love, but she spurned him, partly for family reasons,† and partly because she loved her husband. She quoted the Bible to him on the subject of immorality, and he sent her away in irritation. (The notion that any woman would dare to offend Emperor Tewodros is hardly credible, but Mekonnen proceeded with this story.)

The angry emperor forced her to march naked with her husband and two children before the populace, which offended the people, but they did admire her fine figure. Her uncle, Ras Tedla, rushed forward to cover her with his own shawl and told Tewodros that he himself felt naked and would not permit such humiliation.

"She scorns me, and you, Tedla, feel sorry for her and not for me," the emperor shouted, and ordered the execution of her husband and children, but the people protested and he let the children live.‡ Mekonnen's insertion of these fictitious children was a device to emphasize the cruelty of Emperor Tewodros. However, Tewodros

---

*Mekonnen Endalkatchew's book, *Taytu Betul*, was banned by Emperor Hayle Selasse even though the author was his own prime minister. Mekonnen's son, who was ambassador from Ethiopia to the United Nations in 1966, answered my query as to the reasons for the proscription. "Criticism came from certain people of Gondar ... particularly those who claimed family connections with Emperor Tewodros." Though the book may be regarded as "historical romance fiction" it was taken seriously enough to be banned.
†The only possible family reason could be that Taytu's cousin, Terunesh Wube, had married Emperor Tewodros in 1860 after the death of his wife, Tewabech Ali, in 1858.
‡Considering the time frame and Taytu's probable age, it was unlikely she had any children, let alone two. The empress never referred to any child, or deceased children, in her conversations with the doctors she consulted such as Dr. Martin and Dr. Vollbrecht. There was a Ras Tedla from Mikre (in Begemder) at Tewodros's court, who was somehow related to Taytu. He was noted in Heruy Welde Selasse's thumbnail sketches as "a noble famous for his generosity." His daughter, Altash, was a familiar figure in Taytu's suite and lived into the 1940s. She recounted her relationship to Taytu to Zewde Gabre-Sellassie: "There were others more closely related to the empress but she showed much affection and consideration to me because of the gratitude she felt for my father who had helped her at the time of her husband's execution by Tewodros."

was also known for compassionate treatment of women and children. One witness recounted that after shooting some rebels, "their wives were brought forward, stripped to the waist. The king ordered them to be covered and on learning that their only crime was that they were the wives of the condemned ... said it was no fault of theirs that they had bad husbands. The women were supplied with food and clothing and set free."[20]

In Mekonnen's story, Ras Tedla took her away and cared for her until the death of Tewodros.* The story then jumps 15 years to her marriage to Menilek of Shewa. Antonelli and Dr. Paul Mérab fill in the interval with marriages to other soldiers, one named Dejazmach Tekle Giyorgis. Then, "capriciously, this high-strung woman divorced him. But preferring conjugal life, she gave her hand to the governor of Yejju, Janterar Udie."†

Taytu's preference for conjugal life was not whimsical. It was preferred by all women, for "the woman who sleeps alone risks being struck by the *zar*." The *zar* was one of the demons in folklore who was believed to look exactly like the handsome, light-complexioned Abyssinians and acted as the carrier of physical and mental illness. A married woman might explain the birth of a deformed child by saying that a *zar*, jealous of her husband, had coitus with her.[21] A rational reason for Taytu's choice of husband could have been his high status. *Janterar* was a title reserved for the man who guarded the fortress of Ambasel in Yejju, a safe place to be after the death of Tewodros while Wagshum Gobeze and Dejazmach Kasa Mercha fought for the throne. Kasa Mercha won, became Emperor Yohannes IV, and imprisoned the *janterar* of Ambasel, and Taytu went home to her mother in Debre Mewi, Gojam, "to succor mind and body."

It is a fair assumption that, since her stepfather administered the monastery at Debre Mewi, Taytu would have acquired her adeptness at law and theology there, though wherever she lived she must have pursued an education. She had unusual accomplishments for a woman: she could read and write Amharic; she knew Ge'ez, the

---

*Mekonnen Endalkatchew described her weeping beside the body of Tewodros on 13 April 1868 despite his cruelty to her. This is hard to believe, considering Taytu's survival instincts. That she would be lurking at Meqdela fortress while the British bombarded it prior to storming the gates is not credible.
†Antonelli could be completely wrong and may have confused Taytu with her sister, Desta, who was married to a "Wonde of Ambasel."

recondite language of the sacred texts; she composed poetry, played chess and strummed the _begenna_ (lyre).[22]

According to Antonelli, Taytu was drawn from Debre Mewi to Shewa by the death of her brother, Alula, in about 1881. Another source says that she went to the court of Emperor Yohannes to visit her aunt, Itege Dinqinesh,* and thence to the court of Negus Tekle Haymanot of Gojam.[23]

All sources agree that Taytu married Kenyazmach Zikargatchew, the brother of Bafena, consort of Menilek, in 1881-2. Zikargatchew, described by Antonelli as "the man most elegant and fashionable in Shewa," was jealous and impetuous. He beat Taytu, and she left him, taking a great deal of property and many servants, on the pretext that she was going to visit her mother, but instead, took refuge with her brother Wele in Yejju.

Beating one's wife without good cause (for example, on account of bad cooking, lack of respect or flirting) was an acceptable reason for divorce. Apparently Taytu did not bother with a divorce settlement, since she took away with her all the property she wanted. Nor did she tarry to ask for a prescription from the _hakim_ (medical practitioner) to prevent wife-abuse: "Take a hair from your husband's head, say the magic formula as you bury half of the hair in the ground and carry the other half in an amulet around the neck." Nor did she give Zikargatchew time to carry- out a prescription against a wife's flirtation: "Take seven flies ... mix with hyena dung and massage your genital organ while repeating the magic formula 49 times, then have sexual intercourse with her."[24]

Antonelli has Taytu meet Menilek in August-September 1882, at the time of his reprimand by Emperor Yohannes for his war with King Tekle Haymanot. Taytu has gone to inquire about the fate of those retainers of hers who had been serving Menilek. They agree on a communion marriage and she travels back to Shewa with Menilek. But on the way Menilek stops off for one last scandalous

---

*This relationship is not clear. Dinqinesh was the sister of Kasa Mercha and held the title Itege when her husband declared himself Emperor Tekle Giyorgis. When her brother defeated her husband in battle in 1871 she insisted on sharing her husband's captivity. After his death she married Ras Gebre Kidane and had a son, Seyum. The Lemlem chronicle (BN) has her marry Gebre Medhin, which would make her a distant relative by marriage of Taytu, but Zewde Gabre-Sellassie says this is an error. When Dinqinesh died, in August 1907, aged 92, her sagacity in politics and skills in poetry and music were eulogized. One mourner said there had been two unique women in the country, now there was only one, Empress Taytu.

dalliance with Bafena who had tried to escape his ardor at a convent in Firkuta. That Bafena was in Firkuta is confirmed by the diary of Father Ferdinand, a Catholic priest who had evaded the expulsion order, and was corresponding with her because he lived on land belonging to her.[25]

Menilek's behavior with Bafena so disgusted Taytu that she married someone else, according to an oral source whose family knew the man. When Menilek decided he still wanted Taytu he, in effect, bought him off: knowing that the man was fond of drink, Menilek gave him land in Begemder where he could keep plenty of beehives to make honey-wine.[26]

Amidst all the gossip and stories there is one certain fact about Empress Taytu's marital history. She was married several times before she was 30. It is also certain that before marrying the king of Shewa, she had suffered hard times: carried heavy loads, endured bitter cold nights sleeping on the ground, felt sharp stones against her bare feet and tended the gaping wounds of those impaled by spears or gouged by a bullet. She would have cared for people sick with cholera, a disease that causes vomiting and purging, revolting to sight and smell. Smallpox too was endemic, but Taytu's much admired skin had no scars. It is also clear that she married opportunistically, as in all accounts it is Taytu who is bestowing her hand, and not the other way around.

Taytu, it was said, was motivated by a seer who told her in her youth that she was destined to wear the crown. She clearly organized her life around the courts of three royal figures to provide optimum conditions for the fulfillment of the prophecy. Her renowned youthful beauty was probably less potent a reason for the ease with which she acquired husbands than the importance of her family, especially Wele, who managed to be loyal to Menilek without coming into open conflict with Emperor Yohannes. Wele must have promoted Taytu's marriage to the Shewan king, though in the recollection of one of Menilek's foreign retainers, it was her sister, Desta, who attracted Menilek's attention first. "But when he saw Taytu, Menilek complained to Wele, 'Why didn't you show me the prettier one first?' "[27]

A photograph of Taytu taken about the time of her marriage to Menilek does not testify to any extraordinary beauty. Her best features were her lustrous brown eyes, set in a perfect oval face (though she had a slight indentation on her right jaw), her delicate

The earliest known photograph of
Taytu, taken in her early 30s, showing
her "northern" hairstyle

Menilek, about 1888, five years after
his marriage to Taytu

hands with "fingers like slender reeds," and her well-shaped feet. She
was almost 1.6 meters tall, with a figure tending towards plumpness.
Her early hair-style was "northern," with rows of tight braids
covering her head and caught at the nape of the neck, then released
in a loose cluster. She later changed the style, leaving her hair
unbraided, and used the imported Italian hair oil given to her by
Count Antonelli, instead of the rancid butter with which most
Ethiopian women (and men) dressed their hair. Her neck was
encircled with a lacy design tattooed in dark blue ink, just visible
beneath her jewelry. A fine straight nose, the *sine qua non* of classic
Ethiopian beauty, is not apparent in the photograph, and her lips
appear fleshier than those considered ideal for the usual Amhara
beauty.

It was Taytu's mind and her family connections in provinces other
than Shewa that appealed to Menilek. He admired her shrewdness
which was evident in her mastery of the way the power structure
worked and her diplomacy with the ubiquitous clergy. And to
Menilek, who was famous for saying *"Ishi, nega"* ("Yes, tomorrow"),
Taytu Betul Hayle Maryam's decisiveness — she was famous for
saying *"Imbi"* ("Absolutely not") — must have seemed an impressive
quality.

3

King Menilek and Queen Taytu, 1883-9

After the Easter communion service in April 1883 uniting Menilek and Taytu in their irrevocable bond, the new queen's first question for her husband, according to the chronicler, was "May I build ... a church dedicated to Our Lady?" Menilek agreed to her choice of site at Entotto and there he placed the requisite symbol, a replica of the ark of the covenant, before leaving on a military campaign to subdue the Oromo of Itu. He was clearly not so besotted with Taytu that he could not bear to leave her. In this account the chronicler establishes the new queen as a devout churchwoman, and in the subsequent 50 pages preserves all the minutiae about Entotto Maryam church from the size of the roof beams to the number of sacks of red pepper required to prepare the food for its dedication. It took three and a half years to build the church and the chronicler omits most of the political events of this period. Taytu rapidly gained a reputation for piety and charity. Only a few months after the April marriage, Father Ferdinand, over 150 kilometers from the scene, wrote, "She has studied the psalms of David, is an enduring [sic] woman and gives charity to the poor."[1]

A more credible question for Taytu to have asked her royal spouse would have been: "What lands are you granting me?" or "Who is that foreigner you spend all your time with?" The foreigner was Count Pietro Antonelli, on his second trip to Shewa. He was bringing guns and gifts for the king and carrying credentials for the Marchese Antinori to represent the Italian government in a treaty with Menilek. As the Marchese had died in August 1882, Antonelli became the diplomat.

From the day of his arrival at Ankober, where the royal wedding had taken place the week before, Antonelli spent most of his time with Menilek and never mentioned in his reports that the king had just married. "The welcome given me by the king excited jealousy and envy because for three days no other European could see him and I stayed from morning to evening." Menilek did see Paul Soleillet, the French arms supplier, and in Antonelli's comment can be seen his proprietary attitude towards Menilek: "Signor Soleillet ... pretended to be a representative of the French government, wanting to establish a consulate in Shewa, but did not succeed." That Menilek was to be the puppet of Italy and be under the influence of no other power was an illusion held tenaciously by Count Antonelli for 13 years.

Menilek and the Italian discussed a treaty in which Italy and Shewa would exchange diplomatic missions, and would have full freedom of movement for both men and goods in both countries, exemption from duty for Shewan goods at Assab (now an Italian port), and respect for each other's religion. The treaty was to provide Italy with extraterritoriality, namely, that Italy should have jurisdiction over criminal cases involving its own citizens in Shewa except in cases where both nationalities were involved, which would be judged by a joint Italian-Shewan commission.

Despite her alleged xenophobia and her reputedly overwhelming influence over Menilek, Taytu did not prevent the king from signing this treaty with Antonelli on 21 May 1883. Her role may be detected in the great care that Menilek took over the Amharic translation and his alertness to any exploitation, as remarked by Antonelli. This treaty signified the beginning of official diplomatic relations between Shewa province and Italy, and laid the foundation for Italian support of Menilek's ambition to overthrow his suzerain, Emperor Yohannes. Menilek was not an innocent pawn; he gave Antonelli every reason to think that Italian protection was the answer to his prayers.

While Menilek was off on his military campaign, followed by an elephant hunt, Taytu organized her household at Entotto which, by tradition, was completely separate from that of the king. She also collected materials for "her" church. Soon, the red umbrella, a color exclusive to her and the king, was seen around Entotto as, astride an ornately caparisoned mule, she oversaw her various projects.

Upon Menilek's return, a family of experienced carpenters from Gondar arrived and thousands of laborers were commanded to appear at Entotto. They brought food with them to last a month. When their food was finished, they returned to their farms and were replaced by 5,000 new workers. A French visitor at the time complained, "We could not interview the monarch any longer as he was too absorbed in directing the work; he comes and goes, surveys, encourages with voice and gesture, takes measurements and does not hesitate to put his own hand to work; he is very clever as he designs plans and elevations, constructs little models in wood and seems to have a bent for engineering."[2]

In late November 1883 Menilek ceased this work and went to Arsi with Ras Gobena on one of his many attempts to conquer these unwilling subjects of Shewa. Taytu remained at Entotto.*

At the end of August 1884 Emperor Yohannes summoned Menilek to a conference at Borumeda, halfway between their two capitals. Taytu accompanied Menilek. Yohannes announced the good news that Great Britain had guaranteed the return of Ethiopian districts, over which Yohannes had been negotiating for eight years since his defeat of Egypt. The agreement was called the Treaty of Adwa, or the Hewett Treaty after the vice-admiral who headed the British team. Among other provisions, it promised duty-free transit of Yohannes's goods through the port of Massawa. Britain, by taking over Egypt in 1882, had assumed responsibility for Egypt's colonies, of which Massawa and Harar were two. For his part of the bargain (to get back what belonged to Ethiopia) Yohannes agreed to make common cause with Britain against the Mahdists, a religious-political movement in the Sudan, which was threatening Ethiopia as well. Yohannes promised to guarantee the safety of the Egyptian garrisons under Mahdist siege as they were being evacuated through Ethiopia to the port of Massawa. He also agreed to proscribe slave-trading, and he and Menilek issued proclamations against the business.[3]

At Borumeda, Yohannes secured Menilek's cooperation against fifth-column Mahdists. He also secured Menilek's promise to prevent rebellious clan groups from attacking while he was engaged on his frontiers. Menilek saw his daughter Zewditu for the first time since 1882, in Yejju, where she had begun to co-habit with her husband, Araya Yohannes. For Taytu, it was an opportunity to meet her stepdaughter and also to visit her brother Wele and his seven-year-old son, Gugsa.

Count Antonelli, on his third trip to Ethiopia, met Taytu for the first time at Borumeda in October 1884. Antonelli not only fulfilled his contract by delivering more guns to Menilek, but also satisfied "his dearest wish" by bringing a physician, Vincenzo Ragazzi. Menilek already had the services of Dr. Raffaele Alfieri who was off with Ras Gobena on military duty at this time. Dr. Ragazzi was sent on ahead to Shewa where he was to combine medicine with directing the Italian geographical station. Antonelli stayed behind

*In an earlier version of the chronicle, analyzed by Hussein Ahmed, Taytu went with Menilek on this campaign. She was never reluctant to take credit for fortitude so I believe the account was untrue and amended by her later.

to journey back with Menilek and Taytu.

Antonelli, who had known Bafena and called her *l'arbitra irrequieta* (the tireless go-between), did not take long to recognize that Taytu was now the person whose cooperation must be gained. "Menilek is a warrior king, and intelligent, but loves the weaker sex too much — too often they have a dominant influence over him." During their first encounter Taytu questioned Antonelli about the wife of King Umberto; Antonelli could say truthfully that Margarita was a pious and charitable lady. He did not tell Taytu that Margarita was also bigoted, xenophobic and despotic, words that he frequently used to describe the Ethiopian queen. Taytu assured Antonelli that she always favored Italian interests and preferred Italy to any other nation. He found her informed about his business with Menilek and interested in its success. The "business" was a trade route from the port of Assab via Aussa to Shewa, which would make Shewa independent of the French port of Obok (later moved to Djibouti), thus by-passing Harar which was under the control of Anglo-Egypt.

Menilek had assured Antonelli that he would name a mission to Italy which the Italian fervently desired as dramatic proof of his diplomatic and commercial successes. Almost two years had elapsed since the promise, and now with Taytu's advocacy, the head of the mission was named in February 1885.

Two weeks later the mission was canceled as the Italian navy and 1,000 *bersaglieri* occupied the fetid little island of Massawa with the knowledge and consent of Britain. This agitated Emperor Yohannes more than Menilek because the latter could receive his goods through either Italian-controlled Assab or French-controlled Obok. Yohannes protested to Queen Victoria, for Vice-Admiral Hewett had promised in the treaty that shipping through Massawa would not be impeded; it was also the emperor's clear understanding that if Massawa were turned over to any one country, it would be to Ethiopia. He had refused to make a treaty similar to the one Menilek had made with Italy, though it had been offered, because he had accepted Britain as the guarantor of his rights on the Red Sea. He saw Massawa's occupation by Italy as an English betrayal, which it was.[4]

When the news reached Shewa, Menilek asked Antonelli for an explanation. Taytu was present and could hardly contain her anger against Italy, reported Antonelli. Antonelli had not been informed in advance by his government of the move into Massawa,* so he improvised quickly on the theme that Italy was peace-loving, and that Emperor Yohannes was upset because he did not understand this. Would Menilek, who comprehended Italy's peaceful aims, offer mediation between Yohannes and Italy?

The emperor declined Menilek's offer of mediation, and himself received a conciliatory delegation (Vincenzo Ferrari and Dr. Cesare Nerazzini) in May 1885, which calmed him for the moment. Antonelli reminded Menilek of his huge debt for the guns delivered to date, and Menilek made no further issue of the Massawa occupation. The Shewan king was planning his own occupation of Harar and wanted Italian "understanding" of that move; he also wanted more guns.

The Italians did not confine themselves to Massawa, and in classic colonial style advanced on to the mainland and up into the highlands with the rationale that their soldiers needed fresher air for their health,† and that the trade route required armed protection. Yohannes left matters in the hands of his chief general, Ras Alula, while he and Menilek went to Wello to subdue a rebellion against Araya (Yohannes's son and Menilek's son-in-law) provoked by the murder of an important Wello leader. Menilek's cooperation in this campaign allayed the emperor's constant doubts about his loyalty, and to test him further Yohannes ordered Menilek to expel all the Italians from Shewa. Taytu agreed with Emperor Yohannes. Menilek sent his secretary and translator, Aleqa Yosef Neguse,‡ to tell Antonelli to leave the country. Antonelli penned an arrogant note to Menilek avowing that he had been insulted by this message brought by a "simple clerk" and saying that if Menilek wanted him to leave he should put it in writing over his royal seal.

---

*The operation was known only to about five men. Neither Admiral Caimi nor the army commander, Tancredi Saletta, knew their destination when they embarked at Messina. Only at Suakin was Saletta provided with a map of Massawa by the English colonel. The landing was unopposed, which was fortunate, because all the firearms were stored in the ship's hold, and inaccessible.

†Not without grounds as Saletta reported that one-third of his troops were sick and dispirited. Thirty-seven deaths from disease were reported at Massawa for the first year of occupation. The temperature at Massawa could reach 70°C, a fact that was censored from newspaper dispatches to Italy.

‡Yosef Neguse learned French at the Catholic school in Massawa, c. 1863. He came to Shewa in 1869 on hearing Father Massaia was there. He gave up Catholicism upon taking service with Menilek, returning to Ethiopian Orthodoxy, and became indispensable to the conduct of foreign affairs.

Later the same night Antonelli was summoned to the king's tent and found there Taytu and two chiefs sympathetic to Yohannes. To this committee Antonelli argued that after seven years of work, travel and service to Menilek — his only motive was to strengthen him as king of Shewa — this expulsion order dishonored Menilek's name. "My words were discussed and found reasonable. The queen, a woman of superior intelligence, but mired in Ethiopian intrigue, upheld feebly the conduct of her spouse." The next day Menilek persuaded the emperor to annul the order and Antonelli self-righteously informed Rome that "perseverance and firmness" were the way to deal with Ethiopians.[5]

Lighter moments with Taytu were reported by Emperor Yohannes's doctor, Nicolas Parisis,* also in Borumeda. "King Menilek was good enough to introduce me to his queen, who is sufficiently good-looking and very kind, having something European about her. She played backgammon and dominoes with gusto."[6]

Antonelli nurtured his and Italy's reputation by a constant flow of gifts, and repaired his fractured relationship with Taytu after they all returned to Shewa. He transmitted a letter (drafted by himself) and a gold necklace from Queen Margarita to Queen Taytu, and helped Taytu return gifts with a thank-you letter in which she said that if God gave her life she would use it to strengthen the friendship between Italy and Shewa, via "our friend, Count Antonelli." Menilek was preparing for the Arsi-Harar campaign when Taytu's letter was written on 6 November 1886. It followed several of his own, also written with Antonelli's guidance, justifying the forthcoming conquest as retrieval of ancient lands.[7]

All these contretemps, gun contracts and treaties with Antonelli meant nothing to most of the Shewan people. Questions which concerned them were: Who would tax them, reward them, punish them? When would they be called to battle? Producing food, getting married and divorced, observing religious holidays and fasts, holding funerals and baptisms — these were matters of substance and importance. Guns and cartridges were significant of course, when

---

*Antonelli and Parisis had a severe quarrel over a letter translated by the Greek doctor. It was a letter from Umberto to Menilek (23 July 1885) in which he said, "We took Massawa to keep the peace." Parisis made this look to Yohannes as though Italy had urged the Shewan king to rebel. Yohannes allowed Antonelli to demonstrate the errors, and then showed his displeasure with Parisis by refusing his services a few days later after a fall from a horse.

war was a biennial feature of their lives and cartridges had begun to replace bars of salt as currency.

The paternalistic-maternalistic nature of the Ethiopian monarchy was epitomized in the state banquet. The quality and abundance of food and the number of days spent eating and drinking reflected the throne's power to sustain the life of the people. One's proximity to the "parent," that is, the king, in the seating arrangements, was a measure of one's relative standing in the hierarchy, as it is in most societies. The ultimate favor was to have a morsel of food placed in one's mouth by the host-king-father, the provider of all good things. Foreigners accepted this honor with varying degrees of equanimity, depending on the amount of red pepper that struck their oral cavity.

The official description of the feast to bless Entotto Maryam church disclosed much information about the growth of Taytu's power and wealth in her four years of royal privilege. She had *gult* (crown grants) of the districts of Bulga and Geren, both richly fertile. Of the 36 feasts mentioned in Menilek's chronicle, this celebration, managed by Taytu, on 1 October 1887 lasted five days and became the standard by which all similar events were measured.

Taytu had not only her own house at Entotto, but also her own stockyards, dairy farms, grain storage facilities, beekeepers, beer-makers, flour millers, cooks, water-carriers, *berbere* (red pepper) pluckers and grinders along with an administrative head for each activity. The potters, ironworkers and weavers were separate communities of low status, so were not part of the resident workers at court. Their products were purchased. There were servants whose privilege it was to hold the basins for hand-washing before the meal, servants whose only function was to serve arak and hydromel (elixir of honey), and special people assigned to cut the throats of the steers and cows in Christian kosher fashion.

On the occasion of the great October feast, Menilek loaned workers from his establishment to Taytu, and ordered his district governors to contribute cattle. The chronicler noted that exactly 5,395 heads of cattle and sheep were slaughtered to feed some 20,000 people over the five days, and the service was so efficient that no one had to wait long for his food. As a food critic, the chronicler was very emotional: "When they took the covers off the bread dough to cook it, the scent of cumin, mint and coriander separated the soul from the body, and caused the heart to flutter — that is why the bread of Shewa is more famous than any other bread." The chronicler praised the ingenious efficiency by which the hydromel was made to flow from huge tubs down through hollowed-out tree trunks into cups held up by the imbibers. The elixir was the color of wheat and tasted exquisite, and though everyone had all he wanted to drink, no one became drunk or quarrelsome.

The chronicler even recorded an argument between the royal couple of such bourgeois flavor that it is unique in royal chronicles. Taytu is reported to have said to Menilek that after three days everyone must be getting tired of the same food, but Menilek replied that there were too many guests to change the menu. Taytu responded, "Don't give it a thought. I can do it. Just give me five sterile cows." With the help of 15 women she proceeded to concoct two dishes, one of beef and one of mutton, and she invited all the high-ranking women present to taste them to make sure they were neither too bland nor too spicy. Everyone was dumbfounded.

There are indications that the wife of Menilek was a hard taskmaster. She was "disgusted" with some workers who got drunk; she became "upset" because the outside gallery of the church was not yet finished. The soldiers complained because they had been barred from the best source of water, and the servants were "exhausted." Jules Borelli, a Frenchman who attended the second day of the feast, said there was an accident when two soldiers were killed during the firing of cannon and guns, and added that the priests distinguished themselves with zealous drinking.

The diary of Borelli is a great source of anti-Taytu lore. On arrival in Shewa in July 1886, Borelli became extremely irritated when Taytu declined to receive him and wrote, "This woman is abhorred." What is also clear from Borelli's diary is that he was disliked by everyone. He was treated rather badly by Menilek and other people at court, but he records his own insolence and disrespect with such arrogance that his unhappy situation appears quite justifiable.

By the time the would-be explorer of Keffa was ushered in, Menilek had already picked over Borelli's luggage and had taken a great many gifts that Borelli had planned to distribute on his travels. Menilek demanded his watch, which Borelli refused since it was his only one; he asked Borelli for his field-glasses, offering an old pair in exchange; and he took 25 guns though Borelli had planned to give him 10. As Menilek eyed the silk stockings and embroidered slippers in his cases, the Frenchman asked that these be offered to Taytu in his name, but

Menilek refused saying that although Taytu's feet were small they were too wide for these dainty samples.

Hardly a day passed without Borelli's being pressed for a gift by someone connected with the court. He fumed and fussed as he waited months for Menilek to give him guides and an escort for his trip to Keffa. Finally, when a messenger came from Menilek asking for a hatchet, Borelli exploded: he was sick of making gifts, for all he ever received in return was a *gembo* of beer. He heard later that when his outburst was reported to Menilek and Taytu, "those august persons looked at each other in astonishment." Two hours later, a decrepit old mule, adorned with a harness and collar, was trotted up to his house as a gift from the king and queen.

Borelli illustrated Taytu's niggardliness with a story about Gabriel, a palace interpreter who had decided to marry one of Taytu's favorite slaves "so as to attract her favor." Borelli attended the wedding and was greeted by the ugly bride swathed in a handsome blue cloak given her by the queen. Within a few weeks, however, Taytu demanded the return of this cloak, to the great embarrassment of Gabriel who was already regretting his marriage. He could not tell Borelli why either he or his wife deserved this sign of displeasure. However, Gabriel was well known as an "absinthe guzzler."

The explorer made a friend of Dejazmach Weldiye. Weldiye told Borelli that Taytu had complained to Menilek because he (Weldiye) was disinclined to dismount from his horse and bow whenever she passed by. When Menilek had chided him about this he had replied, "The queen of today may be just an ordinary woman tomorrow," which gave rise to a laugh from the king. This anecdote in Borelli's diary had a long life. Ten years later it was retold: "Weldiye treated her [Taytu] like a prostitute and for that reason she never forgave him and disgraced his son out of malice."

Borelli told how one of Menilek's cousins, Welde Giyorgis, was saved from the consequences of Menilek's anger at the small amount of gold he had brought in as tribute, because he was married to Taytu's cousin, Yeshemabet*. Menilek threw the small purse at Welde Giyorgis's head, but no further penalty was exacted. Borelli managed to offend Yeshemabet as well. She sent him a gift of a small wooden flagon which he disdained, saying, "Take it back ... it is not good

---

*Yeshemabet was the daughter of Taytu's aunt, Yewub-dar Hayle Maryam, by a husband whose identity is thus far not known.

enough even for my domestic." It may have been a puny gift, but Borelli won no friends this way.

"Her relatives have been elevated," wrote Borelli. "One of her favorites, Mekurya, became head of stores in 1886, a very powerful function at court, and was given Taytu's niece as wife."* Having said that Mekurya was a favorite of Taytu's, the foolish Borelli proceeded to insult him, calling him and his son-in-law "*nègres*." Borelli then went to visit Ras Gobena and described his wife, Ayeletch, as a woman of "sordid avarice." This was the gracious lady who was such a friend and protector of Father Massaia from 1866 to 1879.

It is from Borelli that we hear that Taytu's ex-husband, Zikargatchew, was chained, having been caught in *flagrante delicto* with the wife of Kenyazmach Ayele, his nephew, who had leprosy.† Borelli accused Taytu of having a hand in Zikargatchew's sudden demise "after drinking a cup of coffee." "He was odious to the king and queen because he was the former husband of Taytu … and was a gossip." Borelli conceded that Zikargatchew was not mourned, "being one of the land owners best known for extortion." If Zikargatchew was indeed murdered, the perpetrator would more likely have been his cuckolded nephew or a victim of his avarice.

Borelli's most damaging story about Taytu was that she refused to permit some chloroform to be taken from the royal pharmacy for an operation on the gangrenous foot of a European visitor. "It was impossible to make her understand that the least delay could lead to the death of the unfortunate man." The amputation went ahead without anaesthetic. Whatever the validity of Borelli's charge, neither the surgeon, Dr. Traversi, nor the patient, Henri Audon, mentioned the episode. It is possible that to Taytu the amputation of a foot or hand was no crisis as it was the common punishment for stealing, endured by convicted Ethiopians without a sound.‡ It is also possible that the supply of chloroform was exhausted. Audon

---

*The identity of this niece is uncertain. Taytu's niece, Aselefetch, did marry this man, but much later, after the death of Yilma Mekonnen in 1907.

†Ayele was the son of Bafena, and if he did have leprosy, it was grounds for divorce for the wife.

‡Stealing was the most serious crime; by contrast a murderer could get off by paying a "blood price" to the victim's family. Borelli reported that Menilek had punished a young lad at court for stealing by amputation of his hand. Dr. Martin wrote in February 1901 that "people are hung or shot — cutting off hands or legs is not in vogue."

did write that Taytu was a "big woman with a pleasant face ... but in her morals was wicked, vindictive and greedy."

After the feast of Entotto Maryam, the entire court descended from the mountain to Finfini* to soak in the hot springs. At the urging of his wife, Menilek decreed that the site would be known as Addis Ababa, "the new flower," because of its flowering mimosa trees. Borelli punned snidely that Taytu might be the "sun" which opened the rose, but said that the sun was pale and the perfume of the "new flower" nauseating, referring to the smell of the sulphurous springs.⁸

Within two years, Addis Ababa was completed as Menilek's new capital and Entotto was abandoned, except for church celebrations and Menilek's coronation as emperor. It is true that the winds of Entotto were chilly, the plateau was narrow, trees for firewood had been cut to stumps and potable water had to be carried some distance, but these were not the only reasons that prompted the move. Menilek's rheumatism and Taytu's preference were factors that dictated the move to what is now the capital of Ethiopia.⁹

The year 1887, marked near its close with a memorable feast, had begun with two violent events, one in the south with Menilek's conquest of Harar, and the second in the north with Ras Alula's ambush of a 550-man column, which came to be known in Italy as the Dogali massacre.†

The Italians, moving inland from Massawa, had occupied the town of Wa'a in late 1886. Ras Alula demanded that General Gené remove his troops since Ethiopia and Italy were now friends, otherwise "this friendship is at an end." Gené replied that his soldiers were in Wa'a to ensure peace. The inability of Ras Alula to see the logic of this mystified the Italians, but Alula had been instructed by Emperor Yohannes to restrict the Italians to those highland spots required for rest and recreation.

His ultimatum ignored, Alula took into custody a group of Italians who were on their way to Gojam at the invitation of Gojam's king, Tekle Haymanot. Alula threatened to execute his hostages if Italian troops did not immediately evacuate. No reply came from Gené. Alula attacked another Italian-occupied village, Sa'ati, and was

---

*Finfini was an Oromo designation. It would soon be called Filwuha, the Amharic word for "hot water."
†The site is called Tedale in Ethiopia. Caulk considers this ambush as the first battle of the Italo-Ethiopian war that continued in 1895.

forced to retreat after heavy losses. Encouraged by their success, the Italians sent reinforcements towards Sa'ati, and it was this force of 550 soldiers that Alula's men annihilated. There was a hasty withdrawal from Sa'ati, Wa'a and Arafali.

The disaster ignited nationalistic fervor* in Italy. Parliament voted two million lire for revenge and the families of the hostages raised ransom money. Before it arrived, Alula released them with instructions to ask their countrymen, "What are you doing in our country with guns and soldiers?"[10] This simple query was the purest expression of Ethiopian reaction to Italy's incursions and had been asked in one form or another by Emperor Yohannes since the occupation of Massawa in February 1885.

In the same month as the Dogali massacre, on 6 January 1887, the king of Shewa conquered Harar. Menilek had stepped up his diplomatic offensive in 1884 after it became known that the British masters of Egypt were instituting economies by evacuation of Egypt's colonial possessions, including Harar. Menilek wrote twice to his new "friend," King Umberto. "I beg Your Majesty to defend me against everyone ... as I don't know what European kings will say about this ... let others know that this region is ours."

Menilek's desire to take Harar was delayed by obligations to Emperor Yohannes. Then, in April 1886, the emir of Harar provided the irresistible pretext. The emir's soldiers slaughtered an expedition of Italian explorers and traders, immediately after a similar outrage on a French group who were bringing arms to Menilek. The Shewan king met with his queen and his other advisers. They deemed that the murder of the Italians might invite the occupation of Harar by Italy. With Emperor Yohannes's blessing, Menilek acted.[11]

He had already deployed Welde Gabriel to Itu which was contiguous with the target area, and his uncle, Ras Darge, had taken a force to Arsi. He sent spies into Harar, and in April 1886 ordered 1,200 soldiers to work under his Swiss adviser, Alfred Ilg,† to build a bridge over the Awash river to facilitate the movement of his army.

---

*It also ignited the creative impulse of A. Castelletto who wrote a play, *The Daughter of Ras Alula*, based on a novel by Luigi Gualtieri about the love of Alula's daughter for an Italian officer; the plot was not based on fact.

†Ilg came to work for Menilek in 1879 along with two other Swiss from Zurich's Polytechnic Institute. The latter two stayed only a few years while Ilg was engaged in a variety of technical, purchasing and diplomatic capacities for Menilek for 27 years.

The objective was secret when Menilek and his army left in the direction of Arsi on 12 November 1886. He took with him the two Italian doctors, Alfieri and Ragazzi, and delegated Ras Gobena and Taytu to keep order in Shewa. This was Taytu's first duty of this kind. Menilek had vetoed Taytu's request to accompany him, and after he left she refused to return to Entotto from Filwuha, the hot springs where the army had mobilized. She commanded Ras Gobena to build her a house and kitchens there.[12]

Taytu showed her administrative mettle within a month of Menilek's departure. Some hundreds of soldiers had deserted the army of Welde Gabriel, who had been camped two days' march from Harar since the middle of 1886. These deserters were unaware that Menilek was on his way to reinforce them, and on their first approach to Harar had been frightened away by a sudden eruption of rocket fire.

When Taytu learned that these deserters were in her vicinity, "though anger boiled in her heart," she sent them this message: "If all these soldiers have come to guard me, I congratulate them; but if they intend to run away, their heads are mine and their belongings will go to those who capture them." She sent couriers to the governors of nearby districts with this caution: "The soldiers who have been with Welde Gabriel are going to come to you with the pretext that you must feed them. On Tuesday, I intend to chain all the deserters [near me]. You, on that same day, collect the guns of those who have reached you and put them in stocks." The chronicler explained that stocks were necessary because there was a shortage of chains.

As the men straggled in, they headed for the royal tent crying for mercy and begging for food. "Weyzero Taytu responded sweetly, 'You did well to come to me. I will get busy and find you some food. Just rest there.'" She broke up the crowd by giving *laissez-passers* to some of them to take to the governors whom she had alerted. If they had been able to read, they would have read these notes which said, "According to the orders you have already received, be so kind as to take these men and keep them safe." Thus deceived, they walked into the trap, and by the pre-arranged signal they were chained or put into stocks. "The whole country was amazed at what Weyzero Taytu had done!"

Her perspicacity in moving from Entotto to the plains was further proved when Ras Gobena was injured in a fall from his horse. The elderly Gobena,* although an Oromo and suppressor of their independence, was also considered their protector and his accident caused a ripple of unrest throughout Oromo communities. "They wetted with blood the place that he fell and Amhara priests made a hellish racket trying to exorcise this bad omen."[13] "As for the Galla [Oromo], seeing that Weyzero Taytu was settled in the plains and a city was starting there, they understood that Menilek was still in good health and they calmed down everywhere." It was Taytu's way of "showing the flag," and for Menilek's being "in good health" read "able to make war on them."

Menilek had taken Harar on Ethiopian Christmas, the time of year when a feast was in order after a fasting period. However, the annexation of Harar was not celebrated until Menilek's return to Shewa on 6 March 1887; and Taytu composed a gruesome verse to mark the occasion:[14]

Although the *senga* and the *shihir*
Which were on their way from Entotto
Did not reach him in time, the
King of Shewa feasted by slaying
Moslems in Hararge.

A week later, cannon were fired to celebrate Alula's victory at Dogali (Tedale). Pietro Antonelli was discomfited as he watched the Shewans cheer deliriously a victory over his countrymen, and he soon made Menilek understand the possible consequences of Italy's desire for revenge. Antonelli was instructed to sound out Menilek on cooperation with Italy to overthrow Emperor Yohannes; his reward would be the throne of the "King of Kings." Yohannes, however, well aware of Menilek's predilection for his armament supplier, took care to write Menilek a simple summary of his position, specifically disclaiming having given Alula any orders to break the peace with Italy. The gist of his letter was that (a) he had exchanged gifts with the King of Italy and received his consuls as well (Branchi in May 1883 and Ferrari and Nerazzini in May 1885); (b) the English ambassadors came and he had told them that he wanted peace with Egypt and accepted their proposal (Hewett Treaty, 3 June 1884); (c) he did not know what the English had said to the

---

*After Menilek's return from Harar, Gobena was accused unjustly by certain chiefs of planning a coup. Avedis Terzian said Gobena's "nerves gave way" and he crawled on his hands and knees before Menilek and confessed. Menilek refused to dishonor him saying it had taken him 30 years to "make him."

Italians but they occupied Massawa after the English left (February 1885), which was why Alula broke the peace, though he did not give him orders; and (d) Italy had made no accommodation and they did not let anything through the port of Massawa, not even wine for the Holy Eucharist.

Antonelli obtained a summary of this letter from Aleqa Yosef Neguse, but it did not help him with Menilek. Menilek told Antonelli that he loved Italy so much that he felt "half Italian," and had no greater wish than to go there and see it, but he was bound by his oath of loyalty to the emperor. After an assiduous campaign of "rich gifts" to Menilek and Taytu, and pay-offs to Ras Darge, Azaj Welde Tsadiq and the two interpreters, the best Antonelli could extract was Menilek's promise not to use the Remington rifles, furnished by Italy, against Italians. Antonelli promised that Italy would never annex any Ethiopian territory.

For Taytu, Antonelli produced another letter from Queen Margarita, in which the Italian queen hoped that "your efforts, like my own, will help to consolidate the reciprocal attachment of our two countries." Taytu indicated to Antonelli her preference for gifts of decorations for Entotto Maryam church, instead of the jewelry, perfume and silk he was partial to giving. Testy, short notes from her showed her impatience when the church decorations had not arrived, and Antonelli pressed his foreign office to check the orders, as she was making life difficult for him.[15]

Menilek's loyalty was tested in December 1887. Emperor Yohannes, every conciliation effort having failed,* called on Menilek to help defend the nation.† Menilek's army of 120,000 men and women was en route at the end of December. Again, Ras Gobena and Taytu were left behind as co-administrators of Shewa.

At Yohannes's back, the Mahdists were massed on the Sudanese frontier at Metema, and Yohannes deployed King Tekle Haymanot of Gojam to confront them, as he faced Italy. On 18 and 19 January

---

*Britain had intervened with the Portal mission in early December 1887; Portal brought conditions unacceptable to Yohannes, as all disputed territory was offered to Italy.
†Compared to the dire threats that accompanied Menilek's calls to war, Yohannes's call to arms was inspirational· "When you march you must realize that you will be defending your country which corresponds to the love of a mother, the glory of a crown, the kindness of a wife, the joy of a child and the charity of a grave..." An 1872 order by Yohannes was more typical, "Anyone who does not kill one of these rebels is not a strong man but a timid and fearful one like all women." (See Bairu Tafla translation of a chronicle of Yohannes.)

1888, the Mahdists defeated the army of Gojam, killing and capturing some 8,000 Gojamese, including a son* and two daughters of King Tekle Haymanot. Hundreds of men and women were taken as slaves to Omdurman. Tekle Haymanot escaped and was bitterly angry with Emperor Yohannes for not having reinforced him as he had requested urgently. The Mahdists then made a strategic retreat after burning 40 of the 47 churches in Gondar, the old imperial capital, and still a center of ecclesiastical learning.

What Emperor Yohannes now faced on his northeastern frontier was a slowly uncoiling snake whose backbone was a railway line being built up the escarpment from Massawa. The commander, General di San Marzano, a cautious and prudent man, took four months to move his troops 300 kilometers. He deployed troops on both sides of the "backbone" to protect the workers. The goal was to occupy those towns that Italy had been forced to evacuate by Ras Alula in January 1887. In fact, at this time, there was no threat to the troops and workers because the feisty Alula had been relieved of his rule of the Mereb Melash region of Tigray; still, di San Marzano was in great fear of a surprise attack. He knew that the English mediator, Gerald Portal, had reported that Yohannes had at his disposal at least 160,000 soldiers, and his own strength was 20,000 men whose morale was very low. Sustaining the patriotic call to duty to avenge Dogali was difficult under the hardships of boredom, primitive health care, and water that tasted of leather because it had been brought from Massawa in bags loaded on the backs of camels and mules. If anyone fell sick, he would be returned to Massawa to the same shack of a hospital that had doctored the 1,000 men involved in the 1885 Massawa debarkation. Moreover, a simple infraction of discipline meant confinement in the airless oven of a jail cell at Massawa, where the temperature alone could cause a man to die. The soldiers grumbled that they preferred two years in jail in Italy to two weeks at Massawa.

An advance party of Italians reached Sa'ati, 10 kilometers from where the railway line had stretched in early March. It was fortified, iron pylons were erected to carry a telegraph line, floodlights functioned with a generator, and an observation balloon was hoisted. When Ethiopian forces made camp in sight of Sa'ati in the last

---

*Another son, who was married to a niece of Emperor Yohannes, chose to die when his wife was captured rather than follow his father's example of escaping. (Antonelli, "Scioa e Scioani," 100)

week of March 1888, those lights piercing the night were a frightening sight.

To the surprise of di San Marzano, an envoy arrived from Emperor Yohannes on 28 March. He asked that the Italians respect the Hewett Treaty (which Italy had promised to do, but after Dogali they had blockaded all shipments to Yohannes), and invited them to join him in a holy war against the "dervishes." "I am a Christian, just as you are; we are brothers; discord between us serves only to make others laugh." The nearest he came to the apology and reparations demanded by the Italians for Dogali was to say, "That which happened was the work of the devil." He repeated what he had said many times before: "You stay in your country and I will stay in mine."

The newly-hung telegraph wires hummed between the Sa'ati outpost and the foreign office in Rome; the final response to Yohannes's appeal was "No" to everything. By then Yohannes had to make a decision about the Mahdists and face the fact that his armies were weak from dysentery, and lack of food and water, and depleted by desertions; in addition a mysterious disease had attacked his transport animals. On the evening of 2 April, the Italians were relieved to see clouds of dust as the Ethiopians broke camp and moved away from them. Yohannes's failure to eject the Italians from Sa'ati was the turning point that allowed Italy to consolidate its control of the gateway to Ethiopia.*[16]

Menilek and a vast army were advancing north with deliberate slowness (just as Antonelli had hoped) and did not reach the environs of ravaged Gondar until 18 April. They evinced no eagerness to fight the Mahdists. Yohannes ordered Menilek and his army back to Shewa because "they were eating up the country." Menilek's return route was through Gojam instead of Wello, the shorter way. In Gojam he met its disaffected king, Tekle Haymanot, in mourning

---

*Antonio Baldissera replaced di San Marzano in July 1888. He had this interesting viewpoint: "Let us give up saying that we will bring civilization to Abyssinia. We wish to bring it to Abyssinia indeed, but not for them, for us." Baldissera extended the area controlled by Italy by assigning the defector, Kefle Iyesus, to occupy Keren; established close ties with surrounding clans (the Habab and the Asawerta); built roads, fortifications and hospitals, and improved the financial and postal services; regularized customs, taxes and placed all the merchants at Massawa under Italian law. Kefle Iyesus's loyalty was so doubtful that they arrested him in May 1889 and he died sometime after in prison at Assab.

for his daughter, Mentewab, who had died while a captive of the Mahdists.*[17]

The two kings concocted an alliance which could only be aimed at overthrowing Emperor Yohannes. As soon as he reached Entotto on 28 June, and hardly taking time to discuss it with Taytu, Menilek called in Antonelli and asked for a pact with Italy against Yohannes. Taytu declared herself Yohannes's most ruthless enemy and "as she goes," wrote Antonelli, "go many others." This did not mean that she favored war against the emperor. In fact, another Italian source in Shewa said she was absolutely opposed to it.[18]

Despite his knowledge of the Tekle Haymanot-Menilek conspiracy, Yohannes communicated in a friendly way with Menilek in October 1888, explaining that he would return Menilek's daughter, Zewditu (widowed four months before by the death of Araya Yohannes), as soon as he could send her with appropriate gifts; at the moment he was financially embarrassed. Menilek replied, "You are the father of my daughter; may she return when it pleases you." The sign that their relations were at breaking point was that for the first time in 10 years Menilek did not send his annual tribute.

Menilek called his army to war on 24 November 1888. "The man who handles a lance and does not come on this expedition is a woman and no more a man; he shall be called by the name of his wife, and have no share in their common wealth; she may take everything."† But Menilek's coup was over before it began. On 16 December he heard that his co-conspirator, Tekle Haymanot, had made peace with the emperor, and that Yohannes had determined to show Menilek in person who was emperor of Ethiopia.

Though Menilek ordered his uncle, Ras Darge, to swear in writing to Yohannes that all the plotting had been instigated by the Gojam

---

*Before dying, Mentewab composed a poem that became popular in Gojam: "My father, the *negus*, my brother, the ras, went to Gorgora where my husband fired catridges in vain. O men ... who did not stay with me, tell them she died eating cats." This appears to be a lightly veiled rebuke to those who did not protect her. Aleqa Lemlem wrote that in her prison at Metema she cried, "Those who return to our country, tell them, 'She died from eating garbage.' "

†Aleqa Yosef translated this for Antonelli. The chronicle differs: "Men of my country, you have heard what happened in Gojam; I am ready to die for my country; you know it is better to fight at the frontiers, kill your enemies or die, rather than expose your children, your wife and your property to death and ruin ... so hasten to come." It would be amusing, but only speculation, to imagine that Empress Taytu, who was closely involved with writing the chronicle, asked for the less sexist revision.

king, Yohannes kept on marching towards Shewa, while negotiators shuttled back and forth. Even as Menilek vowed to Yohannes that he had always been loyal and that Yohannes's lack of trust in him was the root of their problem, Menilek was asking Antonelli why the Italians did not create a diversion in the north to draw Yohannes away from him. Yohannes returned Zewditu to her father on 29 January 1889 with a herd of cattle, an extremely valuable gift at this time of famine. At the eleventh hour, the invasion of Shewa was called off as Yohannes learned that the Mahdists were massing at Metema for another attack on his empire. He wheeled his armies from Shewa to oppose them.[19]

The battle went well for the Ethiopians, but toward evening on 10 March 1889, Emperor Yohannes was wounded and died the following day. On his deathbed he named his "claimed" son, Mengesha Yohannes, as his successor. The Ethiopian offensive collapsed in confusion upon the death of their emperor, and the Mahdists routed the uncertain soldiers, overtook Yohannes's death train and cut off his head as well as the heads of other nobles fallen in the fight. They withdrew to Khartoum where they hoisted the severed heads on poles and marched in a victory parade.[20]

When news of the death of the emperor reached Menilek, he and the queen were in Wello, at Wuchale, a fief belonging to the queen. Also present in camp was Antonelli who had just delivered 5,000 Remington rifles. Via Antonelli's courier, Menilek informed the King of Italy that he would like Italian soldiers to occupy Asmara, in order to discourage the imperial pretensions of Mengesha Yohannes. Thereafter, he said, "God will give me the throne that for many years I have had the right to have."[21]

He called for oaths of loyalty from the rulers of all provinces, and received them from all but Mengesha Yohannes and Alula in Tigray, although pressure had to be exerted on Ras Mikael who had been fighting at Yohannes's side at Metema. Almost immediately, Taytu's brother, Wele, governor of Yejju, was granted a vast increase in territory and the title of Ras.

On 2 May 1889 Menilek signed a treaty at Wuchale with Antonelli. Menilek signed as "King of Kings of Ethiopia," though he had not yet been crowned. Of the 20 articles in the treaty, one set up the borders of a new colony which would be called Eritrea. The Italians would then be allowed to occupy within a few months, and without bloodshed, the main centers of the region: Keren on 2 June, and

Asmara on 2 August.

Today, Menilek is blamed for giving away the land from Asmara to the sea.[22] The apologia for Menilek was that he was forced to rely on Italy to control Tigray as he was in no position to do so himself. Menilek's opportunistic bargain created Eritrea.*

The import of one article of the Treaty of Wuchale went unnoticed by the sovereign, his spouse, and his interpreter. The Amharic version of the treaty in Article 17 says that Ethiopia *may* use the good offices of Italy in foreign affairs. The Italian version says that Ethiopia *consents* to use Italy as its representative with foreign governments. Whether or not this was deliberate trickery by Count Antonelli is a matter that has occupied historians to this day.[23] For a year no issues were raised in connection with this treaty. In the meantime, Menilek announced his accession to Queen Victoria, Kaiser Wilhelm, President Carnot and King Umberto. He informed Italy that his cousin, Dejazmach Mekonnen,† would head the Ethiopian delegation to Rome to witness ratification of the Wuchale treaty, and Taytu prepared for the coronation.

---

*The Ethiopian citizens of the Italian colony of Eritrea would within a few years become better educated than the people of central and southern Ethiopia and their attitudes were altered subtly by their proximity to these Europeans. Eritrea did not become a part of Ethiopia again until 1962, though it federated with Ethiopia 10 years earlier. Even today it is a stronghold of separatism from the Ethiopian state.

†By 1889, aged 37, Mekonnen was the same young man who carried Menilek's homework to Pierre Arnoux in 1874. He was made governor of Harar in January 1887, promoted over many more senior officers in Menilek's service. Welde Gabriel, many said, should have had the post since he had helped to conquer Harar.

4

A queen becomes empress

Menilek's coronation as emperor, and Taytu's as empress, did
not take place until 3 and 5 November 1889 respectively, eight
months after the death of Yohannes. There were many reasons for
the delay, not the least of which was the time required to make
the celebration a glorious event, one that would shimmer with
imported silks and satins and glitter with gold. The court jeweler,
an Armenian named Dikran Ebeyan,* set to work making whatever
jewelry and *objets* that could not be imported from Europe or
Cairo. The political reason for the delay was the refusal of
Mengesha Yohannes and his proud military organization, headed
by Ras Alula, in northern Ethiopia, to concede that Menilek was
emperor. When Menilek asked the advice of his priests as to
whether he should make war on Mengesha, he was advised to wait
until after his coronation as there was so much death in the country
from hunger that he would be blamed if more death was caused by
a conflict.

Ethiopia in 1889 had a greater enemy than the Mahdists or the
Italians: a devastating famine. Infected cattle from India had been
unloaded at Massawa by the Italians to feed their troops. Rinderpest
had spread rapidly through all the beasts, wild and domestic, and
thousands were dying every day. As their plough animals dropped,
the demoralized farmers made no attempt to cultivate their land with
implements, so there were no crops to harvest.[1]

From Wello, where the news of the death of Yohannes had been
received, Menilek and Taytu went to Lalibela to pray, as the cattle
epidemic was seen as a "scourge sent by God" to punish Ethiopia
for laxity of faith. The 11 rock churches of Lalibela, each a monolith
carved out of 11 gigantic stones, were a mecca of Ethiopia. One of
the wonders of the world, they were built sometime in the 13th
century in an attempt to reproduce the Holy City of Jerusalem.[2]
Menilek's and Taytu's pilgrimage to ask God's mercy went
unrewarded.

---

*He received honorable mention in the chronicle of Menilek, the only foreigner singled
out for such favor. A number of Italians are mentioned by name in the account of
the battle at Adwa; Antonelli is named, but the reference is pejorative.

There was momentary diversion from the problems created by the famine in August 1889 when Menilek met a new type of European. Vasili Mashcov was the first Russian* to reach Shewa. Menilek, probably after a short geography lesson from his Swiss adviser, Alfred Ilg, opportunistically told the visitor, "We all love Russia." He remarked to the slightly-built Mashcov that he had thought all Muscovites would be very tall, have long beards and cruel faces, but now he saw how wrong he was. Mashcov countered that in Russia they had the same wrong idea about the Abyssinians! This caused an outburst of laughter when it was translated to those present.

Though Mashcov was only an unofficial visitor, he espoused an air of official relations based on a doctrinal affinity between Russian and Ethiopian Orthodoxies. Menilek, seeing that here might be another foreign power to counterbalance his dependence on Italy, gave a generous amount of time to the Russian. Menilek regretted that the seasonal rain would prevent Mashcov from seeing his beautiful country, but urged him to remain for the celebration of Mesqel on 27 September and invited him to the coronation, which had been postponed, he said, because his crown had not yet been completed. If Mashcov would stay, he would take him on an elephant hunt.

Mashcov was impressed that "this sovereign of a nation of eight million people in a country many times larger than Italy" was so attentive to an unknown traveler and was so eager for information about the great land of Russia. "How far away is it? Is it big? How many soldiers do you have? Do you have many rases? Why, if you are co-religionists with us, do you not come here, when, as you say, Russians visit countries where there are heretics?"

The Russian, speaking French, gave ingenious answers. To describe distance, he said it would take 11 months to reach Russia on foot from the coast at Zeyla. Yosef Neguse, the translator, had great difficulty with population figures: Mashcov would say, "Russia is 1,100 times more populous than Ethiopia," and the translator would

---

*Nicholas Ashinov made a doubtful claim that he had met Emperor Yohannes in Tigray in January 1886, though he did see Ras Alula. Ashinov made two more trips to Ethiopia, in March 1888 and January 1889, with the aim of setting up a Cossack settlement on the coast. In January 1889 his shipload of settlers was shelled by a French ship at Tajura, thus ending the project. Mashcov was among the 150 Cossacks. He left Ashinov at Tajura and proceeded to Shewa.

cover his head with both hands and groan the Amharic equivalent of "Oh my! Dear me!"

Mashcov could not accept Menilek's invitation to stay; he was embarrassed by his shortage of funds and inability to put on a good show to reflect the glory of Russia. On his return home, Mashcov was applauded in geographic and scientific circles as a great explorer and as the pioneer of new frontiers for politics and religion. He wrote a number of articles which gained for Ethiopia the respect and awareness of the general public as well as of the Ministries of War and Foreign Affairs. The Czar honored Mashcov with a decoration and questioned him in private audience about his Ethiopian experience.

The Italians had been correct about the trouble Mashcov would cause and were beside themselves at this possible competition. In print Mashcov libeled Count Antonelli, describing him as pushy, vain and ignorant, and saying that he was mocked for his inadequate command of Amharic and tolerated by the Abyssinians only because he was prodigal with gifts. Mashcov wrote that on one occasion Antonelli told Menilek he would bring back some silk from Italy on his next trip. Instead of using the Amharic word for silk (*har*), he said "*ar*" which meant "excrement," thus shocking everyone into titters. Mashcov did not meet Antonelli and he got the story second-hand, probably from Yosef Neguse. Mashcov implied that he knew even worse stories about Antonelli but would restrain himself.[3]

As Addis Ababa was at that time no more than a collection of huts around the hot springs, Menilek's coronation was held at Entotto which was also no more than a collection of huts, but boasted a church, Entotto Maryam, as an architectural feature.

Dikran Ebeyan finished the crowns. The imported velvet coronation robes encrusted with silver and gold embroidery arrived.* Quantities of new clothing for court dignitaries, both men and women, were hand-sewn by the wife of Dikran Ebeyan. The one sewing machine in the whole kingdom was used by Menilek's Greek tailor. Father Massaia had imported it many years before and the king himself learned to take it apart, repair it and re-assemble the parts.[4]

The coronation of "The Conquering Lion of the tribe of Judah, Menilek II, elect of God, King of Kings of Ethiopia" took place on

---

*The robes were on display at the National Museum in Addis Ababa. The only other object belonging to the empress displayed was a pale blue enamelware drinking cup.

3 November 1889.[5] The chronicler reached into antiquity to link
Menilek's coronation with that of Yekuno Amlak in 1270.* The angel
who had given the formula[†] for the oil of anointment to Yekuno
Amlak commanded that it not be used for any other emperor except
the one who would appear 619 years hence. The passion of the
chronicler for the perfectly foreordained event strains credulity more
than usual.

Only Taytu, Abune Matewos and the highest ranking nobility of
the empire witnessed the anointing inside the church. Afterwards
a public ceremony was held on a dais set up outside. A ladder-like
invention made it possible for the guests to ascend the platform to
make obeisance to Menilek. The ladders — actually they were more
like ramps with depressions carved out to fit the feet — were painted
red, yellow and green, and must have been the idea of engineer Ilg
who was given a place of honor and handsome gifts by his newly
elevated employer.

Menilek was a dazzling sight — his umbrella, slippers, sword,
scepter and crown were all of gold — as he distributed cloth, money,
salt, horses and mules. His most welcome gift to his people was the
cancelation of all debts and amnesty for all fugitives from justice.
Booming cannon and rifle fire resounded and covered the summit
with a cloud of smoke as the people acclaimed Menilek, kissing the
earth and shouting to heaven, "May God grant thee a reign of a
thousand years."

The feast that followed was on the same lavish scale as the
dedication of Entotto Maryam church in 1887. It defied the scarcity
of meat with the help of the king of Keffa, a province not yet
seriously affected by rinderpest. The Keffan king brought thousands
of heads of cattle as his required tribute to Menilek.

Two days later, scarcely recovered from the excesses of that
memorable feast, Taytu was crowned as Itege (literally "sister of the
country"). Such a ceremony had not taken place since the crowning
of Itege Seble Wengel by Emperor Lebna Dengel early in the 16th
century, though many other empresses since then had borne the

---

*It was believed that Yekuno Amlak had restored the Solomonic dynasty after some
140 years of genealogically suspect kings (the Zagwe) with the help of the Christians
of Shewa.
†The recipe: mix basil, myrrh, jasmine, spikenard, mandrake, lemon and apple juice,
and grapes in a chalice with three handfuls of incense; pray seven days then clarify
with a lump of coal; mix with water and add to the balm. It will become bubbly
after 18 psalms and 22 different prayers are recited over it.

title.* As dusk descended, "in a single moment 82 lamps were lit and flaming torches were held high in the air," and Taytu began the distribution of gifts. A thousand people passed before her. Court women were given gold necklaces, earrings, ankle bracelets, clothing, and pins to hold their head scarves. As recipients decreased in rank so did the value of their souvenir, but no one received less than a piece of silver jewelry. Gold had always been reserved for royalty and was never given out so liberally again.

Once the gifts were distributed, Emperor Menilek made his entrance and sat on his throne. To his right a throne was placed for Taytu. Although the ceremony took place out of doors in front of the church, the thrones were surrounded by a curtain made of cloth "new to Ethiopia — those inside could see out, but those outside could not see in."† Then came a procession of priests headed by the bishop, their bright vestments, gold crosses and silver and gold embroidered umbrellas glistening in the light of torches.

Only Menilek witnessed the actual coronation of Taytu by Abune Matewos, after which Menilek granted her the title of Itege which has come to mean "queen of queens." Then the curtains were drawn and the resplendent Taytu could be seen by all. The chronicler confessed his inability to find words to describe the splendor of her clothing and her sparkling jewels.

The clerics performed their dances and composed a new song in honor of the occasion. Clerical dancing is unique to the Ethiopian Orthodox Church; its movements are specific and may be changed only by decisions made at the highest ecclesiastical level. The solemn and graceful choreography is accompanied by the tambourine and the sistrum. The spectators prostrated themselves. There were 51 rounds from the cannon. Taytu's own troops fired so many times that the sound was like the "thunder that precedes the rain," and smoke again billowed over the summit of Entotto. "There was such a commotion of joy and singing it was as though earth and heaven had come unhinged."

---

* Among them Itege Admas Mogasa (wife of Minas, 1559-63); Itege Maryam Sena (wife of Sertsa Dengel, 1563-7); Itege Mentewab (wife of Bekaffa, 1721-30). More recent bearers of the title had been Itege Menen, mother of Ras Ali; Itege Tewabech, wife of Emperor Tewodros and Itege Dinqinesh, the sister of Emperor Yohannes and widow of Emperor Tekle Giyorgis.

†The fabric was probably something like mousseline de soie, imported from Italy or France.

"Thus, the empire, having been misled for 15 years under Tewodros, three years under Tekle Giyorgis and 18 years under Yohannes ... returned to the glory of the house of David, Solomon and Menilek." Though his mathematics were faulty and his view of history biased, the chronicler was correct that Ethiopia would achieve prominence under the new regime. With Menilek's accession, the political center, which for centuries had been in the north, moved to the geographical center of the empire. A major issue in the religious establishment was settled. Abune Matewos, having secured the privilege of crowning Menilek and Taytu, resolved his own precedence over Petros, who had been his superior when Emperor Yohannes was alive. Matewos's superiority was not officially blessed, however, until the following year by a letter from the Alexandrian patriarchate.[6]

There was no doubt that Empress Taytu was at the apex of the feminine power pyramid. Every ras and *dejazmach* had to make a personal oath of loyalty to her, an act which cannot have been relished by those proud men and their equally proud wives who had come great distances to attend. Notable among the absentees were her brother Wele, whom acute famine had kept in Yejju; Mekonnen, who was in Italy for the ratification of the Treaty of Wuchale; and King Tekle Haymanot, the one "king" who justified Menilek's title of "king of kings." He too had severe famine problems. The empress took the unprecedented step of adding to her title the cognomen, "Light of Ethiopia," which would henceforth appear on her royal seal.[7]

The monarchs repaired to the hot springs of Filwuha in the plains below Entotto "to avoid contagion caused by the hydromel, food and bread that had fallen on the ground" during the festivities. From there, on 17 December 1889, Menilek led an army north to deal with the contumacious Tigrayans who had not acknowledged his hegemony.*

---

*Menilek was not as passive about Mengesha Yohannes's failure to recognize him as emperor as the chronicler implies. In March 1889 Menilek asked the Italians to prevent arms from reaching Mengesha and in May he had sent Dejazmach Seyum Gebre Kidane (even though he was a Tigrayan and the son of Emperor Yohannes's sister, his role as Menilek's agent made him unacceptable in Tigray) with 1,500 well-equipped troops to impose his will on Mengesha and on Ras Alula. On the very day that Menilek was being crowned in Shewa, Seyum fought the Tigray ras and made "peace" with him, but Mengesha fled during the night. Ras Alula refused to meet Seyum, saying "I have no king but Ras Mengesha," and on 6 November Alula forced Seyum to flee to Asmara. There Seyum conferred with the Italians, who rearmed him (and Sebhat and Bahta Hagos). From 2 to 5 December 1889, the Italian-backed forces battled with the three rases (Mengesha, Alula and Hagos) but the latter won the day. It was this failure of Seyum Gebre Kidane that caused Menilek to leave Addis Ababa on 17 December 1889.

The empress accompanied Menilek as far as Desse, the junction of trade routes for the provinces of Shewa, Wello, Begemder and Yejju. At Desse, protected by her own troops, Taytu was commissioned by Menilek to keep these divisions of the empire at peace. "What Itege Taytu accomplished at this time, even a brave warrior could never have done." Though there is no confirmation from any other source that these events happened in the way the chronicler told them, one finds in his account all of the characteristics for which Taytu became famous.

These traits — her ability to keep her head, her strategy, her willingness to risk her personal safety, her adroit use of family connections and her rhetorical gifts — were amply demonstrated by the way in which Taytu handled a crisis in the absence of Menilek. Her brother, Wele, had gone with Menilek on his campaign. A message came from the soldiers of Weldya, capital of Yejju which Wele governed, to inform Taytu that Wele's wife and children were endangered by the rebel, Zegeye. "We are afraid, as there are not enough of us," went the message. Her response: "If you flee, there will be trouble. Stay where you are and if Zegeye comes nearer, warn me." Summoning Welde Gabriel and Lul Seged she ordered them to attack an ally of Zegeye. The people with the empress at Desse were upset. "The army is here to guard the empress, it must not go." She also sent a small force with 300 guns to Weldya. In Weldya marketplace her proclamation was read: "Men of my country, it is to prevent suffering that I have come here. Since the time of Gugsa [Taytu's ancestor from this area] until today, we have had no quarrel with you ... Take care that no dissension explodes between me and you. As for Zegeye, if I should hear that you permitted him to enter and govern Yejju, or even if I learn that you allowed him to drink water in Yejju from his cupped hand, we will become, you and I, mortal enemies."

The people of Weldya pulled themselves together and got word to Zegeye that they were ready to fight him; fortunately he declined the challenge. The other rebels were captured. Taytu's plan had worked and "a great calm settled from one end of the empire to the other."[8]

All was not calm in Tigray, however. On 26 January 1890 General Orero had occupied Adwa, the capital of Tigray. He had taken advantage of the absence of Mengesha Yohannes and Alula who had taken their troops to search for food. Orero's action was a clear and gross violation of the demarcation lines in the Treaty of Wuchale. The Italians, however, were joyfully welcomed in both Adwa and nearby Aksum because they brought food to distribute and because the population preferred them to any governor that Emperor Menilek might impose on them.

Menilek protested to Orero, who explained that he had moved in only to ensure peace until Menilek could handle it himself. This sufficed for the moment. On 23 February, at Meqelle, Menilek presided over the submission of the Tigray leaders, except for Mengesha Yohannes, who made an appointment to submit 20 days hence. In Meqelle, Menilek was joined by his dear friend and cousin, Mekonnen, and the rest of the delegation returning from their six-month visit to Italy and Jerusalem. Menilek's anger at the Italian occupation of Adwa was assuaged by Mekonnen's news that 10,000 new Wetterly rifles and several million cartridges were on their way.[9]

Mekonnen also told Menilek he had signed an additional convention to the Treaty of Wuchale on 1 October 1889 stipulating that the borders of Italian territory were to be fixed as of their *de facto* position on that day. The Italians knew, but Mekonnen did not, that the day he signed the convention, Italian forces had advanced well beyond what Mekonnen understood as *de facto*. Count Antonelli, who had returned to Ethiopia with Mekonnen, was also surprised at how far forward the Italians had gone, but persuaded Menilek to leave matters in the hands of his representative in Tigray, Meshesha Werqe. Nor had Antonelli told Mekonnen about the letter Prime Minister Crispi had sent to 12 European countries and the United States on 11 October 1889, in which he informed them that "Article 17 of the Treaty of Wuchale signified that in all matters dealing with other governments, Ethiopia would be represented by Italy." However, an Ethiopian who had been sent to Italy by Menilek to learn "science" read in the newspapers that Ethiopia had become a protectorate of Italy and quickly informed Mekonnen. Mekonnen asked Antonelli about it and Antonelli insisted that this Ethiopian, Afewerq Gebre Iyesus, read badly and understood nothing.[10]

Menilek was not yet aware of the Italian interpretation of Article 17, for the Amharic wording of this article said that Ethiopia *may* avail herself of the services of Italy in foreign affairs. Stories abound that Menilek simply turned a blind eye. One Ethiopian source said he warned Menilek about Article 17 at the time he signed the treaty and was banished from the court for his pains. In Mashcov's remark to the French resident at Obok that "Menilek will never accept a protectorate by Italy," some historians see an indication that he and Menilek discussed it as early as September 1889. Partisans of Empress Taytu say she warned Menilek:

A man from Eritrea learned about the Italian interpretation and rushed to the palace where a banquet was in progress. He was so angry he forgot to remove his shoes. Everyone was shocked and shouted, "How dare you enter with shoes on." Empress Taytu took him aside, listened to what he had to say, then turned to the astonished assembly and said, "Will all the men of Tigray and Gondar rise — we are going to fight the Italians," and when her brother Wele did not get up, she said to him, "Here, you take my skirt and I will wear your trousers."[11]

In any case, Article 17 was not brought up during Menilek's discussions in Tigray with Antonelli, though many hot words were hurled at Mekonnen and Yosef Neguse over the 1 October convention. People said they must have been paid to betray their country after "stuffing themselves with rich food and good wine." Menilek endorsed Mekonnen by promoting him to ras and enlarging his domains in Hararghe.

The Shewans folded their tents after Mengesha Yohannes's submission on 16 March 1890. Menilek permitted an Italian resident to remain at Adwa, and made the first of his many attempts to keep his hand on Tigray by delegating Meshesha Werqe as his representative and as administrator of Adwa and its environs.

Though they had not fought any battles, Menilek's army was afflicted by hunger and disease on the homeward journey, leaving a trail of dying men and women to mark their route. The empress provided relief when they reached her camp at Desse. Though Taytu had no doubt been informed about the border controversy with the Italians, she had not yet allowed herself to be perturbed by it, at least not on 6 March when Dr. Leopoldo Traversi saw her. They were old acquaintances as Dr. Traversi had been in Shewa off and on since 1885. Traversi had gone to Italy with the Mekonnen mission and returned to Tigray with them, but had left for Assab while the talks were in progress. He was escorting a caravan of silver talers, minted in Europe, for the Ethiopian exchequer from Assab. "If la Taytu looked with favor on my arrival, I would not know, but it is certain that the money cheered her enormously and she gave me

a pleasant welcome — she who has never been fond of Europeans."
Traversi continued from Desse to Shewa but was called back to Desse
in mid April when Menilek's army arrived, to treat the sick who
had survived starvation. "I was impotent in the face of such misery
— it was heartbreaking," he wrote.[12]

It took two months for the emaciated army to reach Addis Ababa.
Then, on 6 June 1890, King Tekle Haymanot came to pay homage
to Menilek and further strained the royal resources as he and his
large escort had to be feted for nine days. After his departure, the
royal couple went up to Entotto and built next to Maryam church
a shelter for the homeless and hungry people begging piteously for
food. Every property owner, "to acquire merit," took in a few people
to feed. *Injera*, normally served as a large pancake topped with spicy
ragout, was, in these straitened days, cut into small pieces; beans,
chick peas and wheat were mixed together in lieu of meat and
distributed by the emperor and empress. But there was never
enough and the soldiers of the emperor spent their days burying the
dead.

Beset with these horrendous problems, Menilek was presented with
another mouth to feed on 9 July 1890. Count Augusto Salimbeni,
the new Italian resident, presented his credentials. Salimbeni had been
selected by Count Antonelli over three medical candidates: Dr.
Traversi, "a pugnacious personality;" Dr. Nerazzini, "too easy to
influence;" and Dr. Ragazzi, "too taciturn and lacking in
initiative."[13]

Salimbeni's diary of his sojourn in Shewa is one of the most artless
documents of the Menilek period. His prejudices, his injured ego,
his petulance and bewilderment at finding himself in an untenable
diplomatic position — are all exposed. A 45-year-old engineer who
had spent three years in Gojam (1883-6) building the Temsha bridge
for King Tekle Haymanot,* Salimbeni had also been one of the
hostages held by Ras Alula in 1887. He had accepted the bridge job
with Tekle Haymanot, he said, to cure his depression after the death
of an infant son. He had little concern for the depressed wife he left
behind, though he corresponded with her affectionately and she
exerted herself on his behalf at the foreign ministry. While in Gojam,
he had been given an attractive female slave by the king. He gave

---

*The Italian government financed this project out of gratitude to Tekle Haymanot
for the role he played in freeing Antonio Cecchi from his imprisonment by the Queen
of Ghera in 1877.

her her freedom and a daughter. Most of the foreigners had Ethiopian families: Alfred Ilg had two sons, Dr. Traversi a daughter, Antoine Brémond a son, Dubois eight sons and Count Antonelli two daughters.[14]

Gustavo Bianchi painted a nasty picture of Salimbeni's behavior in Gojam, alleging that Salimbeni gave himself up to drunkenness, women, vice and a rotten life of idleness. There is a suggestion of bisexuality in the word "vice" and this is vaguely hinted at in Salimbeni's diaries. But King Tekle Haymanot was perfectly satisfied with Salimbeni's work and life style.

Salimbeni was an escort officer with the Ethiopian mission to Italy, and he, Antonelli and Traversi returned together to Ethiopia. After Traversi left to shepherd the caravan of silver talers, Salimbeni stayed quietly behind the scenes while Antonelli talked with Menilek in Tigray. Antonelli left for Italy after briefing Salimbeni on his diplomatic assignment, which was to "get the borders we want."

The journey from Adwa to Addis Ababa was very slow, though Salimbeni was admirably treated en route, despite the famine conditions. He wrote to Antonelli that he was finding peace and tranquility in the black world, a tranquility that had eluded him in the white world. He hoped that Antonelli would protect him from the "savage whites" as he was well aware that his appointment had been strenuously opposed in Rome and that Italian officialdom at Massawa had treated him with disdain. He hit back at those officials in his diary, detailing the social and sexual scandals of the Italian colony and was equally frank about his Shewan adventures; the diary was not published until 1936. The protagonist of the diary, as its editor pointed out, was the "Treaty of Wuchale," though its title was *Crispi e Menelich*.

5

Taytu and the Treaty of Wuchale

When Salimbeni reached a point some three hours from Entotto he changed into his diplomatic frock coat and plumed hat, necessary attire for his ceremonial arrival at his new post. He was promptly thrown to the ground by his heretofore reliable mule. "A bad omen," he wrote.

He was met on the road by an Italian courier who explained that Dr. Traversi could not come as he was busy cleaning up the mess left at the Italian Geographical Station, Let-Marefià, by Dr. Ragazzi. The courier was followed by the interpreter, Yosef Neguse, who knew Salimbeni from the Mekonnen mission to Italy. Yosef apologized for the ragged appearance of his soldier escort. It was raining. In fact, a constant downpour pervades the Salimbeni diary for the next two months. He was disappointed with his first glimpse of Entotto, and compared it unfavorably with the cheerful aspect of Samera, the imperial residence of Emperor Yohannes:

9 July 1890, Entotto. The royal dwelling looks grandiose, but is not handsome. It is a kind of entrenchment with parapeted walls and palisades ... haphazardly built. The path is terrible and I reached the summit of the little hill on which it perches, breathing heavily. (102)*

Salimbeni was taken through a series of enclosures. Finally, he entered through a small door, to see the emperor sitting on a verandah that looked to Salimbeni like a capon-fattening coop in the corner of a barn. He climbed up the short ramp and Menilek gestured to him to pull over a stool. This was not Salimbeni's idea of the way an envoy of His Majesty, the King of Italy, and sponsor of a loan of four million lire should be received. So when the emperor inquired about his journey, he stressed that everywhere along the way he had been welcomed "like a king." Salimbeni, looking around the large room while Menilek read the personal letter of introduction written by Antonelli, noticed that Yosef Neguse, "so high and mighty in Italy, is meek and humble here. I think he is ashamed, as he must

---

*The numbers in parenthesis refer to the diary as published and annotated by Zaghi; footnotes are provided for other references. Though Salimbeni used "king" and "queen" throughout, I have used "emperor" and "empress" to be consistent with the post-coronation era.

recall the splendid reception he was given in Italy compared to this wretched, humiliating, disgusting one given to me." Salimbeni was dismissed without being offered the customary glass of *tej*, and told Menilek he would deliver his mail (letters from Queen Victoria and Kaiser Wilhelm) on the morrow. Davico, the courier, who had accompanied him to the reception, wept with mortification when they returned to the miserable hut assigned to Salimbeni, and then got so drunk that Salimbeni could not talk to him.

The next day, Salimbeni decided to be diplomatically ill and sent Davico to make this clear to Yosef Neguse so that it would be relayed to the emperor. Yosef appeared shortly and avowed that the demeaning reception had been the idea of Empress Taytu who had advised Menilek to be distant with lesser mortals now that he had become an emperor.

Salimbeni's mission was to secure Menilek's agreement to a boundary line between Tigray and Eritrea that was advantageous to Italy. Sitting in his soggy hut Salimbeni marshalled his arguments before taking them up with Menilek. First he was to convince Menilek that Italy *needed* the Mereb-Belesa line to keep order in Tigray; second, as Prime Minister Crispi had already told Parliament that he had the Mereb-Belesa line, it would be embarrassing for him to confess it was not settled; and third, if Italy were to help Mengesha Yohannes instead of backing Menilek, Italy would be given the border by Mengesha. Salimbeni says in his diary that Italy should exacerbate the rivalry, rancor and jealousy between Tigray and Shewa to achieve its goal, a strategy akin to the *divide et impera* policy of Great Britain. Then he offers a bribe of 1,000 talers to Yosef Neguse if he will help persuade Menilek to agree to the boundary line.

For two more days Salimbeni declined to go to the emperor. He was visited by Eloi Pino, a trader in Ethiopia for eight years, who was planning to return to France having just bought some land to leave to his woman and his son; he was visited by Gebre Egziabeher, a godson of Menilek, "a very beautiful lad," who just wanted to meet him and was apparently not looking for hand-outs.

When Salimbeni decided he was well enough to accept Menilek's invitation, he arrived at 10 o'clock in the morning to dine, carrying two Martini carbines and a Belgian elephant rifle, and leading two dogs that Menilek had asked for. He was kept waiting a long time, and just as he was about to leave in a huff, Yosef Neguse rushed out to say that the emperor was distributing grain and money to

the poor and would appear shortly. Salimbeni describes the meeting
with Menilek:

13 July 1890, Entotto. He was very appreciative of the guns and dogs. I
gave him the letters from the Queen of England and the Emperor of Germany
and those from our King and Queen, Crispi and Pisani. When he opened
the English one, adorned with scrolls and flowers, he began to laugh and
said he could see this was from a woman. Oh, if the conceited British could
hear that! (106)

The letters were sent off to be translated, while Salimbeni and
Menilek discussed the bridge that Salimbeni had built for King Tekle
Haymanot in Gojam, and the advantages of iron bridges over
wooden ones. Salimbeni went home pleased with himself, unaware
that the letter from Queen Victoria contained a time bomb that
would soon explode and shatter Salimbeni's diplomatic future.

Antonelli had briefed Salimbeni on the important role played
by Empress Taytu in Ethiopian politics, and the Count was
becoming anxious about her delay in receiving him. Salimbeni
offered another bribe, to her secretary, Aleqa Afewerq, when he
went to tell him that the religious paintings ordered by Taytu from
Italy had arrived by caravan from Harar. The bribe was given
in the hope that Afewerq would put in a good word for him
regarding an audience, and to gain his influence on Taytu regarding
the borders.

15 July 1890, Entotto. Raining so hard I could not go out. Dikran [the
Armenian goldsmith] brought me some lettuce, oil, potatoes and celery.
Gabriel [the interpreter who married Taytu's servant in 1886] wants me to
work with him on the translation of the letters but I told him I did not feel
up to it. Anxious to see Traversi, as I hope he has not sent the news to Italy
about my poor reception as it will alarm the foreign office. Menilek has
promised to send me grain, honey, myrtle leaf, *berbere* [red pepper], salt,
mutton and coffee regularly. I thanked him in Amharic and heard later that
he marveled at my skill. Finally, Traversi came! Told me he was received
badly at court yesterday. He thinks it is utopian to imagine we can get the
Mereb river as our border and advises me not to bring it up yet. He was
very surprised that I had not yet been presented to the empress. (108)

The letter that Salimbeni had declined to help Gabriel translate
was Victoria's acknowledgement of Menilek's accession, of his desire
to send envoys to London and Paris, and of his plea for the right
to import arms. Victoria wrote, "Inasmuch ... as the Italian
government have notified us that by treaty concluded on 2 May 1889
... the King of Ethiopia consents to avail himself of the government

of Italy ... for the conduct of all matters with other ... governments, we shall [send to] ... our friend, the King of Italy, copies of Your Majesty's letter and of Our reply."[1]

Dr. Traversi, and not Salimbeni, took the brunt of the explosive reaction to this letter. He, a doctor who had given his medical skills to Menilek unstintingly for six years, did not expect to be "treated like a dog." As for Taytu, that "notorious whore," she was dissatisfied with the pictures made in Rome and had told Traversi, "The Italians have 'eaten' my money." She raved at Traversi, and she raved at Menilek whom she called "weak and stupid." Traversi recounted Taytu's anger: "The beautiful harlot contemptuously mocked Menilek and said, 'How is it that Emperor Yohannes never gave up a handful of our soil, fought the Italians and Egyptians for it, even died for it, and you, with him for an example, want to sell your country! What will history say of you?'"

The two Italians knew they had a problem, but were not yet fully aware of how insoluble it was, both believing that time, patience, threats, bribes and gifts would resolve everything.

Salimbeni's health worsened as his perception of the intransigence of the Ethiopian emperor sharpened. He decided to wait until after the rains before he informed Rome of the unpalatable truth, moderated as much as he could so as not to offend Antonelli, to whom he owed his present position, however thankless it had become. Traversi returned to Let-Marefià after securing a promise from Salimbeni that he would let him know as soon as he was received by Empress Taytu, and inform him of the manner of the reception.

Salimbeni had a difficult session with the emperor, who told him, "This country is mine and no other nation can have it. I thought we had settled everything when I put my seal on the treaty ceding territory which you asked for; then when I was no longer poor and had become emperor, you asked for more and I gave you all of Hamasen. Now you want still more?"

Yosef Neguse called on Salimbeni to ask what gifts Queen Margarita had sent to the "celebrated Taytu." Salimbeni rose from his sick bed to root around in his luggage for the designs of a throne chair, a coronet and a statue of the Madonna and gave them to Yosef, who also asked him for more money. Salimbeni regretted that more funds were out of the question; he had not only just made a loan to Dr. Traversi but his own expenses were higher than anticipated because of the short rations provided by Menilek. Then Salimbeni asked, "When will the empress see me, and why this delay?" Yosef demurred with an allusion to Aleqa Afewerq, "who speaks ill of you to her." It was Afewerq who had said that Taytu did not like the Italian paintings, yet Salimbeni knew they had already been hung at Entotto Maryam church. Yosef explained that Taytu, formerly a queen, was now an empress of Ethiopia and wanted to "pose" for a while, but "soon she will receive you and you will see that she is a good woman."

Salimbeni told Yosef that he had heard complaints that Article 17 obliged Menilek to use Italy in his foreign relations and he could not understand why because "Menilek should have thought about that before signing the treaty." Yosef responded testily that the Amharic version of the treaty did not say that Menilek *must* use Italy, only that he could if he wished. It dawned on Salimbeni that he had not seen the Amharic translation and he asked Yosef for a copy.

Gloom reigned in Salimbeni's diary; he saw only failure ahead of him, and the diminishing likelihood of being believed in Rome, even if he did write the truth. He sat around yearning for the good old days in Gojam with King Tekle Haymanot, in the company of Giyorgis Fotis, his Greek companion of those days. He followed Traversi's advice and gave Abate, a young favorite of Taytu's, some gifts, and at the first opportunity asked for his intercession with the empress. Abate promised an immediate appointment — soon.

Salimbeni adjudicated some business quarrels between two Armenians and spent time with Richard McKilvie,* an expatriate Irishman who had worked with him on the bridge in Gojam and was now making a catch-as-catch-can living in Shewa. McKilvie was also doing odd jobs for Alfred Ilg, whom Salimbeni had not yet met because Ilg was off on an elephant hunt. When intoxicated, McKilvie told Salimbeni that Ilg was being paid by France and England to influence Menilek. This was a lie. Ilg had been in Menilek's employ for 11 years at a salary of 1,000 talers a year, supplemented by legitimate earnings from trade. In Dr. Traversi's view, one of the worst mistakes Antonelli had made was to offend Alfred Ilg.[2] Antonelli had warned Salimbeni not to trust Ilg.

---

*McKilvie had been one of Tewodros's European captives. Freed by the Napier expedition, he returned as soon as he could to his Ethiopian wife and children.

As soon as he returned from the hunt, Ilg called on Count Salimbeni. "Ilg is a handsome man with a yellowish beard ... I offered him the best my poor house could provide — mortadella, salami, tuna fish and artichokes. Ilg said we would be friends and that though I may have heard ill of him, things were quite different from what people say. He spoke well of Italians." Salimbeni and Ilg got along famously. They were both bridge-builders, though the wooden one constructed by Ilg over the Awash in 1886 had collapsed and he was preparing to build it in iron. A day or two later Salimbeni was invited to Ilg's home.

26 July 1890, Entotto. His house is truly charming and has a wooden floor. I saw his adorable little boy and we had an excellent meal. I sensed he was not happy with Menilek. People around the emperor are saying that he [Menilek] should not be so closely tied to Europeans and for public works he should employ individuals, not representatives of nations. [These critics] rebuke the emperor for making treaties and contracting loans without consulting the great lords of the empire. "Who will pay back these loans? We, and our sons." (125)

Ilg told Salimbeni that he had brought back a telephone from his last European trip. The emperor had been delighted with it until the priests muttered that it was "unnatural." He had brought a lightning rod for the top of a church, but Ras Darge had objected, saying it was a defiance of God. Ilg retorted that it would therefore be a defiance of God to take shelter from the rain and hail, but Darge had said, "That's something else."

Ilg and Salimbeni spoke also of their concern for the security of their children. Ilg had purchased a few parcels of land in the name of his Ethiopian mistress, as he said local law did not protect Europeans. Finally, they talked politics and Salimbeni asked for his advice and cooperation. "Ilg said exactly what I said in Italy. The treaties are worth nothing, as Abyssinian chiefs say they will tear them up whenever it suits them." Ilg, who had been in Tigray during the discussions of February and March 1890, said that Antonelli had told him that the Mereb *must* be the border and if Menilek did not give it for love, he must be forced. Ilg told Salimbeni quite frankly that he had always advised Menilek to impede any inland movement by the Italian army. When Menilek permitted Italy to occupy Asmara Ilg had warned him that he was giving up the door of his house. Now, since it was a *fait accompli*, he agreed that the Mereb made a suitably precise borderline.

On 1 August, Aleqa Afewerq came to tell Salimbeni that he had arranged a meeting with the empress. Salimbeni was to report to Azaj Zamanel, chief steward of her properties in Bulga, Minjar, Metta, Metcha and Merhabete, in his uniform. Afewerq explained that the delay had come about because someone had told the empress that when Ras Mekonnen was in Italy he had received a tardy welcome from King Umberto and Queen Margarita. But Afewerq had assured her that on the day the Ethiopians arrived, the Italian royal family had been out of town, and the moment they returned they had received the delegation. Afewerq asked Salimbeni, "What does the Italian government want from us?" Wearily, Salimbeni went through his justifications for the boundary line and produced a map to illustrate his points. Italy, he insisted, had occupied land up to the Mereb river *before* Menilek had won the submission of the Tigrayan lords, and it was preferable that he recognize this line voluntarily for he could only eject Italy by force: Menilek could feel secure on his throne, he said, if the Italians were in Tigray.

Salimbeni rose early the next morning to clean his uniform, but his appointment with the empress was postponed because she wanted to see the map he had shown Afewerq. On the morning of 3 August, wearing his smart diplomatic outfit with a cape slung over his shoulders, Salimbeni appeared at the royal dwelling. He was so nervous he could not eat, but drank a glass of hydromel before entering Taytu's private apartments.

3 August 1890, Entotto. Yosef, who as they say, smelled a rat, was there ahead of me. Taytu was seated on a low couch wrapped in her white shamma which covered her entirely except for the eyes. She invited me to be seated and treated me with more courtesy that Menilek had done. Yosef acted as interpreter and poor Aleqa Afewerq was superseded. (129)

Salimbeni spoke in a mixture of French and Amharic as Yosef did not know Italian.

As I had been doing with the emperor, I spoke in a laudatory way about Alfred Ilg as I knew he was high in her favor. I alluded to the depressed countryside and said how ashamed I was to take food supplies from the emperor. As I took my leave I told her about a new Italian hair tonic, and she uncovered her pretty head to show her luxuriant hair.

Salimbeni was quite cheered by this meeting with Empress Taytu and commented that she was far handsomer than she appeared in her photographs, very refined-looking with splendid eyes, fair skin and an agreeable facial expression. He was invited to dine with the royal couple the following day and his appetite was much improved.

4 August 1890, Entotto. The Abyssinian food was wonderful. I admired the cleanliness of the room, the clothes of the servants, the plates, rugs, etc. I presented two lengths of fabric to the queen ... also six bottles of quinine hair oil which she accepted with exquisite grace. She bade me drink some *tej* and some arak of the country, while she lamented the pestilence that has killed all the animals in the country. I suggested measures that would be taken in my country in such circumstances and asked the emperor if he had thought of asking for a veterinarian. It would be futile, he said, for the people are so wicked that they throw the entrails of dead animals into the bushes [so an autopsy for cause of death could not be performed?] Menilek gave me three milking cows. I told him that in these times, such a present was equal to 3,000 cows. I kissed the hand of the emperor as I left, so as to have a pretext for kissing the hand of Taytu, whom I like so much, so much ... (130)

Salimbeni's excellent rapport with Alfred Ilg continued, despite the mischief-making of his minor cohorts, Davico, McKilvie and Giyorgis Fotis, all of whom were making indiscreet boasts about the superiority of Salimbeni's bridge over Ilg's and went about denigrating the character of the emperor. Salimbeni shared their opinions of Menilek, but kept them to his diary.

9 August 1890. I do not find in this emperor the energy, strength, nobility and wisdom of the late sovereign Yohannes ... the dexterity required to keep this empire balanced and united is lacking in Menilek. The Tigrayan people have no attachment to him and hate being oppressed, having once been the oppressor; nor does he have domestic calm ... (135)

Salimbeni's source for Menilek's "domestic" atmosphere was a "young and beautiful woman, one of the empress's cooks, with shapely buttocks, who came to me for a few lessons in transcendental love." She told Salimbeni how Taytu could not stop reproaching her imperial husband for his idiocy, and how she harped on the virtues of Emperor Yohannes who died gloriously for the integrity of the empire. "And when the poor man [Menilek] answers, his carnose matron turns her fleshiest part towards him." The pretty cook said that Taytu's shrewish recriminations echoed from mouth to mouth, and she feared the throne was tottering since it was the first time in Abyssinian history that an emperor had given away part of the country.

Personal safety began to be paramount in Salimbeni's mind. He knew Menilek was in bad humor after receiving messages from his

Tigrayan representative, Meshesha Werqe, and from Mengesha Yohannes. He could not find out what they had said,* but he sent a courier to Dr. Traversi warning him that should he, Salimbeni, be put in chains, Traversi should go quickly to the coast to advise Rome to disregard any letters that he might be forced to write to avoid corporal suffering. Salimbeni was now sure that Yosef Neguse had turned against Italy. Ilg assured him that no steps would be taken against him personally because Menilek still wanted good relations with Italy. "Am I going crazy? Do I have a persecution mania?" wondered Salimbeni.

Just as Salimbeni's morale was at its lowest, Ilg relayed some delightful news. The empress had said, "Antonelli made this mess and left this poor man, Salimbeni, in the middle of it." This was precisely what Salimbeni thought, and he wrote in his diary: *"Brava, bella regina.* You are a fine, intelligent woman."

Yosef Neguse read aloud the Amharic translation of Article 17 at a meeting of the emperor and Salimbeni. "What a difference," Salimbeni admitted to himself. Menilek told Salimbeni he had been tricked by Antonelli and would so state "in a letter to me [Salimbeni] and to the king of Italy."

Menilek and the empress were particularly agreeable that evening. After a meal of legumes and fish stew, the emperor gave Salimbeni four bottles of Bordeaux and asked if he had any European house designs. "The empress showed enormous good will and said, 'Poor devil, others made imbroglios and send you to fix them up.' I kissed her beautiful hand with true enthusiasm."

At their next meal together, they eschewed politics as other Europeans were present. Ilg and Salimbeni presented the advantages of a railroad to carry goods from the interior to the coast, and worked out an estimate of how long it would take to build. Both Menilek and Taytu raised the question, "How many people would die if there were an accident?" Salimbeni replied that hostile tribesmen could cause more deaths on the route used by mules and camels.

Pepper was added to the stew simmering between Ethiopia and Italy when Salimbeni received a month-old instruction from Crispi. This was to inform Menilek that, because of French movement in the Awsa area, Italy was hoisting its own flag there in order

---

*General Orero had tried to make an independent deal with Mengesha over the Mereb-Belesa line, but Mengesha told him he could not give what belonged to Menilek and informed his sovereign of the Italian ploy.

to protect it for Menilek. Concerned about having to make an announcement about the flag, Salimbeni told Empress Taytu at Sunday lunch that he hoped she would be present at the discourse scheduled with Menilek because "the wife is half of the husband, and her opinions will be valuable as she is such an intelligent person." When he brought up the hoisting of the Italian flag at Gildessa in Awsa "to impede any other [i.e., British or French] military expeditions" he had to drop the subject promptly because "the empress rose up in anger." Menilek stated simply, "Awsa is mine."

Unbeknown to Salimbeni, that same day Menilek's scribes completed two polite letters of protest to Italy, only one of which was shown to Salimbeni. The letter Salimbeni read reviewed 24 years of contact with Italy and is a fine example of Menilek's style and Taytu's ideas:

Majesty, I say frankly to you: in our country members of the royal family have never been sent as ambassadors abroad unless forced by persecution. Still, I sent Mekonnen to you in the hope that the treaty would be settled as it was, not that it would be supplemented.

Even so, Ras Mekonnen accepted in the name of friendship those articles which were not to the advantage of Ethiopia. Perhaps Antonelli has forgotten, but I told him at Meqelle about the frontiers. Even before the death of Emperor Yohannes, Antonelli said that Italy only wanted a place with a fresh climate for its soldiers at Massawa and for no other reason. Still, when I signed the treaty, the Italian army had not vacated Sa'ati. And you will note that when Ras Mekonnen signed the supplemental on 1 October, Italy had not gone beyond Asmara.

I was astounded when I saw what Antonelli brought me. Even in our country when merchants ask a price, they ask for more than its value so they can go down to its true value; they do not set a low price so as to increase it after.

When Antonelli demanded the frontier at the Mereb, I told him, "If I am called King of Kings of Ethiopia it is because I have Tigray in my kingdom. If you take up to the Mereb, what is left for me?" The hereditary lords of Tigray protested to me, "How can you let Italy take that country which we kept at the price of our blood fighting the [Egyptians]?" I told them it was better to have Christians as neighbors than Muslims and that peace was better than war ... I ordered Dejazmach Meshesha Werqe to make peace between Ras Mengesha, Ras Alula and your generals. They made peace.

Then I gave all honors to your envoy Count Salimbeni and asked him, "Why is the border delineation not done?" He told me it cannot be done until you possess the Mereb as frontier. I know such words could not come from your mouth as Ras Mekonnen spoke highly of your royal character ... I am waiting impatiently for this frontier to be settled.[3]

Salimbeni thought that this letter was insulting and reiterated his faith in bayonets. Traversi told Salimbeni to calm down but Salimbeni fired off his reaction to the palace.

31 August 1890, Entotto. I said that the people of Tigray, desolate and starving, were emigrating *en masse* to ask Italy to feed them. Your Majesty knows that rebels of every kind infest the country and discord reigns among the chiefs. Can Italy, strong and civilized, remain impassive at such a spectacle of misery and discord? No. That is why we continued on from Adwa to the Mereb. (158)

Salimbeni then wrote to his friends in Italy and to his wife, preparing them for his resignation and/or dismissal. He did not want to take part in this obscene comedy in which Ethiopians were calling Italians liars. He spent more and more time in bed, and worked himself up to a fervid hatred of Yosef Neguse whom he thought was responsible for the "mistranslation" into Amharic of Article 17.

The letter that Salimbeni did not see was a straightforward demand from Menilek to Umberto that Italy notify all European powers that they had made a mistake about Article 17. In some of his more lucid moments, Salimbeni had thought that it would be an act of national courage to do just that. But he always reverted to fulminating against Menilek for being ungrateful to the nation that had put him on the throne.

Ilg and Salimbeni remained friends. Meanwhile Léon Chefneux returned from France with 16 rapid-fire mobile cannon. Despite Ilg's assurance that this was a private business deal with Menilek, Salimbeni was sure that it was some official action by the French government to counter Italy.

Diplomacy had become an unpleasant game for Salimbeni and his thoughts turned to the joys of being an engineer. Though he had discussed bridges, roads, houses and churches with Menilek, he now made a proposal more attuned to Menilek's interests: a fort to be built in the Galla plains. "Oh, how enthusiastic the emperor was! What a shame this accursed Article 17 ... ruins everything," wrote Salimbeni.

Menilek was preoccupied with the problem of how to stimulate initiative in the people in coping with the famine. Salimbeni paid little attention to this as he was wrapped up in his own concerns. The pride and independence of Ethiopians are so profound, he complained, that it will prevent them from accepting Italy as their protector. "If anyone should shout, 'Get out, foreigners,' nine-tenths of the people would repeat it." He fantasized about what a pleasure it would be to see Menilek dance to an Italian tune, but realistically predicted, "Anyone in Italy who thinks a protectorate will be accomplished with kind words ... is a lunatic."

Salimbeni kept up a steady flow of gifts to Menilek and Taytu. "I have the best possible relationship with them, especially the empress ... I write her stupid, idiotic letters, turning phrases into Amharic which I remember from my schoolbooks on the 17th century."

By October 1890 both Salimbeni and Traversi had described the actual situation in several ciphered telegrams that took a month to reach Rome. Salimbeni admitted that he had been unable to prevent Menilek from sending a circular letter to the major powers informing them that Italy had misinformed them about its relationship with Ethiopia. The emperor had taken an even more drastic step. To relieve himself of the embarrassment of the Italian loan he had appealed to the people to help pay it off immediately.

A lewd bit of gossip appeared in Salimbeni's diary on 11 October. The source was Alfred Ilg, who was not prone to scandalous revelations. Ilg told the Italian that he had just seen two officers of Meshesha Tewodros, son of Tewodros and a one-time brother-in-law of Menilek,[4] who had come to tell Menilek about the death of his first wife, Altash Tewodros. Ilg disclosed that when he was in Tigray the lady Altash was seen entering the tent of the emperor, and he heard that "she ate from the same *messob* [woven basket table]," which was a way of saying that she spent the night with him. She became pregnant and "now the poor thing is dead, poisoned on orders of the empress." There was nothing unusual in the story regarding Menilek's sex life, but this is the second "poisoning" laid at Taytu's door — her ex-husband Zikargatchew being the first — and can only be denied on faith. It appears far-fetched as there was no conceivable threat to Taytu in Altash's existence. The implication in Salimbeni's account is that Taytu resented Altash's pregnancy because she herself had failed to give Menilek a child.

It was soon after hearing Ilg's tale that Salimbeni talked informally about hypnosis with the emperor, who was curious to experience it. Salimbeni cautioned that he would be willing to hypnotize the emperor only in secrecy, because if people found out that he had a method of controlling the emperor's thoughts, the reactionaries would have his head. He hinted to Menilek that hypnotic suggestion might help a barren woman conceive, hoping to try it out on Taytu, but was never given the opportunity.

While Salimbeni was indisposed with influenza at Entotto, Dr. Traversi, in a personal letter to his old friend, Antonelli, seconded Salimbeni's summation that the damnable border question, Article 17 and the ill-timed placement of the Italian flag in Awsa were the causes of the present impasse. The only solution was for Italy to admit *mea culpa*. The empress, agreed Traversi, was more furious than anyone else and had forbidden the inclusion of customary niceties in the letters written by Menilek to General Gandolfi when he replaced General Orero. Instead of writing, "Happy that you have arrived safely at Massawa," she substituted, "I have heard you arrived at Massawa," and the traditional "May God illuminate us and keep good rapport," was altered to "May God illuminate you ..."

Salimbeni recovered from his illness during a two-week stay with Dr. Traversi at Let-Marefià where, with its prosperous farm gardens, he found a pastoral heaven. He was enchanted with Dr. Traversi's little girl, "so sweet, fair as a European ... a little jewel." As they puffed on their pipes in the evenings, the two men shared their worries about the future of their progeny. Traversi confessed that if he took his little girl to Europe it would destroy his reputation. "But here — what fate awaits her?" Traversi, like Eloi Pino and Alfred Ilg, had purchased land for his children in the mother's name. On political matters, they decided that Salimbeni should keep a low profile while Traversi should go to Rome as soon as they obtained Menilek's permission to present in person the harsh truth to the powers that be.

Persuading Menilek to allow Dr. Traversi to leave for Italy began with an argument on 11 November 1890. Salimbeni said to Menilek, "There is no one better qualified to interpret the claims of Your Majesty, and he [Traversi] will be able to expedite the arms shipment held up at Assab." Traversi said he could go and return within three months, adding, "It is grievous that a little misunderstanding has spoiled a friendship of so many years. The devil has come between Your Majesty and the king of Italy; the devil must be unmasked." Traversi was clever to use this very Ethiopian explanation for misunderstanding, but he also added the threat that if Menilek did not let him go, the European press would make a case out of it.

Menilek said that, of course, Traversi could go, but what would happen should the need arise for a doctor for a military campaign. "Oh, Salimbeni can do whatever I do," lied Traversi. Menilek changed the subject, asking if the English had made peace with the dervishes. Traversi did not know but answered, "Anything is possible because the English are *tanquolegna*," and explained that the term meant "clever people who use secret weapons without scruple to obtain their aim." He told Menilek to watch out for them. Menilek, without missing a beat, riposted: "The *tanquolegna* are you, the Italians. Perhaps we have been friends too long. I opted for Umberto alone, though offers of friendship have come from many sides."

Before granting permission for Traversi's trip, the emperor discussed the matter with Empress Taytu, who wanted to be certain that it would not look as though Ethiopia were begging for favors. But even as Salimbeni was coding his dispatch on 12 November that Traversi was coming to Rome, Count Pietro Antonelli was on his way to Addis Ababa.

It was decided in Rome, when Menilek's letter of protest arrived on 13 October, that a special mission to rescue the Antonellian Treaty of Wuchale was imperative. Exactly as Salimbeni and Traversi had suspected, all their frankness had fallen on deaf ears. Prime Minister Crispi had even toughened his aggressive policy at a speech delivered in Torino on 18 November 1890; Italy, he said, needed land on which to settle her excess population and soldiers must go to protect these people.

Ignorant of this pronouncement, Salimbeni bade farewell to his sympathetic colleague, and then settled down lugubriously to the chore of keeping on good terms with Their Majesties, the interpreters, and the heads of the church. Abune Matewos and Echege Gebre Selasse assured him from time to time that everything would work out well in the end.

Salimbeni devoted a long memorandum to the insecurity and slowness of communications. He was in a peculiar position, he said, when his official mail was not only handed to him by the emperor but had also to be opened in front of the emperor. Ciphered mail aroused suspicion and he had to improvise news or lie on the spot. He confided to his diary his disgust with the bickering and backbiting among the Italians (Capucci, Gagliardi, Valli and Viscardi), each of whom carried tales to him about the others. He was annoyed with Valli, an artist, who refused to paint murals at Entotto Raguel church, though Menilek had asked him to do so. He was also worried about the growing status of the French. By the French he meant Léon Chefneux (whom he described as looking like an English miss though his face was as wrinkled as parchment) and a retired French army captain who was instructing Menilek's soldiers in the use of the rapid-fire ordnance. Salimbeni even entertained the ignoble thought that terrible suffering from famine was proper retribution for the massacre of the Italians at Dogali.

It was dawning on Salimbeni that he could no longer rely on Alfred Ilg, who had become the foreigner most trusted by the emperor. Ever since Ilg had pointed out to Menilek that he had allowed the Italians to enter the "door of his house" at Asmara, Ilg could do no wrong. Salimbeni and Ilg almost came to blows over the calculation of interest on the Italian loan which Menilek was repaying. Salimbeni, in good faith, believed Ilg's computation to be in error, unaware that a mistake had indeed been made by the Banca Nazionale. He imagined that the only way to demolish Ilg's reputation was for him, Salimbeni, to build a really first-class bridge over the Awash river.

The best and the worst news reached Salimbeni in early December. He was ecstatic because his little girl and her mother had arrived from Gojam. He was stunned at the rumor, not confirmed for a week, that Count Antonelli was already in the country and on his way to Shewa. For Dr. Traversi it was even more of a shock; just as he reached the coast he was ordered to turn around and take the exhausting road back with no time to rest or re-provision himself.

Salimbeni's reaction to Antonelli's imminent arrival was three-fold: relief that he could turn over the whole disagreeable situation to the man who had created it; offense at the lack of trust the government had in him; and a feeling of profound bitterness. He feared that Antonelli might be carrying his dismissal from the diplomatic corps, which indeed Antonelli was carrying, but with instructions to use it at his own discretion. Before Antonelli arrived, Salimbeni went to the emperor to cover his rear, so to speak.

9 December 1890, Entotto. I told the emperor frankly that Antonelli's arrival was a serious rebuff to me and that I had it in mind to notify Rome that my health did not permit me to give further service to the government. I spoke about gold extraction and Menilek seemed disposed to send me on a trip to the gold areas and let me direct mining operations ... I went into the *elfign* [royal apartments, whether on the road or in the capital] and kissed the hand of Her Majesty. We spoke about the borders [concessions that Italy might make] and she said, "But how can they be settled when letters have not yet arrived from Italy?" I explained that my word was worth as much

as the word of the king of Italy as I was his representative. The empress, who, by the way, is much quicker than the emperor in business, told me to write an official note on the matter. (239-41)

Salimbeni dined with the royal couple, and then taught them a game played with a candle, pin and thread. They were very amused, "but I was more so, seeing those two august personages with two wax candles placed on the floor between their legs." In this hilarious atmosphere Menilek promised Salimbeni some land for his daughter, and asked him to go to the Awash to evaluate a new bridge project. The following day Salimbeni brought the memo requested by the empress and everyone drank champagne. The empress indicated her approval of the bridge, and Salimbeni had high hopes of staying on in Ethiopia as an engineer under private contract.

By 17 December 1890, the day Antonelli arrived, Salimbeni had convinced himself that Antonelli would fail, though he would give him all the help he could. In a conceivably Freudian slip-up, Salimbeni went to the wrong trail to meet Antonelli, missed him, and did not see him until the following day. Antonelli went straight to the *gibbi* (royal enclosure, wherever it may be) and spent four hours with Menilek, Taytu and Menilek's daughter, Zewditu.* Antonelli decided that "the situation is not as grave as has been painted. Menilek swore he would never have bad relations with Italy."[5]

The following day Antonelli greeted Salimbeni warmly and showed him the letters from King Umberto. The letters said, roughly, that it was only because Menilek's march to secure Tigray had failed that Italy had undertaken to guarantee the peace there and that they had every intention of favoring Menilek on the border line. As for Article 17, notification had already been made to the European powers, in agreement with Ras Mekonnen (untrue!), who had seen the necessity for Italy to uphold Ethiopian rights in Europe. The letter ended with the import of "have a little faith in us." Salimbeni thought the letters were "too salty."

19 December 1890, Addis Ababa. We dined with the royal family. Antonelli and I sat at a *messob* that had been put on top of a box. We sat in Viennese chairs and talked about bridge building. Menilek repeated that he would provide the materials for me to supervise. Antonelli raised the subject of a telegraph line between Massawa and Entotto which interested Menilek

---

*Zewditu was between husbands at this time. On 28 January 1891 she would marry Gwangul Zegeye to assist her father's peace agreement with Dejazmach Zegeye.

very much. After the meal, Antonelli called on Ras Mengesha Atikem* and
I went to my tent. I am in a bad humor and do not know what to do:
renounce my post or await developments. I think Antonelli is overly
optimistic. He insists that Ilg is discredited, but I know the opposite is true.
Antonelli has disarmed Menilek on the loan interest, telling him that because
the lira is now paying five to the taler, he is getting a bargain on the guns.
(252)

This was a small victory for Antonelli, but two days later he was
in retreat while Salimbeni watched. Antonelli attacked Yosef Neguse
for putting the word "may" instead of the pivotal words "consents
to" in Article 17. "The emperor and the empress answered with equal
vigor — Menilek became so excited he lost his voice." Antonelli
proposed one accommodation: he would undo the implications of
Article 17 provided His Majesty promise not to accept a protectorate
from any other power. Menilek told him to put this in writing.
Salimbeni reported the discussion:

23 December 1890, Addis Ababa. Antonelli had me translate the proposal
into Amharic. We took it to the emperor but he wanted nothing to do with
any clause that said, "in the event that Ethiopia might ask for a protectorate
she would give preference to Italy." The empress was even fiercer than
Menilek. Among other things she said was, "I am a woman and do not love
war, but sooner than accept this I prefer war." (254-5)

Menilek then gave his preferred wording: "Italy makes it known
that the empire of Ethiopia is not its protectorate, and the emperor
will refuse to any other power such a declaration."

On the day of European Christmas, Salimbeni took his daughter
to meet Antonelli's child who had just arrived. "She is very pretty
and well-mannered," reported Salimbeni of Antonelli's daughter.
Salimbeni took both girls to the palace to meet Menilek and Taytu
and commented again on how adorable the little daughter of
Antonelli was, and how attentive the emperor and empress were to
both children.

When Antonelli's beautiful mistress and his second daughter had
arrived, Salimbeni joked, "Isn't he taking the risk of having a third?"
Salimbeni passed a lonely New Year's eve, as Antonelli and Valli
went to bed early and left him to pretend that a glass of *tej* was a
glass of champagne.

There were more stormy sessions at the palace as Antonelli asserted

---

*Mengesha Atikem was nicknamed Weyzero (Lady) because his advice to Menilek
was always on the cautious side.

that if Menilek weakened Italy by embarrassing her before other European nations, it would also weaken Menilek since the Italians were his best friends. With the failure of Antonelli's efforts to blame everything on Yosef Neguse (which was what Salimbeni had been trying to do for five months), Antonelli changed his strategy. He said, not directly to Menilek, but to other lords and to the *echege* whom he knew to be close to Empress Taytu, that the responsibility for any rupture with Italy would fall on the shoulders of Taytu, to whose advice Menilek was in thrall.

A reasonably calm discussion was held with Menilek when he drew what he considered to be an acceptable border line. It was not what Italy wanted, but Antonelli kept quiet in the interest of any kind of settlement. There was much talk about the miraculous recovery of Dikran Ebeyan from a perforated intestine; Dr. Traversi had refused to operate on him as he feared he would die under primitive operating conditions, and he did not want the blame for his death. Traversi had tactlessly backed up his refusal with a bet of 10,000 talers that Dikran was doomed.

6 January 1891 (Ethiopian Christmas), Addis Ababa. I observed to His Majesty that Dikran's case was unique in the history of medicine and that he should not blame Traversi for his wager. I did not know how to turn the subject away from Traversi. Antonelli explained he was a cavalry doctor. "Of horses or men?" asked the empress. At this I could not keep from laughing. She asked me what was so funny. I said it was something she had said earlier which had reminded me of Traversi's bet. She got up and left the room. This makes me think that Antonelli's propaganda has reached its target. (269)

Antonelli was happy about Menilek's amiability over the border, and Salimbeni admitted that he too was pleased. "Still we differed as to what was important — and I knew he had yet to face the realities of Article 17." Menilek brought up the subject the following day.

The meeting began with the usual wrangling between Yosef Neguse and Antonelli, and ended when Menilek dismissed them in an angry gesture after Antonelli had shouted at Yosef, "Up to now you have eaten the money of the Italians, now try eating the money of the French." It was true that Yosef had taken money from both Salimbeni and Antonelli, but money did not buy his admission of being a faulty translator.

Though the two Italian diplomats dined at the *gibbi* several days running, little business came up because Menilek was waiting for

Ras Mekonnen to come from Harar. The royal couple were in excellent humor and Antonelli brought up the subject of medicine, which, after guns, never failed to intrigue Menilek. The emperor related how a man had been miraculously cured from snake bite: the man had sent a proxy to Addis Ababa to take a prescription on his behalf, and the wounded recovered by remote control. Empress Taytu told Salimbeni to record the story in his book* and learn from it. "I write it here," he said, "to show what imbeciles this royal couple are."

After Mekonnen's arrival on 14 January 1891, talks proceeded somewhat more smoothly. Mekonnen rebuked Antonelli for speaking too forcefully to the emperor, and Antonelli tempered his behavior. Agreement was made in several areas: Antonelli agreed to cancel Menilek's freight costs for his guns, and to pay for the grain Menilek had asked Italy to provide for the starving people of Tigray; and Digsa (church property in Tigray) and Gura (where Ethiopia had defeated Egypt) would remain on the Ethiopian side of the border. Article 17 was the one remaining obstacle.

The wretched Salimbeni had very little to do. He was not allowed to open his mouth during the palace talks. He was not even allowed to leave his house except in the company of Antonelli, with the exception of two mercy calls when he treated two young victims of shooting accidents at the request of the empress. He heard only what Antonelli opted to tell him about the talks. Menilek moved from his hard-line position of "Abolish Article 17" to agreeing that Ethiopia would not allow any other nation to protect her, and that Article 17 was to be left as it was in Amharic and as it was in Italian for five years. "The empress interrupted often in a decisive and resolutely hostile way," Antonelli told Salimbeni.

Antonelli had argued that annulment of Article 17 would render Italy powerless to defend the integrity of Ethiopia and that Italy could not change the Italian text without losing its dignity. "The empress broke in with her usual vivacity, '... we too must maintain our dignity.'" Antonelli answered her irritably, as it was after all he who had proposed new wording. The empress would not let it rest: "You want other countries to see Ethiopia as your protégé, but that will never be." Antonelli, flustered, for she had put her finger on exactly

---

*Everyone knew Salimbeni kept a diary, though he took great pains to conceal it.

what he wanted, invited the empress to come up with a proposal herself. Menilek interrupted with, "You write one and we will write one," and dismissed him.

Antonelli prepared two letters, one for the emperor and one for the empress, entreating them not to break the peace. He reminded Menilek of his 12 years' work in Ethiopia, and reminded the empress of how she and Queen Margarita had pledged their mutual devotion to good relations. He reminded the emperor of the weapons, the money and moral support Italy had given him against Emperor Yohannes, and that the bad translation of Article 17 could not be blamed on Italy. He closed with, "We do not want Ethiopia to fall into the hands of France and England." Salimbeni made copies of these letters and they paid Gabriel Gobena 100 talers to translate them into Amharic.

Salimbeni took private comfort in Antonelli's exigencies. "At the ministry they will no longer be calling me a giddy alarmist." On 31 January Salimbeni was taken aback when Antonelli made discretionary use of the letter of recall for Salimbeni and told him to leave with Mekonnen when the latter returned to Harar.

After a bad night thinking about presenting his letter of recall to the emperor, Salimbeni arrived early at the *gibbi* with Antonelli. As they entered, Yosef Neguse did not rise and Antonelli snarled at him, "You swine, why don't you stand up when I pass?" To which Yosef replied, "I did not get up because you don't like me." "I had believed that at the court of Menilek there would be better manners," retorted Antonelli.

When the translator finished reading aloud the recall letter, Menilek said with some agitation to Salimbeni, "Why are you leaving me without building the bridge?" Salimbeni excused himself on the basis of his poor health and the delay in drawing up the terms of his work. Menilek turned to Antonelli and asked who would be appointed in place of Salimbeni. Antonelli replied that it would be either Baratieri or Cecchi. Menilek indicated a preference for Cecchi, and added that he would like Salimbeni to remain until his successor arrived. Antonelli then made the surprise announcement that he too wished to depart because the emperor obviously had no confidence in him. He complained that it was useless to wait for the Italian government's response to the new proposals because Menilek was never going to, accommodate himself to anything. These strong words appeared to rattle Menilek; after a few moments of thought he offered to accept the text as proposed by Antonelli.

Salimbeni withdrew his letter of recall and Menilek instructed Antonelli to draft four letters: one stating how much Menilek valued his friendship with Italy; one in the form of a circular to the European powers describing the exact borders of Ethiopia; one giving approval of a telegraph line from Massawa to Entotto; and one setting down a proposal for an accord between England, Italy and Ethiopia to fight the Mahdists.* Salimbeni expressed his pleasure at the outcome:

3 February 1891, Addis Ababa. A great surprise arrived this evening. Mekonnen sent over a letter of accommodation that is beautiful ... in addition to agreeing to leave the texts as they are, Menilek said he will certainly call upon Italy for help in foreign affairs, not through force, but because of friendship ... Bravo Mekonnen! The official interpreter is now our Yosef of Let-Marefià. That animal, Yosef Neguse, is now out in the cold. This rejection of him is a very clever move, since he seems to have taken 800 talers off Chefneux to piss on Antonelli ... this evening I go to bed happy ... (294)

Everyone was pleased by the outcome, and the empress was smiling over the satisfactory conclusion to the business. Even Antonelli was reconciled with Yosef Neguse. The only unfinished detail was to make an Italian translation of Menilek's agreement, as Antonelli had signed only the Amharic one. Two days passed and Gabriel Gobena did not come up with the translation, so Salimbeni began to work on it. He puzzled over an Amharic word he could not find in his dictionary. He learned that it meant *cassare* (to break, cancel or abrogate). "Damnation! They have tricked Antonelli into signing a document that says 'abrogate Article 17' before he saw an Italian translation."

It was sheer stupidity on Antonelli's part to sign a document in a language he understood poorly. A little skulduggery was to be expected, however, as the Ethiopians had been tricked into signing a treaty which made the country a protectorate of Italy.

The next scene was the one sketched for color supplements in the Italian press whenever they did a feature on this historical period. Antonelli is shown standing in front of Menilek and Taytu tearing

---

*Though Menilek had discussed fighting the "dervishes" many times with Salimbeni and had even offered Salimbeni a commission to command, this was the first time such a joint action had come up.

"La Risata di Taitu," reproduction in *Domenica del Corriere*, 1963, of older drawing showing "the diplomatic rupture between Count Antonelli and Menilek."

up the offending document. The actual scene took place outside the throne room where Antonelli and Salimbeni were waiting after they had sent a message in to Ras Mekonnen who was dining with the emperor.

Antonelli's account is more dramatic than Salimbeni's:

I protested strongly against this treachery. The ras told me to give him the paper to show the emperor. I tore off my signature as well as the resident-general's seal as a precaution before giving it to him. The ras was pained as in tearing off my signature I had also torn off the emperor's seal. We were called in. Present were the empress, Mengesha Atikem, Mekonnen and Yosef Neguse. I showed the emperor the torn document and asked for justice. Menilek maintained that what was sent to me was identical to what we had discussed. I maintained the opposite.

The empress told Antonelli that he had no right to abuse the interpreter, Gabriel Gobena; if it was proved he had blundered it was up to them to punish him as they saw fit. She held out the Amharic version of the Treaty of Wuchale, and asked Antonelli to show her the words in it that said Ethiopia was under Italian protection.[6] Of course he could not, as it existed only in the Italian translation.

Ras Mekonnen, "like the swindlers and swine these blacks are," wrote Salimbeni, told Antonelli that the note sent to him meant exactly what it said, "Abolish Article 17."

That night Antonelli decided that he, Salimbeni and Traversi would tell Menilek that in civilized and Christian countries, when

negotiations yielded no resolution, the representatives withdraw. The
following morning, a farewell letter written by Salimbeni in Amharic
was signed by all three men and handed in to Menilek. Ras
Mekonnen had been forewarned as they had asked to travel to Harar
with him for safety's sake. He followed them as they left the palace,
and told them they were acting like children, an insult not taken
kindly by Antonelli, though his colleagues privately agreed with
Mekonnen.

Salimbeni went up to Entotto to pack, trying to leave as much
as possible for his little girl, so "she won't die of hunger. Poor little
thing! I fell on my bed. I was tired to death."

The audience of dismissal was held at 8 o'clock on the morning
of 11 February and the empress was not present. Menilek was very
glum and muttered that Antonelli had told him that he would not
leave until there was a response from the Italian government.
Antonelli confirmed this, but complained of the insult caused to him
by the copy of the agreement that was different from the original.
Menilek said that he had been confused and that they should go back
and start again. Salimbeni recorded the dialogue:

11 February 1891, Addis Ababa
Antonelli: "To start over send me the map that you and I signed."
Menilek: "No. I will send it to your government."
Antonelli: "I am the government and you must give it to me. If you wish
I will give you a receipt."
Menilek: "No. I will send it."
Antonelli: "All right then. Those maps have no value and I consider them
as though they had been stolen from me." (299)

This puerile exchange was followed by a lecture by Antonelli on
diplomatic usage in civilized countries. He topped that with the
ultimatum that Italy would remain at the Mereb river, defend Article
17 and make no concessions in financial matters. "*Gidyelem* [so be
it]," said the emperor.

The Italians* were to rendezvous at Roge. Salimbeni arrived first
after stopping at a spring where he had gorged himself with figs from
a magnificent tree, and had then set fire to the dry grass. With that
same good will he said he would have set fire to "Menilek, to his
whore, and to all Ethiopia."

On the very day of their departure, Galliardi, who had been ill

---

*Traversi, Antonelli, Salimbeni, Pulini and Valli; Capucci was left behind to be a
source of information.

in the past month, died. Salimbeni blamed his demise on Capucci who "treated him badly and made an onerous if not downright usurious contract with him." Traversi was the next to arrive. He was in a surly temper, having only two months before traveled from Addis Ababa to Assab and returned, and feeling disconsolate about leaving behind his mistress and little daughter. Salimbeni hoped that for once all the Italians could travel together for a few weeks without fighting. They succeeded except for a contretemps after Dr. Nerazzini joined the group at Harar. Salimbeni was furious because Dr. Nerazzini did not show him the respect due a superior in diplomatic rank.

From Roge they crossed a plain abandoned by its population after merciless raids by Menilek's soldiers. Along the route, tragic scenes of starvation and death were always in view. A dead young boy lay on the road; debilitated women dragged themselves along in Ras Mekonnen's train,

making a strange contrast with some more robust young girls who appease their hunger more with charm than work ... crying babies; soldiers struggling to prod along overburdened bony mules ... a shriek here, a collision there ... filth everywhere, fetid and loathsome. We saw a family eating a donkey they had skinned ... a little skeleton of a lad had a piece of the meat between his teeth but had not the strength to devour it. If you realize that in this country they have utter repugnance for the flesh of horse, mule or ass, you will understand how hungry they were. It was indescribably horrible and touched the hardest heart.

Salimbeni reflected as his mule plodded along: Antonelli had been too precipitous and his public abuse of Alfred Ilg was a mistake; he had been too outspoken with Menilek. When two-week old mail reached the caravan and they learned that Prime Minister Crispi had resigned on 31 January 1891, Salimbeni opined, "Antonelli is not just the admirer of Crispi, he is the worshiper. Frankly, I don't understand him anymore. The new ministry (di Rudini) has opened its eyes and ... has realized that Menilek is and always was a ruffian." Salimbeni also read in these old newspapers the first public attack on himself. He answered the journalists' charge that "Salimbeni lacked patience" with a prompt salvo.

After a brief stop in Harar, the Italians proceeded to the coast, and thence to Aden, where Salimbeni regained his strength and divided his time between figuring out how to "get" Antonelli and ogling the wives of the residents. "The lady is a jewel — the husband, a toad ... Her husband is a pig, she is a peach, a strawberry, a love ... Oh, his signora is so young, fresh, pretty, tempting."

Salimbeni, Traversi, and Antonelli took different steamers back to Italy and met again on the Via Veneto at Doney's on 22 May 1891. "We discussed African politics and especially Empress Taytu." Antonelli was writing his two famous monographs, one on Menilek, and one on Taytu, copies of which reached the subjects soon after they were published and angered them deeply.[7]

Salimbeni tried to settle down with his wife, whom he said had grown very fat, and wrote many letters on Ethiopian matters with the message, "See how right I was." He was sent to Harar in March 1892, as the man "most likely to soften up Ras Mekonnen," and spent a year there working on financial matters connected with Menilek's repayment of the Italian loan, but made no perceptible dent in Mekonnen's attitude towards Article 17. Salimbeni's Ethiopian daughter joined him; he had her baptized Augusta Pierini and left her with the French nuns of the Lazarist mission when he returned to Italy in 1893. He led the life of a barely solvent grandee in Modena and committed suicide in July 1895, five months after the death of his wife.[8]

The "protagonist" of Salimbeni's diary, the Treaty of Wuchale, was not yet dead, but did have an incurable disease. Dr. Traversi made two more trips to Ethiopia and both times met with "ostentatious coldness," especially from the empress. He thought Menilek showed occasional signs of cooperativeness, but said he was helpless because of Taytu's opposition. "She was even more suspicious and stubborn than before."[9]

Whatever progress Traversi might have made was undercut in Rome, where it was decided to woo Mengesha Yohannes into granting them some desired border extensions. Mengesha Yohannes went so far as to make a pact with General Gandolfi on 8 December 1891 that "they would love each other's friends and hate each other's enemies." This rash short-term advantage for Italy infuriated Menilek even more when he heard that Gandolfi had addressed Mengesha as "Son of Yohannes, King of Zion, King of Kings of Ethiopia." That was in fact who Mengesha was.[10]

Still, Italy did not give up. Colonel Federico Piano* was sent to

---

*Colonel Piano was an aide to General Baldissera. He and his young son were hostages of Ras Alula from 16 January to 11 March 1887, along with Savoiroux and Salimbeni, against Alula's demand that General Gené withdraw his forces from Ethiopian territory.

Addis Ababa in 1894 to take over from Dr. Traversi. Piano experienced the shortest diplomatic posting on record: two weeks. Menilek received him in mid-June 1894 with his face hidden in a shawl, a sign of displeasure, and asked, "When will you be leaving?" Piano answered, "When your Majesty wishes." Menilek said, "Why not leave with Dr. Traversi tomorrow?"[11]

"The dismissal of Piano meant the absolute end of the Treaty of Wuchale and it happened without diplomatic notes, without letters and without discussion, in a purely Abyssinian style," concluded Traversi. In their final report, Traversi and Piano recommended that Ethiopia be isolated diplomatically and deprived of European contacts, not foreseeing how enthusiastically France and Russia would thwart such a policy.

Traversi reported that just before Colonel Piano arrived, Empress Taytu had said to her husband, "What! You want to be friendly with yet another Italian?" "Do not worry," answered Menilek, "after Dr. Traversi has left and before the other arrives and gets to know our country as the doctor knows it, we will have set our affairs in order the way we want them."[12] Thus, serving his own ego, Traversi was evidently blind to the signs that Menilek *had* set his affairs in order. Nourished by anger at Italy, a spirit of unification was abroad in the land, but it was also a product of Menilek's patience, prudence and steadiness.

The diary of Augusto Salimbeni provides evidence that Empress Taytu played a significant role in the process of unification. She clarified issues for Menilek, and she had an individuality and warmth as a woman that was rarely seen by foreigners.

6

Four years of famine; Mengesha Yohannes of Tigray submits

The horror of starvation and disease tormented the people of Ethiopia for four terrible years. From 1888 to 1892 more than a third of the population died, and untold families sold themselves and their children into slavery. Hyenas were so sated from eating human flesh that even they could be caught and eaten in turn by humans; the dung of animals was picked over for edible straw.

There was no system to cope with the desolation, but Menilek certainly did more than hold out his hand for God's help. Admittedly there was a great deal of praying night and day, and a proclamation by the monarch thundered that laxity in church behavior had brought God's angry hand on Ethiopia. He ordered that those who had been walking out of church while mass was being said must stay and make the proper liturgical responses. The deacons who patrolled the three entrances to the church (one for women, one for men, and one for clerics) must stop interfering with those who wanted to enter. The implication of this rebuke was that deacons were making arbitrary decisions regarding the purity of prospective communicants and should desist. Customarily, menstruating women, women who had given birth less than 40 days earlier, and men and women who had engaged in sexual relations during the previous 24 hours were forbidden to enter the church. There was no record of how many people had to pay eight liters of flour to the church, the penalty for non-compliance. The dietary and fasting requirements were obviously overlooked during these times, as people ate their donkeys or any wild animal they could trap.[1]

Menilek and the empress set a personal example of austerity, and though the court was always supplied with food, the area outside the palace gates was swarming with people who came from all parts of the realm to seek sustenance at the seat of absolute power. A relief station was set up beside Entotto Maryam church where the emperor himself handed out pieces of *injera* to thousands of grasping hands.

The chronicler was not embarrassed to say that there was favoritism in the distribution of relief supplies. To "people of high birth" they gave clothes and mules, to "some Galla men and women [slaves], cows and steers," while "the peasants" received cows, steers and money. "Thus, by combining their resources, the sovereigns succeeded in reviving the desolated land." Empress Taytu sent to people living on her crown-grant land in Begemder 300 cows and steers, along with men to cultivate the soil, slave women to dig up weeds, and potters. As described, this effort had all the earmarks of a resettlement project and perhaps to those slaves who were sent, it offered a measure of freedom. Reports of the success of the enterprise were brought back to Addis Ababa: "At the sight of this livestock, people who had escaped death came from [neighboring areas] ... and gathered up cow dung which they took away with them as its smell seemed like perfume."[2]

Though the famine simply took its course, some practical measures were attempted. Menilek directed the governors of provinces to go out and work with the hoes and pickaxes that he had sent them, and to show the people how to make furrows when they had no oxen. He did this himself day after day in the hot sun. The putting of hand to manual labor was philosophically repugnant to most high-born Christians. The emperor tried to import grain but caravans were pillaged going through Somali and Danakil country where the people were also starving. Grain hoarders selling at usurious prices were hunted down and soon sold their stock at reasonable prices to avoid having it confiscated by the emperor's collectors.

Two measures had far-reaching consequences. One was a change in the criminal law. A man convicted of serious crime was usually chained, his goods confiscated and his land sold. This left his family destitute. A convicted murderer who escaped, for example, could cause his family to be deprived of their land for three generations. The law was amended to permit the forfeiture of belongings, but not the family-owned land. Paired with this was the partial restoration of lands to their Oromo owners. For 20 years Menilek and his generals had been taking over vast tracts of land southeast and west of Shewa; the residents (who were not all Oromo) then became tenant farmers of the soldier who was awarded land for his participation in the conquest. Menilek showed in this ruling some awareness that the motivation of a tenant farmer to grow food, a large percentage of which went into the storehouse of his *neftegna**

---

*The meaning of this word, "he who has a gun," conveys the essence of the relationship of the farmer to the soldier.

(soldier-settler), might be improved if he had land he could call his own and pass on to his children.[3]

Menilek dealt compassionately with the appalling cases that came before him, even the "woman of Ensaro who ate seven children." "Have you really eaten human flesh?" he asked. She confessed to having strangled and eaten the seven children. He could scarcely restrain his tears and murmured, "Oh God! How my country has fallen into ruin." He ordered that her bony body be clothed, gave her some food and released her.[4]

The business of empire was somehow carried on and the years 1891 and 1892 saw a sharp increase in the influence of Empress Taytu through the promotions of her brother and her nephew. The latter, Gesesse, was the 20-year-old son of her sister, Desta. He had spent nine years under his aunt's guidance at court and now was named a *dejazmach* and assigned the government of Semen, responsible to his uncle, Ras Wele. Wele's dominions were expanded to include Begemder. He was thus handed the problem of Ras Zewde whose reputation for rough justice was causing anxiety to the crown. Rumors had reached the capital that Ras Zewde was hanging more people for stealing food than there were people dying of hunger. In a letter to the emperor Zewde declared he would kill Ras Wele. The threat, as it appears in the chronicle, was not nearly so offensive as his grammar. Empress Taytu was outraged on behalf of her brother, when Zewde employed verb forms that were used for servants and children. "He dared to humiliate and *tutoyer* Ras Wele whose father had been lord over [Zewde's] grandparents, forefathers and who himself was superior to Zewde."

The poor people of Begemder were subjected to the eat-as-you-go armies of Ras Wele and Ras Mikael who hunted Zewde and his men for six months before capturing him. Zewde spent 15 years in prison, a sentence brought on, it was said, by Empress Taytu's implacable hatred of him.[5]

At the beginning of 1892 Menilek and Taytu and their respective armies and retinues were camped at Desse and being provisioned by Ras Mikael. War on Ras Mengesha Yohannes of Tigray was discussed and rejected. Mengesha Yohannes's cooperation with the Italians throughout 1891 and his courteous but firm refusal to make obeisance to Menilek were provoking but did not yet amount to treason. Famine stricken Tigray could not, in any case, support an invading army.

Before Menilek and the empress returned to Shewa, there was a wedding. Ras Mikael claimed his reward for the capture of Zewde by asking Empress Taytu to grant him the hand of Shewa Regga Menilek. When Menilek objected because Mikael was his "adopted son,"* Taytu pleaded Mikael's case with a biblical precedent† to show that an exception might be made in this case. She also supported Mikael's demand that the ceremony take place immediately, again over the objections of the emperor.

Shewa Regga appears very suddenly in the chronicle as the elder daughter of Menilek. Empress Taytu had "found her living in libertinage," according to one source. Another source, who swore that the truth was told to him by a servant at Menilek's court, says that a priest located the long-lost daughter.[6]

It was Hugues Le Roux‡ who told the following highly romantic tale of low credibility about Shewa Regga. Menilek, as a young man, was so preoccupied with great thoughts about what he would do for his country that he had no time for women and "lived like a grandson of Ecclesiastes." This was patently untrue because Menilek had lived for about 17 years with Bafena, all the while producing assorted children from a variety of women. Among the women who served his table, continued Le Roux, was a lovely young thing who showed a special grace while pouring *tej*. Her name was Dessela.[7]

One night a servant whispered in the girl's ear, "Come walk quietly in the shadows; the Lion of Judah gives you the honor of his bed." She had such a beautiful throat and such a clever mind that Menilek loved her in secret for months. When he left suddenly on expedition the waist of this girl was already thickening, but she dared not tell the emperor.

---

*It was Emperor Yohannes who stood as godfather at the conversion and baptism of Mikael, but Menilek referred to Mikael as "his son and friend."

†The Bible (Numbers: 36) says that Moses commanded that daughters marry within the tribe so as not to lose their inheritance to outside tribes. The *Fetha Negast* (135) interdicts marriage between the adopted son and his "sister."

‡Hugues Le Roux was invited by Alfred Ilg to come to Ethiopia in 1899 and write a book to enhance the image of Ethiopia in Europe. Le Roux did some serious exploration between Addis Ababa and Welega and went as far as the border with Sudan. On his return he told Menilek he had "discovered" certain mountains and rivers which he had named after Ilg, Chefneux, President Loubet of France, himself and his companion (Baron de Soucis), and of course Menilek and Taytu. None of these names was placed on the map of Ethiopia, where, in fact, no geographical landmarks are named after individuals, with the exception of Lalibela, after the 13th-century emperor.

The court was full of aristocratic women who wanted to be the love of their master and sit beside him on the throne. They took umbrage at the fecundity of this servant and between themselves said, "Just because of a child, our king may become attached to this girl," and they chased her away.

Everywhere in the world, life is sad for the girl who carries a baby without a father. Barefoot and alone she walked north hoping to meet the army of Menilek, but her time came, and she gave birth on the path. She smiled at her baby as she had the look of the lion and named her Shewa Regga [Shewa meaning calm].

The child and her mother walked hand in hand over the years, working as bread makers. When Shewa Regga was seven years old her mother died with these words on her lips:

I can be buried beside the church because I have always been a good Christian and no Muslim has ever been able to say I served in his house for money. You, my daughter, must eat the bread of others until you are grown, then show that letter I have placed in the amulet around your neck, which is written for your illustrious father.

For 10 years the little orphan, loved by all for her beautiful smile, sparkling teeth and the eyes of a lioness, served old women by riding behind them on their mules and helping them to dismount. She followed soldiers to war and they paid her with love. When she was 18, her officer-lover in Harar asked her what was in the amulet and he called a priest to decipher it. The priest became very agitated as he read and advised the soldier, "If you value your life, take this girl to the emperor this very day. She is his."

First she was taken to Empress Taytu who had no children. When she saw Shewa Regga she was astounded at the girl's resemblance to Menilek. She kept her hidden in the women's quarters while she polished her deportment and improved her appearance. Dressed like a princess she took on such regal airs that no one could prevent themselves from bowing to her. The empress considered carefully the right moment to present this daughter of past desire to the emperor. "Do you remember," she said one day, "when you left to make a war in the north after loving a servant in secret and that on your return you were unable to find her?" "I remember," said Menilek, "Why did she leave?" Taytu told him how she had been hunted from her quarters by jealous women and had died seven years after giving birth to a baby girl. His eyes filled with sadness and Menilek entreated Taytu to find her. The empress left the room and returned a few moments later with a group of her women. The emperor was annoyed. "Taytu, I beg of you, get busy with your promise." She replied, "I have."

It was then that Menilek realized that a test had been prepared for him. He studied the women all dressed alike and stopped before one, recognizing on her face his features and the smile of the woman he had once loved. He embraced her and wept, for this child was his first-born, and he had just been bereaved by the death of a son.* "I must keep you here for a while, then I will marry you to one of my rases."

This tale by Le Roux omitted the few available facts about Shewa Regga. She was married first to Wadijo Gobena by whom she had a son in about 1884, and she and her mother had lived under the protection of Ayeletch Abarasa, Shewa Regga's mother-in-law in effect. It was Ayeletch who convinced Menilek that he should claim Shewa Regga. The terse but reliable Heruy Welde Selasse wrote that Wadijo divorced Shewa Regga which "made Empress Taytu very angry." There were always doubts cast on whether Shewa Regga was really Menilek's daughter, but there was no doubt that Menilek claimed her as such.[8]

Before Menilek left Shewa for the aborted confrontation with Mengesha Yohannes, he welcomed Vasili Mashcov who returned on a second visit in October 1891.† Mashcov maintained that Menilek was so pleased to see him that he delayed his departure for the north when the Russian became ill, concerned that "in Russia they might think we were unable to take care of him." Mashcov said that the empress sent someone to inquire about his health every day, but he did not specify any encounter with her, generalizing only that "women's estate is very good here. They go about uncovered and enjoy great freedom, which to tell the truth they make wicked use of. The Abyssinian woman has great ascendency over men and exercises considerable sway in political life."

Mashcov delivered a letter from Czar Alexander III which affirmed friendship and respect for Ethiopian independence, and some 509 cases of gifts containing arms, scientific instruments and

---

*Menilek's son, Asfaw Wessen, died in August 1888.

†Mashcov was accompanied by his wife, Anna, the daughter of a wealthy Swedish banker, and his batman, the Montenegrin who had come with him on the first trip. The foreigners enjoyed speculation about the relationship between the handsome batman and Mashcov's wife.

photographic equipment. Two Russian Orthodox priests had come with him, their aim being to establish an affinity between the Russian and Ethiopian churches. Such an affinity was impossible on strict theological terms, but Menilek permitted discussion for his own aims, aims that became clear in the letter Menilek addressed to the Czar asking his support against Italy's interpretation of Article 17 of the Treaty of Wuchale. He told the Czar about Italian intrigues with Ras Mengesha Yohannes, and vowed that Italians would be punished as brutally as their brothers had been at Dogali if they did not stop causing unrest in his country.

When the Mashcov party reached Harar on their outward journey, Ras Mekonnen gave them another letter, addressed to the Czar and dated 12 June 1892, in which he spelled out a request for arms and artillery instructors; he also made it clear that Ethiopia's leaders had no illusions about French or Italian activities in the horn of Africa:[9] "... the west Europeans in their desire for new land have encircled us ... have crossed our borders to deprive us of our independence ... we have heard [that there is] no Orthodox kingdom except Moscow."

As Mashcov and his wife were leaving Harar, a correspondent for the French newspaper, *Le Temps*, arrived. This was Casimir Mondon-Vidailhet, who acted also as a quasi-representative of the French government. He wrote his first column from Harar on 1 May 1892 and stayed there until November writing features on the trade and people of Harar. He ingratiated himself sufficiently with Ras Mekonnen to be introduced to his wife, Yeshemabet, "who was full of distinction and had an agreeable face."* For his researches into customs, Mekonnen advised him to ask the women, saying "they know it all."

Mondon-Vidailhet reached Ankober in the company of Alfred Ilg and Léon Chefneux who were returning from Europe where they had been carrying out some assignments for Menilek. Mondon-Vidailhet and Chefneux were friends, and it was at the latter's behest that he secured the Ethiopian assignment from *Le Temps*. While in France Chefneux had persuaded the French government to award Menilek

*Mondon-Vidailhet erred when he wrote that Yeshemabet Ali was the daughter of Ras Darge. She was the daughter of Welette Giyorgis, a one-time mistress of Darge. Welette Giyorgis was the mother of Darge's son, Desta. Darge arranged the marriage of Yeshemabet to Mekonnen. The French correspondent did not know that while he was in Harar she gave birth to a son, Teferi, the future Hayle Selasse I.

the Grand Cordon of the Legion of Honor for his efforts to abolish slavery and bring "civilization" to his country.*

Menilek examined with evident pleasure the richly embroidered cushion on which the decoration rested as well as the fine notepaper used by the French president. The emperor provided champagne for the formal presentation, which was staged as a great show with a thousand horsemen caracoling in lion's mane head-dresses. An *azmari* (poetess) on horseback, her long blue cape floating in the wind, improvised songs of glory to honor France and Ethiopia.[10]

February 1893 was a decisive month for Menilek. In rapid succession Menilek announced that Ethiopia would have its own coinage,† and that it had finished paying off the Italian loan, and in almost identical letters dated 27 February 1893, he declared to the governments of Italy, Germany, France and Great Britain that the Treaty of Wuchale would be null and void as of 1 May 1894.‡ He carefully included a phrase that he was not nullifying his friendship with Italy.

The angriest person in Addis Ababa in February 1893 was Dr. Leopoldo Traversi. He had just delivered a caravan of two million cartridges to Menilek and been humiliated by being required to prove by demonstration that there was still life in them. This was not unreasonable to the purchaser, Menilek, since these cartridges had been sitting on the docks at Assab for a year and a half.[11]

There was no doubt that the emperor of Ethiopia was flexing his muscles. He had been given a large tribute of ivory by Abba Jifar of Jimma, and he had begun to receive substantial income from the

---

*Chefneux presented decorations to both Menilek and Mekonnen, and Dr. Traversi sneered that it was the "first time France had used the Legion of Honor to flatter blacks." Chefneux brought a letter from Lagarde, governor of Obok, saying that France could not provide personnel but would help with arms. The French government did not provide arms, as these were handled by private entrepreneurs.

†The coins were produced but never caught on. The people trusted only the Maria Teresa taler and melted the various denominations of Menilek's coinage into jewelry, despite repeated edicts forbidding such practices. The officers of the Northern Frontier district in Kenya as late as 1923 were making the three-penny bit size with Menilek's image on it into cuff-links to reward long-serving officers.

‡Aware that he might be given trouble over early denunciation, Menilek adhered to Article 16 of the treaty which provided for review after five years from the date of signature.

diversion of the coffee route through Shewa* (instead of through the Sudan). Even the arrogance of Ras Mengesha of Tigray had crumpled, and he had sent an envoy to Menilek to arrange the terms of his submission.

In the midst of all this good news there was a plot to depose Menilek, the first court-centered plot since 1877. A member of Empress Taytu's establishment, Aleqa Admasu, was involved. Admasu had been selected for his post after serving as a courier between Abune Matewos and the royal household, in the course of which he had impressed the empress with the "purity of his language." "He will help [on the imperial council] in spiritual matters and will recite the Psalms of David for us," the empress said. He had free run of her apartments. Soon, it was reported to the royal couple that Aleqa Admasu had spoken ill of them and had repeated confidences heard "inside." "Oh, it is just envy and jealousy," was Their Majesties' response. But one day Admasu fell ill and in his delirium raved against the monarchs. Thus his disloyalty was exposed. In fact, there was a trial and no doubt considerable discomfort for Admasu before his confession. Admasu had been seen with Tekle Maryam† and Meshesha Werqe, both of whom made no secret of their discontent at being passed over for higher offices. Meshesha Werqe complained that Menilek had promised him the title of Ras when he had plotted his escape from Meqdela. He had served Menilek as his representative at Adwa where he had been insulted by the Italians and forced by Mengesha Yohannes to leave. These grievances carried no weight in court and the three malcontents were tried and condemned to be hanged.‡ The death penalty was remitted over the vociferous objections of all who had heard the evidence and the culprits were remanded for their own safety to the personal jails of three prominent lords. Tekle Maryam died the following year (poisoned it was said), but the other two men were

---

*In their conquest of the southwest, Welde Giyorgis and Tessema Nadew had taken control of the coffee trade and forced the caravans taking the Gojam-Metema route to go through Shewa where Menilek could collect taxes and they could take their share.
†Tekle Maryam (known also by the name Gulelate) had a royal claim through his father Meridazmach Hayle who had been involved in the 1877 rebellion with Bafena. Tekle Maryam's son, Tayye, and his two daughters remained respected at court and all married well.
‡Ras Darge's son, Desta, was said to have been involved in this conspiracy, and when Desta died in late 1893, Traversi reported that his father suspected he had been poisoned for this complicity. But Traversi also alleged that the empress and her brother were involved, which is not credible.

restored eventually to positions of trust. Aleqa Admasu spent seven years in custody before becoming guardian and tutor of the heir to the throne. Meshesha Werqe, always known as a close ally of Empress Taytu, was back in favor within two years and became the chief Ethiopian emissary to Jerusalem, Cairo, Istanbul and Germany.[12]

The celebration of Easter in April 1893 was marked with prodigal feasting; the famine was clearly on the wane. Lavish provisions were supplied by Ras Darge when Menilek and Taytu went to Debre Libanos in May 1893. The occasion was the dedication of a church, the construction of which had begun 12 years earlier. It was also an opportunity for political talks. Rases Wele's and Mikael's dislike for each other had erupted again and Menilek had to make peace between them. The impending submission of Ras Mengesha Yohannes was surely discussed during the nine-day assembly, and it was said that Taytu privately assured her brother that Menilek would not grant Mengesha Yohannes the title of Negus (king) as part of the deal.[13]

The public business was the reformation at Debre Libanos, from which one deduces that there was clerical behavior that needed disciplining. The new rules specified egality of privilege and increased austerity, for example, "Monks are forbidden to go to private houses for more appetizing food," and "Applicants must know the Psalms of David and cannot bring in any possessions they are unwilling to share." Menilek decreed corporal punishment for sinners, and left to Abune Matewos punishment for their souls (excommunication). The *echege*, the highest ranking Ethiopian churchman, had more responsibility for these rules than Abune Matewos, who was not a particularly busy man. "His sole duty seems to be making ceremonial appearances and ordaining priests which he does in a simple outdoor ceremony. He anoints them individually, accepts a taler, and gives them communion."[14]

This Menilek-Taytu-Echege-Abun reorganization at Debre Libanos was one more step towards the unification of dogmas, which was considered so important to the state.* Shortly afterwards Menilek

---

*Debre Libanos was the most influential monastery in the country and had been a center for the "three-birth" believers who were declared heretical in 1878, although, apparently, many holding this dogma were still around. One "three-birth" who had escaped the heresy trial of 1878 turned himself in, in 1891, expecting tolerance on the grounds of Menilek's sufferance of Muslim, animistic and Catholic believers. Two weeks of imprisonment propelled him on the path to Orthodoxy.

embarked on another expedition with religious overtones though neither the empress nor Abune Matewos accompanied him.

The emperor took many soldiers and his engineer Alfred Ilg to Lake Zwai, about 100 kilometers south of Addis Ababa. They crossed the Awash River in record time, testing the new bridge of iron constructed by Ilg and his co-workers. Lake Zwai contained five islands, on each of which was a monastery or religious community. These groups had never acknowledged Menilek as their ruler, nor been subject to the hegemony of the Orthodox church. [15]

After the failure in 1886 to coordinate a landing on these islands, Menilek now prepared an appropriate strategy. On the banks of the lake his soldiers made papyrus barques, each of which could hold about four men and a cannon. Sixty of these boats were built. As the flotilla approached the largest of the islands, a cannon was fired. In the ensuing talks held between the "king" of the island and the emperor, Menilek persuaded "King" Alibo that his aim was only to regularize baptisms and communions by sending properly ordained priests, while Alibo convinced Menilek that he was descended from an emperor and was re-appointed governor. The Lake Zwai Christians said they had been prevented from leaving their islands by pagans. Menilek took care of that problem by attacking the surrounding Oromo lands and ordering the inhabitants to stop interfering with the people of Zwai.

A priestly delegation landed to inspect the Lake Zwai libraries, which had been famous as depositories for religious books since the 16th century when they were hidden there from Muslim predators.* Menilek ordered all the books to be brought to Addis Ababa. The chronicler made a pointed reference to one of these manuscripts which contained proof that adherents of the "three-birth" heresy should be excommunicated, an indication that the religious establishment was still nervous about the influence of this schism.

On his return to Addis Ababa, Menilek stepped from the 16th century into the 19th century, guided by Alfred Ilg. Ilg designed and constructed a piped-in water supply for the palace. The chronicler was so impressed that he recorded that 7,000 talers had been spent importing pipes from Europe and that a concrete viaduct had been made and pumps built to bring the water from the river. One set of pipes carried filtered water for drinking, and another set water

---

*The aggression of Ahmad ibn-Ibrahim from 1527 to 1543.

for washing clothes and watering the gardens. "From then on, nobody [from the palace] had to go to the river to wash linen." Ilg not only amazed people by making water go uphill but also installed a device to direct the water to the side of the palace where it was needed. A poem was composed to commemorate this achievement but it gave no credit to Alfred Ilg:[16]

We have seen wonders in Addis Ababa.
Waters worship Emperor Menilek.
O, Menilek, what more wisdom will you bring?
You already make water soar into the air.
O, Menilek, how great you are becoming.
He makes water rise in the air through a window.
The dirty can be washed and the thirsty can drink.

The religious establishment was quiet on this occasion, but the priests raised a fearful rumpus over photographing the reception for King Tekle Haymanot of Gojam, an event which took place immediately after. One of the photographers was Gaston Vanderheym, an agent of the Franco-African Trading Company.* He reported that Menilek shouted at the protesting clerics that they were "idiots," and that he would have them beaten if they said another word about the "devil's work." Empress Taytu, whose last known photographs had been taken in 1883 at the time of her marriage to Menilek, invited Vanderheym to take her picture. "I spent an interesting afternoon posing the empress, the princesses and court women, all dressed in their finest. I hardly tasted the meal the empress served me. In gratitude I think she doubled the pepper." Vanderheym thought that the empress deliberately set off her own fair skin by selecting darker ladies-in-waiting.[17]

A 17-day reception began on 7 February 1894 for King Tekle Haymanot, who was meeting Menilek for the first time since he had formally acknowledged him as emperor in 1890. The province of Gojam had (and still has) a long history of independence from the power center, whether it was in Gondar, Debre Tabor or Addis Ababa, an independence fostered by the enormously deep gorges of the Blue Nile. Gojam had suffered much from the Mahdists, had been prostrated by the famine, and its king had lost substantial revenue when the coffee-ivory-musk-slave trade route had been

---

*"A young man who had dissipated some 40,000 francs ... wanted to end his life ... but his relatives persuaded Savouré to take him on without contract or promises," as related by Stévenin.

diverted from passing through his kingdom to go through Shewa and Harar to the Red Sea coast. The Gojamese, just raising their heads from the famine, must have greeted Menilek's decree imposing "10 per cent tax on agricultural products"* with derision. Still, Tekle Haymanot had never announced open rebellion against the emperor, as had the lord of Tigray.[18]

The water system and new reception-cum-banquet hall could not fail to impress the Gojam king with the resources available to the emperor. Looking up he could see the multiple candelabra, each holding 48 candles. Looking out he could see that the windows "let in light, but not the wind." On the bank of the river there was a demonstration of rock removal with dynamite. At the palace he was given a new crown.[†] The culinary management of the empress was, as usual, superb. On alternate days, when her kitchens provided the banquet, it was the "best and most savory," and the chronicler asked, "Isn't it true that what is prepared by women surpasses what can be done by men?"

Menilek was so pleased with Ilg's water system that he requested the Swiss engineer to proceed with the railroad project that had been under discussion for 15 years. A concession agreement was signed on 9 March 1894. Opposition had been based on fears more real than priestly superstition. Even the "progressive" Ras Mekonnen was opposed to the railway: what carried goods in and out could carry in an invader. The Ethiopians were well aware that the British had built a railroad to transport supplies for the attack on Emperor Tewodros and that the Italians had built a line from Massawa to Sa'ati in 1888 to facilitate their settlement in the highlands. However, by 1894, Menilek felt secure against a foreign invasion. He had control of much of the region through which a railway would pass, and the French occupying the coast were sympathetic to him, and not to Italy. The project was so fraught with international political and monetary problems that construction did not begin until four years later.

---

*This meant 10 per cent of what was grown, not cash. It was an attempt to establish government granaries from which to feed the military, rather than allow them to act as predators.
†Tekle Haymanot received his first crown from Emperor Yohannes in 1881; the next year Menilek captured the *negus* at Embabo and Yohannes compelled Menilek to deliver the man and his crown to him. Yohannes returned the crown to Tekle Haymanot in a basket, like a lost-and-found object, to indicate his disgust for the Gojam king's quarrel with Menilek.

Menilek looked outwards in minor ways as demonstrated by some public relations gestures towards France. On hearing that the President of France, Sadi Carnot, had been shot by an Italian anarchist on 24 June 1894, he wrote a letter of condolence to the widow and directed that a wreath in his name be placed at the Panthéon in Paris. He fulminated on the nationality of the assassin to Gaston Vanderheym and only calmed down when he heard that the man had been executed. He sent another letter of condolence to the widow of the Comte de Paris* and reminisced with Vanderheym about the treaty his grandfather had signed with France.[19]

After the departure of the king of Gojam, the empress and her staff began preparations for the arrival of Ras Mengesha Yohannes, the next major event on the political-social calendar. The proud Tigrayan and his army of 6,000 left their province in April and took two months to reach Addis Ababa. Menilek ordered 12,000 soldiers of his own into the capital area to ensure that the visiting army would be outnumbered. He also collected all the arms in the hands of private merchants so that the Tigrayans would not be able to buy or barter for them.

Mengesha Yohannes, his mentor Ras Alula, and other chiefs prostrated themselves with the obligatory stone on the neck at an outdoor ceremony on 9 June. Menilek sternly pronounced a pardon, and all the spectators kissed the earth to the simultaneous booming of 31 cannons and the rifles of the imperial army. As well as the oath of loyalty which bound Tigray to the empire, other agreements were made: the province of Tsellemt was granted to Empress Taytu; Zewditu Menilek's crown grant, bestowed by Emperor Yohannes at the time of her marriage to his son, was renewed; the emperor was to replace the *nebura-ed*† of Aksum, who as the Italians said, was "an enemy of the Shewans, in particular Menilek, and does nothing in Tigray without consulting us."[20] Tigray was to pay taxes into the imperial treasury, and Ras Alula, that most feared and capable general, was to stay in Addis Ababa with Menilek.

---

*The Comte de Paris was the grandson of Louis Philippe, with whom Sahle Selasse was supposed to have signed a treaty in 1843; there was a draft, but no signed treaty. One of Menilek's earlier public relations efforts was in 1870 when he offered assistance to France in paying its indemnity after the Franco-Prussian war.

†This religious office was unique to St. Mary's church at Aksum where the Ethiopians believe the ark of the covenant brought from Jerusalem in the 10th century B.C. rests. The *nebura-ed*, Echege Tewofilos, acted also as the governor of Aksum and its environs.

The personality and attractive looks of Ras Mengesha Yohannes impressed Empress Taytu, though not to the extent alleged by a gossipy Frenchman who wrote, "after his departure Taytu was consoled, no doubt having found a new love — he [Mengesha Yohannes] wanted the throne, not the alcove."[21]

Male beauty is often specified in the chronicle, while that of females is expressed in terms of their clothing or the extensiveness of their retinues. The prince of Tigray was described as a young, handsome fellow, full of vigor, with elegant manners and conversation. He was then about 32 and had been married at least twice, once to Tewabech, daughter of the herditary chief of Agawmeder, who had died in childbirth.* An Italian journalist described him as

the handsomest Abyssinian I have ever seen. There are Italians who are not as fair-skinned as he is. He wears the same hair-style as his father, Emperor Yohannes, plaited in even rows to the nape of the neck. He has large, black and gentle eyes, a perfect aquiline nose, wears a small glossy moustache curled to a point and allows a little beard on his chin. Altogether the figure of a medieval cavalier with a frank, easy smile and exquisite manners. His speech is soft and his Amharic most pure and aristocratic.[22]

Taytu and Menilek showered gifts on Mengesha Yohannes every day of his stay in Addis Ababa, but the Tigrayan was not given the gift he wanted most: the crown of *negus*. The monarch certainly discussed the Italian problem with Mengesha and Alula. Coinciding with his visit was the Piano-Traversi mission which was so abruptly dismissed; the nullity of the Treaty of Wuchale had come intó effect. It is believed that Menilek counseled Mengesha Yohannes to be patient and not make any rash moves against the Italians. Mengesha's flirtation with the Italians, and theirs with him, from 1891 to 1893, had ended in mutual disillusionment as Italy gradually recognized its folly in trying to use Mengesha against Menilek. Mengesha was eager for war and had to be restrained.[23]

The rains came in Ethiopia every year from June to September. It was a time for planning, conferring and simple indoor amusements, as there was a sea of mud outside. People visited the hot springs to soothe their rheumatism and warm their chilled bones. Wednesdays and Fridays were devoted to fasting and prayer, and the most devout, such as Empress Taytu, observed a 30-day fast in June. In August everyone over the age of six fasted for 16 days in honor of the Virgin Mary. It was also a time for soothsayers and

---

*The son of Tewabech and Mengesha Yohannes was Ras Seyum.

prophecies. In the rainy season of 1894 the soothsayers were opposed to Menilek's next campaign.

In late August, Menilek announced war against the Welamo, but did not head out until November, an unusual length of time between the call to war and its commission. Luigi Capucci, who was the only Italian left in Shewa, reported that the reason for the delay was unanimity among the predictors of doom. The empress, Ras Darge and Ras Mikael in turn tried to dissuade Menilek from going to Welamo. "As a last resort the empress fell ill and ... said to Menilek, 'We are threatened here in the capital and you leave — what will happen to us?'" The emperor promised that the campaign would take only three weeks. Capucci predicted that the emperor would be so elated to be free of his wife and the cares of state he would prolong the expedition. He was gone for two months, not for those reasons, but because the Welamo resisted so fiercely.[24]

The chronicler reached back into antiquity to justify the Welamo campaign. In the 13th century, he recalled, the country had been governed by a pagan who had kidnapped Egzi-Haraya, the wife of a Shewan peasant. Just as she was forced to submit, St. Mikael swooped down from heaven and carried her back home to Bulga to her husband. They then had a son who performed miracles when he was but 15 months old and therefore a saint; he was the most important saint in the Ethiopian pantheon, Abune Tekle Haymanot. When he grew up he went to Welamo to convert his mother's kidnapper. Later, in 1632, a Muslim, Ahmad ibn-Ibrahim al-Ghazi, destroyed Christianity.

This was the excuse Menilek used for the conquest of Welamo. The real reason was that it was a heavily populated and a fertile cotton-producing region; Menilek told Capucci that there were more people living in Welamo than between Shewa and Massawa. It was inevitable that Welamo be brought under Menilek's hegemony. Had Tona, the king of the Welamo, accepted Menilek's ultimatum, as the king of the rich province of Keffa had done in 1886 (though not without casualties), 118,987 Welamo (the chronicler was very precise in this instance) would not have been killed or enslaved, nor would there have been 80,000 dead or wounded men and women on the imperial side. The slaughter was terrible and a description by Gaston Vanderheym, who accompanied the army, did much to tarnish the image of a beneficent monarch that Menilek had enjoyed in France. One old warrior told Vanderheym that it was the worst carnage he had ever seen. The women and children captives were forced to carry the severed genitals of their husbands and fathers, though Vanderheym said that Menilek tried to forbid these atrocities. Soldiers snatched infants from their mothers' arms to relieve them of a burden that might slow them down on the march back to Shewa.

Menilek's Christianizing-colonizing objective was achieved, but at a terrible cost. Despite the fact that Menilek, "in his mercy," gave the Welamo back some of their herds, the cattle he took back to Addis Ababa still numbered 36,000. Menilek also returned their king to them, after he had been baptized, and Christianity was imposed on everyone. Legend has it that 11,000 people were baptized in one day.[25] Menilek was greeted on his return with the usual celebration, and some very bad news.

Without orders, Mengesha Yohannes had tangled with the Italians in Tigray and been beaten, losing 1,500 men and all of his baggage and correspondence. Furthermore, a Catholic convert, Bahta Hagos, leader of the Akele Guzay people, who had defected from his Italian allies, had been defeated and killed in a sudden Italian thrust. Though Menilek praised Mengesha's courage publicly, he rebuked him privately, "I cannot say the Italians were wrong — you attacked them. How could you do such a thing?"[26]

The day Menilek returned to Addis Ababa was also the festival of Timkat, a day when all Christians renew their baptism by bathing in the river. It was also a time when many weddings took place and Empress Taytu attempted to arrange a marriage between one of her nieces, a widow,* to the recently widowed Ras Mekonnen. Mekonnen's rejection of the lady led to rumors that Taytu would have him removed from the governorship of Harar. It was alleged that Ras Mekonnen believed that Taytu had poisoned his beloved wife, Yeshemabet. The story came from Pietro Felter who was resident in Harar in 1894, the year of Yeshemabet's death. Seven years later, Felter passed on the story to Ferdinando Martini as they discussed the marriage-in-name-only of Ras Mekonnen to yet another niece of the empress.[27]

---

*Capucci said she was the widow, aged between 22 and 25, of Kenyazmach Adera and that she strongly resembled the empress. Her relationship, if any, to the empress cannot be verified.

Felter: "I have always believed it was his religious behavior and wish to remain chaste after his wife's death that brought the empress's hatred down on him ... therefore the poisoning of his wife — which was the work of Taytu."

Martini: "Poisoning?!"

Felter: "Certainly. Mekonnen was away and a certain priest came to see his wife, sent by the empress. He hung around the house of Yeshemabet and the woman soon sickened and died."

Martini: "Proof?"

Felter: "Dysentery and hemorrhage from a certain infusion of stramonium and other things are used to poison women in Abyssinia. The symptoms were such that no one ever doubted that the priest had done it on orders from Taytu. Mekonnen himself believes it, as there is so much hate between him and Taytu. Until Menilek dies this hate will be dissimulated, then the empress will reign herself or put her brother on the throne. Mekonnen will line up against them, if the years have not changed his character and determination."

Relations between Taytu and Mekonnen had soured much earlier, at least by 1890, when he returned from his mission to Italy. She had entrusted him with money to purchase, on her behalf, a house for Ethiopian pilgrims in Jerusalem. This he accomplished, but difficulties over the transfer of title to the house exacerbated their relations.

Mekonnen had paid 8,000 talers for the house, "a bargain," commented the chronicler, and had then left the paperwork in the hands of the Italian consul in Jerusalem. In December 1890 Mekonnen reminded the consul in a letter from Harar that the house was to be registered in the name of Empress Taytu. Three months later the consul informed Mekonnen that the Turkish governor of Jerusalem had ruled that Ethiopian subjects could not own property there. The hapless consul's next chore was to get the caretaker of the house out of jail and advance him money for his urgent needs. The priest-caretaker had been sent to Jerusalem by the empress. He was arrested for barging into the house of the chief of police and striking him for mocking him on a public street. The empress sent another priestly agent, with a letter carrying her imperial seal ordering the Italian consul to consign her house to the letter-bearer. But not until February 1893 were Turkish objections overcome, and the legal transfer effected at the Italian consulate. Dr. Traversi, who was in Addis Ababa at that time, had the pleasure of informing the empress. She did not believe him, he said, until it was confirmed by one of "her" priests who arrived from the Holy Land. In June 1893 the empress wrote to the Ministry of Foreign Affairs in Rome that her

Jerusalem agent had informed her he had not been given the
document that proved ownership, and "without this deed, according
to European custom, how can I prove my rights to it?"

"The empress is very angry with me," Ras Mekonnen wrote to
his friend, Antonio Cecchi, the Italian consul in Aden, "as the
Jerusalem people say they have no paper which declares the house
was bought by the empress. Please do this in her name." Finally,
in September 1893 Traversi forwarded to Rome a letter from Empress
Taytu thanking the Italian government for their efforts on her behalf
in Jerusalem. Traversi commented, "Don't overlook the 'venom in
the tail' where she says she has heard only from us about the deed
to the house, but has heard nothing yet from Hayle Maryam [her
agent]."[28] All these problems poisoned the relationship between
Taytu and Mekonnen, but he was never dislodged from his position
of trust with Menilek. Mekonnen's post in Harar was much envied
as it was a lucrative customs collection point, but his accounting
was scrupulous enough never to have given the emperor cause to
replace him, despite allegations by Dr. Nerazzini, that the "emperor
thinks Mekonnen pockets it [the riches of Harar]."[29]

Mekonnen was consistently summoned to the capital to advise
on foreign affairs. He was one of the few Ethiopians who had seen
military parades in Italy, ships at sea, railroads, the Suez Canal, and
Jerusalem. His dynastic credentials were almost as good as Menilek's,
and it was widely assumed that if the emperor died Mekonnen would
succeed him.

Such a succession would have aroused jealousy in Empress Taytu,
whose ambitions for her own family were already obvious. However,
she was not such a fool as to poison Mekonnen's wife, or even to
try to destroy his rapport with Menilek.

In the five years since Menilek's coronation, however ruthlessly
it had been achieved, Ethiopia was in a promising economic and
political condition. Emperor Menilek was known in the foreign
offices of London, Berlin, St. Petersburg, Rome and Paris as a man
with more than pretensions to independence, though his denunciation
of the Italian treaty had caused scarcely a ripple of reaction in Europe.
Italy was absorbed in its Banca Romana corruption scandal as well
as in a revolt in Sicily where the peasants were starving. In Berlin
the government was trying to control runaway food prices and
industrialize at the expense of agriculture. Russia was recovering from
a famine and at the same time persecuting Roman Catholics and

Protestants, killing Jews, and repressing revolutionary activities. In London, "Home Rule" for Ireland was being debated and Edward, Prince of Wales, was praised for giving up his annual trip to the south of France in order to be active on the Royal Commission for the Aged Poor. Meanwhile, numismatists and philatelists of many countries were eager to acquire for their collections the first issues of coins and stamps by Ethiopia.[30]

Menilek had not resolved the threat of Mahdist attacks. In fact the Italians did it for him by occupying the fort at Kasala in July 1894. Instead of thanking the Italians* for holding down the "worst enemies of Christians," Menilek authorized negotiations with the Mahdists, offering part of the coffee trade and unmolested trading in slaves to keep them from attacking any part of his kingdom. The Italians never reckoned with Menilek's pragmatism. This most devout Christian emperor went so far as to propose an alliance with the most devout Muslim *khalifa* (caliph) against their common enemy, Italy. "When you were at war with Yohannes, I was also at war with him. Between us there has been no war. Now we have a worse enemy who will make slaves of you and me. I am black and you are black … unite with me." This highly unusual appeal based on skin color† reflected a new consciousness in Menilek and others of the ruling class of attitudes held by the white foreigners who had come among them. The saying, "One can recover from the bite of a black snake but a bite from a white snake is fatal," became current in the country at this time. The *khalifa* was more faithful to his anti-Christian principles than was the emperor to his anti-Muslim sentiments, and he spurned Menilek's offer.[31]

An Italian assessment of Ethiopia was:

Menilek is weak, uncertain, and in the hands of his wife. Everyone is sick of his long rule, and awaits with resignation the arrival from Jerusalem [whence the "first" Menilek had come] of a European who will bring peace to the country. To the ignorant Ethiopians all Europeans come from Jerusalem. Public opinion is prepared for the downfall of Menilek. At the first blow the empire will fall to pieces.[32]

---

*Ras Mikael and Negus Tekle Haymanot had sent letters of congratulations to the Italians for their victory over the Mahdists, leading the Italians to think that these two men would not cooperate with Menilek against them.
†Emperor Yohannes, a far more rigid Christian than Menilek, also appealed to the Mahdists (26 December 1888), asking for cooperation against "Turks" and Europeans, and based his appeal on their common ethnic tie, claiming the Sudanese as *habesha* of the same stock. This did not work either.

The Italian evaluation was wrong and was compounded by the return of Francesco Crispi as Prime Minister on 15 December 1893. The megalomaniacal Crispi took over both Foreign and Internal Affairs, and in January 1894 promptly betrayed his Garibaldian heritage by ordering troops to fire on a peaceful demonstration by Sicilian peasants, leaving 30 dead and 50 wounded. His predilection for the use of force to impose law and order on a restive and economically depressed Sicily would be extended to his approval of forceful measures to gain Italian objectives in Ethiopia.

Crispi appointed, as undersecretary of Foreign Affairs, Pietro Antonelli, the architect of the treaty Menilek had denounced over and over. "That son of a priest,"* as Empress Taytu derogated him, wrote promptly to Menilek about his appointment and added his hope that all their difficulties would be resolved.[33]

No one in Ethiopia believed any longer in the good intentions of Italy, but still Menilek resisted pressure from many in his entourage to use military force to remove Italy from Ethiopian territory. The pro-war faction was said to be led by the empress herself, "surrounded by monks and soothsayers; hatred of Italy has blinded her ... from seeing any other danger." The Italians were never to give up the convenience of blaming Empress Taytu for their troubles.

Assertions that Empress Taytu could not stand the sight of foreigners of any kind generally came from Italians. She had been considerate to Mashcov, helpful to Mondon-Vidailhet, had invited Vanderheym to take photographs, and had seen Alfred Ilg and Léon Chefneux whenever they wished to discuss business. The empress's attentions were selective and based on expediency, a trait not uncommon in heads of state. She would dispense her favor to an even greater degree to the delegation that arrived from Czar Nicholas of Russia in 1895.

*He was the nephew of Cardinal Antonelli.

7

The Russians are coming

At the beginning of 1895, as Menilek considered what to do about the Italian rout of Ras Mengesha Yohannes in Tigray and mourned the death of his four-year-old granddaughter, a child of Zewditu,* rumors reached Addis Ababa that a Russian mission was coming to visit him. "No one takes these rumors seriously," reported Capucci.[1]

A Russian mission was indeed on its way, having embarked on a ship at Odessa on 3 January 1895. It consisted of Professor Elisseiv, Dr. Zviaghin, Nicolas Leontiev, servants, interpreters and a representative of the Russian Orthodox Church, Father Efrem. The Italian ambassador was recalled from St. Petersburg for his failure to stop the mission which Rome believed to be aimed at supporting Ethiopia and that "rebel Menilek" with military supplies and advisers. The Russian government assured the Italians it was only a geographic expedition with spiritual overtones.

The leader of the mission was a distinguished explorer, Alexander Elisseiv, a man of culture and sensibility from a prominent Moscow family. His second-in-command was Zviaghin, a military doctor with the rank of captain. The third member of the mission, Nicholas Leontiev, was a 34-year-old lieutenant in a reserve regiment. He had two powerful connections: the editor of the important newspaper *Novoe Vremja*, and the Procurator-General of the Russian church, a man second in power only to the Czar. Leontiev had been expelled from his regiment for not honoring his gambling losses. He was well known as a scrounger and a cheat who had pawned his sister's patrimony to pay some of his debts. On the basis of his travels to India and Persia he had managed to insinuate himself into the Moscow Geographical Society, even though during those travels he had indulged in more shady dealings. The Procurator was still

---

*Capucci said she was four and a half, so she must have been the child of Gwangul Zegeye, and not of Wube Atnaf Seged, Zewditu's current husband. The usual irresponsible accusations of "poisoning" were leveled, though Capucci for once did not accuse Empress Taytu. Doubt that Zewditu ever married Gwangul is inherent in three Ethiopian sources, Heruy Welde Selasse, Kebede Tesseme and Tekle Tsadik Mekouria, who do not mention him as a husband of Zewditu.

dreaming of the expansion of the Russian Orthodox Church within the movement called "Pan-Slavism" and anyone who shared this dream, as Leontiev said he did, was forgiven for past transgressions.

As the Russians sailed towards the east coast of Africa, the Italian Minister of Foreign Affairs was beside himself with anxiety. Plans for a possible military offensive against Menilek were just beginning to take form in Rome, and until now the policy planners had considered France as the only possible hindrance to the enterprise. The French were always delighted when the Italians were upset and the British were always worried about what the Russians were up to, so the European press was awash in speculation during the Russians' three-week voyage.

The emperor of Ethiopia had also come to the conclusion that he would have to take the offensive against Italy. Capucci, the Italian informer in Addis Ababa, wrote to Rome that "All Shewa is unhappy about it, but Menilek will not listen any more to the advice of anyone." Menilek was no fool: if the Russians were coming, he would welcome them. He needed support from any quarter against Italy.

The French governor of Djibouti welcomed the disembarking Russians, feted them with full honors, and assisted in the making up of their caravan in record time. In Harar, Ras Mekonnen provided salvos, feasts and gifts, and judiciously vetted their intentions before expediting their onward journey to Addis Ababa. Unfortunately, Elisseiv suffered a sunstroke while crossing the Danakil desert and had to return to the coast; Leontiev replaced him as leader of the expedition.

The Russian expedition was transformed when Leontiev took command. He became "Colonel" and "brother of the Czar;" Dr. Zviaghin became "General;" Father Efrem became "Bishop" and the French-speaking Ethiopian interpreter they had picked up between Djibouti and Harar became "Lij" (child of noble birth) Redda, and the whole Mission was upgraded to an official Russian government embassy to Ethiopia.

Capucci, ever watchful, was for the first time frustrated in getting information; his usual sources were not used as translators at the meetings. "Colonel" Leontiev even kept his own colleagues out of the sessions between himself and the emperor. "Never has a mission to Abyssinia been conducted with so much mystery," Capucci complained, and added that all the women at court were angry because they too had been shut out. Ras Mekonnen was called from

Harar to join in the final days of talks. Before leaving Harar, Mekonnen told Pietro Felter that he hoped to appeal to Menilek's reason and free him from those pernicious influences that often made him lose his head. Felter interpreted this to mean "lose his head and go to war with Italy."

Leontiev was a tall, well-built and handsome man, the opposite in physique and manner of Mashcov, the diminutive, meek Russian whom Menilek had enjoyed meeting in 1889 and 1892. Leontiev had a persuasive, dramatic way of speaking and just how much he promised the Ethiopian emperor in the form of Russian aid is not known, but he certainly exceeded any instructions the group had received before leaving St. Petersburg. Almost a month after their arrival, Leontiev produced a letter from the Czar. Capucci provided a clue to the delay: "The emperor has begun to perceive he is being fooled ... he, the empress and the court have had enough of Leontiev's outbursts, whims, pettiness and vulgar boasting." Leontiev was unaware that raising one's voice is offensive in Ethiopian etiquette, but must have sensed a certain distaste for his presence at the palace. He therefore concocted a letter from the Czar to boost his importance. It did not deceive Menilek, but the emperor said nothing.

The Ethiopians tolerated through clenched teeth the religious displays staged by the Russian mission, accepted the benedictions of the "Bishop" Efrem ... scandalizing their own clergy. Ethiopians know the Russian religion is different from theirs, but they understand the exigencies of the moment. Even Empress Taytu, who is so fanatically religious has permitted herself to be blessed by the Russian monk.

Abune Matewos, the head of the Ethiopian church, boycotted the Russians completely and distanced himself from the court. He sent a sharp rebuke to the emperor for allowing himself to be blessed by this foreign priest. It was the number-two *abun*, Petros, who lent himself to the charade, as he had done in 1892 with Mashcov and his clerical colleague.

Menilek was extremely busy with other matters during the Leontiev party's month-long stay. He closed the route from the coast to Harar, through Danakil country, to Europeans. He increased his collection of mules both for his own use and to sell to Léon Chefneux for the use of the French in their conquest of Madagascar (both the emperor and Chefneux making considerable profits at each step in the transfer). He also sent protests about the Italian sacking of Adwa, where they had destroyed a church, to the Czar and the presidents of France and Switzerland. The emperor held many sessions on projected strategies for a military confrontation with Italy, which was becoming an inevitable reality as Italy had occupied not only Adwa, but Adigrat and Meqelle. There is little doubt that his conversations with Leontiev were about military affairs, and that he profited from Leontiev's experience as a soldier.

Despite being suspicious of Leontiev's reliability, Menilek was ready to use any means to strengthen his European support and he therefore authorized an Ethiopian mission to return to Russia with Leontiev. It would carry a letter to the Czar asking for war supplies as well as diplomatic support, though its official brevet was to congratulate Nicholas on his accession to the throne in November 1894 and his marriage to Alexandra.* As gifts, Menilek sent a crown, a gold cross, an illuminated manuscript and assorted Ethiopian products of ivory, horn, cane and leather. The empress sent a letter to Alexandra, accompanied by a *messob* and an assortment of gold jewelry crafted by the court jeweler.

Only when the Ethiopian-Russian group reached Cairo did Czar Nicholas and his foreign minister learn from the Russian consul there that an Ethiopian delegation was heading for St. Petersburg. It was permitted to proceed as it was decided that it might be embarrassing to stop the delegation. By the time the group landed at Odessa on 29 June 1895, all the capabilities of the Russians for glitter and pomp had been mobilized.

During the delegation's two-day stay in Odessa, the military commandant and civil and religious authorities entertained members with parades, banquets, a picnic, a theatrical performance and, of course, religious services. The *Novoe Vremja* correspondent wrote, "Their primitive and savage costumes harmonizing with their dark faces are alarming at first glance. But from the mouths of these apparently wild men come speeches made in quite fluent French."

No doubt these "dark" people were a curiosity to the Russians. There may have been a handful of people who remembered seeing the black American actor, Ira Aldridge, play the role of Shylock in

---

*Alexandra of Hesse, granddaughter of Queen Victoria, married Nicholas a week after his father's funeral. His coronation did not take place until May 1896 to accommodate the mourning period. Alexandra would gain a reputation not unlike that of Empress Taytu, for "having too much influence" over her husband and for "meddling in affairs of state."

Odessa in 1858-9 and some would have seen the two Ethiopian priests who attended the 900th anniversary of the Russian Orthodox Church in 1888. Literate Russians believed that their most popular poet, Alexander Pushkin, was of Ethiopian descent.* Only the privileged had seen the "Ethiopian" guards of the Czar and Czarina at Tsarskoye Selo outside St. Petersburg. Recruited from the tallest and strongest blacks found in the slave markets of Constantinople, they were trained, then garbed in scarlet trousers, gold embroidered jackets, curved shoes and white turbans. On this occasion, the delegation's stay in Odessa aroused public interest, stimulated by newspaper articles describing Ethiopians as their "brothers in religion," and describing Ethiopia as the only independent military state on the continent of Africa.

The train carrying the exotic visitors stopped at Kharkov where they were greeted by the Archimandrite of the Pakrovski monastery, and when they reached Moscow they were held up for a day by an impressive reception given by the military commandant while the mayor and the city council offered their guests the bread and salt of custom. They had a tour of the city and ended the day with a call on Grand Duke Sergei Alexandrovich.

Though their arrival in St. Petersburg had not been publicly announced, there was a great crowd at the station along with the welcoming committee of high officials from the foreign office. They were taken to the most luxurious hotel in St. Petersburg, and permitted a short time to repair the ravages of travel before being escorted to St. Peter's Cathedral for mass, and thence to the tomb of Czar Alexander III where they placed the gold crown they had brought with them. A journalist explained that in Abyssinia it was not the custom to put wreaths on tombs, but to decorate them with royal crowns, an explanation he invented on the spot.

Leontiev performed his sleight of hand on the Ethiopian delegation, promoting Damtew and Genemye to be Menilek's highest-ranking generals and close relatives; Belachew became "Prince" and the priest, Gebre Egziabeher, became "Bishop." During the ten days that elapsed before they met the Czar they hobnobbed with the highest officials of the church and the bureaucracy, with numerous grand dukes, and were given tea by Romanov princesses, going everywhere in imperial

---

*Vladimir Nabokov, in the preface to his translation of Pushkin's *Eugene Onegin*, raised doubts about the author's Ethiopian ancestry.

carriages attended by flamboyantly dressed Cossacks.

The high point came on 13 July 1895 when "General" Damtew's carriage, drawn by six white horses, led the cortege of equally sumptuous conveyances to call first on Dowager Empress Marie Federovna and then on Czar Nicholas and Czarina Alexandra. The letters and gifts from Menilek and Taytu were handed ceremoniously to the Russian monarchs by Damtew with an appropriate speech. He said that the Emperor of Ethiopia and his people had been distressed to hear of the death of Czar Alexander, but he was honored to convey their congratulations to Nicholas for his accession to the throne and his marriage, and was delighted to present him with a decoration, "The Star of Solomon." The Czar and Czarina kissed the gold cross that was presented by "Bishop" Gebre Egziabeher who expressed the delegation's gratitude for the enthusiastic welcome they had received. Leontiev presented the colorful basket from Empress Taytu which had been filled with flowers and told the Czarina it had been carried on the head of an Abyssinian domestic from the mountains of Entotto to the sea. The Ethiopian jewelry was presented in separate boxes.

Nicholas and Alexandra then presented their gifts: a gun in a sheath encrusted with emeralds and diamonds and the "Order of Alexander Nevski" for Menilek, and for Taytu, a silver toilet case, a diadem, necklace, bracelet and earrings. For Damtew there was a sabre with a hilt set with precious gems, a diamond ring and a pocket watch in a case engraved with the Russian imperial eagle. A shower of valuable objects and decorations (St. Anna, second class; St. Stanislaw, third class, etc.) rained on everyone, including the servants, the interpreters and Leontiev and Zviaghin. Decorations and medals were awarded to the French governor of Djibouti and his staff, *in absentia*, for having helped the Russians in and out of Ethiopia. Ships, trains and horse-drawn carriages were incredible enough to the unworldly Ethiopians (except for Genemye who had been to Italy with Mekonnen). Then came an astonishing display of the riches of the Russian empire, the beautifully dressed women and gold-braided uniforms of the men, the polished floors, brocaded drapes and gigantic crystal chandeliers to amaze them further.

Despite the fact that Damtew and Genemye were relatively low-level appointees from the Ethiopian hierarchy — a fact which consoled the Italians — they acquitted themselves extremely well. The Ethiopians stipulated that they would attend no social function at which an Italian was present, and they consented to meet only one foreign ambassador in St. Petersburg, the French ambassador, Count di Montebello, who commented, "I was struck by the vivacity and intelligence of these inhabitants of Africa ... with exquisite tact and *politesse* Damtew asked me to convey to the government of France Ethiopia's gratitude for its attentions to his country, and expressed his government's happiness with the Franco-Russian alliance."* Damtew, said di Montebello, was obviously overwhelmed by the Czar's reception and was enchanted with the portraits of the imperial couple presented to them in the name of the women of Russia.

Count di Montebello also complemented Kenyazmach Genemye who took part in their conversations with "all the ardor of a man keenly interested in and very knowledgeable about new inventions. The precision of his observations and his questions proved true intelligence." The French envoy asked the Ethiopians, "What about these plans to campaign against Italy?"

Damtew told him that these were rumors spread by the Italians so as to get money out of their parliament. "We only want to defend ourselves, not attack." Damtew told him the history of the Treaty of Wuchale and di Montebello commented, "The emotional protestations of the general were very impressive." However the request of the Ethiopian mission to stop in Paris on its return trip was turned down by the Quai d'Orsay as the French were still not quite prepared to twist the knife in Italy's back.

The excellent press given to the Ethiopians was due to their graceful deportment at all public events, their obvious devotion to religion — they went to all of St. Petersburg's great cathedrals in the course of observing daily mass — and partly to Leontiev's assiduous public relations. In one interview he said, "Menilek is loved by his people for his generosity and affability. He belongs to an ancient race. The Abyssinian soldier is a warrior born, lover of liberty and independence, and will fight to his last breath. They can field a million more or less armed men ... they do not give battle in ranks but will make guerilla war on the Italians. The Italians? Excellent soldiers ... but they will never beat the Abyssinians."

---

*This was an agreement between France and Russia to assist each other should Germany attack either one. There was an exchange of notes between 27 December 1893 and 4 January 1894 formalizing a military convention worked out 18 months before.

Ten days after the Czar's reception, the newspaper *Grazdanin* asked some embarrassing questions:

Who is Leontiev? Who is Damtew? Is he really a prince? The Ethiopians, if that is what they truly are, have never been properly identified. Ethiopia has no bishops, yet Leontiev has brought one.* This so-called "Prince" Damtew has strewn decorations with 'emeralds' right and left, and this newspaper has learned that they are really colored glass and were made up in St. Petersburg.

Leontiev responded in an interview that these charges were the ravings of madmen, but was careful to state that he would rebut them in detail only after the Ethiopian mission left the country. Regarding their prodigality, Leontiev insisted that only 14 decorations had been given out, and admitted that only six of them had real emeralds, "but many governments are not rich enough to give precious stones." In succeeding reports, the newspaper revealed Leontiev's previous indiscretions and accused him of having promised Emperor Menilek military assistance in the name of the Czar without authorization. He had also passed himself off as "Count." He had tried to saddle the mayor of St. Petersburg with the cost of the gifts the Ethiopians had offered to the Czar and Czarina. He had told people that the bronze bells being taken back to Emperor Menilek were to be paid for by Ethiopia, when in fact they were being funded by the Moscow diocese. He had petitioned, without the knowledge of this mysterious delegation, for them to visit other Russian cities so they might repeat on a regional scale the generous welcome they had had in St. Petersburg.

Their Russian hosts concentrated on getting the Ethiopians on their way before dealing with these allegations. To hasten their departure, the Ministry of Foreign Affairs consented to pay the costs of their stay, estimated by the French ambassador to be almost one million francs, not counting expenditures by the religious establishment. These Ethiopians, an informer told Count di Montebello, had managed to drink 160 rubles' worth of champagne every day, the major consumer being "Bishop" Gebre Egziabeher who drank two bottles at breakfast every morning in the guise of coffee and milk.

The champagne toasts at the embarkation in Odessa on 9 August 1895 were drunk by Russians fewer in number and lower in rank

---

*Ethiopia had a bishop, Matewos, but the priest with the delegation was a *memher* (literally "master;" usually abbot of a monastery).

than those who had greeted the Ethiopians on their arrival. The armaments Menilek had hoped for amounted to a last-minute gift from the Minister of War of 135 late model Berdans. Leontiev was allowed to accompany them as far as Djibouti but was instructed to return immediately to Russia to account for his behavior.

When the travelers reached Constantinople the sultan placed at their disposal his beautifully appointed barques and carriages and entertained them at his palace. When they reached Alexandria, they remained aboard ship, though they had been programmed to visit the Ethiopian convent, Der-es-Sultan, in Jerusalem. The excursion was canceled at the last moment for mysterious reasons said to be connected with the fear that their visit might incite one of the unpleasant incidents that erupted regularly between the Ethiopian resident priests and rival claimants to this holy place.

On 2 September 1895 they docked at Djibouti where they were met by an escort from Ras Mekonnen. They proceeded to Harar and then to Addis Ababa, where, on 17 September, Menilek proclaimed mobilization for war.

Leontiev returned to Russia, but took his time about it, stopping off in Paris to see Léon Chefneux about opportunities in the private arms trade. In the meantime, "Lij" Redda, who had remained in Russia from a "fear of incurring the anger of Emperor Menilek," made a clean breast of everything he had conspired in with Leontiev to Grand Duke Vladimir:

Leontiev said [to Menilek] that Russia would furnish Abyssinia immediately with 100,000 guns ... and build a powder mill at Entotto. Since all this has been proven untrue, I cannot return home, as I would be condemned to death. Not knowing Leontiev, I believed him and just translated everything he told me about being the brother of the Czar. I now beg help from the great monarch of Russia with tears in my eyes, to save my life, and to write to the great Negus Menilek and ... Mekonnen that I am not to blame for this trick. I was only the translator of the words of a dishonest man. If the great monarch of Russia cannot write to my sovereigns, I beg him to give me asylum for I can never return to my beloved country.

The Czar provided money for the repatriation of Redda, and the Holy Synod wrote letters to Menilek, Mekonnen and the governor of Djibouti in which they affirmed that Redda had performed ably on behalf of his country while in Russia, and was not to be blamed for Leontiev's dishonesty.

Once again, Leontiev was saved by his verbal acrobatics. Barely

a month after it was reported that he had been disgraced and
rusticated to his mother's village, he was seen dressed in full uniform,
wearing the medal given him by the Czar, at the celebrations in
Odessa for the birthday of Dowager Empress Marie Federovna,
shouting denunciations of Italy to the press. Then Leontiev had the
temerity to offer himself as peace mediator to the Italian ambassadors
in France and in St. Petersburg. (He had used a false name to gain
admittance in Paris, and Mr. Stanhope of the *New York Herald* had
helped him in St. Petersburg.) Leontiev told both ambassadors that
he was the only person in the world to whom Menilek would listen.
He promised to use his charms on Menilek's "very powerful consort,"
from whom he had "just received a letter." When Leontiev eventually
wrote a book, he said the opposite about Empress Taytu: "She has
no decisive influence on her husband though she is intelligent and
energetic. As Menilek said to me, 'Either you fool around with
women or you do business.'" A few days after seeing the Italian
ambassador in St. Petersburg, Leontiev was confiding to Prince
Lobanov that the Italians had offered him two million rubles to
induce him to make peace with Menilek for them, but that he had
disdained their money as he had such great devotion to the Ethiopian
cause.

Though the Italians alleged that Russia gave extensive military aid
to Ethiopia, all that was ever provided was the shipment of 135
Berdan guns. Russian officials had considered concrete assistance, but
Leontiev's machinations cooled these intentions and they concluded
that Russia's interests were in Europe and the Far East and not in
Africa. Leontiev's espousal, albeit a self-serving one, of the Ethiopian
cause, and the publicity surrounding the exchange of missions,
however misleading, resulted in a climate of moral support for
Ethiopia that strengthened Menilek's hand in his dealings with Italy.

In Italy, public interest in their Eritrean colony had petered out
and was not revived until the press reports of Ethiopians in St.
Petersburg. There had been a flurry of interest in the interim,
however, caused by the arrival on leave of General Baratieri and
by Menilek's arrest of the engineer, Luigi Capucci.

Capucci's arrest in mid-May 1895 followed the defection of one
of his couriers, though the comings and goings of Capucci's
messengers and his use of a cipher had long been known to the
emperor. The arrest was part of a calculated move to tighten his
security. A week later he ordered Ras Mekonnen to deport the one

other Italian, Pietro Felter, from Harar.[2]

Luigi Capucci had been in Shewa for 10 years and had adjusted easily to Ethiopian life with a mistress by whom he had a son. He had put his hand to a variety of projects: gold smelting, gunpowder mixing, flour milling, trading in guns and cloth, and the construction of houses, churches and bridges. He had begun his "information" service in 1894 at the request of the departing Piano-Traversi mission, and had built up a network of informers among the secretaries and interpreters at the palace who provided him with gossip as well as with copies of letters sent to and from emperor and empress.

Capucci, who had sensed clear signals of personal danger for at least four months prior to his arrest, said that the empress wanted him assassinated. He had therefore asked the Italian government to grant him official status for his own protection. He sequestered mules in case he needed to escape, was "a little more careful about politics," and applied himself with renewed energy to the construction of two churches.

On 20 May 1895 Menilek summoned a jury of male foreigners to hear the evidence against Capucci and asked their advice on his punishment.* Léon Chefneux counseled the emperor to put Capucci where he could do no harm, as such a merciful gesture would earn him credit in Europe. Capucci was sent to a mountain fortress where, except for a few hours when he managed a brief escape, he spent the following 14 months in chains.

Alfred Ilg, Menilek's usual adviser on matters involving foreigners, was in Europe at the time of the Capucci trial, attending to business for the emperor. He failed to gain admission for Ethiopia to the International Postal Union because Italy had blocked it with its description of Ethiopia as a nation of savages led by a barbarian. Ilg had alerted the French foreign office that Menilek was preparing for war because of Italy's obsessive refusal to disavow a protectorate claim over Ethiopia. He assured the French at the same time that Menilek had no intention of depriving Italy of its Eritrean colony. But Ilg's efforts to draw France into an active role in rebuffing Italy failed, as France was more interested in making a deal with Italy over its own occupation of Tunisia.[3]

Menilek made his first military deployment in early May 1895,

---

*There were two Armenians and one Greek as well as Captain Clochette, Léon Chefneux, Trouillet, Stévenin and Mondon-Vidailhet. Mondon-Vidailhet was criticized for telling Menilek that spies caught in France were shot.

just before the arrest of Capucci, and that excellent spy reported that it was accomplished with great difficulty. Ras Alula was ordered to take his 3,000 Tigrayans north to rendezvous with Ras Wele; they joined reluctantly because they preferred the easier life in Shewa to a return to impoverished Tigray.

Alula and Empress Taytu, Capucci reported, were pressing for war. But, in a second dispatch the same day Capucci reversed this statement, claiming that it was Menilek who was determined to go to war without listening to anyone else's advice. Word was that the empress opposed his plans and was angry because she was not included in discussions. Capucci may have meant that she was opposed to the particular strategy adopted. Ras Wele must also have been against going to war, since he refused his cooperation when Ras Alula arrived in Yejju and would not cede him a district in which he could quarter his soldiers. Menilek, rather than have an argument with his powerful brother-in-law, directed Alula to proceed to Sokota and wait out the rains. Alula was helpless when Menilek detached most of his soldiers and sent them to Ras Mengesha Yohannes. Alula had left Addis Ababa believing he would command a combined force of 12,000; he ended up with less than 2,000 and gave in to the wishes of the commander-in-chief.[4]

The emperor established a supply dump at Were Ilu where he stored about one and a half million cartridges and thousands of guns, and also set up granaries in several locations.

While Menilek made these obvious preparations for war, General Baratieri left Eritrea on home leave. A wildly enthusiastic welcome for the general was whipped up by the government. When he entered the Camera on 26 July 1895 there were cheers, a standing ovation and congratulatory handshakes even from those opposed to the whole African venture. King Umberto eulogized the general for the triumph of civilization over barbarism, and in one speech Baratieri boasted that he would bring Menilek to Rome in a cage.[5]

Baratieri did warn of a possibility of war in the colony by October, but was confident that his 10,000 soldiers were sufficient to confront the divided leadership of the undisciplined Ethiopians who numbered between 20,000 and 30,000. He was granted a modest increase in his appropriation, enough to raise 1,000 "native" troops and purchase 700 mules.

The Italian government had a recess for most of August and part of September. Meanwhile, Menilek continued to accumulate supplies (Ras Mekonnen raided thousands of cattle from the Ogaden), smooth out alliances, threaten the sultan of Awsa should he betray their long-time "friendship," and calculate the excellent returns from a special tax levied in 1893. The empress not only kept the weavers, potters and food-producers on her estates busy with constantly increasing orders, but also equipped and organized her own army with Menilek's support.[6]

Even as he dealt with larger issues the emperor could still engage in petty quarrels with men such as Stévenin whom Menilek asked to repair the cartridge-making machine. Stévenin refused because the emperor had not yet paid him for two years' work on some flour mills he had assembled. The emperor threatened to chain him hand to foot. Stévenin countered by saying that if anyone came near him he would blow them and himself sky-high with dynamite. Knowing how desperately Menilek wanted the cartridge machine to work, Stévenin sent his friend Trouillet to offer his own services in return for a loan of 3,000 talers. Menilek took the bait and gave him the money.

At the machine shop the following day, Menilek saw Stévenin working. "What's going on?" he mumbled. Stévenin blandly admitted the subterfuge. "That money was mine [with a cut for Trouillet for his collusion] and now that I've been paid, I'll work." Menilek tolerated from foreigners an insolence that would have earned one of his subjects a brutal whipping at the very least.[7]

When the rains ended, Menilek was ready. On 17 September 1895 the slow beating of drums summoned the populace. Pennants flew from poles in front of the imperial compound. The brilliantly colored umbrellas of the clerical establishment mingled with the stark white of ordinary dress and the glittering shields and lances of Menilek's palace guard. This proclamation was read:

Assemble the army, beat the drum. God, in his bounty, has struck down my enemies and enlarged my empire and preserved me to this day. I have reigned by the grace of God. As we must all die [sometime] I will not be afflicted if I die ... Enemies have come who would ruin our country and change our religion. They have passed beyond the sea that God gave us for our frontier. I, aware that herds were decimated and people were exhausted, did not wish to do anything [about it] until now. These enemies have advanced, burrowing into the country like moles. With God's help, I will get rid of them. Men of my country, up to now, I believe I have never

wronged you, and you have never caused pain to me. Now — you who
are strong, help me ... and you who are weak, help with your prayers, while
you think of your children, your wife and your faith. If ... you refuse to
follow me, look out! You will hate me for I shall not fail to punish you.
I swear by St. Mary that I will never accept any plea for pardon. Men of
Shewa await me at Were Ilu and may you be there by the middle of *teqempt*
[about 25 October].[8*]

The proclamation contained two false statements. Italy did not
aim to change the religion of Ethiopia and the sea had not been
Ethiopia's frontier since the Ottoman empire's occupation of the
littoral in 1557. One interesting feature of the proclamation is the
emperor's apology for not having taken action sooner because of
the famine; another is his implicit acknowledgement of the pressure
brought to bear on him by the Tigrayans whose province was the
land through which the Italians were "burrowing." The song-makers
of Addis Ababa composed more warlike sentiments, "You, base city
of Rome; Menilek, saviour of the world, will not leave even one
of your seed to bear your name."[9]

As the mobilization date neared and soldiers were reporting for
duty from every village, the churches were filled with weeping
women. So general was the anguish that Dr. Nerazzini, at Zeyla,
believing some national catastrophe to have taken place, relayed the
rumor that Menilek had been struck by lightning and was dead or
paralyzed.[10]

General Baratieri stepped up his departure from Italy, not because
of Menilek's proclamation, but because his deputy, General
Arimondi, informed him that Ras Mengesha Yohannes, with about
5,000 men, was in the area of Debre Hayla, less than 150 kilometers
from the Italian fort at Adigrat. Prime Minister Crispi, on vacation
near Naples, saw Baratieri off and assured him of his complete
confidence; he expressed his regrets that the government had not
increased his budget by a greater amount. Baratieri was unperturbed,
and on arrival at Massawa went directly to Adigrat where he
conferred with Arimondi and dispatched two columns to encircle
the forces of Ras Mengesha Yohannes.

On 9 October there was a skirmish which lasted about an hour,

---

*The tone of this call to war was quite different from previous ones. For example,
in 1888, Menilek had proclaimed, "The man with a lance ... if he does not come is
a woman ... and shall be called by the name of his wife and will share no more in
their common property ... for his wife is better than he is and has the right to take
everything."

but the ras eluded capture. One Italian column pushed further on
to Amba Alage, releasing Ras Sebhat from prison. Sebhat offered
to collaborate with the Italians so that he could fight the man who
had imprisoned him, Mengesha Yohannes. Sebhat remained at the
mountain fortress with 300 men under his command, taking orders
from Major Toselli with his battalion of 1,850 men.

Amba Alage was 58 kilometers from Adigrat, the nearest source
of supplies. Beyond Amba Alage lay the vastness of Ethiopia. As
Lt. Bassi wrote, "I do not believe ... this can be interpreted as a
glorious success. It gives us a wider territory disproportionate to our
resources." Major Gamerra concurred: "We push on to Amba Alage
and ... step by step like reckless children who stir up a wasp's nest,
we provoke the just resentment of all the Ethiopians."[11]

On 9 November, when Menilek was at Were Ilu with more than
100,000 troops, Baratieri was reporting, "Internal and external
situation tranquil." One of the reporters covering Baratieri said that
the intelligence service was so appalling that the general did not even
know how many cannons, guns or lances Menilek had at his
command.[12]

The Ethiopians tried to make peace with Italy right up to the
outbreak of war, posing only two simple and fair conditions: Italy
should move back behind the borderline agreed upon by treaty in
1891, and Italy should renounce publicly its claim to a protectorate
over Ethiopia. Even with long experience of Ethiopia, the Crispi
ministry and its man in the field, General Baratieri, had misjudged
its adversary. They relied too heavily on the propensity of Ethiopians
to fight each other, and underestimated their ability to unite to fight
a foreign invader.

8

War with Italy: Amba Alage, Meqelle, Adwa

The emperor, the empress, and their respective armies moved out of Addis Ababa on 11 October 1895, leaving the elderly and infirm, some women and children, a few priests and a handful of foreigners to be governed by Azaj Gizaw. Menilek's elderly uncle, Ras Darge, represented imperial authority and was to be alert to any rebellious actions by the conquered peoples of the southwest; Mekonnen's elder brother, Dejazmach Hayle Maryam, was to guard the caravan route for Menilek's guns from Djibouti to Harar and ensure that there was no interference in the passage from Harar to Shewa. It was foreseen by both Menilek and Mekonnen that the Italians might try a diversionary invasion through the southern coastal door to Ethiopia. This was, in fact, the Italians' intention, but the British would not let them use their port of Zeyla.[1] The capital became a quiet hamlet for more than seven months.

This was the first time that Empress Taytu had gone to war with Menilek, although she had witnessed and lived through several campaigns with her previous husbands. Having been a persistent advocate of force against Italy, she was prepared to share the hardships consequent upon that policy despite her age.

This war would differ dramatically from the one Menilek had fought against the defenseless Welamo. This time his forces would fight an army commanded by the redoubtable white men. While the Tigrayans were veterans of successful battles against the European-commanded Egyptians in 1875 and 1876 and of several conflicts with Italy's Eritrean army, the soldiers of Shewa, Gojam, Wello, Begemder and Yejju had never fought such an enemy before. At the first stop from Addis Ababa, Menilek addressed the foreigners whose custom it was to bid him farewell at this stage of every departure, "Not only do I dread this war, but the thought of shedding Christian blood also saddens me."[2]

The empress traveled with a suite of about 100 women, including Princess Zewditu Menilek. They were protected by some 5,000 troops, for whose food and arms the empress was responsible. They kept almost the same pace as the emperor, who did a great deal of reconnoitering from side to side, wearing out several mules a day.

Taytu, her guard and followers on the march, *c.* 1898

The empress, her escort and her soldiers were described by Mondon-Vidailhet, who added that the empress had been ungallantly and falsely portrayed by Count Antonelli:

> Her escort had not the same unconstrained character [as Menilek's]. Her soldiers kept perfect order. The women were mounted on mules, astride ... and kept silent, which must have been hard on them, for the daughters of Eve are the same in all latitudes.
> Her Majesty ... like all Ethiopian women, is very brave. She has a strong character — sometimes haughty — and is of interesting appearance. Her features and coloring are like those of an Andalusian. Her look is commanding and at the same time has finesse ... In sum, she is a great lady, who perhaps in another milieu would have been a Christina of Sweden or a Catherine the Great.[3]

The logistics of a military campaign were heavily dependent on the thousands of women who carried on their backs what could not be loaded on a mule. Only the high-born women of Empress Taytu's suite rode mules and were sheltered from the harsh winter sun by umbrellas carried by men running along beside them.

The Ethiopian army may have looked from above like an inchoate mass, but in fact there was a plan of organization and a chain of command that was rooted in antiquity, with a few modern improvements. The army did not march in ranks, but there were units based either on the soldiers' place of origin, such as "men of Welega," or on the soldier's allegiance to a particular ras, *dejazmach* or *fitawrari*. The non-military personnel overlapped, but were in general a replica of the peacetime stationary palace staff.

All functions were governed by rank. The empress's special responsibilities included the transport of the royal clothing, both for personal use and for gift-giving in the field, and the 50 or so containers made of horn and decorated with silver which were filled with the highest quality *tej*. The carriers of these items had a higher status than the carriers of the undecorated horns and leather pouches filled with ordinary *tej*. Each section of the army had a special corps whose job it was to carry the tents to be erected the moment the emperor gave the signal. These tent-carriers were also armed, as they were in the forefront and vulnerable to attack. The imperial tent was made of red velvet, and once it was positioned each detachment knew its precise place in relation to it. This tent had a name, *desta*, which meant "joy" for the obvious emotion it inspired in the tired trekkers. The signal to raise the tents was usually given before the sun dropped below the horizon; if the signal came later it had even more pleasant implications as there would be a full day's rest before march was resumed.

The empress's tent was lined with green fabric "so her eyes would not be dazzled by the light," and was the second to be raised. After she dismounted and while waiting for her tent to be readied a portable blue silk canopy was set up to protect her. She would then walk to her accommodation, her bearers carrying the blue silk over her."

Behind the royal tents were placed at least five housekeeping tents: one for making bread from the refined flour reserved for the sovereigns and their party; one for mixing the ordinary bread; one for the *wat* (stew) made from superior ingredients; another for the lesser-quality *wat*; and one for turning the best honey into beer when the stock brought from Addis Ababa ran out. All the distinctions for the upper classes were preserved on war campaigns. Beside the emperor's sleeping tent was a huge reception canopy where he held war councils, passed judgments and dispensed hospitality. It was carpeted with rugs, fitted with cushions and a portable *alga* (throne-couch). Tents were erected for the mules, horses and their fodder. About 20 tents in all comprised the royal compound which was then enclosed by a cloth fence with guarded entrances.

Within an hour of the moment when the emperor gave the signal, a city had been installed. The women put down their loads and went out foraging for wood to build the fires for cooking the cattle and goats that the butchers had just slaughtered. After the food and drink were consumed, torches were snuffed and the entire camp slept.[4]

It took 18 days for the city-army to reach the designated collection point at Were Ilu, scarcely more than 150 kilometers from Addis Ababa. This distance is calculated as the crow flies, and does not account for ravines and mountains. The slow pace gave time for units from other districts to reach Were Ilu, and for the conduct of business and local justice. At least one slave trader was caught and hanged along the way, and at least one regional chief who had waited to see which way the wind was blowing made his submission to the emperor. The army swelled from 50,000 to 150,000 during the march, and the deadline determined by the emperor in his proclamation (the festival of Timkat) was met.

On 25 October the emperor authorized Ras Mekonnen to offer peace talks to the Italians. Mekonnen's messenger took three weeks to reach the coast at Zeyla. In the absence of Pietro Felter to whom the letter was addressed, Dr. Nerazzini relayed it to General Baratieri, not by the available telegraph, but by sailboat, which took nine days! It was an indefensible dereliction of duty. By the time Baratieri received it, Ras Mekonnen's advance-guard army was in sight of Amba Alage, where Major Toselli and his 2,150 troops were ensconced with the Ethiopian defector, Ras Sebhat.

Offended by the failure of Italy to respond to his letter offering talks, Mekonnen nonetheless made one more effort. On 26 November he wrote directly to Baratieri, via Major Toselli at Amba Alage. Toselli relayed the message by telegraph and Baratieri asked for instructions from Rome. In the meantime Major Toselli told Ras Mekonnen by messenger that if he really wanted peace he would withdraw his troops to Lake Ashenge. Ras Mekonnen replied on 2 December, "I have come to make war. I cannot send back people who have been called to war. Friendship for Baratieri persuaded me to act as peace mediator. As I have had no answer I must advance because my emperor [is behind me]." Major Toselli fired off a feisty answer: "Your advance contradicts the offer to mediate. To advance means war ... in my view, departure is in the power of man, and arrival is in the hands of God. At Meqdela and Sa'ati* the fate of

---

*Meqdela was the site of the defeat of Emperor Tewodros by the Anglo-Indian expedition of 1868. At Sa'ati, Emperor Yohannes IV had faced the Italians, ready for battle, in 1889. It was not a defeat however — Yohannes simply withdrew to fight the Mahdists.

two great emperors of Ethiopia was determined. Italy was pleased to assist the third emperor [Menilek] to assume the throne of Solomon, and it can, today, destroy its own work of the past seven years." Eventually a message came from General Baratieri to arrange a meeting with Mekonnen, but it was too late.[5]

The battle at Amba Alage

Major Toselli, standing on the heights of Amba Alage on the night of 6 December, could see in the middle distance the immense enemy camp as a "magic spectacle of illumination ... fires along the horizon in order, three great columns to the right, and on the left ... other fires ... of dispersed groups." Toselli broke into song, singing the Ave Maria sonorously into the dark night. Confident of his position, confident that he would be relieved after the first assault by the enemy, Major Toselli serenely bid his batman goodnight and went to sleep.

At dawn, on 7 December, the three rases, Mekonnen, Wele and Mengesha Yohannes of the advance force, authorized a reconnoitering column to mark out a flanking movement around Amba Alage, having no intention of attacking the small fort. Under the command of Fitawrari Gebeyehu, some 1,200 men left the Ethiopian camp at 6 o'clock in the morning. An hour later they ran into an Italian look-out post and shots were exchanged. The men in the look-out retreated up the escarpment into the fort with Gebeyehu's men in pursuit.

There was confusion in the Ethiopian camp at the surprising sound of gunfire; no attack had been ordered. Many soldiers snatched up their guns and leapt on to their horses, though Tesfaye Antalo, the right hand of Ras Mengesha Yohannes, shouted at them to halt. This was not a strategic place for a battle. The Italians could fight them off simply by raining stones on their heads, let alone bullets. But there was no stopping the rush. It was obvious to the three rases that they had to go to the support of the scouting party. Fitawrari Gebeyehu had started the war though the main body of the imperial army was still over 300 kilometers from this zone.[6]

Major Toselli, awakened by the gunfire, trained his binoculars on the action; he immediately sent a message to General Arimondi, who was only 25 kilometers away, to come with reinforcements. Baratieri forbade Arimondi to move from Meqelle. He was to order Toselli to hold his position as long as he could, then fall back slowly in as much of a delaying action as he could manage. But Toselli never received these instructions because Arimondi never sent them.

Fighting went on furiously for six hours. The Ethiopians sustained terrible casualties as they tried to scramble up the steep sides of Amba Alage. Their dead mounted to 500, but they won the day. The Italians and their askaris and Ras Sebhat's men were almost wiped out. Only 400 wounded, exhausted survivors of a force of more than 2,000 made their way to Arimondi's post in the rear. Ras Sebhat eluded capture and Major Toselli was dead.

Italy had found a hero. Queen Margarita wrote to a friend: "This death of Toselli is so sublime ... that tears, not of grief, but of admiration spring to the eyes ..." She expressed her immense pride that a small band of Italians (forgetting the equally brave askaris) had fought and died for the honor of the flag.[7]

Neither the house of Savoy nor Prime Minister Crispi faced the utter folly of losing on one day almost a quarter of the military strength of the Italian colony. Crispi's answer to the parliamentary furor was that it was not his fault: "Not mine the victories ... therefore not mine the defeat. The only act completely my own was the Treaty of Wuchale which gave us the Eritrean plateau. And who has failed this treaty? Italy? No! Menilek has betrayed it, inspired by hostile influence [France and Russia]. Our aim was to oblige Menilek to stop the slave trade. He didn't like that and it was one of the reasons he betrayed the treaty."

There was a clamor to recall all troops from Africa and end this "adventure." "*Viva* Menilek" was heard in Rome's piazzas and student forums. The final vote in the Camera, however, was confidence in the government, an increase in the appropriation, and an appeal for new troops for immediate transport to Massawa.

On the Ethiopian side, the hero of the day was Gebeyehu. "That week, great and small, Amhara and Tigrayan, shouted his name, calling him 'Gobez-ayehu' ['I have seen a brave man']." Nevertheless, notes the chronicler in a dry and unexpected postscript, Gebeyehu was put in chains for three weeks as a punishment for starting the battle without orders.

The Ethiopians buried their dead, and despite the objections of the brothers of Bahta Hagos, gave Major Toselli an honorable funeral. The brothers objected because it was Major Toselli who, after fighting Bahta Hagos in 1894, had left his body unburied, a prey to hyenas.[8]

The victory at Amba Alage was a tremendous lift for the Ethiopians. Fear of the white man's invincibility was laid to rest. The enemy with its cannons, uniforms and "magic wires" had been beaten. When the news reached the emperor's camp far from the battle site, there was ecstatic rejoicing. At the same time, after two months on the road, the army was running low on food.

Coincidentally, the 40-day fast before Ethiopian Christmas had begun and with logistical precision, the required "oil of *noug*" arrived from one of Empress Taytu's estates as the substitute for the proscribed clarified butter. Muslims in the army followed their own dietary laws and had their own butchers. Christians observed the daily hours of fast from sunrise until early afternoon; they were allowed honey, grain, chick-peas and *berbere*, but they could not eat blooded animals, nor the products that derive from them. The chronicler does not state that the head of the church, Abune Matewos, had lifted the fasting rules because of the exigencies of the military campaign, so one must conclude that he had not.[9]

The fast simplified the supply problem and did not appear to impair the vigor of the troops and that of their female carriers. The chronicler emphasizes how well the army had been fed up to this time, and says that the only concern of the soldiers was that the war might be over before they got to it.

The narrow passes of Alamata lay before Menilek's army. They began the passage through them on 14 December and it must have been exactly as Antonelli described a similar maneuver in 1887:[10]

Imagine 70,000-80,000 mules and 20,000-30,000 women burdened like the beasts themselves with utensils to grind flour, make bread and cook jars of liquid strapped by two leather thongs to their shoulders and waists. These women, bent under their loads, dressed in torn clothing, go along singing, laughing and frolicking as if they were at a party. In the midst of it all, you will see under a bright umbrella the swathed head of a priest carrying a *tabot* [replica of the ark of the covenant], with another neophyte ahead of him sounding a little bell. No one pays the slightest attention to this traveling church or its ministers. In open spaces the throng moves along quite well, but come to a precipice or a deep ravine which is difficult even for goats — and it is hell incarnate. Shouting, cursing, shrieking, groaning ... pots breaking, then screams when a beast or person falls over the side — sometimes to their death.

If a general and his retinue insist on passing through to the opposite side — and it may look impossible — with a hail of blows, shoves and pushes, the mass somehow shrinks and permits them through. Afterwards, everyone laughs. The women resume their songs, which are often quite bawdy, and onward they go.

When Menilek's army reached Lake Ashenge there was a military parade before the emperor and empress, not only to celebrate the victory of Amba Alage, but to take account of the numbers who had made it through the passes and also to present a show of strength to some minor chiefs of Lasta who had been waiting to witness Menilek's strength before committing themselves. Indeed, General Baratieri's hopes for collaboration with some anti-Menilek chiefs had gone up in the smoke of Amba Alage; his belief that the Muslims would rise up against Menilek had vanished with the disappearance of Sheikh Tohla-ben-Giafer of Wello, who fled after taking the first assault at Amba Alage. The Awsa Muslims were at that very moment being surrounded by forces commanded by Welde Giyorgis, Tessema Nadew and Welde Tsadiq to make sure the Sultan of Awsa would not honor his promise of full cooperation with Italy.

The emperor changed his route out of the Lake Ashenge area in late December, to avoid the camp of Ras Mikael where an epidemic had broken out among the horses and mules. On 24 December his army was augmented by the 5,000-man army of King Tekle Haymanot of Gojam. This was another blow for General Baratieri, who had counted on Tekle Haymanot's neutrality, as the Gojam king was known to have had little sympathy for the Tigrayans, to have held many grudges against Menilek, to have suffered awesome losses while fighting the Mahdists and to have enjoyed good personal contacts with a number of Italians for nearly 20 years.* With the joining of King Tekle Haymanot, the Ethiopian empire was as unified as it had ever been.

Menilek had achieved something of a diplomatic edge on Italy as well: the French continued to let his arms go through the port of Djibouti; the sympathy of Russia was well known, and he had two unofficial French military men with his army. Menilek wrote to his Swiss adviser, Alfred Ilg, in Zurich at this time, "Be assured, I will not make any treaty or peace agreement, or give up land. I am not afraid of a few soldiers ... for I am a friend of Russia and of France, who comfort me."[11]

---

*Gustavo Bianchi (1880 and 1883-4); Dr. Raffaele Alfieri (1880-2); Augusto Salimbeni, Giuseppe Andreoni, Francesco Colaci, Cesare Diana, Gherardo Monari (c. 1883-4); and Giacomo Naretti on those occasions when Tekle Haymanot came to see Emperor Yohannes IV.

The siege of Meqelle[12]

The Italian public avidly absorbed the emotional reports in their
newspapers of the "45-day siege of Meqelle," eager to believe that
a small, brave band of their countrymen had held out against
repeated assaults by "war-crazed black barbarians." Subsequent
study had shown that the siege lasted only 15 days. Nevertheless,
there remains every reason to praise the defenders of Meqelle fort
as brave men and women.

Meqelle had been one of the principal residences of Emperor
Yohannes IV. It consisted of a small village nestled in a hollow
surrounded by low mountains. On one slope was a quite astonishing
"castle" that had been designed and built by Yohannes's "architect",
a carpenter named Giacomo Naretti,* with the assistance of
Engidashet Schimper, a German-educated half-Ethiopian. One of the
two churches in Meqelle was an ancient one, Enda Iyesus, built at
an elevation of 2,225 meters. The Italians took over the church, after
paying the priests 1,000 talers and giving a guarantee that they would
build another in its place. They proceeded to burn down all
habitations in the vicinity to eliminate places for ambush, and
summarily executed a 50-year-old priest and his acolyte who were
accused of threatening one of their askaris.

Major Galliano was in command with about 1,300 men and their
women; the latter included some camp-followers while the others
were wives of the soldiers. At midnight on 7 December, terrible cries
were heard from the women's quarter. The survivors of Amba Alage
were straggling in.

Lt. Moltedo rushed from his bed dressed only in overcoat and
boots. He saw an askari on the ground, covered with dust and blood.
The man groaned, "Salaam, Lieutenant ... the Abyssinians are here
... the askaris of the fourth battalion are all dead ... all dead."

"The women quickly gathered," continued Lt. Moltedo, "and were
tearing their hair, beating their feet on the ground, crooning
monotonously. A wife and a sister recognized the husband and
brother they thought were dead ... and their cries of joy brought

---

*Naretti had worked for Yohannes in 1871-2 and become much trusted. He married
Teresa Zander, the half-Ethiopian daughter of a German worker at the court of Emperor
Tewodros. Teresa, who spoke French, Italian, Arabic, Amharic, Gallinya (Orominya)
and Tigrinya, and her husband were both employed by the Italians at Massawa at
this time. Naretti's brother, Giuseppe, made sketches for Italian journals to illustrate
their war stories.

tears to my eyes." Another observer, more cynical, wrote, "The Sudanese* widows were the most inconsolable, or at least their grief was the loudest. The Abyssinian women wore the tarbushes of the dead which they put on their heads with ill-concealed coquetry ... one would not have thought they were three-day widows."

The population of the fort at Meqelle was increased by more than 100 wounded survivors, who gave Major Galliano as much information as they could on the Ethiopian army that had attacked them. Galliano was certain that his complement of more than 1,300 could resist any frontal thrust and if he needed assistance he could call on General Arimondi, three days' march away at Adigrat.

Ras Mekonnen made his camp a few kilometers from Meqelle and for a month, aside from isolated sniping episodes, neither side made an aggressive move. Messengers went between the Enda Iyesus fort at Meqelle and Mekonnen's camp with polite communications. Mekonnen wrote to Galliano on 12 December saying that he regretted the shedding of Christian blood at Amba Alage, which had been attacked without his orders, but that he was prepared to resume talks. Galliano queried General Baratieri on this offer. Baratieri referred it to Rome. No action was taken because Prime Minister Crispi's thoughts were not on peace, but on revenge for Amba Alage.

In another gracious exchange, Mekonnen wrote to Galliano: "How are you? I am well, thanks be to God. Your soldiers? Are they well? Mine are fine. In the name of the Emperor Menilek, I beg you to set free our land, otherwise I will be forced to make war. I beg you. Go away with your soldiers. Your friend, Mekonnen."

Galliano, with equal courtesy, explained to Mekonnen that his king had ordered him to stay where he was, therefore he could not withdraw. "Believe this," he wrote, "I have here the very best guns and some excellent cannon. Your friend, Galliano."

On instructions from the high command, Galliano, on 18 December, sent Lt. Partini to keep alive the notion in Mekonnen's camp that Italy was keenly interested in negotiations. Partini left the fort with an interpreter and was met about 20 minutes down the pathway by an escort of 50 men who guided him to Mekonnen's tent. He was allowed to sleep in the tent of Lt. Scala who had been captured at Amba Alage. They spent the night talking of Scala's

---

*Sudanese men and women had been recruited into the Italo-Eritrean army and had proved to be particularly adept gunners.

experiences and guessing the strength and intentions of the Ethiopians. When Partini returned to the Meqelle fort at 6 o'clock the following evening, he said, "Mekonnen has many guns, many mules, many women ... about 25,000 soldiers." Partini then rode 192 kilometers to Adigrat to report, covering the journey there and back in four days, with only four hours' rest. Partini's movements as well as all the mail received in the fort were through the courtesy of Ras Mekonnen who patrolled all access routes.

By 26 December, Mekonnen had run out of patience with the obviously deliberate delays from the Italian side. He informed Galliano that "where the Emperor bids me, I will shed my blood ... we no longer believe in the sincerity of Italy." Mekonnen's reputation was at serious risk. His persistent efforts to avoid war were considered treasonous by some of his compatriots.

Still, three days after this note, Mekonnen requested, and Galliano granted, the services of Dr. Mozzetti to care for the distinguished Ras Mengesha Atikem who had been injured in a fall from his horse. Dr. Mozzetti returned from this errand of mercy somewhat shaken in his conviction (after more than 10 years in the colony!) that they were dealing with "savages." He was struck by the aristocratic manners, courtesy and hospitality he had received, and found his patient's question, "Why are the Italians invading my country," rather embarrassing. He also noted the luxuriousness of the enemy's accommodation (carpets, camp beds, good food) compared with the crude conditions in the Italian fort.

The next Italian to enjoy the comforts of the Ethiopian camp was Pietro Felter, whose *bona fides* with Mekonnen began to be utilized after he arrived at Adigrat. Baratieri asked him to do everything he could to delay movement of the enemy for 20 days to give time for reinforcements to arrive from Italy. Obediently, Felter kept in touch with Mekonnen and in his own words, "gained time for the occupiers of the fort at Meqelle to strengthen their defenses." He left Adigrat for Mekonnen's camp where he arrived on 5 January 1896. Just before Felter's arrival, Mekonnen had sent what amounted to an ultimatum to Galliano: "I have not come to make war on such a small fort; we are numerous and have no fear of your guns. Remember Amba Alage and the end of Toselli. Give up the fort!" Mekonnen offered to have all the people in the fort escorted safely to the port of Massawa. He would send their baggage after them. Then he offered reimbursement for the medicine sent to his camp and for the services of Dr. Mozzetti.

The army of Emperor Menilek was joined to Ras Mekonnen's forces on 6 January 1896. The great assemblage could be seen from the fort at Meqelle. "In the space of an hour the hills were literally covered with human beings ... giving the effect of a sudden growth of a forest of pines and firs. In this sea of tents, suddenly, there was erected on a little hill the red tent of the king of kings." It was also the day before Ethiopian Christmas when the fasting period ended. Empress Taytu's nephew, Dejazmach Gesesse, arrived from Semen with sheep, cows and great containers of butter, another tribute to her masterful planning.

Pietro Felter awoke on the morning of 7 January to the sound of machine-gun fire. This time it was not the hot-headed Fitawrari Gebeyehu who had started a battle, but a runaway mule. The owner chased after his valuable beast and the occupiers of Fort Enda Iyesus fired on him. The emperor gave the order to return fire and thus began the real siege of Meqelle.

It had been Menilek's intention to bypass Meqelle, leaving a detachment there to keep the Italians bottled up in the fort while he proceeded with the bulk of the army towards the main Italian strength at Adigrat. Instead, for the whole day, each side lobbed shells at the other with no appreciable damage being done.

Stung by murmurs that he was "soft on Italy," Ras Mekonnen volunteered to lead an infantry attack on the fort. This assault began at 10 o'clock on the morning of 8 January and was met with a stalwart defense. Ras Mekonnen was slightly wounded, and some 500 casualties lay on the slopes when he ordered retreat at nightfall. Inside the fort there were six dead and nine wounded from the artillery barrage. As an Italian officer described it, cannon balls would land on the sandbags alongside the parapet and the askaris would collect them into piles. "Captain Olivari arrived late for mess carrying an enormous platter of cannon balls which he offered with a flourish to his fellow officers: 'Here is a dish not on the menu — His Majesty Menilek sends it with his regrets for not having cooked it.'"

Empress Taytu, her brother Ras Wele, and Ras Mengesha Yohannes were reported to have opposed this frontal assault which had ended as they had foreseen with many dead and no penetration of the fort. It was Taytu's idea, and her idea alone, the chronicler records, to capture the water supply of the Italian redoubt. The emperor gave his approval after reconnaissance had been carried out by Liqemekwas Abate, trained by Capt. Clochette in handling cannon and artillery, and by Azaj Zamanel, seneschal of Taytu's establishment, who agreed that it could be done. The chronicler says that Taytu addressed her own troops, a highly improbable action; both she and the emperor had people who spoke for them. Her words, however delivered, were these:

You [soldiers] have been saying you would be happy to go into the fort and fight. But, with an army as large as ours, and with only one small point to attack you might kill each other and the massacre would be worse than what the Italian guns could do. Those of you who boast of fighting, I hope you will not be afraid to die in the plains. Those who volunteer will be honored — I will make the *teskar* (funeral remembrance) for those who die and I will care for their children. May the Lord be with you.

Obviously Ethiopian soldiers had to be persuaded that taking the enemy's water supply was as brave a thing to do as hand-to-hand combat.

Just before dawn on 9 January, 900 men from the empress's contingent crept down into the ravine. They built a barricade to protect themselves from enfilading fire, though in fact there was no possible line of fire from the fort to the ravine. They then settled down for the next two weeks, well supplied by the empress with food and drink.

Major Galliano ordered immediate rationing of fluids. He was concerned, but expected a relief column to free him and his people from any uncomfortable hardship. Each Christian askari was allotted one-third of a liter of water per day and a tot of beer, wine or rum. The teetotal Muslims and the Italians each received half a liter of water. Italian officers continued to draw their wine ration. Galliano ordered a reduction in population of the fort. Women not legally married to an askari, and their children, of whom there were about 100, were ordered to leave the fort. However, many of the expelled women returned at night and their male friends threw them ropes and drew them up over the parapet. As the siege continued, some of these women may have regretted their commitment, for as Yosef Neguse wrote from the emperor's camp, "The women for whom the Italians had no pity became so obsessed by thirst they threw themselves off the walls in their agony."

There were desultory attacks on succeeding days by soldiers of Ras Mekonnen. After the losses they took on the night of 10-11 January, the emperor wept silently, embraced his cousin Mekonnen and said he was sorry he had suspected him of too much sympathy for the Italians. On 13 January Ras Mekonnen requested an armistice so that he could bury his dead. Galliano refused unless Mekonnen would order his army to retreat 11 kilometers. Well aware that Galliano could use any retreat as an opportunity to replenish his water supply, the Ethiopians declined, and the stink of rotting bodies below the fort was an additional plague for those inside.

Apart from occasional firing by either side, dead silence prevailed after 13 January. As Dr. Mozzetti wrote, "This waiting is irksome, insupportable ... we can see people coming and going tranquilly about their business in the enemy camp." Morale worsened as the water in the barrels turned green. There was still a little wine. Mules, horses and cows began to die as they were given no water at all. A terrible stench filled the air. "We officers," wrote Lt. Moltedo, "have not washed for seven days except by dampening our towels in the morning dew. We still joked at table however. We were so sure that we would be relieved by troops from Adigrat."

A woman messenger from Adigrat succeeded in reaching the fort on 18 January. She told Major Galliano that not a single soldier had moved out of Adigrat to relieve him. She returned to Adigrat taking Galliano's message, "The fort resists, but we have only two rations of water left. Our fall is near." That he would be relieved was an illusion in the mind of Major Galliano; he had been informed repeatedly that no challenge to the vast Ethiopian army surrounding the fort was intended. Negotiations for their evacuation were in progress, he was told.

Meanwhile, Menilek had remembered that Pietro Felter was in his camp and summoned him to talk. There are conflicting versions of who was the more forthcoming. In one, Menilek said to Felter:

You have come to conquer us and have not even tried to help those poor devils in the fort. If my wickedness were equal to yours, I would let your people die of thirst. Tell this to Baratieri: the Evangelist tells us to love our enemies. I am a Christian, not a pagan king. So that these Christians may not die, send some men to lead them away. If you want to fight us, just wait! I will come.

In Felter's version, he said that Menilek was so depressed by his losses that he sued for negotiations.

By 17 January, Menilek and Felter had reached an agreement and Felter galloped to Edaghamus, some 65 kilometers away, with Menilek's terms. The emperor would permit the besieged to fall back to Adigrat with their arms and their baggage. For this Felter had promised Menilek more than he could deliver. Menilek's primary condition was the immediate opening of peace talks embracing the whole Ethiopian problem with Italy. Baratieri agreed, but did not include this condition in his telegram to Rome.

Inside the fort on 19 January, the quartermaster distributed the last drops of water. "He called each man and woman by name, peering carefully into each face to make sure that no one tried for double rations ... the wife of one of the Sudanese gunners delivered a baby that day and wanted water to wash the baby. It was refused."

Later that evening an emissary arrived with a letter from General Baratieri. As Galliano read it his eyes filled with tears. "In the name of His Majesty King Umberto, cede the fort at Meqelle to the *negus* of Abyssinia."

The Italian officers may have regretted that their heroic defense had ended in capitulation, but the dying askaris and their women were overjoyed. It was not until the following afternoon at 5 o'clock that the garrison was permitted to draw 30 barrels of water from the stream. During that day the able-bodied men in the fort destroyed their ammunition. One unfortunate victim had a cartridge blow up in his hand and the sound of that explosion caused anxiety, both in Pietro Felter and Ras Mekonnen who were in charge of the details of the evacuation, that some reckless trick had been concocted.

The miserable Galliano was received by the emperor honorably the following morning and given a handsome mule; the exodus of the Italian force began. It took them two hours just to cross the encampment which was seething with people. The next few days were spent arranging the purchase of transport animals for the wounded. There was only enough cash in the fort's strong box to pay for half the required number, but Menilek agreed to advance additional mules against future payment.

The Ethiopian flag was raised over the fort. The Italian forces were permitted to take their rifles, cannon and loaded machine guns with them, over the fiercely expressed objections of the Tigrayan chiefs and Empress Taytu. The evacuees had to be protected by Ras Mekonnen's men from soldiers who did not share Menilek's repugnance for winning a victory by creating a drought.

Escorting the Galliano battalion to a camp near Adwa served the emperor well. The Meqelle area had been denuded of provisions and fuel and he knew that there would be no attack by Baratieri as long as these survivors were in his train. Menilek was well aware that reinforcements were arriving from Italy at the port of Massawa every day, but he was also counting on the start of peace talks as Pietro Felter had promised, and as he had proposed to the King of Italy in the letter Felter carried back to Baratieri. The Italian general forwarded Menilek's letter to Rome, noting that the contents were insolent. The part that offended Baratieri was, "Giving proof of our Christian faith ... we are sending, with all their belongings ... and in good health ... those who were in the fort of Enda Iyesus, even though they were exhausted by thirst, hard-pressed ... and almost trampled under our feet."

Rome agreed that this truth was insolent, and instructed Baratieri not to negotiate until there was an Italian victory. Sparring for time, Baratieri sent Felter back to Menilek to say that Major Salsa "would be coming" to discuss matters. Menilek was visibly angry, said Felter. It had been 10 days since Menilek had permitted the evacuation and Felter had promised that a plenipotentiary would be on his way immediately. Major Galliano was called to the emperor's tent and told that everyone could leave for Italian lines, except 10 officers who would be kept as hostages until the envoy arrived.

Major Salsa was in fact on his way, but when Galliano reported that some officers had been held back pending the arrival of Salsa, the foolish Baratieri recalled Salsa, stubbornly insensitive both to his own weak position and to the promise made to Menilek.

When Salsa had still not arrived by 3 February, the 10 nervous officers kept by the emperor noticed a stiffening of attitude in their previously pleasant guardian, the French-speaking Balamberas Amanuel. Rumors reached them that they were going to be executed: "Empress Taytu and her brother want our death, but Ras Mekonnen and Ras Alula oppose them." Silently saying their prayers, the officers were taken to a space near the emperor's tent and kept waiting for two and a half hours until Lt. Partini was called to see Ras Mekonnen. The ras made everything clear:

The emperor has a right to do with you whatever he wishes, for your government has broken its word by not sending Major Salsa; your death was resolved on, but our emperor is generous and good and does not wish to take revenge on the innocent for the faults of others, so he gives you liberty. Leave at once. Tell Baratieri that if he does not wish to send Salsa, he may send Felter, and if he does not, Christian blood will flow again ...

The Italian officers, still convinced that they would be killed one way or another, moved with trepidation out of the camp as insults were flung at them. It took four hours to reach their own lines, where they were greeted by gunfire. "Good heavens, they are firing on us. We have escaped Abyssinian rifles and now face our own! We wanted to raise the flag that Lt. Partini had saved from Meqelle, but it was too big and we didn't have a pole. Finally they heard our shouts and let us pass."

Balamberas Amanuel presented himself under a white flag the following day, and told General Baratieri that the emperor was waiting impatiently for the Italian representative. Only then was Major Salsa authorized to proceed. On 11 February he arrived, and the empress, skeptical as usual, observed to her intimates: "That man, it seems to me, has not come for reconciliation, but to spy on us." Her suspicions were borne out by the ridiculous terms brought by Salsa: "Renew the Treaty of Wuchale and give back to Italy all land that has been seized from her."

Menilek's answer, in effect, was, "I didn't come all this way to tear down the Italian flag in my country and then raise it up again." When Ras Mengesha Atikem brought Salsa's terms to the tent of the empress, her reaction was dramatic. "She raised her eyes to heaven and cried out sadly, 'O God of Israel, be witness to this injustice! Trusting their cannon and their guns, they have spoken their heart's desires, but they do not know that strength comes from God. We, trusting in the help of Christ — we are not afraid.' "

On Salsa's return to the camp of Baratieri to inform him of Menilek's total rejection, he also told him that the Ethiopians had "20,000 tents and 70,000-80,000 guns." Undaunted, Baratieri sent word to Menilek, "Negotiations are broken off and from this moment each army retakes its freedom of action."

On the night of 13 February, Ras Sebhat and Hagos Teferi defected from the Italian side.* The defectors arrived in the Ethiopian camp with some 500 followers equipped with recently issued rifles. Much more valuable, however, was their knowledge of fortifications, reinforcements, and the route of the Italian telegraph and supply lines. Their return to the Ethiopian cause was couched in patriotic terms: "We did not want to attack our own country with people we

---

*Both men were related to the old Tigrayan family of Sebagades and believed that they had been unfairly treated by Ras Mengesha Yohannes; Sebhat had fought beside Toselli at Amba Alage in December 1896. Hagos Teferi's collaboration with Italy began in 1893.

do not know who have come from overseas." They had been attacking their countrymen for some months. Nevertheless, they were welcomed and Sebhat was able to provide a timely warning. A unit that had left to attack the Italian line was approaching a particularly well-fortified point, and based on Sebhat's advice, Menilek recalled them.

A few days later the defectors proved their renewed loyalty by engaging Italian troops marching from Adigrat to Enticho, inflicting some serious casualties, though not as many as Sebhat claimed to the emperor. They cut the telegraph line and disrupted caravans bringing food to the troops at Adigrat. One officer there wrote to his family that mail was not getting through because of these continuous attacks by Sebhat and Hagos Teferi. He said that although they repaired the telegraph line often it was costing them men and munitions each time, and although they had "flour and rice, they had neither wine, cheese, vinegar, nor writing paper."

The women living in the area around Adigrat were taking an active role in the harassment. Dr. Ambrogetti, returning with some wounded men who had been repairing the telegraph, said that he had seen a woman firing at them. Another repair detail brought back two women whom they had found trying to cut the wire by rubbing it between two stones.

As Menilek moved his armies in the direction of Adwa, Lt. Bassi, for one, was afraid. "Here we stand with 7,500 black troops and 7,500 whites on Mt. Sawriya along a 4-mile [6.5-kilometer] front. The white soldiers [mostly new recruits just arrived from Italy] are poorly assimilated and they are underfed." These naïve new troops chanted a little ditty: "Hey, beware of these black folks with woolly hair! Menilek, you're dead — here comes a shower of lead."[13] The Italian correspondents covering the war sent stories exposing the lack of supplies and poor training of the troops, and for their pains, two of them were expelled.

By 23 February, in the hollow of Adwa, surrounded by mountains, the entire Ethiopian army was spread out. An Ethiopian* wrote to a friend in Russia, describing the situation. He said that they were amply supplied with water and food, since a shipment of beef on the hoof had arrived from Harar, as well as fodder for the animals, so the pack mules were very frisky.

---

*Bahta Amoneous was the name on the letter. Just who he was and how he acquired a friend in Russia is a mystery. He is not listed as a member of the delegation to Russia in 1895.

We are working night and day to prepare stockades and trenches in the
European way, to defend our camp if we are attacked. We have cut down
thousands of trees, dragged them here and piled them as high as your house
in Kronstadt ... and so thickly I believe a cannon ball cannot pierce through.
The women and children have helped us with great enthusiasm. Our king
of kings passes here many times which is why we take great care. We hold
an excellent position. There are five superb mountains before us ... four
in a circle, and one nearer to us in the middle. Our king of kings is stationed
at the middle one, and his *gibbi* is in the most delightful situation he has
had thus far. I can see his tent from where we are and hear the singing of
women and priests. Yesterday [25 February] was his third visit to our work,
and all the rases were with him.

Ras Mekonnen, who is now cured of his injuries at Meqelle, rode past.
I dared to say to him that his cape was torn at the shoulder. He laughed
and answered that he thought the Italians might give him a new and better-
looking one.

The sick were left at Meqelle and though our medical services do not
function like the military hospital I visited with you they work quite well,
especially since we have the help of some [captured] Italians who were happy
to have their chains removed in return for their services. Many soldiers have
been foraging into the countryside to learn the terrain.[14]

The Ethiopian army was not only learning the terrain, but also
scouting for food. General Baratieri, misled by deliberately planted
misinformation, drew the false conclusion that these sorties
represented widespread desertions from the emperor. At a meeting
with Generals Arimondi, Ellena, Dabormida and Albertone on 28
February, Baratieri asked their opinion on whether they should attack
or fall back to Asmara. He admitted that their own provisions would
run out in four days. His generals, to a man, were opposed to a
retreat. Baratieri closed the session, saying he would let them know
his decision on the morrow, pending some intelligence he expected
to receive that evening.[15]

Baratieri's critics said afterwards that he was unbalanced, drinking
too much, affected by the barely concealed contempt of his generals
(especially Arimondi), and under pressure from Prime Minister Crispi
to save the honor of the army and the prestige of the monarchy.
They even said that he acted because he had found out that he was
to be replaced, and he therefore wanted to retrieve his reputation
by some stunning victory. It was true that the government had
secretly replaced him. General Baldissera was at that very moment
traveling under a pseudonym towards Massawa. That Baratieri knew
this has not been proved.[16] Whatever his reasons, Baratieri issued
a battle order effective at 9 o'clock on the evening of 29 February

— it was a leap year — for his 17,700 troops to move to the attack. In the dark of night, four battalions moved out. They had inadequate maps, old model guns, poor communications equipment and inferior footgear for the rocky ground. (The newer Remingtons were not issued because Baratieri, under constraints to be economical, wanted to use up the old cartridges.) Morale was terrible as the veterans were homesick and the newcomers too inexperienced to have any *esprit de corps*. There was a shortage of mules and saddles. In the darkness, one battalion became confused and crossed another. It took the men an hour to extricate themselves from the subsequent confusion. They arrived at dawn, hungry and tired, at four assigned positions. These were the 17,000 men who were to challenge an Ethiopian army that was at least 100,000 strong, whose morale was buoyed up by the news that had arrived from Azaj Welde Tsadiq that the collaborators of Italy, the Muslims of Awsa, had been smashed.

The battle of Adwa[17]

It was 1 March 1896, a Sunday, about 4 o'clock in the morning. The night was black and the silence profound. The camp, between Adwa and the mountains, slept. The emperor and empress were up, having left their tents without ceremony, to go to divine services. I was there also with Rases Mekonnen, Wele and Mikael.

Everyone was deep in prayer and contemplation when a courier ran in and threw himself on the ground before the emperor. There was a rumbling, a muffled thunder of troops on the move. The emperor shrugged off this warning and continued his prayers. More messengers arrived and finally the emperor realized that danger was imminent. Trumpeters sounded assembly and in very short order the troops were ready.

Everyone in the church took holy communion. The green-yellow-red flags were dipped before the crucifix. The communicants bowed, beseeching the God of Combat, St. George, to help the country, the emperor and the faith. As dawn illuminated the scene, the army got under way with its customary shouting.

The identity of the Ethiopian author of this account is not known, but as the editor of the journal in which it was published commented, "It lacks technical character, but its episodic form gives interest and credibility to the story."[18]

At exactly 6.10 a.m. General Albertone, who was trying to locate one of his units under Lt. Turitto, heard a fusillade and realized that Lt. Turitto had gone too far forward. The battle of Adwa had begun.

The anonymous source continues:

The emperor allowed no one else to command. King Tekle Haymanot ... was
deployed with 12,000 men on the right wing ... Ras Alula and Ras Mengesha
Yohannes hastened to stop the enemy towards Kidane Mehret with 13,000
Tigrayans. In the center were the Harar troops of Ras Mekonnen, the Gallas
[sic] of Ras Mikael, and the Amhara under Ras Wele. The emperor and his
imperial guard occupied Enda Abba Garima. Each man carried 40 cartridges
and could be re-supplied.

And the empress? Her Majesty went with the emperor to the outer limits
of the camp and organized the defense perimeter with the 5,000 men of her
personal army. What happened then would have made Europeans laugh. The
empress collected the ten or twelve thousand women in the camp and issued
water jugs to all of them. This army of another kind filled their jugs at the
river and were ready to carry water to those who fought, wherever they stood.
Hundreds of women remained in camp, prepared to care for the wounded.

Menilek's chronicler writes that some of the Ethiopian commanders
were kilometers away at Aksum attending church and picking up food
requisitioned from the resentful clerics there, and so this early dawn
call to arms was somewhat disorganized: "The servant could not find
his master, the soldiers their chiefs ... but each marched ahead of
Menilek into combat ... as though they were monkeys in sight of a
haystack." This strange metaphor was not a denigration, but a
metaphor for eagerness, "as these men were not afraid to face death
nor did they tarry to pick up the wounded, who themselves urged
their comrades to pick them up on their way back."

The chronicler places Empress Taytu at the side of Abune Matewos,
surrounded by her soldiers and women. Before them were the clergy
of Aksum (who had come to complain about the food requisitioning,
but then had to stay for the battle) and the trumpeters. Instead of
organizing the water and medical services, the chronicler has Taytu,
face to the ground, praying while the shells were falling "like drops
of rain."

At this moment, the empress removed her veil and under a black umbrella
advanced on foot, as did the other royal women, among whom was Weyzero
Zewditu, daughter of the king of kings.

Empress Taytu, seeing some soldiers hesitate,* cried to them with all her
strength. "Courage! Victory is ours! Strike!" The soldiers ... could not run
away when encouraged by a woman and [returned to the fray]. Taytu shed her

*There were several "hesitations" in Berkeley's analysis of the battle. Martial de Salviac
collected one story in which it was thought Menilek had been killed, but Empress Taytu
quickly identified the dead man who did resemble Menilek, and restored confidence.

femininity and became a valiant warrior ... her cannoneers to the right of where she stood fired so continuously that they succeeded in breaking the center of the enemy army.

That this was a distortion by the chronicler of what actually happened must not be glossed over. It took the troops of four Ethiopian generals, at least 25,000 men, to "break the Italian center." Ethiopian women used much more blood-curdling exhortations than "Courage!" before and during battles. More typical would be, "Kill! Kill! The brave man will bring me a trophy [genitalia of the victim]."[19]

The fighting was intense in every sector, but the war was essentially over by 12.30 p.m., when General Baratieri began preparing his retreat* although firing continued at many points until late afternoon. The emperor himself did not return from Abba Garima until late in the day; meanwhile many combatants were streaming back with their wounded comrades and their Italian prisoners. The empress again assumed authority: "Where are you going when your king has not yet returned? Give me your wounded and go back."

The "sister" of the empress, Azaletch,† joined in exhorting the soldiers to return to the battlefield and the admiring chronicler wrote, "The goodness of Menilek made brave not only the men, but even women and monks. At the battle of Adwa, Empress Taytu and the women with her deserve special praise, for they spent that day doing a task not usually that of women."

The empress sent a message to Menilek asking him why he did not come back: "Has not the enemy been defeated? Don't you see night has fallen?" So Menilek returned, and the empress went to her tent. "She bowed down before her throne and then took her place — one could not have said she had spent the day at a battle ... though her face, usually so luminous, became dark under the flow of tears for the dead."

A vivid description by the Russian, Nicholas Leontiev, based on information gleaned three weeks after the battle, adds some details to this day of death.

---

*At his trial in June 1896, Baratieri was charged with leaving the field prematurely.
†"Sister" can mean simply a close relationship. Azaletch was the daughter of the sister of Taytu's mother, thus her cousin. Azaletch was married to Kenyazmach Walelu, had a son (by another man) who rather unusually went by his mother's name. He was called Desta Azaletch. (Zewde Gabre-Sellassie) Avedis-Terzian named as one of his sources a man who had taken Taytu's name, Gizaw Taytu.

As soon as the *negus* saw he was victorious, he ordered his men not to kill those who gave themselves up. The women who carried jugs of water to the soldiers, set their burdens on the ground and helped take prisoners. The dead lay in heaps ... streams of blood turned into rivers ... and the enormous field of killing looked like some horrible chess board where fate, with a merciless hand, had interfered in a terrible endgame. The intoxicated conquerors began to loot. Clothes were taken from the dead. The Abyssinians set fire to the grass and as the flames spread, in their fiery glow could be seen in outline, shadows rising from the earth. These were unfortunate Italians, some wounded, some lying as if dead to avoid capture. They were compelled into resurrection to save themselves from being burned. They were seized and led to the emperor with the triumphant cry, "Sing, black vultures, sing ... here is human flesh for you to eat."[20]

Sudden torrential rain ended this terrible day. One Italian prisoner who saw the empress returning to her tent after witnessing a long procession of prisoners, wrote of his agonizing walk across the drenched encampment:

It was a city without end ... an inferno of drums beating, deafening screams ... agonizing weeping and continuous firing of guns into the air. My tenuous grip on reality snapped and I lost track of how long it took before I was tied down to a cot. Men jumped up and down hysterically around me. One man tried to get a ring off my finger and just as he was about to cut the finger off to get it, an old man, invoking the names of Menilek and Taytu, shouted at him, "Swine, ass ... this man is a Christian, leave him alone." I was covered with a black cape riddled with fleas and fell into a nightmarish sleep.[21]

Leontiev reported the terrible mutilation inflicted on the *bashi-bazouks* (the Eritreans, or askaris, who fought with the Italians, and technically citizens of the colony therefore not treasonous), with a contorted justification of the action:

When they were paraded before Menilek, he, as usual, did not make the decision, but looked at Abune Matewos, while all the soldiers were shouting, "Slice them up!" The bishop ruled that since they had been treasonous their right hand and left foot should be cut off. More than 400 men endured this gruesome operation without a sound. To us this may sound barbaric but it must be remembered that in Europe, at this time, traitors are shot instantly. Hysteria was rampant after the victory and Menilek had to appease his soldiers. Feeling against these turncoats was such that no one would give them water, and no one would bind their wounds.

In truth, many women in Adwa, as well as relatives of the victims, were able to help them, secretly. Many survived to spend the rest of their lives as beggars, though some received tiny pensions from Italy and some were fitted with prosthetic devices. But the atrocity and the fact that a few Italian bodies were emasculated by the "trophy"-collecting Ethiopians appalled readers of the European press.[22]

The fact remained that the Ethiopians had won a war against a European army. As *The Spectator* commented on 7 March 1896: "The Italians have suffered a great disaster ... greater than has ever occurred in modern times to white men in Africa." It was the first victory on the African continent of black troops against white since the Zulus had won the battle of Isandhlwana in 1879. But Adwa was the bloodiest of all colonial battles, leaving 11,000 dead from both sides.[23]

Pictures of Menilek and Empress Taytu appeared on front pages in various parts of the globe.[24] The notion of a "warrior queen" caught the popular fancy and evoked references to Zenobia, Cleopatra, Joan of Arc and Catherine the Great. While interest in the Battle of Adwa persisted sporadically in France, Germany, Russia and America, in Italy it remained a daily and dominating news story for two more years.

The Italian press had little to report about the peace process that began in Menilek's camp on 9 March. Journalists tried to satisfy a public clamoring for information on which of its sons, brothers and fathers were alive and which were dead. It was almost two weeks after the battle before lists of survivors began to appear and only on 25 March did the first hospital ship reach Naples.

When news of the calamity reached Italy there were street demonstrations in most major cities. In Rome, to prevent these violent protests, the university and theatres were closed. Police were called to disperse rock-throwers in front of Prime Minister Crispi's residence. Crispi resigned on 9 March. Troops were called out to quell demonstrations in Naples. In Pavia, crowds built barricades on the railroad tracks to prevent a troop train from leaving the station. The Association of Women of Rome, Turin, Milan and Pavia called for the return of all military forces from Africa. Funeral masses were intoned in churches for the known and unknown dead. Families began sending to the newspapers letters they had received before Adwa in which their menfolk had described their poor living conditions and their fears at the size of the army they were going to face. King Umberto declared his birthday (14 March) a day of mourning. Italian communities in St. Petersburg, London, New York, Chicago, Buenos Aires and Jerusalem collected money for the families of the dead and for the Italian Red Cross.

To defuse the general rage at the government, the new prime minister, di Rudini, declared amnesty for the Sicilian protestors who had been in jail since 1894 for demonstrating against food shortages. And on the ludicrous side, the now ex-Minister of War, Mocenni, fought a duel over some slight to his honor. King Umberto's wife, Margarita, refused to contribute to an association formed by the Countess Santa Fiora to send help to the prisoners held in Ethiopia, not because the Countess was her husband's mistress, but on the grounds that the prisoners should be freed by a new expeditionary force.[25]

A special illustrated gazette, *La Guerra Italo-Abissinia*, was issued between February and August 1896. Empress Taytu's photograph was published three times and an article cribbed from Antonelli's pamphlet of 1891 reviewed her many marriages. Another feature horrified its readers with the "revelation" that Empress Taytu bathed in the blood of virgin girls to keep her beauty. Her reputation as a "Jezebel" became firmly fixed in Italy and playing children could be heard singing "Tie-too, Tie-too." She was blamed for the mutilation of the askaris, the threat to kill Italian officer-hostages, and even for the war itself. But for her, they would say, Emperor Menilek would have come to some reasonable compromise.[26]

The invective in Italy was almost matched by the hyperbole in Ethiopia. "Armed as a man she rushed in, cheering on the warriors, reminding them of their duty and ordering the monks to excommunicate anyone who dared to glance behind him during the battle."[27] "Armed as a man?" It is possible that she may have held a shield in front of her to deflect a bullet, but considering the functions she was directing — caring for the wounded, supplying water, and possibly preparing ammunition — it was improbable that she ever shouldered a rifle, or held a pistol or a lance. This does not prevent the folk painters of the Battle of Adwa from picturing Taytu astride a horse and aiming a gun that is spitting bullets. "She and the other women tore up their shammas and capes and wrapped gunpowder in the scraps for putting in the cannon," said a distant kin of the empress.[28]

The exaggerations must not be allowed to diminish the empress's justly deserved fame for courage and intelligence. She relinquished the protection due her rank in order to be an active participant. This was elegantly and subtly summed up by an Ethiopian poet: "Why did you go out into the sun, O Taytu? Was not the parasol created just for you?"[29]

A failure of nerve on the part of Menilek has been alleged by both Italian and Ethiopian sources. In one it was said that "Menilek wanted to quit after the first two engagements, but Taytu and her brother, Wele, said, 'Never.' " In another it was said that "Ras Mengesha Yohannes shouted at him [when he wanted to retreat], 'For years I have fought the Italians and you aren't brave enough for even one day!' "[30] Despite these stories, Menilek II of Ethiopia was the architect of victory. His far-sighted purchases of munitions enabled his people to fight with something better than lances, spears and old muskets, and he had won their loyalty and obedience, the indispensable weapon in winning a war.

9

Peace negotiations; prisoners of war; the Russian Red Cross

When Major Salsa rode over the battlefield on 6 March 1896, the unburied bodies were already putrefying. Salsa's first goal was to obtain permission from the emperor for a burial party to come from the Italian side, and his second goal was to identify as many survivors as he could. The latter was a virtually impossible task as some 600 prisoners had already been marched to the rear.

A military review was held on 7 March which Major Salsa watched, standing beside Ras Mekonnen. Mekonnen was recovering from light shrapnel wounds under the care of Dr. Mauri, one of the prisoners, but managed to stand with Salsa for seven hours as some 80,000 men marched past. It was both a show of strength for the benefit of Major Salsa, and a way in which the Ethiopians could count their own survivors.[1]

Lt. Roversi, who accompanied Salsa, described their meeting with Emperor Menilek two days later at Fares Mai:

At dawn we started off ... without knowing where they were — our escorts didn't know either. After two hours' ride, Fitawrari Desalegn [with the Mekonnen mission to Italy in 1890] with excellent eyesight and a lorgnette — what a dandy he was — saw an immense cloud of dust in the direction of Fares Mai. There was the army. We had to cross the plain of Yeha which was bisected by a small river where we saw many of our dead with their faces down in the water. The plain was literally covered with cadavers. It was eight days since the battle and the hyenas had not touched them — bodies were on top of each other as far as thê eye could see ... I kept my handkerchief to my nose and my eyes half-closed. Even today this horrible scene is frightful to recall.

At 9 a.m. we halted under a tree and could see the army approaching. It was divided into six columns — a melange of soldiers, women, children and animals. They came down the mountainside slowly, silently ... like an immense column of ants.

At about 10.30 we saw a group of horsemen followed by armed soldiers on foot in perfect order. It was the escort of the emperor. He was in the middle, but not easy to recognize as he always had at his side two people dressed exactly like him ... their harnesses and saddles were worked with silver — a magnificent and picturesque sight. At noon Empress Taytu arrived, astride a mule and sheltered by her own umbrella of brilliant red. She was followed by her dames of honor, servants, slaves and an escort of armed men. She passed quite near us, wrapped in her embroidered cloak, and to avoid seeing us lowered her umbrella to make us disappear.

At three in the afternoon we saw go up, quite suddenly, the red tent of the emperor and in minutes thousands upon thousands of tents of various sizes and shapes and colors were erected. It was done with such rapidity and order it stupefied me.

At 4 o'clock we were taken to Mekonnen. He gave us a medium-sized tent of mediocre cleanliness. They brought us some rugs and a camp bed that Pietro Felter had given Mekonnen in better times. They allowed us very few servants which connotes bad will. Things did not look promising. At 8 p.m. Mekonnen called us to his tent and gave us a drink and we chatted about nothing.

The next morning, 10 March, we were taken to Menilek's quarters. Twice we were searched. The inspector felt me on all sides, had me lift my tunic and looked into my helmet. He confiscated a small pen knife I use to sharpen pencils, then I was escorted to the imperial tent and found myself face to face with the famous sovereign. I bowed and went towards an empty chair next to Major Salsa, but Menilek had me approach the sofa where he was half-extended supported by silk cushions. He held out his hand, asked me some meaningless questions with good humor, and invited me to sit down.

He continued his conversation with Salsa which had begun before I entered. I was dumbfounded at the insouciance of his attitude and language. He talked of silly things, such as asking if it was true that in Italy there was a variety of chicken that hatched huge eggs. He was laughing, amiable and had the air of a bon vivant in quest of a moment of distraction, rather than a sovereign debating questions of state with an adversary.

Soon I realized it was a tactic. He asked about various Italians he had known and expressed satisfaction on learning they were safe and sound, but on hearing that Baratieri was well, he made a slight grimace. It seems he had heard he was dead.

After a while I stopped paying attention and looked around at the rases, whom, except for Mengesha Yohannes and Alula, I was seeing for the first time. In sharp contrast to the bonhomie of Menilek was the look of that imperious savage, Alula. I noted the plumpness of Tekle Haymanot next to the angular figure of Mekonnen. There was Mengesha Atikem — small, thin, shriveled; the athletic form of Ras Mikael; the ugly Tesfaye Antalo; the unusually good looks of Ras Mengesha Yohannes. They were all squatting oriental style. One could see only their heads, immobile and dumb as mummies while Menilek moved about on his divan, from time to time showing his feet which were enormous and covered with white cotton socks. He talked, interjecting pleasantries, droll anecdotes and bizarre questions as Major Salsa, whose demeanor never changed, proposed serious matters.

Even though we were escorted as we left the tent, we were unceasingly insulted by people calling us disgusting names. The women, above all the Tigrayan women, were especially rabid. We paid no attention, but I muttered to Salsa who said, "My friend, this is nothing compared to what awaits you tomorrow for we are going to see the empress who resents this whole proceeding. I know from a good source that she has sworn not to spare us. So prepare yourself."

At our next meeting with the emperor, we asked for the honor of being received by Empress Taytu. Menilek covered his face with a fold of his cape and after a second uncovered himself and said, "I will transmit your compliments myself ... it would be better that way for you."

During these days we saw our miserable Italian soldiers, nude, exhausted — literally dying from hunger, reduced to begging from the Abyssinians who mistreated them with relish. Major Salsa petitioned Menilek to assemble them and distribute them among different chiefs who could provide them with nourishment. His request was granted immediately. Salsa even obtained transport to Adwa for the wounded.

I did not go every day with Salsa to see the *negus*. I went about collecting objects, letters, notes and snapshots belonging to our men so I could give them to their families.[2]

Major Salsa took Menilek's terms to General Baldissera who had replaced the disgraced Baratieri. The terms were: Italy must publicly renounce its pretensions to a protectorate over Ethiopia; and she must evacuate Adigrat and permit free transit of goods between Eritrea and Ethiopia. Menilek was prepared to accept provisionally the border between Tigray and Eritrea to which he had agreed in 1890. The Salsa team returned after a 36-hour stay at the Italian headquarters, bringing a caravan loaded with cases of medicine furnished by the Italian Red Cross, some cases of liqueur, food, candles and soap. The medicines had been requested by Menilek. The liqueur was offered to the rases. Major Salsa also brought back a totally unacceptable counter offer. Italy would renounce its claim to a protectorate, but Menilek must agree not to accept protection from any other European power. This infuriated Menilek who promptly broke off negotiations and asked for the return of his letter of terms (Fares Mai, 16 March 1896). He ordered his armies to break camp on 20 March and directed that Major Salsa be detained in the camp of Ras Mengesha Yohannes until his letter was returned.[3]

Lt. Roversi summed up:

We were well-treated materially and with courtesy. Ras Sebhat, who had defected from us, even sent one of his lieutenants to greet us and begged our pardon for what he had done. Menilek never showed animus to us and if Major Salsa did not succeed in his mission it was due to the influence of the rases and probably the empress, who, though she did not show herself to us, took as usual an active part.

Major Salsa failed in his mission because of the absurd demand that Ethiopia agree not to accept the protection of any other power, and not because of some imagined obstruction by the rases or

Empress Taytu. The emperor broke off negotiations for additional reasons: his army was tired and short of food. Ras Mengesha Yohannes was charged with containing the Italians, but Menilek was content that Italy would not try again. He had 1,900 guarantees in his hands, namely the Italian prisoners of war. He left the rases of Tigray well armed and gave them 30,000 talers to help the sorely bruised province that had been ravaged by his own soldiers as well as by the Italians.[4]

Empress Taytu, in the Ethiopian way of securing loyalty,* arranged the marriage of her young niece, Kefey, daughter of Ras Wele, to Ras Mengesha Yohannes. This required a quick divorce for Mengesha from his current wife, of whom he was said to be very fond, and a quick divorce for Kefey from Nadew Abba Wello. Kefey Wele was not a bad bargain. "She is very tall for an Abyssinian, has a graceful figure ... is beautifully dressed with very good taste," wrote Augustus Wylde who met her a month after the wedding. He added that she had the reputation of being very clever and opined that "all the women of the upper classes are much cleverer than the men."[5]

Liqemekwas Abate† took the cannon captured from the Italians by a slightly different route so he could reach Addis Ababa before the emperor. He had distinguished himself at Amba Alage, Meqelle and Adwa with his management of the artillery, so it was fitting that he be in charge of the captured matériel. Accompanying him were the ironworkers, the leather stitchers and those prisoners among the Italians who knew how to shoe mules.

Menilek and Taytu and their armies took two months to return to Shewa. Abate was ready with the cannon and a deafening salvo was fired as the emperor entered the capital on 22 May 1896. Some POWs helped to man the cannon. The weary, ragged Italians witnessing the humiliating spectacle recovered quickly as Menilek opened the doors of the *gibbi* to treat them all to a fine banquet.

Among those present at the banquet was Casimir Mondon-

---

*Not solely an Ethiopian way: the marriage of Vittorio, son of the king of Italy, to Elena of Montenegro that same year was hailed as an augury of improved Russian-Italian relations.
†Abate had been raised at Menilek's court and was much favored by the empress. His father, Bwalu of Menz, was castrated after his birth, so Abate was called *"fettene"* which meant that if his father had not hurried to procreate him, he would not again have had the possibility. Abate was called behind his back *"tchecagn"* or "cruel."

Cover of *Le Petit Journal* of 9 February 1896, showing Crispi of Italy as a fat
fool falling to the ground as Menilek stuffs a baguette of bread labeled
"Makalle" in his ear

Le Petit Journal

Le Petit Journal
CHAQUE JOUR 5 CENTIMES
Le Supplément Illustré
CHAQUE DIMANCHE 5 CENTIMES

SUPPLÉMENT ILLUSTRÉ
Huit pages : CINQ centimes

ABONNEMENTS

SEINE ET SEINE-ET-OISE
DÉPARTEMENTS
ÉTRANGER

...tième année   DIMANCHE 29 MARS 1896   Numéro 280

S. M. TAÏTOU
Impératrice d'Abyssinie

Cover of *Le Petit Journal* of 29 March 1896, showing a photograph of Taytu taken 13 years previously, tinted and doctored slightly to remove some flesh from her face

Vidailhet* who complimented the emperor on how well he looked, making a little joke over the report that Menilek had been killed by the Italians: "Had they shot you twice you would have been even more robust." He praised the emperor for the way in which he had treated the POWs, and Menilek assured him that this was his custom. He invited Mondon-Vidailhet to look at the great pile of letters he had received from various parts of the world congratulating him on his victory. Some were from cranks and others were from stamp collectors hoping for the new and already rare Ethiopian stamp to be affixed to a reply. Some were from "Jews proposing to take over Menilek's treasury," some from "Australian pastors citing biblical passages in praise," and others from "Venezuelan adventurers offering to enter Menilek's service." In this pile of mail was a copy of *Le Figaro* with a cartoon of Menilek depicted as a coarse blackamoor, which the emperor had the "grace to laugh at." The empress "managed a smile though she is as fair as our southern women and I think in her heart she felt insulted."[6]

Italian opinion considered Mondon-Vidailhet obsequious for always addressing Menilek as "Your Majesty," and resented his report that the prisoners of war were well treated in Ethiopia. Another Frenchman, the trader Stévenin, was very pro-Italian.

One of my Abyssinian workers warned me one day that he had seen some whites at the door of the imperial palace, completely nude. I went out of my little workroom and saw them — Italians. One of them expressed himself quite comprehensibly in French — said he was a *bersagliere* and told me he and the others had preceded the main group of POWs by a few days. I went to the governor of the city and told him Italian prisoners were here and

*Now about 60, Mondon-Vidailhet had been in and out of Ethiopia since 1892 and had been a sympathetic commentator on the country. He had, to a degree, a scarce quality among foreigners to Africa: some comprehension of the need to understand cultural and historical factors. He was rabidly anti-Italian and anti-English, and it happened that the actions of both nations at this time provided him with great scope to exercise these prejudices. He closed his eyes to French actions in Madagascar, Indo-China and North Africa. He learned Amharic but one story of his proficiency made the rounds: he said to the empress, "Listen to me," ["*Yis mugn*"] but altered one vital syllable and said "Kiss me" ("*Yisamugn*") which she did not find amusing. He had no columns in *Le Temps* during the second half of 1896 because of a "ridiculous accident that almost cost me my sight." The Italians returned his hostility in *La Tribuna*, 6 July 1897, with "He is an old, ugly, coarse, gouty person," and said his eye trouble was caused when a "young girl defending herself from him ... poked a finger in his eye. Everyone hates him, including his compatriots." However Mondon-Vidailhet was in the good graces of both Menilek and Taytu. Menilek had Aleqa Yosef send him detailed accounts of what happened at the battles of Meqelle and Adwa.

they were starving. He answered, "May their fathers be cursed." I said, "If you refuse the food you would give an animal, may I take them with me?" I took them to my house, had a sheep killed and they all ate and wept with joy. I gave each one a shirt and a pair of slippers ... then went to look for something to cut their hair and beards.

Stévenin had to borrow scissors from Mondon-Vidailhet, who turned a deaf ear to a request for money and was thought contemptible for turning his back on people of "his own color."[7] In the memoirs of some prisoners, dislike of the French community (except for Armand Savouré and Stévenin) crops up. Italian officialdom as well as the rank and file remained convinced that France had abetted Menilek, armed him and had sent French officers to aim his artillery. The French defended themselves vigorously, saying with some truth that it was the Italians themselves who had armed Menilek, and that no Frenchman had participated in the battle.* The Ethiopians knew that many of their rifles and cartridges had come from Italy and a verse was sung, "What fools are these? They made instruments of death and gave them to us. With the guns they brought, the cartridges they sent, Menilek has roasted ... the barley [Italians] that came from overseas."[8]

Countering the propaganda that the empress never did anything for the prisoners, Mondon-Vidailhet described a meal she provided for them in the open area outside her private apartments. All ranks, with General Albertone presiding, were served in completely European style: "They sat at tables, had plates, forks, spoons, napkins, various wines and even flowers on the table." Mondon-Vidailhet ventured that some of these men had never in their lives sat down with their officers at such an elegant meal.[9]

Batches of prisoners were assigned to different chiefs and some were four months on the road before reaching Addis Ababa; some remained in remote districts until released by the peace treaty of October 1896. As each batch of prisoners arrived in the capital, they would be treated to a banquet on the royal compound and asked if they had any special skills. Watchmakers, gardeners, carpenters, mechanics, painters and certainly doctors were kept busy in Addis Ababa. The most important captive, General Albertone, was given into the care of Azaj Zamanel, commander of Empress Taytu's army

---

*Clochette and Carrère reached Adwa on the eve of the battle, but manned no guns. They had both taught the use of weapons, paid to do so by Menilek, and not by France.

and peace-time major-domo. Dr. d'Amato accused Empress Taytu of trying to impress Albertone with her generosity and humanity, not appreciating that her respect for rank was a very Ethiopian concept. Albertone had a tent to himself, a horse and servants. One of his aides wrote that the general, in spite of these privileges, was often intemperate of language and gesture, his mood fluctuating from great pride to depression, but that his prestige was such with the Ethiopians who guarded him that "he seemed to be commanding them."[10].

Of the almost 1,900 Italians who were prisoners from 1896 to 1897, only a handful wrote books about the experience. A contemporary historian, Angelo del Boca, believes that the paucity of the record is attributable to the glacial welcome received in Italy by the returning prisoners for having lost a war, and the fact that they were subjected to long interrogations when they debarked, were defrauded of part of their back pay, had their mementoes confiscated and were ordered not to talk to journalists.[11]

Italian prisoners and Ethiopian women[12]

Lt. Nicoletti-Altimari found himself lying on the ground inside a *tukul* (thatched round hut) the day after the battle. A bullet had passed through his chest, and the slightest movement caused him agonizing pain. An old woman came in, opened his bloody jacket, pushed aside the wad of bandage and examined the hole closely. As she did this, a number of other women entered, "murmuring like a choir," and Nicoletti-Altimari, who had been in Eritrea more than five years and knew the language quite well, heard the old lady say, "This wound is not dangerous."

His attending "nurse," gathering up all her strength, suddenly spat on his wound, and then, one after the other, each woman repeated the act, whispering encouragement to him. He was surprised, disgusted and helpless, but vaguely understood the significance of this strange medicine, though it "bothered me to see my chest become a cuspidor." To his amazement, his wound began to heal within a few days.*

---

*Nature's healing balm, saliva, is instinctively used by animals when they lick their wounds and when a human puts a finger in the mouth after cutting it. In 1981 scientific investigators defined the factor, NCF, a mysterious protein discovered in the 1950s which is secreted by nearly every type of body cell.

The women, especially a little girl he called "Tuata"* fed and protected him. He grew to love the little girl who declared again and again that since her own father had been affectionate with her and had never cried when he was wounded, and since Nicoletti-Altimari acted the same way, she would call him "father." Tuata earned herself a blow on the head one day when she defended the Italian in front of all the villagers. Nicoletti-Altimari had shouted that he was sick of listening to the minstrel sing of the Ethiopian victory over Italy. At the first opportunity, the convalescent took aside the man who had struck Tuata and sermonized, "Jesus Christ said suffer the little children to come unto me." He then warned him with his fist never to strike another child.

Though Nicoletti-Altimari spent only 10 days in this small village whose residents helped him back to the Italian lines, he had enough adventures to fill a book that was serialized at the end of the year in Italy.

Giovanni Tedone, a sergeant of the *bersaglieri*, was 24 years old the day he was wounded at Adwa. When he regained consciousness he had been denuded, except for his plumed helmet and a medallion of the Madonna around his neck. The bloody crotches of two comrades who lay dead beside him, and two Ethiopians fighting over his jacket, were the first sights he saw. Eventually he was given some clothing, a little nourishment, and began the four-month walk to Addis Ababa. As he did not have any special skills to offer in the capital, he was obliged to continue his journey, and he spent the next six months in the villages of Chercher being rotated between custodial families.

Before leaving Addis Ababa, he and a friend succeeded in replacing their tattered clothes in the market and acquired a chicken. They were in the process of cooking it over an alley bonfire when they saw all the inhabitants rushing out of their houses to prostrate themselves as Empress Taytu was passing by. The two Italians stayed where they were, squatting on the ground. One woman in Taytu's entourage came over to them and said, "Stand up and salute when 'la Taytu' passes by." Tedone's friend muttered the Roman equivalent of "Drop dead." The empress sent a minion to reprove them for their lack of respect but also sent some *injera* with a message that she

---

*This is not an Ethiopian name.

would not hold their bad behavior against them as she was a good and pious woman.

Tedone, writing in 1915, many years after these events, insisted that the empress had never become friendly with any of the prisoners, contrary to the gossip that her apartments had been a place of merriment for the Italians. Tedone had the good fortune to end up in the care of a relative of the empress, Weyzero Zandietu,* who told him the familiar story of Taytu's rise from a nobody to the legitimate spouse of the king of kings.

Tedone wrote that he knew immediately that he was in the company of a superior person:

Frankly I was surprised by the cleanliness of her hut. It was whitewashed inside and out. In the corner were two copper pots, a bottle and two glasses ... very rare objects. Here was a cousin of the empress, a beautiful young widow who had lost her husband at the siege of Meqelle and her teenage son at the battle of Adwa. She was under 30, with a supple, graceful, full-breasted body. Her face, a perfect oval, was lightly tinted and enhanced by two large, almond-shaped black eyes. I was sure I would not be welcome in this ambience where death had harvested a full crop, but the *weyzero* allayed my anxiety, "Be tranquil, you will be treated well. You have suffered much not being used to our way of life and I could not be so unfeeling as to abuse you, defenseless, for the death of my own family. You are not to blame. You did what you were commanded, as did my menfolk — only they were unlucky. God decides and we cannot prevent his will from being done."

A *messob* was prepared and it was the first time that a black person had invited Tedone to share a meal. Two servants brought *injera* spread with hot chili sauce, boiled goat meat, sour milk and a glass of *tej*. His hostess placed in his mouth a portion of meat wrapped in *injera* and dipped in hot sauce. It was too big for him to swallow all at once. He sneezed, coughed and threw up everything. "It was a serious insult. Everyone was horrified saying I was unworthy of such a favor. I apologized saying it was an accident because of an illness in my throat."

Tedone's fellow dinner guests were the two women who had delivered him to Weyzero Zandietu. After the meal he saw them off, and then sat on the ground outside admiring "this wild place in sepulchral silence with only the howl of the hyena to be heard." It

---

*Just how she was related to Empress Taytu is not explained in any source so far researched. Most certainly her name was "Zewditu,", not "Zandietu."

was dark when a man tapped him on the shoulder and motioned that he should enter the house. Zandietu ordered the servants to leave and she and Tedone sat near the fire. He lit up his pipe and began to relax. He stretched out on the ground, his head supported by a smooth stone and dreamed of far-off Italy. Dozing off he burnt his tongue from his pipe, came to, and refilled it.

He saw Zandietu was watching him:

My indifference seemed to displease the black diva. So much so, that she took my right hand between hers and with a weeping voice like a baby asked me, "You are Italian?"

"Yes."

"Do you know our language?"

I was a little vexed since the question was silly, as we were speaking in Amharic.

"Yes."

She cast her eyes down as if to hide her own ignorance and said, "I ask you only just to speak to you, not knowing how to ask more interesting questions of a man coming from over the seas."

In this way the ice was broken and we talked for two hours. The theme was on the customs and manners of our women, though we also spoke of politics and religion. She wanted a report on our royalty, on the Pope, and her eyes opened wide when I described the Quirinale and the Vatican as being respectively larger than all of Addis Ababa put together. I could not persuade her that ever on the face of the earth could there be a building larger than the palace of Menilek.

Zandietu told Tedone that she had spent her early youth at court and had met some Europeans. Of them all, she said she preferred Italians, especially Capucci because he did not get drunk and molest women as did her own countrymen and other Europeans like the Russians.* "At court," she said, "Ethiopians sometimes held their noses when Russians went by, exclaiming, 'Moscovi are loathesome.'"

Tedone reports, as though it were amazing, that Zandietu had a decided aversion for men who beat women, and during their nightly talks would repeat, "They should act like Italians ... my own husband beat me despite the fact that I brought him the huge dowry of 50 cows." She also did not like Ras Mekonnen, the "exploiter of widows

---

*If Zandietu is defining her "youth" as six years earlier, the only Russian she could have met would have been Vassili Mashcov in 1889 or 1891. Leontiev's party of about 10 Russians arrived in 1895, hardly Zandietu's youth. It is possible but not verifiable that she was the "relation of Taytu," spoken of by Capucci in 1894, whose marriage to Ras Mekonnen did not come off.

of soldiers killed in the war," whom he made to work from morning to night in his own house in Harar for a single handful of grain. "It was only through the influence of my cousin, Empress Taytu, that I managed to escape his claws."

Zandietu slept in her corner of the hut and Tedone in his. Tedone described their relationship:

I could see she was not the usual, ignorant and vulgar Abyssinian woman, therefore I had to change my attitudes and retrieve some gentility — something I had lost these past few months.

In the morning I betook myself to the brook very early to wash. She wished to go with me and chattered all along the way. She told me that once in Addis Ababa she had seen a European wash his face with milk. It was soap of course, of which she was ignorant. She told me about the orders given by Menilek for the care and feeding of prisoners. Each one was to be changed every 15 days between two Amhara families while a selected number of Galla [Oromo] families had to provide daily food in turn. In my case, since I had tossed to the dogs what the Gallas had brought, she would provide my meal.

The Gallas were so poor, I would give back their fetid *injera* which overjoyed them. Many times, knowing that I smoked, they substituted food rations with a few leaves of dry tobacco.

One evening Tedone heard the dogs barking and ran out to find a man unconscious on the ground in a pool of blood. He had been bitten on the foot.

We carried him into the *tukul*, trying to bring him to with extract of wild mint. I tried to cauterize his wound with a hot poker. Then he was carried home. I was allowed to go to treat him every day and in compensation, when he was cured, he brought me good leaves of tobacco and sometimes a fresh egg. He never stopped thanking me.

In this village I passed the nicest period of imprisonment. This pseudo-imperial highness tried to content my every whim ... and what is more important, no one gave me any trouble.

Tedone impressed the villagers with his muscular strength, inviting them to engage in arm wrestling, a contest which he always won.

They are weak because of poor diet and besides they are afflicted with syphilis and scrofula ... it means the inexorable end of these people.

I also taught them not to mock me. Two of Zandietu's relations were visiting one day. I heard them talking about me and of the villainy of Italians in general. "Shut up, and get out," I shouted. They understood because I spoke in Amharic. But they did not move nor stop their insults. Fed up, I picked up a stick and beat one up. They exited in a hurry.

Not only did Tedone get away with this risky behavior but the local people also laughed and said, "He has strength ... good ... good." On another occasion, during one of the frequent condolence visits paid to his hostess when people came to "get drunk" in memory of her dead husband, one guest said to Tedone in Italian as he offered him *tej*, "Drink this, it will cure you of the beating you took at Adwa." Furious, Tedone asked him how he had learned Italian and when he heard that he had been in the service of Ras Sebhat, whose defection from the Italian side had substantially helped the Ethiopians, he asked the man, "Why did you betray people who treated you well, who freed you from the chains of Ras Mengesha Yohannes and to whom you swore on the cross to be faithful forever? Why?" The man replied that he had done so because the Italians were weak, and Menilek was strong. To which Tedone retorted, "You are a coward. Here. See how much weight there is in the hand of an Italian." Tedone slapped him. No one punished Tedone and no one came to the aid of the visitor. He slunk away.

The man whose foot he had treated came to tell Tedone that the previous evening he had seen some Europeans heading for Addis Ababa. Excited, Tedone secured permission from Weyzero Zandietu to go and see who they were, promising to bring back medicine for her boils if they were medical people. She gave him a guard, and he found the foreigners after an eight-hour trek. He described the group:

It was part of the Russian Red Cross. I was directed to an officer in a red jacket and white leggings, but was halted several meters away by a black interpreter who relayed my message. I could not understand what they said but the expression on the officer's face told me to get away as fast as possible.

Tedone's explanation for this hostility was that they were not keen to have an Italian witness their greater dedication to the collecting of animal skins, ivory, gold and coffee, than to the succoring of the Ethiopians.*

Disappointed, Tedone returned to his village. Having watched the women weave baskets he decided in his boredom to make a straw hat. They gave him some straw and a thorn needle. It took him five days to make his hat.

---

*Tedone's observation is suspect. He dated his stay with Weyzero Zandietu as beginning about 1 August 1896. He would have been in the second week of his stay on or about 15 August. The Russian Red Cross mission passed through Chercher in the first week of July as they reached Addis Ababa on 26 July. This group could have been part of the Harar contingent of the Russian Red Cross simply out on a hunting trip.

When the blacks saw it on my head they gave me an ovation. Everyone touched it, caressed it, turned it this way and that. For days people came from all around to admire it. Abba Abanos, the priest for this region and confessor to my Imperial Highness, declared he had seen a hat like it only twice before — once on Menilek and once on Ras Mekonnen.

Orders rained on me. The second one I gave to Weyzero Zandietu, who gave me a new *shamma* for it, and the third I sold to the priest in exchange for a goat and three adorable monkeys.

The monkeys became Tedone's new diversion. He taught them tricks and began to earn eggs, meat and tobacco in exchange for their performance.

The lady Zandietu decided one day to go with Tedone and his guards on a hunting trip. After shooting a couple of dik-dik and a gazelle they stopped by a stream to rest and the guards drew away. Zandietu picked a flower and dropped it on Tedone's chest. "Look," she said, "it is as white as you are." He ignored this flirtatious overture.

Tedone claimed he was never attracted to Zandietu or to any other Ethiopian woman because of their dirty habits and infectious diseases. In this regard he was unlike his co-nationals, he admitted. There were an uncounted number of sad ladies with half-Italian babies in their wombs when the prisoners departed. Tedone knew for certain he had become a leading character in a romantic fantasy of Zandietu's later that evening when he heard her speak of him to her servant: "He is handsome ... and I have no husband." The servant girl did her part by sighing to Tedone that her mistress was beautiful and virtuous and had no husband.

The Italian was outraged one night by the behavior of two house guests, a man and a woman from Addis Ababa who kept him awake all night with their vigorous sexual activity. He complained to Zandietu. She proposed a day or so later to marry him and go to Italy with him. Tedone was wary of offending her and was tactful. Her campaign intensified and she tried to make him jealous saying, "I will have the son of Fitawrari Gabriel sleep with me and make you watch." Tedone's embarrassment was relieved by an order that came from Ras Mekonnen to join a work party chosen to paint the Awash River bridge.

It gave tremendous pleasure to each of the Italians who had been isolated with various families to work together on the bridge, and they were soon up to mischief, trying to stretch out the job. To immortalize their work, they painted on a rock, "The Italian prisoners did this: September, 1896." Their foreman ordered them to paint on another rock, "The Lion of Judah always triumphs," and on another, "Ras Mekonnen is great."

Instead of these tributes, Tedone painted *"Viva l'Italia"* and "Death to the Ethiopian empire." Their illiterate foreman asked them to write his name somewhere. They painted "The chief, Gebru, who escorted us to this work is a donkey."

When Tedone returned to the house of Zandietu, she resumed her talk of marriage, but on Tedone's persistent refusals, she announced plans to marry Tekle, the son of Fitawrari Gabriel, and told Tedone he could no longer remain in her *tukul*. Tedone did not mind. He slept in another hut, continued making his hats and putting his monkeys through their antics, singing at the top of his lungs, *"La donna è mobile."* The tune appealed to the villagers and his hostess enormously.

On her wedding day, Zandietu took a bath of purification, which, as she explained to Tedone, would cleanse her of faults committed before they occur. Then her new husband, Tekle, brought an ox, whose throat was cut, and with the blood Tekle bathed the feet of his wife.* The marriage was consummated while the guests frolicked outside the *tukul* and a 10-day wedding feast commenced.

The day after the wedding, a messenger came from Ras Mekonnen to deliver a shirt and a pair of pants† to Tedone as a token of appreciation for his work on the bridge. The gift was more trouble than it was worth, as everyone begged him for the glass buttons on the shirt, driving him nearly out of his mind.

The rumor that an Italian mission had passed through Harar and was on its way to Addis Ababa became a reality. Tedone received permission (this time from Zandietu's new husband who, by virtue of the marriage, had become his custodian) to go to the main transit route, and to his unutterable joy he saw the plumes of an Italian soldier. He found the group headed by Major-Doctor Cesare Nerazzini, on its way to sign the peace treaty with the emperor.

They embraced. They wept. Nerazzini exhorted Tedone to have courage and be patient. It was on 20 November, more than a month

---

*This ritual has not appeared in other accounts of marriage ceremonies. In Cohen's "Cérémonies," based on observations made in 1909 and 1910, after consummation the bride stepped over the threshold where the blood of a chicken had been spilled.
†The Association of Roman Women had deposited a store of clothing, money, medicine and food in Harar and Addis Ababa in July 1896.

later, that the Nerazzini party, accompanied by Ras Mekonnen and
Léon Chefneux, made the return journey picking up prisoners along
the way. Tedone bade his farewells to the mournful Zandietu. She
made him swear to return for a visit and to bring her gifts of gold,
linen and perfume, while her husband asked for every kind of gun
he could think of, plus a small cannon. Zandietu kissed his hands,
"When you are home, remember me. I wait for you. Good-bye and
safe journey."

All the Italian ex-prisoners were camped outside Harar when
Giovanni Tedone received a summons from Ras Mekonnen. He
found himself under a big tent facing the ras and Léon Chefneux.
When asked if he had written the insulting words on the Awash
bridge, he admitted that he had. "I ought to suspend your departure,"
said Mekonnen, "but because you were honest and because of my
regard for Major Nerazzini ... I give you leave to go."

Leaving in the same contingent as Tedone was Dr. Nicola d'Amato,
who had had a completely different experience. Being a doctor, he
was one of the privileged, and was able to remain in Addis Ababa.
His memoirs concentrated on personalities at court and his bitter
feelings towards the non-Italian foreigners in the capital. He devoted
an entire chapter to Empress Taytu, aspiring, he said, to correct the
impression given in the European press that she was some kind of
odalisque in a harem where slaves and Italian prisoners of war stood
about waving fans. Very few prisoners had any contact with Taytu,
in the way that they had with the "beautiful and good" Princess
Zewditu Menilek who stopped and talked with the prisoners on her
way through the palace grounds to visit her father, and also consulted
the Italian doctors about her eye disease, which they cured.

The only occasion on which Dr. d'Amato talked to Empress Taytu
was during the trek from Adwa to Addis Ababa. He had been
summoned in her name to treat the knee wound of a *shum* (village
chief.) He saw a great crowd coming to meet him, preceded by a
soldier on horseback who made a piercing noise by blowing with
all his might on a horn. Immediately behind, in the center of a dense
crowd, was an imposing, veiled woman, also on horseback. "Taytu
came up to a few paces from me ... asked who I was, then
commended the *shum* to me as her friend. She asked if I needed
anything. 'I need everything!' I said, and she wheeled her horse and
trotted off."

That evening she sent some pasta to the doctor's tent. D'Amato made other fanciful claims and assertions. The empress, he said, had been prepared to set fire to herself if the battle had gone against Ethiopia; she was a frequent visitor to Jerusalem; she wanted to have all the POWs killed and had a "ferocious leer on her face," as they filed past her. For a woman who was always veiled in public, even a "smile of satisfaction" would have been difficult to observe. Such was d'Amato's capricious testimony. The doctor admitted that most of his information trickled out of the imperial quarters.

He described in detail the variety of musical instruments the empress had, and said he heard music coming from her apartments frequently. Other sources confirm that she was fond of music and played the *begenna* very well. He observed that she spent hours in prayer at the Church of the Trinity, dined with her husband almost every evening and that they showed each other "thoughtful and tender attention."

One of Dr. d'Amato's sources of information was a painter, commissioned by the empress to cover the interior walls of the palace with murals. This fellow told d'Amato that she ordered him to paint warriors, scenery and a veritable zoo of animals. One day when the royal couple came to see his work, they stopped to admire his drawing of an elephant. They murmured their approval of his lion, then paused, "ecstatic" over his galloping horse, without a rider. "Giyorgis (St. George)" they said in a single voice, [as if this horse lacked a head] and immediately ordered the addition of a rider carrying a lance in the act of combat.

D'Amato reports that "the queen was interested in scientific matters and wished to discuss them as though she were a woman who had read much in books." He describes how the only lighting at the time was a rag soaked in wax which gave off a sooty flame and a nasty smell, and that Taytu wanted something better. She presented the problem to the engineer, Alfred Ilg, who took some borax and sulfuric acid from the pharmacy to be added to the wax. "She aimed to make candles and establish a national industry."

D'Amato did not see the results of this experiment, but his account of her interest in it is one of the most interesting things he says about Empress Taytu. Many others have alleged that she had no interest in new ways of doing things. The result of the experiment was seen by one of the Russians, Shchusev, who wrote that she "artistically" cast wax candles for domestic use in the palace and for sale in the palace shop which Menilek had constructed and in which he put into circulation the coins minted in France. "In the shop you could buy bread, candles, wax and meat, and taste Abyssinian dishes in a small restaurant. They take any kind of money and give change in Menilek coins."

Sgt. Francesco Frisina told his story 23 years after the war. He resented the preferential treatment given to the doctors, said the medals they received on their return to Italy were undeserved, and praised the Russian Red Cross personnel. In his account, he tells how he attracted the attention of an older woman, a high-born lady, Avesha Avegaz, who, he alleges, seduced him. She showered favors on him and gave him food and drink from the royal kitchens where she had privileges, being an intimate of Empress Taytu. She even gave him the gold headband that the empress had given her for her services at Adwa.

According to Francesco Frisina, Avesha Avegaz was the ex-wife of Ras Wele; in this he was mistaken. Wele's ex-wife was her sister, Desta, whom he also met. Avesha was heart-broken, as was he, when he was dispatched to another province. His custodian there, an Oromo, wanted Frisina to know that he had only one wife whom he respected, unlike the Amhara who had five or six. He was immensely kind to Frisina who abused his generosity by misbehaving with a girl servant in the household, fighting with his benefactor's son, and being sneaky and scornful. At the end of his stay, Frisina apologized for his misdeeds and told his guardian he would remember him like a father for the rest of his life.

In sum, as it was the emperor's intention that the prisoners be treated well and within his capacity to guarantee it, they were. But many prisoners suffered. They were ordinary men, white men, with the convictions of most white men that they were in every way superior to black men. Cross-cultural understanding was not the reason they were in Ethiopia. Their will to survive was strong and they tricked, lied, stole and killed to do so. As their stay in the country lengthened they gained confidence in their ability to outwit "these simple peasants" and with audacity used the Amharic insults they quickly learned, pushed people around, slept with complaisant women and evaded punishment for their misdeeds through the amazing tolerance of the ruler and his people.

The Russian Red Cross[13]

When the Russian Red Cross, headed by Gen. N.K. Svedov, arrived in Harar on 26 May 1896 it had such a military look that Ras Mekonnen warned the emperor. Menilek told Mekonnen to detain them in Harar.

Menilek was not aware that in Russia most physicians were civil servants, and that doctors and male nurses* wore uniforms as they were either students or staff at the St. Petersburg Military Medical Academy, the finest medical school in Russia. He expressed other reservations to Alfred Ilg. His letter had a strong whiff of Empress Taytu's views. "The Russians will come and save the lives of six or seven thousand wounded and then go away; these thousands would not be a great loss for the *negus* as he has many millions, but the people of the country would become accustomed to medical aid, begin to think about it, then claim the same help from the *negus*, which he would be unable to provide." Ilg persuaded Menilek to let the mission come, as long as a third of the group remained in Harar. Two months after setting foot on Ethiopian soil, 41 members of the mission of mercy arrived in Addis Ababa.

Housing was a critical problem for such a large number, though they were equipped with tents. Menilek requisitioned the house of the French trader, Stévenin, who protested: "Majesty, you, to whom the entire world pays homage for your generosity, you who have prevented the mutilation of soldiers, you cannot put me and my wife outside in the rainy season!" Stévenin was delighted when Menilek told him to go and choose any piece of land he wanted. Stévenin chose the estates of two prominent men who had died at Adwa, and with the help of a dozen Italian POWs built himself a comfortable habitation as well as fitting up a dormitory for his prisoners. He had nothing but praise for his indentured labor:

For five months they ... demonstrated a willingness to do anything. We built a horseshoe-shaped courtyard which held the mules with which I did commerce with Harar. All around this rotunda, about two meters off the ground, was built a circular terrace. Here the Italians slept in their respective bunks under the shining stars of Ethiopia. The night was never excessively cold.

---

*Twelve women nurses had volunteered for the mission but were repatriated when they reached Egypt after it was learned they would have to take the more difficult route from Djibouti to the interior because the Italians would not allow them to go through Massawa.

On Wednesday nights Stévenin permitted his charges to invite women in, "to prevent them from going out hunting alone for girls which might result in blows or dangerous talk." At midnight he would send the women home.

When the Russian Red Cross arrived, the emperor and empress supported them enthusiastically. "Menilek loved to be present at operations using chloroform ... he would hold the hands of the patient and when he woke up would say, 'May God help you recover,'" wrote Shchusev.

Shchusev described Taytu:

I saw the empress many times which does not happen to everyone. She was short, rather fat and with such light olive skin you could tell when she blushed. She wore a white shirt, wide trousers with masses of embroidery, a *shamma* and a black cloak. Twice, against all etiquette, she attended operations to extract necrotic bone from those wounded at Adwa. It was a difficult operation. She wept several times in the operating room ... but stayed until the end.

During their 70-day stay in the capital, the Russians treated almost 5,000 patients. Of these only 368 were casualties of war. By far the largest number of patients were suffering from syphilis, skin diseases and chronic gastro-enteritis. As Mondon-Vidailhet coyly phrased the medical statistics: "Though Mars claimed many victims, Venus accounted for even more."

Among the few women treated was an 18-year-old servant of Empress Taytu. She was seen by a neuropsychiatrist, Dr. Goltzinger, who diagnosed her as "hysteric." She was possessed, she said, by an evil spirit. Among his 121 "mental patients" he said he had no cases of neurasthenia, the term for nervous exhaustion, or simple neurosis. From the "natives' point of view," he noted, "all the Europeans are 'sick,' that is to say, neurasthenic." He said that the Ethiopians could not understand the irritability and restlessness of the Europeans, and that they described foreigners as "people who behave as though they were going to die the next day."

At the emperor's request, the Russians produced a primer of medical advice in Amharic. For most ailments such as trachoma, scabies and head lice, the prescription was to bathe often with hot water and *indod* (the soap plant). The book advised that the Ethiopian cure for tapeworm, *kosso*, though effective, should not be taken too often and urged people not to eat raw meat or drink dirty water. It suggested that too much red pepper was bad, advised quinine for malaria and emphasized the infectious nature of syphilis. There was a section on setting fractures, an area in which the *hakim* of Ethiopia were relatively competent.

The Russian Red Cross closed its books on 5 October. There was a grand ceremony at which General Svedov made a farewell speech, and Menilek handed out decorations. The emperor expressed his gratitude to the Czar and the Czarina and in a letter conveyed the wish that friendship between "our two countries will thrive through the centuries." Acceding to Menilek's request, they left a skeleton staff of one doctor, three medical assistants, one orderly, a translator and all their equipment and medicines. As the Russian flag was lowered, the Ethiopians hoisted their own flag and below it flew the emblem of the Red Cross. "The Ethiopian Red Cross was inaugurated under the patronage of Her Majesty, Empress Taytu."

Mondon-Vidailhet was envious of the propaganda impact the Russians had made, and bemoaned the lack of even a shelter under the sponsorship of France. "The Russians, by their good behavior, their totally military discipline and the services they rendered have raised European prestige here."

The politics over the POWs

The Italian government, under its new prime minister, Antonio di Rudini, learned in mid-May 1896 that Pope Leo XIII was dispatching his own mission to Ethiopia to negotiate with Menilek for the release of the prisoners. The Pope had chosen an envoy from the Catholic-Copts of Egypt,* Bishop Macarios, trusting that his knowledge of the Ethiopian Orthodox Church would facilitate rapport. Another mission, under Fathers Wersowitz-Rey and Oudin, was sent by the Association of Roman Women to take donations of clothing, soap, food, medicine and letters from their families to the prisoners. The Italian Red Cross sent its representative, the Count de Choiseul.†

The Vatican mission was completely unacceptable to the Italian government: it was a usurpation of the government's responsibility. As it was politically impossible to forbid such a mission, di Rudini

---

*In 1440, at the Council of Florence, a delegation of Copts knelt before Pope Eugenio, signaling their return to the See of St. Peter. They were "Copt" in the sense of being Egyptian, but no longer associated with the Coptic Patriarchate in Alexandria.

†Father Wersowitz-Rey died of sunstroke after leaving Djibouti; Father Oudin and Count de Choiseul took over leadership and combined their missions.

took steps to thwart it.

Di Rudini asked the journalist-explorer, Augusto Franzoj, who had
been in Ethiopia from 1883 to 1884, to go to Zurich to persuade his
friend, Alfred Ilg, to come to Rome for talks. Ilg agreed, despite
objections from his wife, who feared that his life might be in danger
from some hot-headed Italian patriot, as Ilg was well known as
Menilek's defender and representative. Ilg and di Rudini met in secret
and the Swiss consented to go as quickly as possible to Ethiopia to
urge Emperor Menilek not to make a deal with the envoy of Pope
Leo XIII.

When Ilg arrived in Harar late in June, he found there not only
the representatives of the Pope, the Association of Roman Women
and the Italian Red Cross, but also the Russian Red Cross. Ilg then
unblocked Menilek's objections to the Russians and accompanied
them to Addis Ababa.

Ilg conferred immediately with the emperor and explained the
political sensitivities of the Italian government. When the young,
blond, bespectacled Bishop Macarios arrived on 11 August, Menilek
greeted him but excused himself from further contacts as it was
fasting time, and would be until 28 August. Ilg had not been
completely successful, for the emperor told Macarios (or Macarios
certainly got the impression) that he would have all the prisoners
in the provinces rounded up and brought to the capital. A week later,
a courier from the coast informed Menilek that the Italians had
sequestered a Dutch ship carrying arms ordered by the Ethiopian
government.

"I ... knew that Menilek's favorable intentions had changed and
that the poor prisoners must give up hope of being freed by us,"
reported Macarios. He left the capital on 1 October, bearing a pro
forma letter from Menilek to the Pope and taking only two prisoners
who were very sick. Unofficially the Italian government was
delighted that Macarios had failed.[14]

While the Pope's envoy was in Addis Ababa, the irrepressible
Nicholas Leontiev was meeting Prime Minister di Rudini in Rome.
He introduced himself as the plenipotentiary of the Emperor
Menilek of Ethiopia, ready to start peace negotiations. Here again
was a demonstration of Leontiev's ability to land on his feet. He had
been in disgrace with his own government not one year before for
his falsifications about the Ethiopian mission to St. Petersburg.
Then, in February 1896, just as the Ethiopian army and the Italian

army of Eritrea were positioning themselves for their final confrontation, there was Leontiev at Massawa requesting permission for himself and four Cossacks (two of whom he passed off as doctors) to take a humanitarian mission to the Ethiopian side, carrying the Red Cross flag through the Italian lines. A query to the Russian government elicited their denial that Leontiev had anything whatsoever to do with the Russian Red Cross: "Take him. Arrest him — do whatever you want with him." Entry was refused, and Leontiev and his friends had to take the long route through Djibouti, Shewa and the north where they found the emperor making peace. They had missed the war. Returning to the capital with the emperor, Leontiev was given a letter to the Czar, and granted the privilege of escorting 50 Italian POWs to the coast to honor the Czar's coronation. Leontiev had the temerity to send an announcement of this charge directly to King Umberto "like an equal to an equal." King Umberto did not deign to reply, but di Rudini directed Major-Doctor Nerazzini to go from Zeyla to Djibouti to take consignment of the prisoners and thank the Russian upstart. Nerazzini did so on 27 July and reported to his government, "It is my duty to state how helpful he was — he and his four companions — to the prisoners, both during the trip Shewa-Djibouti and on the painful march from Lake Ashenge to Shewa." Nerazzini also said, "The maneuver of obtaining the liberty of 50 prisoners was as much to establish his personal influence with Menilek, as to show Europe the growing Muscovite influence on Abyssinia — it is a very clever move."

The letter to the Czar was taken by Leontiev's companion, Ato Yosef (the former interpreter for the Italians in Shewa), to Russia while Leontiev played the role of Menilek's ambassador to Italy. Before going to Rome, Leontiev had given an interview to *Le Figaro* in Paris, in which he voiced his disapproval that a person of such low rank as Major Nerazzini had been named to head peace negotiations. Still, in Rome, he was received by the Contessa Santa Fiora, Cardinal Vannutelli and finally Prime Minister di Rudini. On this occasion the prime minister, who was known for his mildness, if not ineptitude, changed into a bear.

After an hour-long meeting with Leontiev, di Rudini transmitted his report to King Umberto:

He is a big man, unpolished, but very polite. He described the miserable conditions for the prisoners and said he was empowered to negotiate peace on behalf of the emperor. He added to the preliminary terms agreed on by

Salsa and Menilek, "payment of indemnity." I told him I already had Nerazzini as my negotiator ... and that if Menilek wanted an indemnity he would have to come and take it by force in Rome. He said my refusal would cause suffering and death of our prisoners. I said it is my duty to refuse any indemnity and it is their duty to die for the dignity of their country. [I told him] we will reimburse Menilek for the expenses of their keep but no more."

In due course, di Rudini would eat these words, but for the moment he dismissed Leontiev from his office. Leontiev went directly to Vienna, where on the morning of 27 August Czar Nicholas arrived accompanied by Prince Lobanov, his foreign minister. No longer the discredited bounder — had he not been received by the head of the Italian government? — Leontiev was seen by the Czar immediately. Leontiev rode on the Czar's train to Kiev (Prince Lobanov died of a heart attack en route) to join the meeting with Ato Yosef who carried Menilek's request for the Czar's good offices with Italy.[15]

The Czar's mediation was not needed after the Italian government authorized Nerazzini to withdraw its insistence that Menilek agree never to accept the protection of any other power. Nerazzini reached Addis Ababa on 8 October 1896. He signed the peace treaty with Menilek on 20 October and departed with the first batch of prisoners on 20 November. The Italian government agreed to pay "indemnity" of ten million lire. Encased in the face-saving euphemism "reimbursement for expenses on behalf of the prisoners," it was to be paid in three installments over a two-year period at no interest.[16]

For Ethiopians, 1896 was the year of the *ferengi*. Never before had so many white faces been seen in their country: close to 2,000 Russians, Frenchmen, Italians and English, excluding the Italians in the army of Eritrea. Their faces looked the same, but Ethiopians began to be able to make distinctions between nationalities. That curious bond of friendship that often occurs between ex-enemies, in this case the Italians and Ethiopians, was established. European medical practices, introduced by the Russian Red Cross on a larger scale then ever before, took their place alongside traditional Ethiopian methods.

Though the day-to-day lives of its people did not change significantly, the country would never again be the same. World attention would be both a burden and a challenge as the 20th century came into sight.

10

Diplomacy: domestic failure and foreign success

Though hostilities with Italy had ceased,* Tigray was a disaster area, short of food and strewn with corpses, its inhabitants still caring for wounded men and women. The national unity brought by the war held in Gojam, Wello, Begemder and Shewa, but the long-time Tigrayan enmity to Shewan hegemony would return in full force though Menilek proclaimed, "I give Tigray to Ras Mengesha, my son and friend."[1]

A witness of the post-war devastation was Augustus Wylde who arrived at Adwa for the *Manchester Guardian* at the end of May 1896. Wylde, who had seen the area 12 years earlier, described the ruins of Ras Alula's house and noted that little was left of the comfortable home of Mercha Werqe, former envoy to England for Emperor Yohannes, and now interpreting for Ras Mengesha. The wife of Mercha, "a venerable and stately old dame whom I had known before was hospitable despite her miseries and troubles. Her home had been sacked by the Italian askaris and instead of full granaries and a cattle yard, she had no grain, no sheep ... [only] three ploughing bullocks and two heifers ... one goat gave only enough milk for the youngest child."

After a chat with his old acquaintance, the grizzled Ras Alula, Wylde attended the wedding of Mengesha's daughter, Attenesh, to Abreha Hagos. It was a match planned to seal forgiveness of Abreha's father, Ras Hagos, for his long collaboration with Italy.

Ras Mengesha was the image of his father, the former emperor, Wylde thought. "The same nervous look and peculiar restless eyes ... good-looking ... but a want of firmness about the mouth." The 16-year-old bride was very pretty, and could read and write a few Arabic words. "It is no wonder the Italian officers rave about these girls. There was no religious ceremony. Her hand was put in the bridegroom's by her father who said a few words then kissed her."

---

*Between 28 March and 7 April 1896, Col. Stevani undertook the relief of an Italian garrison at Kasala under siege by the Mahdists. This succeeded at a cost of nearly 500 dead and wounded on Stevani's side. General Baldissera re-fortified Adigrat in May with aggressive intentions but orders from Rome prevailed and he withdrew from Adigrat as had been promised to Menilek in the preliminary peace talks of 18 May.

Also present at this wedding was Lt. Mulazzani, who had brought gifts for the bride's father honoring Mengesha Yohannes's marriage to Kefey Wele two months before. Lt. Mulazzani took consignment of a batch of prisoners, whose release had been authorized by the emperor. The group included Major Salsa, the negotiator of preliminary peace terms, detained by Menilek's order until the evacuation of Adigrat was completed on 18 May 1896. Wylde said that he helped scrub and shave the prisoners and cut their hair, but that they were in otherwise healthy condition.

Two months later Ras Mengesha Yohannes invited Wylde to visit him in Meqelle, instructing him not to take the route through Agame, an area ruled by Ras Sebhat, as there was unrest there. Wylde answered many questions from Mengesha about England, its army, navy, government and system of justice. He had some difficulty explaining why the two main British political parties never resorted to armed combat. Ras Mengesha, in turn, explained the problem with Ras Sebhat. He was a poor governor and he ill-treated his own people who preferred another man, Ras Hagos, Mengesha's new in-law.

As Wylde prepared to return to Massawa to write his story, Ras Mengesha, who had obviously informed the emperor of Wylde's presence, said, "Wait until I hear from His Majesty." Wylde then accepted an invitation to Shewa so he could confirm for his readers that Menilek was treating his Italian POWs humanely.

Wylde took 45 days to journey to Shewa, a distance that was normally covered in five days. His party was delayed by detours to avoid fighting in Sokota district, by wounded soldiers en route to Shewa who joined them, and by an elderly lady from Semen and her servants wishing protection on their way to visit Empress Taytu. Going in the opposite direction were about 100 men in the service of Ras Wele, taking transport animals to pick up some wounded soldiers and guns Wele had left in storage at Adwa. Wylde's caravan crossed with priests on their way to Jerusalem.

Supplies were also a problem. The women in one village fought and knocked down with sticks some of Wylde's escort soldiers to keep them from preying on their grain supplies. They passed near a caravan that included a sister of Ras Mengesha Yohannes. "I found out she was considered 'fast' and was being sent by her brother to a nunnery to keep her in order." The young lady sent a servant to ask Wylde for an umbrella and wanted to know if all "English" were tall, with red beards and moustaches. As Wylde was suffering from fever he did not get a chance either to show her the color of his hair (not red) or find out more about "nuns."

Ras Wele, whose reputation for xenophobia was said to equal that of his sister, Empress Taytu, was, however, extremely cordial. His house, "the best I have seen in Abyssinia," was furnished with a couch and two chairs of Austrian bent wood. "We dined with knives, forks and spoons, which he knew how to use." Wele confided to Wylde that Yejju was difficult to govern, and that he had been forced to execute many people to keep his province in line. Still, said Wylde, "He is popular and taxes a little over 10 per cent." Wylde may have been the only foreigner to describe Ras Wele as "charming."

Wylde's interpreter was Engidashet, the half-Ethiopian son of the German botanist, Wilhelm Schimper.* Engidashet had served in Italian intelligence during the recent war and was nervous.† Wele was pleasant to him as well, and kept him up half the night asking about the banking, revenue and commercial figures in a *Whittaker's Almanac*. Engidashet was unable to explain to Wele's satisfaction why so little coverage of Ethiopia was given in the publication.

Continuing on through Wello the party encountered Italian prisoners in good health, happy with their Ethiopian women companions. They passed through the corn, butter and honey producing areas belonging to Empress Taytu, met hundreds of people taking livestock to the Borumeda market and saw a heavily loaded caravan going to Tigray with wedding presents from Empress Taytu to her niece, Kefey Wele.

By the time they reached Addis Ababa the peace treaty with Italy had been signed and Menilek asked Wylde to have it printed in the *Manchester Guardian*. As Wylde continued out of Addis Ababa on his way to the coast, he met the French delegation on its way to establish formal diplomatic relations with Ethiopia. Its head, Léonce Lagarde, erstwhile governor of Djibouti, did not even say "*Bonjour*," wrote Wylde, a foretaste of Lagarde's attitude towards Englishmen.[2]

---

*Schimper, the Baron de Fahrenbach (1804-78), lived for over 30 years in northern Ethiopia. He was sent there by the Jardin des Plantes, Paris, and is said to have introduced the potato. Engidashet trained at the Polytechnical Institute in Karlsruhe, and returned to Ethiopia in 1878, serving Emperor Yohannes in a variety of areas, technical and diplomatic.
†After Wylde left, Menilek had him flogged. Engidashet escaped and went back to Eritrea, but returned to Addis Ababa in 1907 to work at the German legation.

The peace treaty, signed 26 October 1896, is dealt with summarily in the chronicle. "[Major Nerazzini] abolished Article 17 which was the cause of the war and thus freed the Italian prisoners."

The following passage in the chronicle is concerned mainly with Empress Taytu and the events surrounding the visit of Ras Mengesha Yohannes to Addis Ababa. Were it not for the fact that the relations between Tigray and imperial authority were a matter of utmost seriousness, the story could be seen to contain hints of Taytu's self-congratulation on her generous efforts to placate Ras Mengesha Yohannes.[3]

The Tigrayans arrived on 6 January 1897. The ras was provided with a fine house and food was sent daily to him and his suite. "The intendants of *Jan-hoy* [His Majesty] and the *itege* took turns supplying hydromel, arak of honey and wine."

The mention of "wine" diverts the chronicler into a short historical review of wine production in Ethiopia: its demise in the time of Emperor Tewodros, and its revival 30 years later by Taytu. The latter's success at viticulture, must, the chronicler asserts, "be given a prominent place in our story." The empress had some Italian POWs working as gardeners under her Armenian supervisor; still it was remarkable that in the nine months since her return from the war theatre she managed to serve domestic wine to Ras Mengesha Yohannes.

From wine production the chronicler segues into an assurance that Empress Taytu loved Mengesha Yohannes very much, to the extent of granting her niece to him. He tells that during the month of his visit Mengesha spent his days in the great reception hall and his evenings in the private apartments, and "never wore the same clothes twice." This daily change of clothing was provided by the empress. On the day of departure, all the Tigrayans received new clothes, harnessed horses, saddled mules, beef on the hoof and some slaves, while Mengesha received 60,000 talers to pay his soldiers.[4]

Yet, after all this generosity, Mengesha Yohannes rebelled against Menilek. The chronicler turns back to events in the past to explain this betrayal, ascribing it to the evil influence of "Tesfaye Antalo and Basha Tewelde, both of whom were sons of peasants." The latter spent his time in Addis Ababa visiting clerics and nobles, boasting, "The reason we came ... was that Ras Mengesha Yohannes be named Negus."

The empress summoned Tesfaye Antalo. "Basha Tewelde is going about ... demanding that Mengesha be named 'King!' What does this mean?" Tesfaye Antalo professed ignorance but went straight to Ras Mengesha to warn him that the empress was in a towering temper.

Early the following morning, Ras Mengesha presented himself in his traveling clothes at the empress's apartments. Taytu was still at her morning prayers and shocked by his appearance at this unconventional hour; her first thought was for the safety of "her daughter" Kefey Wele, who had been left behind in Tigray. "Tigrayans were hot-tempered and might do the girl harm." She had her sandals brought, ate her breakfast, and then invited him in.

She saw his angry looks, but made the customary inquiries after his well-being and motioned him to sit down. He remained standing and came directly to the point. He had come to Addis Ababa to warn the government about threatening events on his borders (the campaign of Anglo-Egypt to take control of the Sudan from the Mahdists) and to say that he did not want to be named "King." "If God wants to grant me a crown, he knows where I am ... why would I ask intercession by others?"

Despite this haughty declaration, she replied, "My son, I am your mother ... I love you well, God knows that. If the emperor ... heard these things he would turn against you and humble you before everyone. I wish to spare you this." She told him the history of the lords of Tigray, none of whom from the time of Mikael Sehul (1740-80) had held any title higher than Ras. She urged him to busy himself making his area prosperous and reminded him sarcastically that half of Tigray was still occupied by Italy. This remark must have infuriated the Tigrayan prince since Italy's continued occupation of part of Tigray had been legitimized by Menilek in the peace treaty. Ras Mengesha took her maternal advice "in a bad way" and left for Tigray, vowing never to return.

Not naming Ras Mengesha a Negus may have been a critical error. The title would have cost the emperor very little and might have moderated the bad feeling between him and the Tigrayans. Since Empress Taytu had the dominant voice in giving the bad news to Ras Mengesha, it is reasonable to assume that she had a strong vote in the decision not to promote him. With the title of Negus went the privilege of naming others as Ras or Dejazmach, and Menilek had not let that power out of his own hands since his coronation, when he confirmed the title granted to Tekle Haymanot of Gojam by Emperor Yohannes. This privilege was an instrument of the centralization of power.

It was that power which was responsible for an influx of foreigners to Ethiopia so great over the following three months that the emperor complained to one visitor, "What do they all want?"[5] A summary of the court calendar for March, April and May 1897, exclusive of domestic, religious and political activities, is given below.

9 March   Reception for French diplomatic mission, headed by Léonce Lagarde
9 April   Reception for French expedition to the Nile, jointly led by Gabriel Bonvalot and Charles de Bonchamps
10 April   Reception for Count le Gonidec, Prince de Lucinge; audience with Ensign Bénito Sylvain, Haitian navy
13 April   Reception for Duc Henri d'Orléans, Edmond de Poncins, Nicholas Leontiev
15 April   Reception for envoys of Khalifa Abdulahi (responding to visit of Menilek's envoys to Omdurman in early 1897)
30 April   Reception for British diplomatic mission, headed by James Rodd (later Lord Rennell-Rodd)
19 May   Reception for Italian diplomatic mission, headed by Major-Doctor Cesare Nerazzini
? May   Reception for Turkish diplomatic mission

While most of the visiting foreigners had come to Addis Ababa under the aegis of one or another European power, a small number were enterprising individuals on one-man missions.

The French

The government mission of 11 men, including three doctors and an artist who wanted to paint Menilek's portrait, was escorted by a smart contingent of Senegalese troops. Lagarde, chief of mission, had spent a month in Harar making an agreement with Ras Mekonnen that Djibouti would be Ethiopia's official port of entry, in return for which France would guarantee that arms destined for the Ethiopian government could pass through duty-free.[6]

Mondon-Vidailhet, still writing his column for *Le Temps*, and also acting as Menilek's "Minister for Post and Telegraph,"* "Minister for Forestation," and "Minister for Public Instruction," was very proud that his nation was first to salute Ethiopia. This "first" had been contrived by Léon Chefneux, in Paris on business for Menilek,

---

*Stamps had been printed in Paris and postcards produced for the POWs, but the telegraph was not yet operating.

who had urged the French government to beat the British diplomatically.[7]

Lagarde settled down to business with Menilek, while the doctors started treating patients and Paul Buffet, the artist, went out sketching. The emperor granted permission for the Franciscan Sisters of Calais to operate a school in Harar and for the return to Tigray of the Lazarists, who had been expelled by General Baratieri. He renewed the mythical 1843 Treaty of Friendship with France and on 20 March 1897 signed a secret "Convention for the White Nile" in which he agreed to help France establish herself on the upper Nile in return for a border with French Somalia that favored Ethiopia. Secrecy was agreeable to both sides: to Menilek because it would otherwise damage his relations with the Mahdists and compromise him with Great Britain, whose envoys were on the way; to Lagarde because France was about to make its ill-fated challenge to Britain's dominance of the upper Nile.

Léonce Lagarde did several peculiar things. He hinted to Menilek that he would like a title. Menilek granted him the comical distinction "Duc d'Entotto" which Lagarde took so seriously that the foreign colony never ceased making fun of him. Then, knowing full well that the designated agents of France, Commander Bonvalot and Charles de Bonchamps, were soon to arrive and expedite the "Convention on the White Nile" that he had just signed, Lagarde gathered up his delegation and departed for the coast, leaving behind only a factotum to set up a legation and Buffet, who had not yet finished his portrait of the emperor. Compounding this neglect of duty to coordinate the expedition to the Nile, he ordered Captain Clochette and two of his lieutenants to start for the Nile.[8]

The Bonvalot-Bonchamps group arrived in Addis Ababa raging at Lagarde whom they had crossed on the way. He had instructed them to stay no longer than eight days in the capital. On arrival, Bonvalot was handed a note from Clochette which said, "I could not wait for you ... have yourselves dismissed." Clochette was only 50 kilometers north of the city and Bonvalot could not comprehend why he did not return to effect cooperative plans. After several meetings with the emperor who said he could provide only nine camels, Bonvalot was at boiling point. He left Bonchamps in charge and returned to the coast to retrieve the two collapsible boats that Lagarde had so far failed to forward. Bonvalot never returned. Bonchamps took charge and he and four colleagues left on 19 May for the Nile with their nine camels and about 60 escort soldiers, provided by Menilek, but paid for by the French.[9]

The French aristocrats in Addis Ababa had assorted reasons for being there; Henri d'Orléans was there because he had met the artful Russian, Nicholas Leontiev. Son of the pretender to the French throne, d'Orléans was a bona fide world traveler and author. He had a tenuous connection with the Nile exercise, having once been asked to head it. Two members of his party were only interested in hunting. The emperor saw them all. Menilek enjoyed the company of d'Orléans who presented splendid gifts, but he was annoyed with Prince de Lucinge and Count le Gonidec who had killed five elephants en route — ivory was a crown monopoly. Le Gonidec fell ill with syphilis and had to be carried back to the coast on a stretcher. The fourth Frenchman, Edmond de Poncins, had nothing good to say of Ethiopia, concluding that "the Somali and Danakil were incomparably superior to the Abyssinians ..."[10]

The British

When the mission was announced in London, *The Spectator* of 27 February 1897 said: "That Menilek governs very roughly, that his queen cares little for human life, that his generals allow great outrages is all possible enough; but this is a native dynasty of dark men, nominally ... Christian, therefore improvable and striving ... to become orderly enough to be received into intercourse with Europe."

Eight Englishmen were sent to receive Ethiopia into "intercourse with Europe." On 29 April 1897 they made a stunning entrance into Addis Ababa. Averaging 1.90 meters (over six feet) in height, the Englishmen were garbed in bright uniforms glittering with decorations and plumed headgear, and escorted by even taller be-turbaned Sikhs. One of the men was Captain Charles Sayer Tristram Speedy, a still vigorous 70-year-old ex-army officer who had lived in northern Ethiopia from 1861 to 1862, and had been at Meqdela with the Napier expedition in 1868 and with the Hewett Mission to Emperor Yohannes in 1884. Some Ethiopians recognized him and greeted him with excitement, but his initial reception by Menilek was cool. The emperor said sternly, "You were a friend of my enemy, Tewodros." However, their relationship improved and Menilek gave him many gifts. Speedy must have told the emperor about Alemayehu, the son of Tewodros, whom Menilek had seen as an infant at Meqdela, and whose affectionate guardian Speedy had become in 1868 when he was taken to England. The boy had become a great favorite of Queen Victoria between terms at Rugby, and when he died at the age of only 18, he was buried at Windsor Castle.[11]

Diplomatic negotiations were in the hands of James Rodd, an aide to Lord Cromer in Cairo. He was aware that Menilek had just seen envoys of the Mahdi, whose militants were the only force standing in the way of British control of the upper Nile. Menilek knew the British had abetted Italian ambitions in Ethiopia. A bargain was struck on the border of Ethiopia with British Somalia whereby Britain ceded 34,500 square kilometers of Somali-inhabited territory and Menilek agreed not to help the Mahdists.[12]

Just as England had been capable of duplicity with Yohannes in 1884,* so Menilek parleyed with Rodd despite his secret agreement to help the French block the British on the Nile. Though Henri d'Orléans pretended that the reception of the British was cold compared to the warm welcome to the French, there was little difference in panoply and ceremony.[13] The British presented Menilek with bear skins, silver, guns, and a beautifully printed book on the life of Alexander the Great, replicating a manuscript looted by a British officer from Meqdela.[14]

Dr. Pinching answered Menilek's questions about the latest in medical science, and the emperor reiterated his interest in the "Roentgen machine," with which one could see the bones of the hand without cutting through the skin. Pinching said they had been reluctant to bring such equipment for fear of resentment by the clerics. Menilek riposted indignantly that Ethiopians were not as backward as they had been in the past. Dr. Pinching gave Menilek a microscope in compensation for his disappointment.

The empress received the British mission, and was presented with a diamond and emerald necklace, a looking-glass and some silk embroidery. She bowed slightly acknowledging the gifts, then through her interpreter asked about the Queen of England. She marveled when she heard that Victoria at the age of 78 had just taken her annual holiday, via ship and train, to the south of France. "She has never seen modern travel like a train," commented Rodd. She wanted to know if Victoria's children were all by the same father, and the occupation by Victoria's progeny of thrones scattered around

---

*Augustus Wylde called Britain's failure to live up to the Hewett Treaty in handing Massawa over to Italy "one of the vilest bits of treachery that has been perpetrated in Africa or India."

Europe* fascinated the Ethiopian empress.

Just before the mission left in mid-May, Yosef Neguse brought a signed letter from the empress to James Rodd in which she regretted that a minor indisposition prevented her from saying farewell. She enclosed a small gift for Queen Victoria with a polite greeting. "It was a quaint double-gold necklace, built up of small plaques of filigree work connected by golden rings and beads and was a replica of one worn by the Queen of Sheba." Actually, it had just been designed by the court jeweler, Dikran Ebeyan.

Despite her "indisposition," the empress was sitting beside the emperor on the balcony of the *elfign* as the British caravan departed. Surprised, the delegation dismounted and, standing in a line, bowed solemnly three times. A wave of the hand by both monarchs acknowledged their salute.

The Italians

Four days later Dr. Cesare Nerazzini returned briefly to present Major Federico Ciccodicola as the new minister for Italy, and Dr. Lincoln de Castro who would accompany the last POWs to the coast. Nerazzini took back with him two Italian officers, not prisoners of war, who had been held in southwest Ethiopia for three months on Menilek's order. Lts. Vannutelli and Citerni were the sole survivors of a foolhardy Italian expedition that had ventured into southwestern Ethiopia just as Menilek was returning from the battle at Adwa. Their temerity was based on arrogance and ignorance. The expedition had been led by the unscrupulous Captain Vittorio Bottego, who had selected the healthiest and worst criminals from the Italian jail at Massawa to be his escort. With Lts. Citerni and Vannutelli and a scientist, Dr. Maurizio Sacchi, they had killed their way across the Somali plains to establish an Italian outpost at Lugh on 18 November 1895. There they helped Lt. Ugo Ferrandi build a fort, left him 45 askaris to defend it, and went on their way, skirting Ethiopian territory, unaware that Italy and Ethiopia were at war. Their objective was exploration and the charting of the Omo River; once this was accomplished, they crossed back into a plateau alive with soldiers of the emperor. Menilek knew they were there, but instructed

---

*The description was very "Ethiopian": the Prince of Wales' wife is the daughter of the Queen of Denmark and the sister of the King of Greece; the wife of Czar Nicholas is the sister of the Prince of Wales' wife; the heir to the Kaiser is the grandson of the Queen of England, etc.

his people to let them wear themselves out, then bring these "white men" to Addis Ababa, alive. On 17 March 1897, occupants of the Bottego hillside camp, whose number had been reduced by desertion and disease from the original 124 askaris to 86, were surrounded by 1,000 soldiers. Bottego made no attempt to talk; he ordered his askaris to fire. In three minutes it was all over, and all but Citerni and Vannutelli were dead. Dr. Sacchi, who had left the expedition at Lake Chamo, had been killed a month earlier while taking a rich caravan of illegal ivory to the coast.[15] Nerazzini and Ciccodicola were glad to have the two survivors. Menilek signed a trade treaty, and relations with Italy were regularized in every respect.

The Turks

Little is known about the congratulatory mission from the sultan of Turkey, except that they brought gifts, among which were some diamonds for Empress Taytu.[16]

The Russians

Capitalizing on the high reputation won by the Russian Red Cross, P.M. Vlassov established a legation in January 1898. He brought with him his wife, Emily, and her companion, Miss Proctor. Mrs. Vlassov was English, and her ways, "a little American, must astonish Abyssinian women," wrote Mondon-Vidailhet. By "American," he could have meant either "informal and open" or "coarse and uneducated." According to Lagarde, the nationality of Vlassov's wife intrigued Menilek. "He asked me what I thought. He is simplistic and thinks that since the mission is Russian, and the Russians are anti-English, that it is odd they would select a diplomat with an English wife. I told him this phenomenon was common, but he did not understand."[17]

Russian-French and Russian-Italian relations got off to a bad start as soon as Vlassov debarked at Djibouti. Transport animals were in short supply and Vlassov could not comprehend why they could not be instantly requisitioned. Vlassov sent two men off to find animals. They went to Raheita and that put the Italians in a swivet. The sultan of Raheita was their client, and no one was to deal with him except through Italian good offices. The trouble was not Vlassov's fault. Ensign Babichev consulted the sultan of Raheita on a private deal he was concocting with Nicholas Leontiev. To mollify the Italians, Vlassov ordered Ensign Babichev to return to St. Petersburg. He declined to go, resigned from the navy, and spent the rest of his very long life in Ethiopia working for Emperor Menilek and his successors.*

The strained relations between Russian and French envoys were apparent to Menilek. Lagarde thought he had Menilek eating out of the palm of his hand, but Menilek favored the Russians, no doubt because they had brought a six-member medical team. Menilek ordered a proper and permanent hospital to be built for them.

All that Lagarde could produce in the way of medical aid was a veterinarian, Dr. P. Wurtz, and his assistant, Gilbert Fenski. They tried for months to develop a vaccine to protect cattle from disease but were distracted because they had also brought smallpox vaccine with them. Menilek ordered his people to report for vaccination, and Wurtz and Fenski inoculated 20,700 in seven months. They trained two Ethiopians and left enough vaccine for 250,000 more on their departure.[18]

There is one more Russian to account for — A.K. Bulatovich. He was with the Red Cross mission and had remained to help maintain the medical service. When this young Cossack learned that Ras Welde Giyorgis was going into the relatively unknown area south of Keffa, he asked the emperor if he could go along. Unlike Babichev and Leontiev, he took the trouble to remain "inside" the Czarist establishment by riding all the way to Djibouti to obtain the permission of the arriving diplomat, Vlassov. The trip there and back took 23 days, the length of time normally required for a one-way trip under optimum conditions.

Bulatovich spent four months in the company of Ras Welde Giyorgis, "the noblest, most energetic, intelligent and honorable person I have ever met." Scattered about in Bulatovich's report on geography, flora and fauna, and customs of the tribes being brought under Menilek's hegemony, were references to Abba Jifar and his mother and two close female relations of Empress Taytu.[19]

He thought the Jimma residence of Abba Jifar was more elegant than Menilek's palace in Addis Ababa. After they had sipped some coffee, he was asked by the young prince to treat his sick mother. Bulatovich was given a chair outside her house which was screened by white fabric. He regretted that he could not prescribe for her

---

*Babichev had come with the Red Cross mission in 1896 and met Leontiev then. He married an Ethiopian lady, became an administrator in Welega, and died in Addis Ababa in 1955 at the age of 84.

heartburn, coughing and headaches without seeing her. Bulatovich was permitted to enter and had a rare glimpse of this powerful woman who had persuaded her son to avoid conflict with Menilek and accept his rule rather than have his people slaughtered.

The queen mother sat on a carpet-covered divan dressed in a black silk cape with gold embroidery over a long silk skirt. Fair of skin and fine-boned, she appeared younger than her 40 years. "Her arms and legs, on which she wore gold bracelets, were so tiny that an aristocratic Chinese might envy her." Her suite of women, who were "positively beautiful," gasped when the Russian leaned over her chest to listen to her breathing. He could do little for her bronchitis but gave her a powder for her cough and wished her well.

Then Bulatovich met the family of Ras Welde Giyorgis, another rare privilege. The encounter took place in a large *tukul* about 10 meters in diameter with white-washed walls. There were two doors opposite each other but no windows. It was sparsely furnished with a few chairs and divans. The guns and swords of the ras were mounted on the wall, and his religious books, each tucked into a leather sheath, hung on straps from nails. "Yeshemabet was light-skinned like her cousin, Empress Taytu, but older and dressed far more richly. She absolutely glittered with gold and silver jewelry, even wearing a little diadem on her head. The ras, her third husband, adores her and they have been united by the rite of religious marriage, after many years of a civil arrangement." He was introduced to a niece of Empress Taytu, Aselefetch Welde Hanna, who would become one of the better-known courtesans of Ethiopia.[20] At this time she was only 14 years old and told Bulatovich that she had already been married three times. She said that she had married her present husband, Dejazmach Demissew, at the behest of her aunt. Bulatovich observed that the life of aristocratic women was very constrained, in contrast to the freedom enjoyed by women of a lower class. For weeks at a time they hardly left their apartments and when they did they were surrounded by a crowd of protectors — "for all that, they are a flirtatious lot." He added that educated women like Weyzero Yeshemabet took over administrative duties when their husbands were absent and often acted as private secretaries handling their correspondence.

In contrast to the genocide that had characterized Ras Welde Giyorgis's conquest of Keffa, the colonization of the area up to Lake Rudolf on this expedition was almost bloodless. The threat, "Give in or we'll shoot," had the potency of the Keffa campaign behind it, and there was evidence that Menilek had become aware that dead people could not farm or produce goods. Bulatovich described their progress: "The ras first sent his troops into Gimirra to convince them of his good will. Despite this, they began driving their herds into the mountains and hid there with their families. Nevertheless the ras hoped that in the end, realizing the impossibility of opposition ... they would come to their senses and he would forbid his troops to undertake hostile operations ..."

As Welde Giyorgis brought southwestern Ethiopia into the empire, Ras Mekonnen and Fitawrari Habte Giyorgis were subduing the Beni Shangul people and the Borena-Sidama region respectively. By these conquests, Menilek established a negotiable basis for his borders with Anglo-Sudan and Anglo-Kenya. Ethiopia had begun to take the shape it has today though the cartographers had many years of work ahead of them.

Menilek himself did not go on another military exercise after Adwa but settled down, except for side trips, in Addis Ababa. This "village of huts draped over sloping green hills" developed into a town dominated by the 15-meter-high royal residence of Menilek and Taytu, and the huge banquet hall with its three-tiered roof and windows of tinted glass. The legations of France, Germany, Italy and Great Britain were constructed. Gutters to carry off rain water made their appearance on buildings, and tin roofs began to replace straw. Eucalyptus seedlings, imported on the advice of Mondon-Vidailhet, Alfred Ilg and Léon Chefneux, flourished and altered the barren aspect of the capital.[21]

Nicholas Leontiev

The Russian, Nicholas Leontiev, did not fall into the category of explorer, visitor or diplomat. He had delivered the first 50 Italian POWs to Zeyla in July 1896. Since that time he had taken upon himself other duties for Menilek, stretching the truth when it suited him. In St. Petersburg, for example, he had told the French ambassador that "Menilek wishes to take possession of Khartoum and is ready to ally himself with the dervishes and scheme against London."

Leontiev had been dining with Roman nobility, Vatican cardinals, the Czar, Leopold II of Belgium, the Sultan of Turkey, the Khedive of Egypt, assorted foreign ministers, ambassadors, generals and munition manufacturers of many countries in the eight months that he had been away from Ethiopia. He had accomplished little, but his public relations on behalf of Ethiopia and himself had been enthusiastic. His source of ready cash was a mystery for he was not reimbursed by Menilek for his traveling expenses until two years later. But Leontiev was a resourceful man and may have collected advances from Russian and French entrepreneurs who saw possibilities of economic investment in Ethiopia.

Now Leontiev wanted his reward, a little kingdom of his own to govern and develop. On 7 June 1897 Menilek handed him a letter which began:

> Upon your return when you have finished the business about which we have spoken, *I intend to name you* [my italics] administrator-general of a border country that you must organize — entering into my service according to the laws of my country. In recompense ... I will give you relief from taxes for five years, at the end of which you will pay taxes just like others ... be it in gold, silver, ivory or coffee. This border country will be in the south of Ethiopia.

Always an original, Leontiev had brought 40 brass instruments and a conductor to teach the Ethiopians how to play them. "The Amhara," wrote Mondon-Vidailhet, "refused energetically to make the acquaintance of cornets and saxhorns, so conductor Milewski was given Welamo and Shanqila men." Over the next four months they learned to play a creditable "Marseillaise," the Russian national anthem, and Milewski's own composition for an Ethiopian national anthem.[22]

A phonograph was another gift from Leontiev and he spent some time with the empress explaining how it worked. Menilek was very impressed and foresaw the phonograph as a new form of writing. "One reads with the ears instead of the eyes," he said.

Though Leontiev had his promissory letter from the emperor, he was dissatisfied with it, in particular with the omission of a specific territory. Before leaving Ethiopia, with the connivance of Gabriel Gobena, the interpreter known as the "absinthe guzzler," he forged a new letter that specified "Equatorial Province." This would be more useful in raising money and recruiting personnel. He went to Paris as d'Orléans had promised his help. On 15 August 1897 he was d'Orléans' second in a duel with Savoia-Aosta, Count of Turin, son of the king of Italy, who had taken offense at d'Orléans' insults to Italian honor in an article in *Le Figaro*. D'Orléans, only slightly wounded, remained Leontiev's friend until the latter's machinations were unmasked a year later.[23]

The man from Haiti

Amidst the princes and dukes whom Menilek received was one Haitian, Bénito Sylvain, who was an honorary naval officer. Sylvain had followed the fortunes of Ethiopia closely since founding in Paris in 1891 a journal espousing racial equality, *La Fraternité*. When Ethiopia won the war with Italy, Sylvain believed that he had found in Emperor Menilek the black hero he sought to ennoble a movement for the "uplift of the black race." He was well enough connected to have letters of introduction to Léonce Lagarde, Henri d'Orléans (with whom Sylvain's brother had been at school), Ras Mekonnen, and to Emperor Menilek and Empress Taytu themselves.

At his first meeting with Menilek and Taytu, Sylvain said that the emperor grabbed his hand, drew him close, pushed back the lace ruffles of his elaborate uniform and said, "Look! He is completely a man of our race." During his several encounters with Menilek, Sylvain urged him to be wary of the colonial powers controlling his access to the sea, suggested that he have diplomatic representation abroad, and asked him to deny what the Italians said of him, namely, that he tolerated slavery and the slave trade in Ethiopia. Menilek assured him that he did what he could to prevent slavery, but that it was very difficult to abolish it altogether. This answer was sufficient for Sylvain to keep his hero on his pedestal. Sylvain departed, bearing a new title, "Aide-de-camp to His Majesty, Emperor Menilek of Ethiopia," and fired with the determination to see that Haiti invite formal diplomatic relations. Menilek decorated him with the "Cross of Solomon." The earnest Sylvain disappeared from all accounts until he returned in 1903 with a black American entrepreneur.[24]

Alfred Ilg

The protocol officer scheduling these visitors to Ethiopia was Alfred Ilg whom Menilek named as "Counselor of State for Foreign Affairs," confirming Ilg in a function he had been exercising for more than 10 years. Ilg purchased an ornate gold-braided uniform and plumed cocked hat to fit his new title. Some idea of the scope of Ilg's duties is found in letters he wrote to his associate on the railroad concession of 1894, Léon Chefneux, who was in Paris at this time.[25]

Ilg had been joined by his young wife, Fanny Gattiker-Ilg, in January 1897. He wrote to Chefneux: "She consoles me when I lose courage." Fanny Ilg must have been an interesting woman but little is known about her. For her to have accepted her husband's unusual life, which included two half-Ethiopian daughters and a son of about 17, was quite remarkable for a Swiss gentlewoman of her time. Of course, Ilg, being a resourceful engineer and having been a resident for 18 years, had as comfortable a house as anyone could have in Addis Ababa. There were three other "white" women in the capital when Fanny Ilg came. All three were wives of traders and there are indications that Mrs. Ilg considered herself socially above them and did not seek their friendship. At the four o'clock tea parties she always addressed her husband as "Excellency." The son born to her in Addis Ababa was christened "Menilek" and the emperor stood as godfather and granted the child the title of Lij.

After expressing his delight at his wife's presence in one letter, Ilg turned to his annoyance with Chefneux for not writing. "It puts me in an embarrassing position. You know how they [Menilek and Taytu] like to know what is happening in Rome. Our railway business has been good news and the telegraph line has begun." A week later Ilg wrote:

I've done my best to calm His Majesty, but I cannot convince him that you cannot find half an hour in which to write. The mining equipment for Comboul* has not yet arrived, though some cases were brought by Clochette which I sent on to Comboul on 29 March. Drouin ... has run out of telegraph wire. Menilek waits impatiently for the silver coins. Hurry! Have them struck at the mint and sent! My wife brought the flag made by Mrs. Fraeful. Menilek was enchanted and had it blessed by Abune Matewos on the first of March. I learned today that they displayed in Paris two flags in honor of the emperor. Hope they were made up to the design I gave you. Sending order for cartridges via Mekonnen. Their Majesties have returned the embroidered gold mantles you sent. The gilt turned black and no one will give 10 talers for them. That expense will be on us. Order some revolvers. The table service is incomplete — lacks 12 spoons, 2 soup spoons, 36 dessert spoons and 4 knives.

In subsequent notes to Chefneux, Ilg reminded him not to forget the fruit trees, especially the extra 50 that Mondon-

---

*Edouard Comboul, a mining engineer, hired on Menilek's behalf by Chefneux, was in Welega, seeking to improve the gold yield.

Vidailhet wanted to give the empress, and that "Taytu is impatient for her jewels [some 200 diamonds and other precious stones had been sent to Paris to be reset] and she wants a Star of Ethiopia made up — spend up to 25,000 francs." Ilg said that the empress noticed the difference in quality of the diamonds in the cross sent by the Czar and the mediocre ones sent by the sultan of Turkey.

He made some criticisms of the foreigners he had ushered into the emperor's presence, of how time-consuming their complaints and demands were. He said Ras Mekonnen had warned him not to get mixed up in the "stupidities of Leontiev," who was running around showering gifts on everyone and "wants to horn in on our gold-mining scheme" which "I will not permit." Ilg asked Chefneux to send the "Roentgen machine" which Menilek wanted immediately, and told him, "Mrs. Ilg was delighted to hear you are sending a piano until she learned that it was intended for the emperor and not for her." Finally he told him that the emperor had advanced 8,000 talers to Carrère to build and equip a hotel, but "you and I must be his guarantors."

Menilek had more on his mind in 1897 than foreigners and their pursuits. He planned to take the "benefits" of Amhara civilization to the "benighted" (that is, non-Christian) population of the economically rich area of Keffa and beyond. He had dispatched three armies in January 1897 under the command of Ras Welde Giyorgis, Dejazmach Demissew Nassibu and Dejazmach Tessema Nadew.

Unlike the king of Jimma who had taken his mother's advice and acknowledged the sovereignty of Menilek in 1882 and was thus able to retain his kingdom as reward, the Keffans and their king fought Amhara domination. The campaign was a fierce one despite the guns carried by the imperial army against the spears of the Keffans. King Gali Sheroko, whom the chronicler admitted was "loved by his people," eluded capture as the army "ravaged the land and exterminated the people." The army of Welde Giyorgis suffered heavy casualties from wounds and disease. The king was finally captured and brought to Addis Ababa in November 1897.[26]

The army under Dejazmach Demissew had conquered Sidamo and Konso by April 1897 as Dejazmach Tessema's army encircled the southwest territories. It was Tessema Nadew who was assigned to guide the French under Charles de Bonchamps to the Nile.

"The Fashoda Crisis"

"The Fashoda Crisis," which was the headline writer's delusive summary of three years of arduous trekking, confrontation by the super-powers of France and England, and the deaths of hundreds of people, began in February 1896. Captain Jean Marchand started from the west coast of Africa in February 1896 and de Bonchamps left Addis Ababa in May 1897 to meet Marchand at the Nile, assisted as per the agreement between Ethiopia and France.

When de Bonchamps and his party reached Gore, Tessema Nadew's capital in Ilu-Babor province, they discovered that Tessema had gone to Addis Ababa and would not return for three months. A frantic message was sent to the emperor, pleading that Tessema return forthwith. The reply came back, "Go ahead if you want, but sign this paper relieving me of any responsibility for your safety."[27]

It was impossible for de Bonchamps' party to proceed without the help of the Ethiopian general. Of their original 56-member escort, 45 had deserted and their camels had run away. The two men who had been sent ahead with Captain Clochette (who had just died) by the French envoy, Léonce Lagarde, refused despite their misery to put themselves under the orders of de Bonchamps until they received permission from Lagarde.

Two members of de Bonchamps' group agreed to go to Addis Ababa to secure that permission and also appeal directly to Menilek for Tessema's help, literally laying their problems on the emperor's doorstep. He and they conferred as they all squatted in the doorway of his *elfign*. "We told him that local chiefs had prevented us from advancing." The emperor replied, "I have already talked to Tessema about that ... these people are imbeciles ... I will give new orders." It was clear that the emperor was fed up with the intrigues and lack of coordination between de Bonchamps and Lagarde and that he used their poor organization as an excuse for his own half-hearted cooperation. He did give them an Ethiopian flag to place beside the French flag should they ever manage the 900 kilometers between Gore and the Nile.[28]

By the end of October, the two men were back in Gore with a letter that they had extracted from Lagarde ordering all Frenchmen to place themselves under the orders of de Bonchamps. Malaria and dying transport animals delayed them further. Their cook went berserk and had to be tied to a mule, and when Tessema Nadew finally came from Addis Ababa, he brought no supplies, no money and no boat. "Twenty-five thousand francs and the boat were still at Djibouti." They blamed Lagarde for all their misfortunes.

Tessema Nadew announced a new Menilekian policy. "Up to now I have made war to kill, ravage, pillage and collect beasts and slaves. Now, His Majesty Menilek wants no more of this kind of aggression. Tell me where you want to go. We will leave in eight days."

Fortunately, de Bonchamps recovered in time from a fever which so deranged him that he tried to kill himself, and the expedition got under way. They said goodbye to Tessema's wife, Weyzero Beletshachew Abba Jobir, at whose baptism before her marriage Empress Taytu had stood as godmother. The young princess was a daughter of a king of Guma, who had been conquered by Menilek. She presented them with a female slave as a farewell present. They took her picture with the camera given them by Madame Lumière, and left her behind. Their group was augmented by three Cossacks from the escort of the Russian minister in Addis Ababa. Minister Vlassov had given these adventure seekers permission to go provided they stayed out of Franco-Ethiopian politics. His orders evaporated under the pressure of shared torments in the swampy terrain.

It was one of the Russians who placed the French flag on an island at the confluence of the Sobat and the Nile on 22 June 1898. The Frenchmen, barely able to stand, had offered money to a local resident, a Yambo, to plant the flag on their behalf. As one historian phrased it, "Modern Soviet propaganda might have wished that Colonel Artmanov had acted with less conversation." Artmanov shouted, "It shall not be said that only a Negro could plant the French flag on the Nile," and plunged into the river. Like lemmings, the other two Cossacks threw themselves in after him.[29]

The whole purpose of the expedition was aborted. Marchand was not there. Though de Bonchamps wanted to wait for him, the Ethiopians, having placed their own flag on the right bank of the river, would not remain in the fetid marshes a day longer and everyone had to return to Gore, arriving with one person fewer in the party. Potter, the artist, was killed on the way back by a lance hurled by a frightened Yambo.

The fiasco was complete when Britain gave an ultimatum to France, "This means war." When Captain Marchand appeared a month later, he was ordered by his own government to evacuate.

He and his men were escorted by a British crew to the point where the Russians had raised the French flag. They were put ashore on the bank claimed by Ethiopia and laboriously made their way to join their co-nationals waiting in Gore.

Menilek was not unhappy as he had established Ethiopian control over his northwest border with the Sudan at relatively low cost. He provided generously for the 10 whites, the 100 Senegalese and the 43 Nyam-Nyam quartered in Stévenin's compound. While they waited for fresh uniforms to come from Djibouti, the Senegalese and the Nyam-Nyam performed military drills that delighted the spectators of Addis Ababa. Lagarde summoned Marchand and told him he wanted the black troops moved down to the Akaki River. "Akaki!" bellowed Stévenin when Marchand told him, "that is a cold place ... there is not a shrub, a bush ... nothing with which to make a fire." Marchand marched back to Lagarde's house and said, "*Merde!* We won't go!"[30]

One Senegalese and one Nyam-Nyam died in Addis Ababa. "The burial was ... a military ceremony watched by a small group of Abyssinians who could not get over the fact that whites were honoring dead men of color." On 13 April 1899 the Marchand-de Bonchamps expeditions left Addis Ababa in their new uniforms, and that was the end of the episode. Léonce Lagarde survived the acrid attacks on his actions in the French press but was never as high in the esteem of Menilek as Ciccodicola, Harrington (British representative in April 1898) or Vlassov.[31]

Apart from ceremonial receptions and religious celebrations, the daily life of the emperor and empress followed a simple routine, though Menilek often enjoyed the 30-kilometer horseback ride to Menengesha forest where his "superintendent of forestry," Maurice Dubois, supervised the cutting of timber. Dubois, who was called a "drunk" by some, was a handsome man. Having worked in Ethiopia since the early 1870s, he spoke excellent Amharic, and "for that reason the empress invited him to her private apartments frequently to chat and have a meal."[32]

The emperor rose at four o'clock in the morning, and after prayers and breakfast (except for Wednesday and Friday which were fasting days) started work:

He has to read a great deal of correspondence which arrives daily from far-away provinces; he is constantly interrupted by demands from court officials to see some complainant. They wait in the ante-chamber playing chess or

tric-trac. Then he walks about the palace compound visiting the workshops
of saddle-makers, carpenters, jewelers and ironworkers and is followed by
a cluster of pages who ... cut-up and fool around as soon as he steps inside
a doorway.

Foreign visitors were entertained at a noon meal, after which the
emperor rested.

Then he resumes his rounds — perhaps to the pharmacy, or the storehouse
where valuable gifts are mixed helter-skelter with bric-à-brac, or to the house
of books and paper where his principal private secretary [the author of
Menilek's chronicle] held sway over scribes and translators. This man's
capability and memory is absolutely incredible. His office consists of a few
copyists. There is no journal of incoming and outgoing correspondence so
he must remember everything.

At state banquets, the emperor ate, drank, coughed, and spat
behind a curtain held at the height of his head to screen him from
profane looks; the holding of this cloth was a privilege vied for by
his officers. About once a month the emperor dined with his
maheber, * a brotherhood whose members hosted dinners in turn.
On these occasions Menilek ate from one basket with his friends.

Twice a week the emperor presided over the "supreme court" with
the *afenegus* who gave legal advice, then announced the emperor's
ruling. Any person in the empire had the right, if he had the stamina
to get to Addis Ababa, to seek redress from this high court.

The empress's routine was much the same: rising early, saying her
prayers, then going on her rounds. She supervised the kitchens, the
sewing and weaving ateliers, jewelers and gardeners. She dictated
correspondence to her scribes. She presided over intimate gatherings
with her husband when they sat beside each other on a low couch.
"Conversation was in a low tone but everyone talked freely. The
cuisine was especially good — the empress was famed for her *doro
dabo* [chicken and hard-boiled egg stew] and her hydromel was
special and never soured as it was made with Entotto spring water
to which she had exclusive rights." Mondon-Vidailhet was a frequent
guest at these family meals and Menilek would ask him to explain
any recent inventions. "The emperor adored this kind of talk ... other
times we spoke of Ethiopian history and geography and he would

*Dr. Martin said that ladies could be enrolled and be represented by a male relative
and that women took turns providing the food. Menilek and Taytu were honorable
members of several *maheber.*

have maps brought. The empress also took part."[33]

Mondon-Vidailhet's rapport with Empress Taytu netted him a fine collection of rare manuscripts, some of them copies that the empress ordered especially for him. He returned the favor in his columns for *Le Temps*. The only unkind thing he ever wrote was that she had become fat from lack of exercise.

Still, she has a grand air ... vitality ... and makes charming conversation. She does not dress differently from other women and is extremely clean ... rare in this country. She receives few women. I hardly ever saw her in the company of other women. This gives the court an air of rectitude which was not there when Menilek was a simple king of Shewa. He had a reputation that Henry of Navarre might have envied. After his religious marriage to Taytu he became a stay-at-home and did not abuse the treasury of indulgence that his people reserve for great rakes. The empress had enough allure and character to merit this fidelity so alien to Ethiopian mores.[34]

Menilek and Taytu were both in good health. Ethiopia had formal diplomatic relations with four countries. Her armies had extended her empire. Her treasury and granaries were full and exports were growing. The firm voice of centralized authority was heard throughout the land — except in Tigray.

11

The "end" of Ras Mengesha Yohannes

Between the angry departure of Mengesha Yohannes from Addis
Ababa in February 1897 and April 1899 when he was brought back,
still angry, as a prisoner, Emperor Menilek had made numerous
efforts to appease him, but these were never enough. The reason
for the young lord's refusal to pay annual homage to the crown was
ascribed to his continued sulking over not being named *negus*; the
fact that he had refused to come was deemed a declaration of
rebellion.[1]

The emperor had sent him money in 1897, and a clerical delegation
with his humble message, "If I have offended you, take pity and
pardon me."[2] The empress must have been deeply involved in the
strategy with Mengesha Yohannes for her letter to him is reproduced
in full in the chronicle.

She wrote to express how shocked she was that he had told the
emperor that he would never again come to Shewa: "Since all we
wanted was to strengthen your house, and have gone to so much
trouble to do so [that is the campaign against Italy] why are you
pulling down this house? Do you think God approves? Satan inspired
the man behind you [Tesfaye Antalo], for you, a Christian, and son
of a Christian, would never act this way on your own."

She begged him to abandon his evil intentions and "break the wings
of Satan." She reminded him that Ras Alula and Ras Hagos had
perished fighting each other — a sad event which brought only joy
to the enemies of Ethiopia.*

"I, your mother and friend," continued the empress, "am so
afflicted by what you have done, I have cried ... and though I would
be happy to sit or stand while thinking of you [an Ethiopian
expression used when facing a difficult problem] I cannot discover
how we have wounded you." She cautioned him against making
excuses or trying to put the blame on others and ended with a plea
not to let the blood of Tigrayans and Shewans, "who are brothers,"
flow again in Tigray.

---

*Alula and Hagos had clashed on 19 January 1897 and Alula, though wounded, was
victorious. He had the captured Hagos executed, then died of complications from
his own wounds on 15 February 1897.

Tigrayans and Shewans were a long way from being "brothers" despite their common historical roots, so this was said more in hope than in fact. Taytu sent her own priestly delegation to speak to Mengesha Yohannes. The priests continued her arguments in so identical a style that it was clear they were carefully instructed by her. What is this they have heard? Is he afraid to come to Shewa for fear he would be chained? If that were true, why had he come to Shewa the year before? Why had he participated in the war with Italy? Does he not know that people overseas are watching Ethiopia? They reminded him that when Emperor Menilek disobeyed Emperor Yohannes, he was not afraid to be called to account. His own father, Yohannes IV, had cursed his own people, the Tigrayans, for their lack of obedience, and "to this day, the chiefs and soldiers and peasants of Tigray have never stopped killing each other." In other provinces, the priests said, peace reigned, and even the dervishes had stopped attacking Ethiopia. So safe was it elsewhere in the empire that "a woman carrying gold on her head could travel alone and no one would bother her." Now, why was Tigray always the site of conflict? "A man like you ... from noble stock, should be a model of virtue." The priests denied that the emperor had called him a rebel: "He would not ever say that even to his closest friends, let alone to your friend Tesfaye Antalo." This point was reiterated. "Menilek has a big hand and a small mouth ... and does not say 'Ras Mengesha Yohannes has betrayed me.'"

The priests reminded Mengesha Yohannes of the fact that Empress Taytu had given him her "daughter" Kefey Wele, an act of extraordinary generosity since she relied on this niece to celebrate her *teskar* (funeral, remembrance ceremony),* as she had no children of her own. "Why did she do this? So that her house would be yours, so that your heart would never be afraid ... for mutual trust." They recalled to Mengesha the tolerance Emperor Menilek had shown other rebels, belying their previous statement that Menilek had never called him a rebel. Zewde, for example, should have been hanged or had his foot and hand cut off, but Menilek had pardoned him, without flogging or harsh words.

Notwithstanding these appeals, Mengesha Yohannes "was

---

*Since Empress Taytu had other nieces, this reason appears as a dramatic turn of phrase. The *teskar* was taken very seriously and was held on the 12th, 40th and 80th day after death. It was followed by banquets that imposed a great outlay of resources on the part of the bereaved.

determined on evil ... called his chiefs and soldiers together and had them swear they would never submit to the Shewans." "Oaths are something they take lightly in Tigray," chides the chronicler, since they had taken an oath to be loyal to the emperor only one year before. The Tigrayans, of course, made the same charge against the Shewans.

Aside from not coming when called, the other "evils" of Mengesha Yohannes were his inability or unwillingness to collect taxes owed to the emperor from the disputatious regions of Tigray, and his independent contacts with the Italians, the English, and the Patriarchate in Egypt. The English had given short shrift to Mengesha's envoy in Cairo, and Governor Martini in Eritrea had only two aims: to keep the peace with Emperor Menilek and to have the provisional border with Tigray drawn in Italy's favor.

The most detailed reporting of events in Tigray comes from the first volume of Governor Martini's diary from the day he became civil governor of Eritrea in January 1898. In addition to the 135 or more paid informers who floated back and forth between Tigray, Shewa, Gojam, Semem and Eritrea, there were the almost daily reports from Martini's two field officers on the border with Tigray, and constant written and verbal communications from Ras Mengesha Yohannes, the priests of Aksum and Adwa, those Tigrayans who were in the process of becoming Eritreans and Ras Mekonnen and Emperor Menilek. There were also telegrams from Major Federico Ciccodicola, head of the Italian legation in Addis Ababa.[3]

Governor Martini, in his late 50s, was a man of probity, intellect and rectitude: not for him the casual morals of the Italian colony.[4] He tried hard to bring about joint Italian-English mediation to clear up the problems between Menilek and Mengesha Yohannes, but Rome procrastinated so long with his request that he could do nothing, though he sent Dr. Mozzetti* to present to Ras Mekonnen unofficially his views on the matter.

Ras Mekonnen had barely returned from the conquest of Beni Shangul when the emperor ordered him to Tigray in October 1898 as all the humble letters and priestly appeals had failed. In Martini's diary of the three months between the arrival of the army of Ras Mekonnen and the surrender of the Tigrayan rases, his caustic

---

*Dr. Mozzetti was known to Ras Mekonnen as he had been sent across the lines in late 1895 to treat the injured Mengesha Atikem.

opinions were directed equally at his Italian staff, Ras Mekonnen, Ras Mengesha Yohannes, the Catholic missionaries, the government in Rome, the English in general, and the Italian press. He was one of the rare observers who had a sense of the significance of women in the world he was living in, and never failed to remark on the whereabouts of the wives, daughters and mothers of the leading characters.

Governor Martini repeatedly made it clear to Mengesha Yohannes that Italy would make no separate deals with him, though he did express in his diary some reservations that if Mengesha Yohannes managed to hold off the army of Ras Mekonnen, the Tigrayans would hate the Italians more than ever for not giving them aid and thus unsettle his border even more than it was at the moment. He phrased his refusal to send Mengesha Yohannes any ammunition with a careful deception by saying that the arsenal of Eritrea held a different caliber of cartridge than that needed by Mengesha.

In return for his "neutrality" which favored Menilek, Martini wanted his border with Tigray settled. Menilek kept putting off the matter with Ciccodicola, to whom it was relegated, and the border wanted by Italy was not settled until July 1900, long after Martini had expedited money and food to help the emperor's forces in Tigray.

Menilek left Addis Ababa with Empress Taytu and an army in early November 1898 to go to Were Ilu, not only to back up Ras Mekonnen but also to emphasize to Mengesha Yohannes that the consequence of his disobedience would be war. Martini's informers told him that Taytu, Ras Mikael and Ras Wele were still trying to dissuade the emperor from the use of force on Tigray.

At Were Ilu where Menilek and Taytu made camp, it was proclaimed on 6 December 1898 that Ras Mekonnen would rule Tigray and the Tigrayans were assured that Mekonnen would bring plenty of food with him so that the peasants need not fear despoliation. Naming Mekonnen as ruler before catching the incumbent was not an atypical procedure in Ethiopian changes of governors. However, it did serve to rally some Tigrayans around Ras Mengesha Yohannes, not because Mekonnen was not a fair and intelligent administrator, but because he was a Shewan of Shewans, an Amhara of Amharas. So Ras Mengesha Yohannes's counter-proclamation included the rallying cry, "Do you want to be ruled by a Shewan?" As one Tigrayan told Governor Martini, "Sure, Mengesha Yohannes is rabble ... yes, it was he who was the cause of the war [1895-6] but ... in Tigray better he than Mekonnen."

For almost three months, Ras Mekonnen's army, except for isolated incidents, followed orders not to take food and animals from defenseless people. Mekonnen recompensed anyone with a provable complaint against his soldiers, and whipped anyone caught in violation. Ras Mikael, who had joined his men to Mekonnen's, disciplined his soldiers by mutilation. This policy paid off, as people began to turn against Mengesha Yohannes. Neither the Tigrayans nor the imperial soldiers were keen on war.

Even as Mengesha Yohannes was forced to barricade himself in the old Italian fort at Edaghamus, he was still making ridiculous claims; he would commit suicide rather than knuckle under to Menilek; at the same time, he was asking Governor Martini by messenger to mediate some face-saving compromise that would enable him to keep an honorable share of land and possessions. He had sent his wife, Kefey Wele, about whom Empress Taytu was so concerned, to an amba for safety; his mother had taken refuge in the church at Aksum. Ras Sebhat, his principal, though very doubtful, ally, had done the same. They had a few cannons, about 7,000 guns and plenty of food in the fort at Edaghamus. From time to time, Mengesha Yohannes would dispatch a gift of food or liqueurs to Mekonnen as a display of wealth. He kept up an avalanche of correspondence with Governor Martini to the extent that Martini called him a "letter maniac" and reasoned that Mengesha was trying to compromise Italy in the eyes of Mekonnen and the emperor.

It was an earthquake, swore the chronicler, that finally shook Mengesha Yohannes. Only this sign of God's displeasure moved Mengesha to "separate himself from Satan." Events were somewhat different in Governor Martini's account, however.

Almost daily, peacemakers went from both Mekonnen and Mikael to the Tigrayan redoubt during the first two weeks of January 1899. Conditions hardly changed from meeting to meeting: he was to pay taxes, pay homage to the emperor by the coming September, cooperate with Ras Mekonnen, and send his son, Seyum, as hostage for his promises. In return, he could retain some authority and possessions. Ras Mekonnen took an oath that he, Mekonnen, and Empress Taytu would "go on their knees with stones on their necks" before Emperor Menilek to obtain a pardon for him.

The "shaking" of Ras Mengesha Yohannes occurred when it dawned on him that he and his men were surrounded. He accepted the terms for peace, and descended with Ras Sebhat from the fort to meet in a church with Ras Mikael and Ras Mekonnen on 18 January 1899. Joint proclamations were issued: in Mengesha Yohannes's name, "I have made peace to spare the country;" and in Mekonnen's name, "Peace is concluded and I have forbidden my soldiers to attack."

Governor Martini sent his congratulations to Mengesha Yohannes immediately and urged him not to wait until September to pledge, in person, his loyalty to the emperor. Martini assured him that Menilek had promised the Italian government that no harm would come to him. By the time Martini's letter reached the deposed Tigrayan lord, he was on his way to see the emperor, already persuaded by the words of Ras Mikael that it would be the judicious thing to do. Mengesha Yohannes insisted that Ras Mekonnen go with him to meet Menilek, so that there would be no reneging on the promises made by Mekonnen.

The messenger who delivered Martini's congratulations reported, "Ras Mengesha smiled, then handed it to Ras Sebhat, then to Ras Mikael." For some reason, this smile, or smirk, infuriated Martini. "He is an animal and a child: aside from shooting a gun, he understands nothing ... and can conceive of help only in terms of cartridges and guns ... I am not happy that Ras Mekonnen is in charge of Tigray — but Mengesha Yohannes is a true son of the corrupt house of Yohannes and has got the fate he deserves."

The fate of the lord of Tigray was that he would never see Tigray again. Empress Taytu and Mekonnen kept their promises to plead for a pardon, but Menilek was immovable, and broke every assurance to treat him with dignity. Menilek had had enough. For 10 years, lurking behind his disobedient acts, was Mengesha Yohannes's claim that he was the rightful emperor of Ethiopia.

Mengesha Yohannes was not put into chains, but was confined and watched constantly. Kefey Wele remained in Tigray until April 1900, well provided for: "The revenue of Temben goes to Gugsa Wele, Seyum Mengesha and Weyzero Kefey." Afterwards she came to see her aunt in Addis Ababa, accompanied by her half-brother Gugsa Wele, to beg for mercy for her husband. This devotion to a husband fallen from power was rare in the realm of political marriages. Kefey sustained it for three more years and gained the right to visit her husband in confinement. She had a child in April 1901, "on the road," after being seized by birth pangs while traveling

back to Addis Ababa from a visit to her husband.[5] When
Mengesha Yohannes was transferred to the state prison at Ankober,
she spent time with him there. The Italian legation doctor, Lincoln
de Castro, who had treated her in Addis Ababa and taken her
photograph, was in the Ankober area in February 1903 when he
received a message from her asking for champagne. He did not have
any with him, but sent some simple medicines back with his
apologies.[6] Later that year, she divorced Mengesha Yohannes and
remarried her former husband Nadew Abba Wello.*[7]

Despite the removal of Mengesha Yohannes and Ras Sebhat (who
had also been confined) from Tigray, the area remained unstable.
In June 1900 it began to quiet down when Ras Wele of Yejju replaced
Ras Mekonnen. Governor Martini was astonished at Wele's success,
as he had agreed with the prediction that "no one will submit to
Wele," and that "Mekonnen was not liked because no Shewan is
loved in Tigray, but Wele is haughty, proud, violent and ... Tigray
will be in constant ferment."[8] Two months after taking over, Wele
had received the submissions of most important Tigray chiefs. He
had also expelled the Catholic missionaries from Agame, and
prevented the Protestant Swedish mission from crossing Tigray to
distribute their newly-printed Oromo Bible in the southwest.[9]

Though Governor Martini was required to be officially concerned
over the expulsion of the missionaries, he privately expressed dislike
for them all, with the exception of the Swedish mission whose work
he much admired. Martini exchanged courteous letters with Ras Wele
and facilitated the delivery of talers and food, arranged through
Menilek's Italian credits. He realized that he could "live" with Wele,
when in July 1900, Menilek agreed on the border preferred by Italy,
an agreement for which Italy would pay five million lire.[10]

The chronicler described the appointment of Ras Wele to Tigray
as the "restoration" of the territory to its legitimate heir. The father
of Empress Taytu and Ras Wele was half-brother to Dejazmach Wube
who had conquered Tigray in 1831, invading it from his ancestral
province of Semen, and had ruled it until 1855. There were marital
connections with Tigrayan rulers† but to say that Ras Wele was

---

*Nadew was a man of some sophistication. He accompanied three other Ethiopians
to Paris in 1900 to represent Ethiopia at the exhibition, and in 1901 went with Abune
Matewos to Jerusalem and Russia.
†Dejazmach Wube's half-sister, Yewub-dar Hayle Maryam, was married to Sebagades,
a lord of Tigray. Kasa, son of Sebagades, was married to a daughter of Wube.

entitled to Tigray by heredity was very far-fetched. His governorship only lasted one year, and he was physically present only half of that time. After Wele the province was divided between three Tigrayans: Desta (the son of Ras Sebhat, still in detention), Gebre Selasse and Abreha Araya. The latter two had received some education in Italy and Gebre Selasse had been on the Italian side of the battle line during the war of 1895-6. Gebre Selassé was forgiven this position for a very good reason: he had kept secret contact with Emperor Menilek the entire time.[11] Gebre Selasse's father* had been a witness at Menilek's marriage to Aletash Tewodros and had become a friend of Menilek's uncle, Ras Darge, when they were all imprisoned at Meqdela.

These appointments boded well for Tigrayan-Eritrean relations, but brought only a temporary lull in Tigrayan-Shewan enmity, and "a new generation of hereditary princes went on with their internal rivalries" in Tigray.[12]

---

*Barya Gaber Farus was 79 years old when he died fighting the Mahdists at Metema in 1889.

12

Political marriage; women's rights; religious law and customary behavior

"Nearly half of Ethiopia is in the hands of her relatives."[1] Such was the geographical estimate of Empress Taytu's control of the country through nepotism, marriage alliances and accumulation of land grants.

Nepotism was the inseparable companion of absolute power as it encompassed the natural assumption that a relative was more trustworthy than a non-relative. There was nothing startling about it in Ethiopia where marriages that were seen to strengthen political cooperation had characterized centuries of the country's history. Taytu's property was a factor of her position as the wife of the emperor. The facile but basically correct formula, "a third of the land belongs to the church, a third to the crown, and the remaining third to everyone else," does not begin to describe the complexities of land tenure.[2]

The empress's holdings were divided between *gult* and *rist* and are listed in the chronicle. *Gult* was granted by the emperor, and the holder had the right to receive income from the people who worked it; *rist* was roughly equivalent to private ownership and was inherited within a family. Women had equal rights in inheritance law.* An Ethiopian savant in 1838 complained, "When women began inheriting land they lost their submissiveness and from that stemmed disrespect for marriage."[3] While Taytu had extensive areas under her control, her revenues (primarily food products) went to keep a huge domestic staff, to maintain many churches, and to arm, clothe and feed her personal army. She lived well but, for a monarch, with neither ostentation nor profligacy.[4]

What seemed to cause unease among foreigners was not only the personality of Empress Taytu, but also the idea of a woman being so powerful. The wives of European monarchs gave parties and cut ribbons; even Victoria, Queen of England and Empress of India, did not interfere unduly in government though she made her opinions known. It was obvious that Taytu was an adviser of Menilek, and

---

*Except in rare cases women had no control over their inherited land which was administered by her husband, son, brother or another male relative.

foreigners perceived this advice to be anti-foreign. Indeed she was more cynical than Menilek about statements made by diplomats in Addis Ababa, and certainly did not share her husband's delight in gadgets invented overseas. She asked questions that he did not: "Where will our poor country find the resources to satisfy the needs you create. Frankly do you think our people will be happier [with a railroad] than they are now?"[5]

The "half of Ethiopia" said to be under Taytu's influence was described in 1900: Ras Wele (her brother) controlled Tigray* and Yejju; Ras Gugsa Wele (her nephew) governed Begemder; Dejazmach Gesesse (her nephew) ruled Semen and Wolkit; Ras Welde Giyorgis (her cousin's husband, and also Menilek's cousin) ruled Keffa; and Ras Mekonnen was presumed to have fallen into her orbit by his marriage to her niece, Mentewab Wele. Governor Martini of Eritrea, who compiled this list, did not place Ras Mikael or Ras Tessema Nadew on it though he might have done were he using the marital or familial yardstick. Tessema Nadew, ruler of Ilu Babor, was married to Taytu's god-daughter, and the children of the widowed Ras Mikael by Shewa Regga Menilek lived under her care in the palace. Taytu's cousin, Bayenetch Merso,[†] was married to a nobleman of Menz, a rich wool producing district.[6]

The empress had good reason to make whatever advantageous connections she could. Menilek did not have an acceptable male heir[‡] and Taytu was childless. What would happen to her if Menilek died? There was no better way for Taytu to insure her future than to maintain close personal relations with all possible candidates for the throne. Yet this very natural, very human prudence was viewed as wicked.

The marital link with Ras Mekonnen, judged by many to be Menilek's choice of successor, or at least of regent for an under-age heir, was the result of years of pressure by Taytu. In January 1901, after a long private meal with the empress, Ras Mekonnen agreed to marry Mentewab Wele. Mekonnen was about 50 and the girl was about 10. Ras Mekonnen took her to Harar, where she was cosseted and guarded by eunuchs who had to undergo daily inspections before

---

*Ras Wele's rule of Tigray lasted only until January 1901 when he returned to Yejju.
†Bayenetch was described by Gebre Heywet as very influential on Taytu, and much hated by her own retinue.
‡The objection to Wesen Seged, Shewa Regga's son by Wadijo Gobena, was based on his physical imperfection — dwarfism.

taking up their duties. "I was told," wrote Dr. Paul Mérab, "that one of these eunuchs, tired of being inspected, said to the ras, "I have been with you since infancy and you want to look at my organ? Is it a stalk of corn that grows each year?" A year and a half later, in May 1902, Mekonnen returned the child, *intacta*, to her aunt and urged the empress to marry her to someone else.* The empress was furious, everyone said, though there was no effect on Menilek's trust in Mekonnen.[7]

Also in 1901, Empress Taytu arranged that another niece marry Ras Mekonnen's son, Yilma. This niece was Aselefetch Welde Hanna, still young but already thrice-married. Yilma was purportedly legitimized by his father at the behest of the empress, but others say he had already been recognized after saving his father's life at the battle of Adwa. Recognition as Mekonnen's heir may have always been intended since Yilma was known to be Mekonnen's son and had been raised with other young nobles at Menilek's court.[8]

The most important political marriage of 1900 was that of Taytu's nephew, Gugsa Wele, to Menilek's daughter, Zewditu. It was Zewditu's fourth and final marriage at the age of about 27. Gugsa Wele was promoted to ras and made governor of Begemder province upon this marriage.

Zewditu's marital history was a sad one. Her first husband, Araya Yohannes, died and left her a widow at 13. He had fathered a son by another woman. She divorced her second, Wagshum Gwangul Zegeye, after only a few months; by him she had a child who died. She divorced her third husband, Wube Atnaf Seged, because he struck her for having an affair with Liqemekwas Abate or insulted her by saying she was not really the daughter of the emperor, or at the insistence of Empress Taytu.[9] Her marriage to Gugsa Wele, who had been described as "one of the most enlightened men of the Ethiopian nobility, a renowned poet, great lover of books, and pious and fair in the administration of Begemder," endured. This notwithstanding, a report in 1903 stated that he was summoned to Addis Ababa to answer a charge by Zewditu that he had mistreated her.[10]

To conclude that Mentewab, Aselefetch and Zewditu were unhappy, unwilling pawns of the empress is to misunderstand the position of the female child in this society, and Empress Taytu's responsibility to them. "Taytu brought all her relations to the palace

---

*She was married to Kebede Mengesha Atikem in March 1903, and died in January 1907.

and considered them adopted — like royal children."[11] It was her duty to arrange marriages that would be economically advantageous for them, and at the same time serve the needs of the state. Opportunities for power-brokering were provided by the deaths of three important men in 1900 and 1901. In March 1900 the court went into deep mourning for Ras Darge who had been like a father to Menilek. He had fought wars for him,* advised him, deputized for him when he had left the capital, negotiated on his behalf with Emperor Yohannes, and had always remained completely loyal. The traders in Addis Ababa would also miss Ras Darge for they could rely on him to press Menilek to pay his bills.

By his three known wives, Ras Darge had had five sons and three daughters. He had been unlucky in his sons: his eldest had died in a fall from a horse in 1882; Desta had died in 1893, allegedly poisoned; Gugsa had gone to be educated in Switzerland in 1894, been suborned by the Italians during the war of 1895-6 and was considered "dead" by his father;† and Asfaw, who shared with his brother Tessema the rich agricultural resources of Salale after Ras Darge's death. He was arrested for treason in 1901. It was said that Darge had warned Menilek before he died that his son Asfaw was somewhat deranged on the subject of succeeding to the throne. Tessema Darge never won Menilek's trust. According to Darge's stepson:

My mother married Tessema Darge. He was very kind, refined and intelligent and since he loved my mother he treated me as his own son. The sad thing was, being afraid of Menilek, he always took precautions I still remember. There was a man ... a spy for Menilek who would stay overnight at our house. My mother said, "He comes to spy," and was fearful. Tessema Darge pretended not to know about him and treated him as a friend ... but was very careful about what he said.[12]

Darge's daughters fared better. Weyzero Tisseme had fulfilled her duty to the state in 1869 by marrying the chief of Lasta to seal a pact made by Menilek, but after a son was born in 1881 she was divorced and returned to Shewa to marry her father's factotum,

---

*Darge's death was not mourned in Awsa which he had conquered brutally for Menilek.

†The disappearance of the "Abyssinian princes" from Neuchâtel in 1895 was in the European newspapers for weeks. First it was said that they were "kidnapped" and then that they had gone willingly. Gugsa Darge and Kitaw Zamanel (son of Empress Taytu's major-domo) were asked in 1900 if they would like to be repatriated at Italian expense. At first they agreed, then changed their minds fearing what might happen to them on their return.

Dejazmach Welde Tsadiq. Weyzero Askale had a son and a daughter
by her first husband, Fitawrari Mạnyahlihal, and then married
Fitawrari Damtew* on his return from Russia in 1895; he died at
the battle of Adwa. The third daughter, Weyzero Tsehaye Werq,
was unusually independent. She refused to marry, but had a number
of "lodgers." She was a good shot, a good horsewoman and "did
not like staying in the house behind a curtain. She knew how to make
shirts and socks and liked to knit gloves as women do in Europe.
She was on good terms with Menilek and Taytu and was called
'*balemwal*' [favorite]," though her political activism caused her to
be placed under house arrest on one occasion.[13]

The last male scions of Ras Darge died in 1906: Asfaw in prison
and Tessema at his home. Weyzero Tisseme's son carried the honor
of the family.[†]

When Gojam's king, Tekle Haymanot, died in January 1901 it was
a less emotional blow for the emperor then the death of his uncle,
but it opened the door to political machinations that plagued Gojam
for many years. Tekle Haymanot had ruled for the better part of
33 years. After his death, his legal wife of 30 years, Laqetch Gebre
Medhin, wrote to the emperor to inform him of her husband's wish
that she rule Gojam after him. But Tekle Haymanot had three grown
sons, each by a woman other than Laqetch. The eldest, Belew, had
rebelled openly against his father in 1890 and fled to Shewa, where
he was arrested and handed back to his father. Bezebeh, another
son, was accused of trying to poison his father in 1891 and was
remanded in Menilek's custody at court. Seyum, about 19, was said
to be his father's favorite, but he too had quarreled with him.[14]

Weyzero Laqetch's claims were not taken seriously,[‡] though she
was said to be capable of holding her own militarily, through the

---

*He had two sons from another marriage, Abebe and Desta. Abebe distinguished
himself in the 1935 defense against Italy; after defeat he lived in Jerusalem until the
end of the Italian occupation in 1941. Desta, who was the son-in-law of Emperor
Hayle Selasse, was shot by an Italian firing squad, suspected of complicity in the
assassination attempt on Marshal Graziani.
†Kasa Haylu was named Ras in 1916 and Leul-Ras (high prince) at the coronation
of Hayle Selasse in 1930. He led an army against the Italians in 1935-6 and went into
exile in Jerusalem and England until the restoration in 1941. He was appointed president
of the crown council, a position he held until his death in 1956.
‡Laqetch was offended by Emperor Yohannes who denied private audience to women.
When she was granted a public reception she defended her husband, Tekle Haymanot,
from the rebuke by the emperor for going to war with Menilek in 1882. It was said
(Vigoni) that she attracted Menilek's attentions when he invaded Gojam in 1877.

army of her son-in-law, Ras Mesfin of Damot. An obvious dislike of Laqetch was the theme of one of the folk songs addressed to her in Gojam, "Defend yourself — yourself! Why, among all of your subjects, do none of them love you?"[15]

Two of Tekle Haymanot's rebellious sons, Bezebeh and Belew, were in Addis Ababa when news of their father's death arrived and they actively competed for the emperor's attention. Menilek postponed the problem of succession in Gojam, meanwhile lopping off portions in the south and northwest to reward two non-Gojami appointees who would keep an eye on the province. He then named the third son, Seyum Tekle Haymanot, to central Gojam. Seyum Tekle Haymanot was summoned to Addis Ababa on the anniversary of his father's death in January 1902 and was required to bring with him some cohorts of his father whom he had chained. Among these cohorts was his half-sister's husband, Ras Mesfin.

Seyum told the emperor that he carried proof in letters written by Ras Mesfin and others that they contemplated treason. The emperor acted as detective and judge, using a scientific method to discern that the letters were forgeries. The chronicler found Menilek's method amazing enough to record: Menilek used a compass to measure the circumference of the seals on the letters, and then compared them to the seals belonging to the accused. In this way he discovered that they were forgeries! The emperor consigned the forger, Seyum, to Dejazmach Tessema in Ilu Babor, and named to the post his half-brother, Bezebeh, to whom he gave the title of Ras.

Empress Taytu did not have any direct ties with Gojam, but would shortly remedy that lack.[16] Bezebeh Tekle Haymanot must have found favor with the empress during his years of detention at court, for in 1903 he returned to Addis Ababa to claim his child bride, Zenebe Werq Mikael, Menilek's granddaughter. Zenebe Werq was the subject of one of those concoctions so dear to European writers, in which a little truth and a lot of imagination fused into a heart-rending story. Hugues le Roux told how Zenebe Werq happened to be living with her imperial grandfather in 1897. When news of her mother's death was brought to Menilek he was in the middle of a religious and military fête, and immediately suspended the celebration. "I want neither songs nor salvos. My daughter [Shewa Regga] is not dead. Her soul is in the child she left behind. Have her brought to me. Ras Mikael can marry another woman,* but I had only one daughter." Le Roux seems to have misplaced Menilek's other daughter, the even better-known Zewditu.

Zenebe Werq was brought up with warmth and affection, "close to the hearts of Menilek and Taytu." She learned to read and write and say her Psalms. Then came the day for her marriage to 35-year-old Ras Bezebeh. After a grand wedding, she went to live at Debre Marqos in Gojam, and one year later she died. "Struck by the sun's rays, complicated by homesickness," was one diagnosis, but *sotto voce* they said other things. Though only about 12 years old, it was sadly possible that she died in childbirth. Her husband, Bezebeh Tekle Haymanot, was convicted in 1905 of plotting against one of Menilek's pro-consuls in Gojam, and died in prison in the same year.[17]

Negadras Agidew's death in October 1900 changed the status of two women, both named Yetemegnu. Agidew's widow, a distant relation of Empress Taytu, "arrived [in Addis Ababa] to mourn her husband whom she deserted when he was sick," said Dr. Martin.[18] Her real purpose was to petition the emperor for retention of her husband's crown grant. Yetemegnu† succeeded and was seen ruling Weldya, a "center of commerce" in Yejju, at the age of 65. "She is president of the tribunal, commands the militia and attends the atrocious mutilations her court hands out as sentences."[19] A neglectful wife was a phenomenon seen often by Dr. Mérab in his practice. "A wife was the last person to be attentive to a sick husband. It is common for a divorce to follow a grave illness, as the woman does not want to be saddled with the expenses attached to funerals."[20]

The second Yetemegnu was Empress Taytu's niece. She would marry the successor to Negadras Agidew, his assistant, Hayle Giyorgis. A man of no aristocratic pedigree, Hayle Giyorgis would develop an unprecedented control of trade through his selection of regional "trade commissioners," change the system of customs collections to raise substantially the revenues going into the imperial

---

*Not long after, Ras Mikael married by communion service a woman named Zenebech.
†Yetemegnu Wele was given the title Bejirond (treasurer) by Ras Wele, according to her grandson Imru Zelleke. She and Wele were not related. The same source says that she had indeed separated from her husband, but neither because he was sick nor because she wanted to avoid expenses of a funeral. Imru Zelleke's account differed greatly from Dr. Mérab's observation, saying even the poorest family could afford the funeral feast because everyone contributed. His grandmother, he said, would not have missed her husband's *teskar* as it was a very large court-attended event.

treasury and his own, and become one of the richest and most important men in Ethiopia. His importance may have partly compensated Yetemegnu Alula for her abrupt separation from her then husband, Shum Temben Gebre Medhin, "without divorce, separation, or even a quarrel, merely her aunt's command. When summoned to the palace, she pleaded indisposition but was told to come anyway. Her suite waited outside for hours. About five o'clock in the afternoon, they inquired about her. The guards laughed. She is being married right now to Hayle Giyorgis."[21]

Undeniably Empress Taytu expanded her power however and whenever the opportunity presented itself. Certainly, the empire of Ethiopia had rarely seen her like before,* but the empire had never been so large, prosperous or stable. Taytu had shared in that development, therefore she shared its advantages. She saw her power as a simple restoration of privilege to those who deserved it. "The Lord never forgets the injustices of the past and recompensed the sons of Dejazmach Betul by having Itege Taytu attain government and by placing on the *alga* of their ancestors Ras Wele and others."

"Half of Ethiopia" in the hands of Taytu's relatives was an imprecise measure but essentially true, and it apparently suited the emperor that it be so. The chronicler summed up her accomplishment: "Itege Taytu applied herself not only to feminine works, but like quicksilver attended to perplexing business usually done by men, and succeeded at it."

This is an exceptional admission for a royal chronicle considering the unequal status of men and women in Ethiopia. No society structured either by custom or religion is equally fair to men and women, and Ethiopia was not unique in its emphasis on the inferiority of women in folklore and religious texts, nor was religious hypocrisy exclusive to this society. What mystified those who observed Ethiopian society was the combination of the absence of the sense of guilt inculcated by Judaic-Christian doctrines, the

---

*Itege Elleni, one of the wives of Emperor Zara Yaqob (1434-68) directed the country, "because she knew how to govern the royal house" during the minority of Emperor Lebna Dengel (1508-40). Her story is related in Lebna Dengel's chronicle. Itege Mentewab, wife of Bekaffa (1721-30), was treated generously in the chronicle of her son Iyasu II (1730-55). Her beauty is stressed and then her administrative ability. Iyasu II said "make my mother reign ... as without her my reign cannot go on." Her hand was firm as she was unpopular with some nobles who mounted rebellions against her. Both of these empresses exercised power in a far less complex geographical area than the expanded empire of Ethiopia in 1900.

ostentatious observance of ritual, prayer and fasting, and the high frequency of divorce. As to why the Amhara and Tigrayans had strayed so blatantly from the ideal of Christian marriage there are a number of hypotheses but no certain explanation.

One hypothesis rests on their geographical position surrounded by a Muslim world, and their demographic mix of Muslim and animist peoples. The Islamic practice of having three or four wives influenced the Christians, asserted one historian, and in turn some of the Ethiopian Muslims, those called Jabarti, adopted the practice of having only one wife who went about unveiled and enjoyed considerable liberty. On the face of it, the Muslim impact was the stronger.[22]

A brief look at history, the book of law, the concept of masculinity and the view of women in folklore, and some observations by foreigners serve to demonstrate the uniqueness of the matrimonial customs of Ethiopian Christians. In having both civil and religious marriage they were not exceptional, but marriage for a stated length of time on a salary (*damoz*) for the female partner was an original contribution.

Imperial marriage in history

Kings, provincial rulers and emperors had been openly polygamous, with a "queen of the right, a queen of the left," and uncounted concubines at their courts. A 12th-century emperor had attempted reform with the edict, "Let every man live with one wife and every woman with one husband." A remarkably brave churchman in the 14th century had denounced Emperor Amda Siyon for his un-Christian matrimonial habits and was beaten and exiled. The first monogamous emperor in centuries was said to have been Lebna Dengel (1508-40), but his example went unheeded. As Francisco Alvarez noted during his stay in Ethiopia from 1520 to 1526, "the man who had plenty of food kept two or three wives, even though he could neither enter the church nor receive its sacraments because of them."[23]

Emperor Tewodros (1855-68) tried by edict and example to bring some dignity into the marriage contract. Emperor Yohannes's celibacy after his wife's death and Menilek's communion marriage to Taytu were indications that they agreed that the free ways of ordinary men and women were inappropriate to a monarchy that boasted of its anointment by God, though Menilek had trouble with the concept of fidelity.

Marriage, divorce and adultery in law and in practice

The *Fetha Nagast*, the law book of Ethiopia, had specific behests on marriage, sex, contraception, adultery and divorce. Marriage was the right of every child, and parents could be sued for failing to fulfil this obligation.[24] Marriage at 12 for a girl and 20 for a boy was the rule of the *Fetha Nagast*, but it was not observed. The adage, "A third marriage is a sign of depravity," was ignored. By that standard, most of the prominent personages in the empire were "depraved," and a good percentage of the population as well. Antonelli wrote that "there was hardly a girl over 10 who was a virgin, or a woman of 30 who had not had five or six husbands," and Mérab said, "The clergy told me that not one girl in a thousand was a virgin at the age of 12." Their statements were not arrived at scientifically, but were certainly supported by individual case histories and by the repetitiveness of the observation by all the other foreigners.[25]

Lust, or concupiscence, as the *Fetha Nagast* terms it, was a terrible thing, but as one man cheerfully confessed to Dr. Mérab, "I am young, I am on fire ... the devil pushes you to infidelity and the girls are so pretty. One can marry in the church only when one's blood begins to cool ... and there are so many separations because of military service or hunting expeditions." Mérab commented, "The Ethiopians transgress the law of marriage with the pretext of better observing it."

Even married sex was a defiler of self for no one could take communion or even enter a church if that person had had sexual intercourse in the previous 24 hours. A menstruating woman or a person of either sex who had had relations in the past 24 hours could spoil the honey beer if they walked into the place where it was being made.[26] Sexual relations were forbidden during Lent and Holy Week. "No impure person may enter the presence of a newly baptized child, nor may a virgin wife know her husband for the first time on Sunday." The taeniacide, *kosso*, would not work "if the shadow of a man who had slept with a woman fell on him," and the *lebasha* (thief-finder) had to be a lad who had never touched a woman. "The churches were empty," commented Pollera, "people congregated outside," and a popular joke made by a gentleman when his wife said, "Tomorrow I will go to church," was "If I wish."[27] What could have been easily lied about was apparently strictly observed and suggests a certain pride in the weakness of the flesh.

The Ethiopian church shared with other religions the belief that the purpose of sexual congress was to have children. "Shedding the seed outside the uterus," was prohibited, and no "poison" was to be given against conception. Relations during menstruation were forbidden as "the genital organ would be spoiled," and "leprosy would befall a child conceived at that time." "A menstruating woman may not enter the church even if she is from the royal family."

Adultery was condemned because a preoccupied adulteress might fail to provide food, the children might lack affection and there could be uncertainty about the parenthood of the offspring. Punishment for an adulteress had to be more severe than for the sinning male because, "the aim of law was to remove difficulties from men." A cuckolded husband might kill his transgressing wife* which would make enemies of his wife's father, brother and mother. That was a "difficulty" to be avoided. The deceived wife could just divorce her husband, take her dowry and a third of his property, a custom that was fair and non-violent.

Adultery by wives left behind during the war of 1895-6 was very common. There were so many reprisals when the husbands returned that an edict was broadcast stipulating that murder was unjustified, a fine of 40 talers being sufficient. Observers in Tigray found adultery uncommon because separation was simple to arrange, and divorce occurred more often because of incompatibility or because the woman aspired to a richer husband, rather than for sexual reasons or jealousy. Ladies were discreet, they said, not because they might lose their lives but because they might lose their dowries.[28]

Beating was the most common complaint women had against men. In Tigray, the victim or her family could demand a fine for this abuse, and a husband only abandoned the practice when he could not afford it anymore. Bodily harm was a ground for divorce in the *Fetha Nagast*, as were also the preference of either spouse for the religious life; the denial of conjugal rights; lack of news from an absent spouse (with the proviso of a two-year wait if he had gone away because of war and a five-year delay if he had been imprisoned); insanity or leprosy if contracted before the marriage and kept secret; impotence; and the lack of femininity in a woman. The last named could mean infertility or frigidity; it could also mean incompetence at domestic duties.

---

*In August 1913 the Minister of Finance, Fitawrari Ibsa, killed the lover of his wife and got off with a small fine.

Sterility, always assumed to be the fault of the woman, did not always lead to divorce. If the couple liked each other, the wife might select a servant to bear her husband's child and raise it as her own. Drs. Mérab and Annaratone found a very high incidence of sterility which they blamed on the prevalence of venereal disease.* Mérab also attributed sterility to marriage at a young age, the use of certain plants by women to induce abortion, and vigorous vaginal douching that he observed women engaging in at the river each morning and night. The *afenegus* told Mérab that abortion was not prosecuted unless the husband was the accuser, and that the Abyssinians believed the foetus had no soul until the fourth month. Both the famous[†] and the common man suffered from syphilis and gonorrhea and the frequent exchange of sexual partners naturally facilitated the spread of venereal disease. The recipe books of local medical practitioners were filled with formulae for treating these diseases.[29]

Men complained about the talkativeness of women. "Three things disturb life — a notorious king, an evil neighbor and a complaining woman." "There is no trouble, no quarrel worse than a loud, bad woman. It is better to live with lions and snakes than her ... catastrophe and darkness is she ... and a woman who gets drunk and roams about and never covers up her sex organs is an unhealthy excitement." These sayings are from the *Book of the Wise Philosophers*, which also advises consultation with others, but never with a woman.[30] The *Fetha Nagast* says: "Women shall not teach nor be made members of the clergy and none but clergy can act as judges," and "nuns, pious widows and virgins must not raise their voices when they speak, or quarrel or sue someone for worldly objects." In actuality, women became skilful legal pleaders and their advice was listened to deferentially. They were popular as soothsayers, dream analyzers and reconcilers of husbands and wives. One novel explanation for the distrust of women was that there had once been an empress who vexed her male subjects with the impossible order for a house to be built above the earth and below the heavens. "Yet in Shewa there are women who surpass men in

---

*What venereal disease caused was not sterility, for conception can take place, but still-births and infants too sickly to survive.

[†]Emperor Menilek, Afenegus Nessibu and Ras Darge for example; the last two named died following a rigorous Ethiopian treatment for the disease. There was a saying among the conquered and forcibly converted Oromo and Keffans, "Marry an Abyssinian and receive syphilis at the same time as the *mateb* [the thread worn around the neck of a Christian]."

pleading ... [she] will stand before the judge ... and stretch out her hand and stamp like a man." One district governor in Eritrea tried to restrict red umbrellas to aristocratic women. "No American or British suffragette could match these women in energetic protest and the order was rescinded."[31]

Women could be as noisy as they liked when it was a question of admiration for a man's virility which was equated with aggressiveness. Killing an animal, capturing a slave, bringing back the genitalia of an enemy killed in battle — men admired each other for these deeds and women encouraged them. Though the *Fetha Nagast* is concerned primarily with the privileged members of the Amhara-Tigray* society, submission in females and aggressiveness in males were the qualities most admired in many other ethnic groups.[32] Neither the *Fetha Nagast* nor the *Book of the Wise Philosophers* glorifies aggressive behavior, but these books were written in Ge'ez, a language far removed from the understanding of ordinary mortals. Moral precepts and the philosophy to get through a life in which demons and evil spirits vie with the power of the supreme being and all the saints in heaven reside in the proverbs and folktales of everyday speech.

The language of everyday life

Proverbs and sayings are without prudery. "The nipple is inside out, the mouth is crooked," is said of a woman not capable of discussing a serious issue. Other sayings run as follows:

There are times of trust when one can show the hair on the genitals; there are times of distrust to make one conceal the hair of one's armpits.
Man is killed by what comes out of his mouth; the woman by what comes from her genitals.
Too much knowledge forces a finger into one's anus.
Women with their indiscretions and dogs with their turds ruin the country.[33]

A bawdy sense of humor was not restricted to the lewd songs sung by women carrying loads on campaigns. Paul Soleillet described a party of women at the house of Ras Darge's wife:

---

*One of the generalizations made by Plowden in the 1850s was that Amhara women were gentle and kind of heart while Tigray women were disagreeable, harsh-voiced, claimed equal rights with their husbands and had little tact, but were more faithful.

Some fat crow sat there. They told me he was the fool or buffoon of the women and that I was not to get angry at whatever he said to me. The women were convulsed with laughter after he said, "I would like many women if their *cul* wasn't so vast; their *cul* is too big, so big that if it were allowed I would put my whole head in, but I would have to hold my nose, as the *cul* of women holds the evil of the world."[34]

Even Empress Taytu enjoyed the "Rabelaisian wit and sly solutions to human problems" of the resident story teller in her entourage. She was said to be so fond of this man, Aleqa Gebre Hanna, that she protected him from Menilek's wrath when he overstepped the bounds of humor and mocked Shewa as "that Galla province."[35]

The empress would not have been amused at some of the poetry she appeared in. "O Taytu, O my Taytu; your news has reached us; you take a man in the evening and lie with him in the morning; then you pierce him," which meant that after enjoying a lover she would kill him and call another to her bed.[36]

Despite the businesslike attitude towards marriage and the mundanity of divorce, romantic notions thrived in songs and poems praising the legs, firm breasts, lips, teeth, calves, neck, ears or eyes of the beloved woman. "Alas! Taste once her lips; all day I go without spitting as I have received communion."[37]

Unusual for its length (91 lines) and style, one poem was the Amharic version of the Cole Porter song, "You're The Top," only the merits of the love object were likened to some outstanding characteristic of a successful person, someone in authority, or a foreign group. For example, "You're [like] Ras Mikael who killed [while] laughing ... [like] the French who know how to talk ... [like] Jivagee [Hindu store owner] who says 'I have money.' " Two lines of the poem refer to Empress Taytu: "You're [like] Empress Taytu who says 'Cut him in two;' " and in the other line she is so jealous of this paragon of a woman that she wants to exile her. Disguised as a paean of praise for the lady, Teruwerq, it was also a political satire and probably won laughs from the assemblage of men before whom it was read.[38]

One occupation exclusive to women was that of singer at a funeral, and those who performed their laments with artistry* were well paid

---

*The more exaggerated, the more artistic, as in the song recorded on the death of Emperor Gelawdewos (1540-59): "Happy the sterile women who have neither conceived nor given birth and whose breasts have no milk. They are happy not to have any children, who would have seen, like we have, the grief caused by [his] death."

and enjoyed high status.[39] Tattooers, hairdressers, potters and basket-makers were women. Otherwise there was the profession of trader, or of wife, which entailed cooking, processing grains, carrying water, fetching firewood, collecting dung, gardening, spinning cotton, and brewing *tej* and *tella* [beer made from wheat]. And there was the profession of prostitute.

The dividing lines between the salaried wife, the "thigh maid" of the military expedition, the courtesan, the *madama* of the Italian soldier, and the prostitute were very fine until the late 19th century. The chronicle of Emperor Iyasu (1682-1706) mentions a fire that broke out in Gondar in the house of a *gelemota*, understood to mean a woman of easy virtue. The same manuscript contains an edict that could be interpreted as anti-licentiousness: "The king had the herald proclaim that girls must not ride astride mules ... tightening the belts of their skirts and holding a spear in their hand following the expedition's march like men."[40]

There were many words to designate the woman who sold her sexual favors, but the one which became the most commonly used was *shermuta*, an Arabic word, popularized by itinerant Muslim traders who were the main clients.

The travelers of the 1840s described unattached women as courtesans and said they were much respected. "What is to us an insult, far from being odious in Abyssinia, is a respectable title. They maintain themselves in absolute independence, display great luxury of dress, and many have retinues like queens; kings have a deference for them which has something of gallantry. The courtesans charge dearly for the love they grant and not everyone who wishes receives the favors of these ladies." "They are not despised here as by us," wrote Cecchi in the 1870s. "Beautiful Ethiopian women were much sought after and renowned in the towns of the coast," and after a time would return home with a small horde of talers and have no trouble finding a husband, wrote Vigoni in 1881.[41]

The *madamas* of the Italians in Eritrea were a proud lot. "Often young girls were offered to us by their parents, for if they came from a low class, their daughter immediately acquired the title of Weyzero, or great dame." The ceremony of alliance consisted of cleaning the girl, and cutting her hair to get rid of the unpleasant smell of rancid butter with which it was dressed. The Italian soldier's obligation was to buy her a *tukul*, furnish it with a bed, a couple of wooden stools and some earthenware pots. Each month she would receive a sack of grain and a small sum of money. One visitor gave this account of her:

Today [1896] there has been a rise in prices ... but they do not carry on over modistes and couturiers [the way European mistresses do]. Nevertheless they are abominably coquettish, even more than Parisians, and if united to an officer, their ambition knows no limits. He has to give them presents — silver bracelets, necklaces, earrings, chemises, shawls, European toiletries and finally goats and even cows. They are very orderly and frugal. But when the time comes for showing themselves off and making visits, they know the art of persuading their lord and master that for his dignity, his *madama* must be elegant ... and here in Africa as in Europe, husbands fall weakly into the snare held by a clever woman. She must have her own mount — for an elegant woman cannot go about on foot. On her calling days, she reminds one of the European *mondaine*. She is preoccupied with her toilet, is nervous and the mule must be clean and glistening and have a rich harness. She mounts astride and with her umbrella in most brilliant red* she is preceded by a sub-officer who carries a gun. The *madama* of a captain takes a superior attitude to the *madama* of a lieutenant.

Outside of her flirtatiousness, so natural and excusable, the Abyssinian woman has qualities not found in civilized countries. Very intelligent, she learns Italian with astonishing rapidity and can sustain a conversation with ease. She adjusts quickly to our habits and it is amazing to see them in a short time learn to cook, wash, sew and iron to our liking. I even saw one in Massawa use the sewing machine. In the conjugal life they are sweet and devoted and never abuse our trust. Extraordinary as it may seem, they are faithful. Rarely during my stay in Eritrea did I hear of a betrayal. But I fear this will change. We will teach these people a lot of things that as yet they do not know exist. Women will hear of independence. This will be too bad for the husbands.[42]

When these Italian soldiers were reassigned, they left their *madamas* relatively well off. Some would take up with another officer, and others might marry one of their countrymen. They were not prostitutes. It was the Ethiopian contract marriage, *damoz*, without the contract.

In a very short time, Eritrea had houses of prostitution *per se*, and their occupants underwent inspection by Italian doctors. In 1900 one of these medical inspectors, Dr. Ambrogetti, wrote a pamphlet entitled *La Vita Sessuale nell'Eritrea*, which enjoyed a brisk sale in Italy. In it he said that *shermuta* were either from poor families who had not yet managed to marry them off, or had been abandoned by a husband for not becoming pregnant.

---

*Only in the Italian colony could she carry a red umbrella; in Ethiopia proper, only royalty could carry red.

He was impressed by their cleanliness, which he said defined them quite clearly from honest married women. The *shermuta* washed herself often from head to toe with soap, but her Italian patron had to get used to the smell of rancid butter and civet of which she reeked. Dr. Ambrogetti had been with the Italian troops during the siege of Adigrat in 1896 and said that cleanliness was so important to a *shermuta* that she never failed to show up for her rendezvous with a little pail of water.

Their pudenda, he said, were bare of hair because they plucked it out.

In their sexual relations, *shermuta* were very reserved, never exposing their private parts in daylight and at night they would put out the light before undressing. They do not allow any position other than the one in which the woman is supine and never touch the genitals of men nor let themselves be touched and never permit cunnilingus. They reject with horror any kind of sexual perversion and for such proposals have a phrase, "Hands are for working, mouths are for eating, cunt is for copulation."

Ambrogetti found only one pair of prostitutes who conducted a lesbian relationship, and opined that the rarity of homosexuality among women as well as among men was the result of the general air of sexual freedom: "This filthy plant [homosexuality] puts its roots down among us in colleges, barracks and prisons."

Prostitution in Addis Ababa was often related to drinking houses where the proprietress sold *tej* or *tella*. In 1908 Dr. Mérab counted about 50 such shed-type houses with about four women in each. Not all *tej* sellers were prostitutes. Mérab recounted how one of his domestics married a young woman who had been the mistress of a European. Two months later they were divorced, and when Mérab commiserated with the young woman over the short length of her marriage she said without regret that she had no need of a husband. "I have my commerce in *tej* which is enough."[43]

"Christ has said he will put fire in the mouth of a person who takes interest money. But he has promised that he will forgive *shermuta*," a prostitute told an investigator. The prostitutes were very religious, going to church on patron saints' days, burning incense, covering their floors with rushes on religious holidays and attending to all kinds of rituals.[44]

No opinions of Empress Taytu on the subject of prostitution appear to have been recorded. It is possible that she appreciated not only the economic alternatives for women but also their equality before

God. She did, however, have opinions on marriage, for, in a conversation with an English woman she said that she thought it commendable that couples become acquainted before marrying. Moreover, Mérab said:

The only thing she liked and admired in Europeans was that in our countries we urge, and rightly so, respect and affection for women. "For this custom," she said, "these European riff-raff should be imitated." She, if not a feminist in theory, is a wary and practical protector of her sex. She listened willingly to complaints that women lodged against their husbands, brothers, fathers or sons.

She backed Menilek in his assessment of divorce damages to be paid to Weyzero Nigist Tekle Haymanot* by her husband, Gesesse Welde Hanna, for his adultery with a Muslim, even though Gesesse was her nephew.[45]

The empress and her clerical advisers were responsible for an edict issued in 1909 threatening dire punishment to anyone who divorced after a communion marriage. The edict was not particularly daring since very few couples united in this bond; admittedly his knowledge was limited, but Dr. Mérab could think of only seven such marriages in Addis Ababa. The edict could have been more of a slap at Abune Matewos, the only one who could grant these divorces, than any attempt at reform. The empress had quarreled with the head of the church about various matters by this time. Mérab's informant told him, "Abune Matewos goes against our religion."[46]

One might conclude from this survey that there were no happy families in Ethiopia. Such an assessment would not be true. Within this bewildering socio-religious system, grace, generosity, kindness, mutual respect, tenderness and laughter abounded. Though childhood is short, children were loved and cared for.

The emperor never touched the subject of child marriage though he made ineffectual edicts to reform behavior at funerals: "Abstain from disorderly demonstrations and follow the procession silently as it is done in Europe." He also made recommendations on health matters: "Be innoculated," and "Boil water, wash clothes and burn

---

*Nigist Tekle Haymanot, having been divorced from Ras Mesfin by whom she had had three children, was the object of competitive marriage bids from Merid Mengesha Atikem and Gesesse. She asked the emperor's advice but he told her to decide; her choice of Gesesse almost resulted in a war between the two suitors which was resolved by the threat of troops going from Addis Ababa to support Gesesse.

dead animals." Not until the 1930s, in two Amharic novellas by
Heruy Welde Selasse, was there open advocacy of the prohibition
of child marriage (that is, marriage under the age of 15) and the
suggestion that arranged marriages resulted in frequent divorce which
the author called the "curse of Ethiopian family life." Contract
marriage is no longer legal, but is said to persist, and a divorced
father still has the right to claim custody of his child at the age of
four.[47]

13

"In Ethiopia they begin to speak by wire"

The laying of a telegraph line that was begun in 1897 and the completion of telephonic communication between Harar and Addis Ababa by 1899 were a triumph over superstitious resistance to any technological idea other than firearms or medical treatment.[1] They were a breakthrough for Emperor Menilek.

In 1890, Ras Mekonnen had returned from Italy with a telephone apparatus. The French man-of-all-work, Stévenin, was called to the *gibbi* and asked to make it work. He hooked up a wire between the royal residence and the house of the imperial treasurer who had a "thunderous voice." The sovereign, surrounded by his court at one end of the wire held the receiver and exchanged a few words with the treasurer. Stévenin described the reaction:

Suddenly, Menilek stood up, leaving the receiver on the table and went out on the verandah to see if by any chance the treasurer was behind the window.

A group of priests suddenly arrived. They said, "Cut it off immediately ... that machine is inhabited by a demon!" Since I was the one who had made it work I was warned by a friendly cleric not to get mixed up in theological matters. Menilek exclaimed, "These priests are cretins ... the machine functions without diabolical interference of any kind. Those priests are raving." Nevertheless Mekonnen urged the emperor not to make an issue of it for the moment.[2]

Two years later the line was put into the house of the *afenegus*, the emperor's chief justice, so as not to excite the priests. Unfortunately, the *afenegus* received a severe electric shock from the receiver one day, and was stunned. The priests took away the set and burned it. It was promptly replaced and eventually the clergy calmed down. Until lightning rods were placed at intervals of 10 to 15 meters, the line between Addis Ababa and Harar frequently did not work because of damage from storms in the rainy season. By May 1904, Addis Ababa was linked to Tigray and through Eritrea to Massawa. In 1905, a line was connected from the capital to Gore (Ilu Babor) and to Ras Welde Giyorgis's capital in Keffa. Telegraph messages could be sent from the capital to Asmara and Massawa, Harar and Djibouti, but the telephone was much preferred, as many customers believed that telegram messages were fabricated by the clerks. The ability of Menilek and his governors to communicate in a matter of hours that which had formerly taken weeks and months contributed more to the centralization of power in Addis Ababa, both in respect to trade and politics, than any marital links arranged by either the empress or the emperor.[3]

The Ethiopians, in their isolation, had skipped both the "age of enlightenment" and the "age of scientific inquiry." This, combined with a view of the world in which supernatural forces vied with the will of God to explain their misfortunes, justified their fear of the telephone and telegraph, whose marvels were indeed invisible. Less comprehensible was their opposition to flour mills, wheeled vehicles and conveyor tracks.

Priests had forced the dismantling of a water-driven flour mill in Shewa in 1843 as the "work of the devil." Emperor Tewodros, forward-looking in many respects, opposed further importation of a corn grinder brought in by his Egyptian bishop, Abune Selama, on grounds other than religious, "What would we do with the arms of women?" Emperor Yohannes thought mills a good idea to replace the "army of women that encumbers us."[4] It was Menilek who persisted and finally achieved the introduction of this labor-saving device for women. One woman told Capucci, the engineer who built the hydraulically driven mill on the Akaki river in 1888, how grateful to God she was for having been kept alive to see this wonderful device.[5]

In 1901, the enterprising Stévenin persuaded Menilek to put money "up front" for hand-powered flour mills to be imported from France, with the argument that the efficiency of the Ethiopian forces on the Adwa campaign had been impaired by the difficulty of providing flour for bread. In Europe, Stévenin obtained the gadgets at a good price, as electric power in France had already made them obsolete. Stévenin and his wife made good use of the mills they kept for themselves, rigging up a belt and pulley system to make them even more efficient, and establishing a bakery in Addis Ababa. Stévenin built the oven, imported a baker from France and made rolls and bread. He presented his first batch of hot, fragrant rolls to Menilek, "so he could see what could be done with good flour and good organization." The emperor instantly ordered "20 talers worth delivered to the palace each day, and Empress Taytu ordered the same. With one stroke, I was assured of orders for 40 talers a day." Stévenin sent for another baker from Paris, and made his next contribution to Ethiopian "progress" in the form of a croissant.[6]

The hand-cranked mills did not get much further than the palace compound, but they were a start. Another hand-cranked object also had made an appearance: the first gramophones, brought by Henri d'Orléans and Nicholas Leontiev in 1897. The reaction of the sovereigns to the sound of *Tannhauser* was not recorded. But when the British delivered a machine in 1898 with a cylinder recording of a greeting from Queen Victoria, that was another matter. "She speaks my name," said the amazed empress. Menilek voiced the opinion that this kind of thing might well replace written communication, and both Menilek and Taytu recorded messages to be sent back to Queen Victoria.

Taytu's message was spoken with a "cultivated manner of speech and has a pleasant tone."* "I, Itege Taytu, light of Ethiopia, say to the very high Queen Victoria, the great Queen of the English ... may God give you health. Your phonograph has reached me. And now, since God has the will to bring my voice to the ear of the honorable Queen, I declare ... God give you health and long life."[7]

A cinematograph sat unused for several years before the resourceful Stévenin was called in to fix it. The emperor provided wire and insulators from his storeroom.

By now he was ashamed of the vociferation of priests and said, "The cinema? What is it?" Once I had explained it to him, he said, "Priests or no priests, I will see this thing." The first reel to be run was of a religious subject, showing Jesus walking on water, so the priests ... though they wanted to, could not speak of the intervention of Satan. What a success! Menilek and Ras Mekonnen were most assiduous attending the cinema. At the first sitting they called out, "These whites are some demons. They can do anything. They dare anything, except building the soul of a person."[8]

Despite this and other divertissements in Addis Ababa, such as the development of a polo field and race course by the foreigners, the building of substantial structures by legations and well-off Ethiopians, and the presence of the Russian hospital, Menilek decided at the beginning of 1900 to build another capital, which like Addis Ababa, was named by the empress. The name she chose was Addis Alem or "New World." The chronicler explained Menilek's decision: "Why abandon a city as beautiful as Addis Ababa? Not because he was disgusted with it, but to have a place in which to pass the rainy

---

*The recordings by Menilek and Taytu can be heard at the British Institute of Recorded Sound, London.

season and find wood more easily."

Wood was the key problem. The area surrounding the capital had been denuded and though the imported eucalyptus trees were growing fast, fuel was in short supply. Coal had been found at Tegulet and at Debre Libanos, but its mining and transport problems had not been solved.[9]

Before beginning construction of Addis Alem, 40 kilometers from Addis Ababa, Menilek established an arsenal at Salamge in Bulga, where Empress Taytu held a *gult* (fief). Near by were some hot springs in which Menilek could soothe his rheumatism. In the first five months of 1900, Menilek and the empress went back and forth to Salamge, a two-day trip in each direction.[10]

It annoyed the resident diplomats that Menilek was away so frequently. When Captain Harrington returned at the beginning of the new century with an unusual set of gifts for the emperor, he had to wait a week for Menilek to return to town. Among the gifts was another reproduction of an Ethiopian manuscript taken from Meqdela in 1868, some fox terriers and two well-bred horses. Both Menilek and Taytu wrote thank-you letters to Queen Victoria. In his, Menilek said, "The dogs were very nice and wonderful runners. In our country we have never seen a dog catch a running hare." The empress thanked Queen Victoria for the book and her photograph which she said she had longed to see, and said the dog she had sent was nice, "but death took him."[11]

In Harrington's party was another treasure that the British had taken from Meqdela, Dr. Charles Martin. In April 1868 an Ethiopian child of about four had been found by a British officer, wandering around the smoking ruins of the fortress. The officer had taken the abandoned boy back to India with him where he had educated him under his own name, Charles Martin. On graduating from Lahore Medical College in 1882, Dr. Martin had joined the Indian Medical Service and after additional training in Edinburgh was assigned to the Burma Service.

Menilek had been told of the existence of this Ethiopian-born doctor by the Rodd mission and had expressed the wish that he come to Ethiopia. Dr. Martin, obviously an independent spirit, quarreled with Captain Harrington during the journey from the coast to Addis Ababa and Harrington complained to the foreign office that Martin was "wanting in respect for him."[12]

On 5 January 1900, along with Harrington and an English

hunting party, Dr. Martin was welcomed at the palace. At the end of the hour-long reception, the emperor asked Dr. Martin to stay in Ethiopia to work for him. Dr. Martin stated his conditions: a written contract stipulating a remuneration of 5,000 talers per year, plus an allowance for medical supplies and funding for a hospital. Menilek offered 2,000 talers and a house. This did not match Martin's salary in the Burma Service, so he declined, but remained in Addis Ababa for 15 months and began his extraordinary diary.[13]

While the dickering over his contract went on Dr. Martin met and treated various notables and their wives. "Fitawrari Ibsa's wife was pregnant and seedy ... Aleqa Gebre Selasse is feeling seedy ... Bidwoded Atnafe has rheumatism ... Lul Seged's daughter is sick." He performed an operation on a woman who had been in labor for five days. He treated the daughter of the palace jeweler (Dikran Ebeyan) for "sore eyes," Sarkis Terzian for "the clap," and the empress's cousin, Yeshemabet, for a "disorder of the menses." He began the study of Amharic and had several talks with Abune Matewos who wanted Martin's help on explaining to Menilek the advantages of an educational system.

Dr. Martin did not meet the empress until almost nine months after his arrival, though he had seen her from a distance and sent her a gift. This unusual lapse of time would appear to confirm the allegation that the empress disliked the ways in which foreign-educated Ethiopians became tainted with alien customs and ideas. Dr. Martin dressed in European style, and that would have been enough to put her off; but in due course she became interested enough to see him. Dr. Martin wrote:

Today, 11 September 1900, is the Abyssinian New Year and there was great rejoicing in the town last night, and guns were fired at the palace. The customary thing is for inferiors to fire guns in front of their superior's house. Yesterday I was received by the queen. She was very gracious and kind and made me eat my breakfast, or rather lunch, before her. It [the lunch] was cooked and served in the European fashion. The food was good but badly served. The Abyssinian attendants did not know anything about serving. The queen, although nearly 60, looked very well and not older than 40. She is fair and good-looking and carries her age wonderfully well. As common people are not allowed admittance to Her Majesty I had to go along without an interpreter. I had a short conversation in my broken Amharic and then retired. Her Majesty was very complimentary and kind. Azaj Gizaw and Ato Welde

Gabriel* were given me as *baldarabba* [intermediaries] and permission was given me to wait on Her Majesty whenever I had anything to communicate. My being an Amhara of Gondar† and Her Majesty being Amhara gives me some favor in her eyes.

A month later Dr. Martin presumed on this invitation from the empress to present the petition of Kentiba Gebru‡ for the return of his lands. Ato Welde Gabriel returned the petition to Dr. Martin with the message that the empress would pay no attention to it because it was none of his business.

As his contract terms were not met, Dr. Martin decided to return to Burma, and asked to pay his respects to the empress before leaving. She sent word that since he was returning to a foreign country there was no need for an audience, and that he could go to whatever country he liked where he could earn more money. Dr. Martin sent her a note begging her not to be annoyed with him, and she answered that she was not at all angry with him.

Dr. Martin expected to be paid 500 talers for services already rendered to the palace, but Azaj Gizaw informed him that the emperor had no money. The *azaj* also told him that in a year or so when some students returned from Russia where they were studying medicine, the emperor would send for him again. Abune Matewos told him that the emperor had no work for him just now, while Alfred Ilg promised that he would arrange an appointment for him with the railroad company in a year's time.

That there was no money and no work for a doctor were blatant excuses. The parsimonious Menilek saw no reason to pay for medical

---

*Martin was wrong about interpreters. Many of them were "common people" and taken in by foreigners. Gizaw had often acted as deputy for Menilek. Dr. Martin considered him an obstacle to his contract negotiations. Welde Gabriel was the head gatekeeper of the inner entrance to the royal apartments.
†Martin, by the time of this meeting, had been identified by a scar on his body by his grandmother. In his diary on 30 March 1900 and on 6 May 1900 he refers to this, saying at first that he was skeptical. She wore a nun's dress and introduced him to other relatives living at Entotto. Later he changed his name to Charles Werqneh-Martin.
‡Known first as Aleqa Gebru Desta, he had become a Protestant convert. He spoke some English and fluent German as a result of being educated in Jerusalem and Germany from the age of 12. He had gone with a German-Italian mission to Zanzibar and Aden, and then was engaged by Ras Mekonnen in Harar. Menilek used him as his envoy to the Khalifa in 1897 as he also knew Arabic. On his return he was rewarded with the administration of Gondar with the title Kentiba (mayor). Suddenly, in 1898, he was arrested and sent to the state prison at Ankober. Released just as suddenly in July 1900, he contacted Dr. Martin and asked him to carry his petition requesting the return of his confiscated property.

services when he had free use of the Russian doctors. He could also
call on Dr. Wakeman of the British legation, and knew that Dr.
Lincoln de Castro was about to return to the Italian legation. For
Menilek's short-sightedness, Ethiopia lost the talents of Dr. Martin
until his return in 1908. The trouble with Dr. Martin was that he
was Ethiopian in appearance but not in behavior, that is, he was
not obsequious in the presence of his superiors. He had difficulty
concealing his disgust at the "backwardness" of his native land, an
attitude he confided to his diary.

Menilek and Taytu were both deeply involved in the building of
the new town of Addis Alem. Captain Harrington wrote at the
beginning of 1901 that the emperor was so preoccupied that "it is
impossible to get him to talk business," and a later report said,
"Menilek is absolutely cracked about this new town."[14] Menilek
had impressed some 20,000 Oromo workers to build houses and an
imperial residence in a unique style, based on the palace of Versailles.

Though the Italians reluctantly moved their legation to Addis Alem
and the Russians set up a clinic there, Menilek eventually relented to
pressure from all those established in Addis Ababa, with a little help
from a vision. "The Virgin Mary appeared to warn him that the site
was ill-omened." However, Addis Alem was not abandoned. The
royal residence there was turned into a church, for, as the chronicler
reported Menilek as saying, "The kingdom of heaven is worth more
than a kingdom on earth, which is what the empress had pointed out
to him in the first place." Menilek settled down again in Addis Ababa
and began concentrating on the development of fuel resources, tree
planting and conservation, and the building of a road that would
facilitate the transport of supplies from the Addis Alem area.[15]

"Menilek has decided to build a road suitable for wheeled traffic
between Addis Ababa and Addis Alem," reported Ciccodicola from
the Italian legation in May 1902. "Taytu has urged me to keep
Menilek determined on this, and she will contribute part of the cost."
Ciccodicola asked for Italian engineers and some skilled workmen to
direct the labor that would be provided by the emperor. He was elated
at the prospect of a reliable Italian contractor building the first road in
Ethiopia* and "would secure the beginning of other important works

---

*Emperor Tewodros had had roads built from Debre Tabor to the base of Meqdela,
under the supervision of the German missionaries in the 1860s. The purpose was to
move his cannon. Ras Mekonnen had already built a road from the railway terminus
at Dire Dawa to Harar.

that will increase the glory of our country ... justifying all the sacrifices made by us for this African land." Approval from Rome came promptly and Silvio Castagna, a quartermaster sergeant with some engineering background, left Eritrea for Shewa at the end of June 1902 to make a feasibility study. The road was started in October 1902.[16]

The empress not only made a financial contribution to the cost of the road, but also spent days following its progress: "She was so happy [about it]; she had a portable parasol covered with red silk and lion's hair from which cloth hung down like a wall, carried over her by a man. The attendants who followed her, both men and women, brought stones ... picked up from around the area ... and competed to see who could bring the greatest quantity of rocks."[17]

While the road was being built, a new village called Gennet ("Earthly Paradise") began to develop, closer to Addis Ababa than Addis Alem. "It is I who will see to this!" said the empress. She had a tent raised and watched the workers the entire day. Water from the Holeta river was channeled into this new hamlet. Houses in Addis Alem were dismantled and materials brought to this new location. Gennet became the new "country retreat" for the royal couple.

On 2 March 1903 a gigantic celebration was called to commemorate the battle of Adwa. Seven years is the obligatory remembrance interval to honor the dead, but it also coincided with the emperor's need for labor. His letter to his governors said:

We must render glory and honor to God. If I ... impose the fatigue [of the journey] on you, it is to thank God for his benevolence in keeping us in comfort and health for seven years; it is not ... to aggrandize my own pride, or strength, or to admire the multitude of my armies and number of my guns. Do not dwell on thoughts of how tiring it is to bring wood and stones [for roads and buildings] but consider how afflicted you would be if I left this earth. Do not, my brothers and friends, celebrate this day because of fear of what would happen to you if you didn't.

This was a novel summons by Menilek in that it did not include any dire threats for non-compliance.

The call for labor had gone out in January, two months prior to the Adwa celebration. With the 20,000 workers supplied by Ras Mekonnen and those sent by other chiefs, the area from Addis Alem to Addis Ababa was seething with people. Soldiers complained bitterly about doing road work and Ras Wele's men even defied orders and refused to do such menial labor.[18]

The empress's financial and personal cooperation in road building belied Menilek's assertion, "The Ethiopians and I, we like progress, while the empress, my nobles and my clergy make war upon us." He "cunningly used her reputation to mask his own reluctance to make a decision and pose as a lover of progress so as to better exploit Europe." That the emperor himself was a source for Taytu's celebrated anti-anything-new attitudes is evidenced by "Don't tell the empress about our discussions as she will harass me."[19]

The ingenuity and creativity of the *ferengi* were impressed upon a few individuals by the emperor. When some of his advisers said that there were too many foreigners in the country and that he should get rid of them, Menilek called a similar number of foreigners and Ethiopians to a spot, had pieces of stone given to them for each to carve as he wished, and told these "anti-whites" to watch. Intricate designs were carved by the foreign workers, and the best the Ethiopians could do was to carve a cross. "There! You see our men have much to learn."[20]

Part of the incentive for the road builders was the lavish food and drink provided on "Adwa Day." The panoply attendant on the celebration was enhanced by the return of Abune Matewos from his diplomatic trip to Alexandria, Constantinople and St. Petersburg.* Permitting the head of the Ethiopian church to leave the country, "to see Patriarch Kyrillos and to visit his parents," was in itself an historic act by Emperor Menilek.[21] Only once before in the empire's recorded history had its Coptic bishop been allowed to leave the country: in 1209 Abune Mikael had left after a dispute with Empress Mesqel Kebra.[22] Abune Matewos would have problems with Empress Taytu after this trip, but for now he was greeted with great joy by those who feared "he would never return."

The chronicler described the tents and reviewing stand with his customary precision, with places set for the "consuls of the kings of Europe." For her care of the wounded and encouragement to the troops at Adwa the empress was singled out for special recognition with a fulsome quote from the Bible: "Be strong, for I have conquered the world."

The parade began at 7 o'clock in the morning. More than 300,000 "guns" marched past. The absence of Ras Mekonnen, Ras Gugsa

---

*Menilek wanted Abune Matewos to press Czar Nicholas to continue providing a Russian medical team, which had diminished to two doctors, a pharmacist and a medical assistant. Despite budget arguments between foreign ministry and the military medical department, the Czar agreed.

Wele, Wagshum Gwangul, Ras Mengesha Atikem, Ras Bezebeh and Dejazmach Gesesse was noted and explained: "Their countries were too far away; it was not because they refused to come." Actually each of them had security problems, though it was also suggested that Menilek thought that too great a concentration of people in the capital would invite an epidemic. The feast consumed, attention turned to the report of Abune Matewos on his trip.

The bishop had succeeded in gaining Russian support for Ethiopian ownership of the Der-es-Sultan convent in Jerusalem. This minor success was completely negated by his failures, for not only had he been unsuccessful in winning such recognition in Jerusalem and Cairo, but he had also compromised himself by signing a document with two other monophysite bishops that validated jurisdiction of the Coptic Church of Egypt over Der-es-Sultan. "As soon as Abune Matewos returned to Addis Ababa, the emperor dismissed him from his position and confined him to his residence for this conspiracy and for arrogating a capacity which he does not possess."[23] This source is in error. Menilek could have made life miserable for his bishop (as Emperor Tewodros had done for Abune Selama) or he could have asked Alexandria to replace him, but he was not invested with the power to dismiss him, nor did he put him under house arrest.

Empress Taytu was furious, and the previously cordial relations between her and Abune Matewos cooled from that time onward. She argued unsuccessfully for his replacement, not by an Ethiopian, but by another foreign co-religionist, a Syrian. Given Taytu's vigorous nationalistic sentiments, this preference was curious.* The whole matter was kept quiet, though the bishop had also used his trip out of the country to move funds back to Egypt. His income from taxes on church land, ordaining deacons and priests, blessing tabots and conducting arbitrations had made him a rich man. He put some of his money into schools for Copts in Egypt, but none of it went for the relief of needy Ethiopians in Jerusalem.[24]

The "Jerusalem problem" was not just the claim to the convent of Der-es-Sultan, but the treatment of Ethiopian priests, nuns and pilgrims. Though Menilek was generous with money for this cause, it was Empress Taytu who took the initiative. She announced a special levy in November 1903, collected more than 300,000 talers and made plans to go to the Holy City herself.

---

*Perhaps because Ethiopia's first bishop in the 4th century had been of Syrian origin.

14

Jerusalem and Ethiopia

Jerusalem, one of the holiest places in the world, sacred to Judaism and all the permutations of Christianity, as well as to Islam, had been governed by a pasha, representing the sultan in Constantinople, since its conquest by the Ottoman empire in 1517. It was the one point on the globe that Ethiopian Christians aspired to visit. Itege Mentewab confessed to James Bruce in 1770 that though she was the mother of kings who had sat upon the throne for more than 30 years, her dearest wish, for which she would give up all her worldly goods, was to go to the church of the Holy Sepulchre in Jerusalem and beg alms for her subsistence for the rest of her life.[1] However, she was both too old and too bound by her status as the revered dowager empress to make the arduous journey. Had she made the journey, Itege Mentewab would have been horrified at the miserable living conditions at Der-es-Sultan, where Ethiopian monks and nuns did indeed beg for sustenance.

The winding alleys of the walled city of Jerusalem can be traversed from the Jaffa gate to St. Stephen's gate in less than half an hour. It has been invaded, defended, destroyed and rebuilt countless times since the time of David. The western wall for the Jews, the Holy Sepulchre for Christians, and the Mosque of Omar for the Muslims, each claims the reverence of its respective pilgrims.

The Holy Sepulchre, the burial place of Jesus Christ, encompasses a number of chapels and convents. On the roof of the chapel of St. Helena is found the collection of about 20 cells called Der-es-Sultan, or the "House of the Sultan;" the dome of St. Helena therefore graces its courtyard. The Arabic name first appeared on a document dated 22 August 1687 describing some repair work at the convent which was paid for by the Copts. The exact date of construction of these cells and the right of the Ethiopians to live there cannot be ascertained. That Ethiopians lived in Jerusalem and worshipped in the Holy Sepulchre in the early 13th century is verifiable, and it is very likely that they lived on the roof of St. Helena's in the "convent of the Abyssinians" by the early 16th century. One list made in 1514 of their residing places mentions that at the Holy Sepulchre, "certain houses one gets to by a ladder," which does suggest climbing up to the roof of St. Helena.[2]

The Ethiopians, far from home, usually knowing no Arabic and very poor, were dependent on the Copts and the Armenians, their co-religionists, who often ill-used them. There were, however, instances of their being treated with kindness, as a Church of England cleric noted in 1823 that "twelve Abyssinians, five of whom are women, receive food from the Armenians."

During a cholera epidemic in 1837 and 1838 all but one of the 24 Ethiopians then in residence died. The Turkish authorities ordered that the furnishings be burned as a sanitary precaution and in the conflagration all the documents proving Ethiopian ownership of Der-es-Sultan were destroyed. The Copts came into possession of the key to a small door that was at the time the sole ingress to the convent area. When more Ethiopians came to replace their defunct brothers and sisters in 1840, the Copts locked them up in the convent every night and let them out in the morning. From then on the small Ethiopian community was tormented by the better-off Copts and Armenians, on whom they were still dependent for food.

The British consul, prodded by the Rev. Samuel Gobat who had studied Amharic with the monks at Der-es-Sultan before going on his mission to Ethiopia at the end of 1829 and who had become the Anglican bishop in Jerusalem in 1846, unofficially mediated for and protected the Ethiopians to the best of his ability. In 1850 about 100 priests arrived from Ethiopia and were "treated like animals and slaves and not allowed to enter their church without permission of the Armenians." Encouraged by the Rev. Gobat, a few of them obtained the key by a ruse. The Armenian priests stormed into Gobat's office. Fortunately, a new Armenian Patriarch who had arrived in Jerusalem took a more conciliatory attitude and arranged a compromise. The nightly internment was abolished, but the key was given to the Copts, and complaints from the Ethiopians had to go through the Armenians to the British consul.

British protection became official in 1852 after a request from Ras Ali and Dejazmach Wube who would shortly make war on each other. The absence of unity under a single authority in their homeland hampered the ability of the Ethiopians to uphold their rights in Jerusalem. After Tewodros became emperor in 1855 he made matters worse because he had such a poor understanding of the politics in Jerusalem's spiritual circles. The Coptic Patriarch, Kyrillos, made an unprecedented visit to Ethiopia and Emperor Tewodros, not without some provocation, treated him as an Egyptian spy. When Kyrillos was finally allowed to return to Alexandria, matters had been smoothed over, but Patriarch Kyrillos's experience had not made him "pro-Ethiopian."

In 1862, the pasha of Jerusalem refused to recognize British protection of the Ethiopians. He reasoned that because the Ethiopians were brothers in religion of the Copts who were Ottoman subjects, they too were Ottoman subjects. In one violent fracas, the Ethiopians managed to lay their hands on the prized key to Der-es-Sultan, but the pasha directed the Copts to change the lock on the door and his soldiers watched while it was done. British protection ceased after Emperor Tewodros imprisoned the British consul in 1864.

There were two distinct lines of contact and conflict with the Copts of Egypt. One involved the appointment of the bishop, or *abun*, of Ethiopia by the Coptic patriarchate; the other was the access to Der-es-Sultan and the well-being of Ethiopian monks, nuns and pilgrims in Jerusalem. The first practical step towards conciliation was taken by a Tigray noble three years before he was crowned as Emperor Yohannes IV in January 1872. "Dejazmach Kasa, head of the nobles in Ethiopia," sent 1,000 talers to the spiritual head of the monks in Jerusalem "for the church in which you hold services and for the place where you live," and asked them not to forget him or his recently deceased wife in their prayers. He promised that if God put him on the throne of Ethiopia they would receive an annual sum of money.

As "Dejazmach Kasa" he had already requested and been denied a bishop for Ethiopia on the grounds that Emperor Tewodros had imprisoned Abune Selama, thereby causing his death. A second request and the payment of 20,000 talers acquired Abune Atinatewos who arrived in Ethiopia in July 1869.

A third source of conflict was the regional rivalry among the monks in Jerusalem, replicating the animosities between Gojam, Tigray, Shewa and Begemder in their native land. In 1870, Welde Semayat, who would become head of the monks of Der-es-Sultan, visited Dejazmach Kasa. He returned to Jerusalem with more money and the trust of the soon-to-be crowned emperor. Emperor Yohannes sent money almost every year and with each contribution he urged the monks to stop fighting with each other. In 1877 and 1878 he sent four crates of gold captured when he defeated two attempted conquests of Ethiopia by Egypt. His generosity was not rewarded by peace among the members of the religious community. With a gift of 20,000 talers in 1886, Yohannes sent his sternest rebuke to date, ordering the monks to stop making life difficult for Memher Welde Semayat and to cease their quarrels with each other. Quarrels or not, the money sent by Yohannes began to relieve the problems of accommodation and worship amongst the Jerusalem community as Memher Welde Semayat was able to purchase land and build the religious center of Debre Gennet, outside the old walls on the Jaffa road.[3]

With the death of Emperor Yohannes in 1889, the focus of power in Ethiopia shifted to Menilek and Taytu, and geographically to Shewa. The shift resulted in even slower communication with Jerusalem than before, and intra-community hostility worsened. Memher Welde Semayat, who had taken the trouble to learn Arabic and who "showed skill and resourcefulness in hiring an architect, giving instructions, and designing himself various decorations including the cross now seen on the church" had to gain the confidence of Menilek and Taytu.[4]

It was probably on the recommendation of Ras Mekonnen, who met Welde Semayat in Jerusalem in 1890 in the process of purchasing a house on behalf of Empress Taytu, that "she entrusted the house to him ... until such time when another person could be sent." That same year, the issue of the key had been resolved by order of the pasha. The Copts had to give them the key, but in a fit of petulance they prevented the Ethiopians from praying in the Chapel of the Four Living Creatures, next door to their convent.

In 1894 Ras Mengesha Yohannes contributed to the intrigue in the Holy City by sending five Tigrayan clerics with 500 talers and medals for the governor of Palestine and the Greek and Armenian Patriarchs, in memory of his father, Emperor Yohannes. "It is a ploy to get mixed up in the convent business — tell Menilek," the Italian consul advised his foreign office. This caution was sent to Rome on 18 May 1894, but Ras Mengesha Yohannes, having finally made up his mind to re-submit to Menilek, arrived in Addis Ababa on 2 June and as far as is known the message to "tell Menilek" did not reach Shewa in time to blight the elaborate ceremony held to mark his arrival.[5]

Memher Welde Semayat traveled to Addis Ababa the following year to describe his squabbles with the Tigrayans. On his return to Jerusalem he presented himself at the Italian consulate with a letter addressed to himself from Empress Taytu authorizing him to take possession of "her" house and all the papers pertaining to it. The letter designated him as the spiritual head of the convent. This is the strongest evidence yet discovered that Empress Taytu was in charge of the "Department of Jerusalem Affairs." The consul was advised by Rome that this letter of authorization should come directly from the empress to him, but having dealt with the *memher* for several years, the consul ignored the bureaucratic advice, entrusted the papers to Welde Semayat and reported that "calm and tranquility" would return to the convent "for a while."[6]

Memher Welde Semayat managed to alienate the Jerusalem community of monks and nuns to such an extent that in January 1899 a petition was signed by 52 men and sent to "The Conquering Lion of Judah, Menilek II, King of Kings of Ethiopia." There were 22 nuns in residence who either were not allowed to sign, could not sign, or did not share their sentiments. The monks' grievances were: Memher Welde Semayat had refused them food (that is, the money for food) sent by Menilek for the previous two years; and the house which had been rented for 120 gold Egyptian pounds to be applied to the cost of food was now a "church of the king of kings in which various weddings go on and where even some children have been born." They complained that the house was neither beautiful nor "big enough for even one of your soldiers."

Last year we went 10 days without food, and this year, one month. Those who have the strength have left, and the weak who remain are ridiculed by the whites. Since the income from this house was taken from us, we are in misery. For twelve years we have used it [the income] to buy grain. Your Majesty, this is the country of Muslims. We beg you to save us from Welde Semayat for he has lost the mercy of Christ.

Welde Semayat rebutted with a letter of his own:

The Gojamese and the Tegrinyi [sic] have turned against us, wanting to take for themselves the whole house of the Ethiopians. They have been led by five people of defiant spirit and fast tongues who are able to write lies as truth. Thus they have depopulated the convent by saying things that were not so. When the *liqemekwas** came from Your Majesty, they

---

*Just who this person is, is a mystery. Ato Yosef (known to the Italians as "Giuseppe of Let-Marefià" went to Egypt, Russia and Constantinople in the company of Nicholas Leontiev to gain Russian support for Ethiopian claims to Jerusalem but did not carry the title of Liqemekwas. A man who had that title, Nadew Abba Wello, was in Jerusalem in 1900. It may have been Aleqa Gebru Desta (later known as Kentiba Gebru) who was sent by Ras Mekonnen in 1891, or the empress's representative Abba Hayle Maryam who did cause tension between the Italians and the *memher*, also in 1891 and 1892. The rebuttal in the Italian archives was not dated, but it was juxtaposed to the petition which was dated January 1899.

excommunicated him and sent him on his way rudely, saying of him, "He is a Galla from Shewa who dresses in animal skin! Who gave the church and house in Jerusalem? Everything is from Yohannes ... and they have tried to take by force the drum and the cross that Itege [Taytu] sent to us.[7]

The chronicler reported none of this, writing only that "monks in Jerusalem informed Empress Taytu that Memher Welde Semayat had put his own name on the house she had purchased." As the on-site representative, Welde Semayat signed registration papers in his own name and had indeed put his name on the house so that Turkish authorities would have no doubts that this was Ethiopian property. Unhappily these actions provided the pretext to slander him. The Italian consul said that the priest had been summoned to Ethiopia; the chronicler, that he just happened to come to Addis Ababa where people recognized him and said, "Is that the man who put his name on the house the *itege* bought?"

Memher Welde Semayat told the empress what he had done and why he had done it, though the chronicler invested him with malign intent: "He confessed that the devil made him do it," and was exiled to Debre Libanos.* "The empress was put to endless trouble because of what Welde Semayat had done and had to write to Istanbul and the pasha of Jerusalem to have effaced what he had written." The disgrace of Memher Welde Semayat was clearly the work of the empress as was the appointment of his successor, a cleric from her inner circle, Memher Fekede. Her intervention was perhaps excessive as the monks in Jerusalem were supposed to elect their own spiritual head, but the results were positive.

The problems of housing and provisioning the Ethiopian community in Jerusalem gradually eased with Memher Fekede's disbursement of funds collected by the empress from 1903 to 1904, supplemented by the 50,000 talers contributed by Menilek. The house Taytu had purchased in 1890 was razed and rebuilt, the dome on the church of Debre Gennet was completed (the church had been consecrated on 24 April 1893) and the compound enlarged and a wall built around it. The statement, "two houses, each with 24 rooms, wells and secret places [latrines] ... were built," implies complete credit to Empress Taytu, but most of the groundwork had been done by Memher Welde Semayat.

---

*Welde Semayat escaped from Debre Libanos and returned to Egypt disguised as a Muslim, with the assistance of the monks of Debre Bizen in Eritrea. He lived until his death in a Coptic monastery. Information provided by Kirsten Pedersen, Jerusalem, September 1983.

Ownership by the Ethiopians of the convent of Der-es-Sultan in the Holy Sepulchre was not conceded. Ato Yosef, backed by the Russian Orthodox hierarchy whom he had seen in St. Petersburg, went to Constantinople in December 1897 to negotiate with the sultan. On his return to Addis Ababa, Ato Yosef reported that his efforts had failed because of obstruction by the French ambassador who contended erroneously to the sultan that France was entitled to represent Ethiopia in Jerusalem. Ignoring the fact that Catholic Italy had already acted as their protector, the empress asked Menilek whether he had turned over to Catholics the right to defend their orthodox faith. Menilek answered that it was some kind of misunderstanding based on a treaty with France in 1843.*[8] Then came the diplomatic gaffe by Abune Matewos in 1902 when he was a party to acceptance of the *status quo*, the control by the Coptic church. So, in 1903, the empress made ready to go to Jerusalem herself, and "do business usually done by men."

While in Europe in January 1903, Alfred Ilg told Ferdinando Martini who was visiting him in Zurich that Empress Taytu would go to Jerusalem if Menilek predeceased her and that she had already put the necessary funds in a European bank. The funds he referred to were with the Crédit Lyonnais in Cairo from which Memher Fekede drew the money for the expenses of repair, building and assistance to pilgrims and clerics.[9]

The empress surprised Major Ciccodicola of the Italian legation in November 1903 by announcing that she would like to go to Jerusalem and asking him to arrange it. Since the visit of the "Queen of Sheba" to King Solomon in Jerusalem in the 10th century B.C., no male or female sovereign of Ethiopia had ever left the country while on the throne.† Ciccodicola telegraphed the Italian consul in Jerusalem to acquire a suitable house. "She plans to take Alfred Ilg as her political adviser, and wants me, who has been handling all her financial affairs [with Jerusalem] to go along also."

The Italian government denied permission for Ciccodicola to go, or even be involved in providing a ship for her travel. They would "put nothing at the disposal of the old, presumptuous, intriguing empress — Ciccodicola would be just a servant and agent for Menilek and a simple valet for Taytu." The empress did not bring up the

---

*The draft treaty did have a clause about "protection of Ethiopian pilgrims."
†Emperor Lalibela in the 13th century was said to have made the trip to Jerusalem, "carried by angels."

matter again, so Ciccodicola was spared the embarrassment of giving
his government's reaction.[10]

On 14 May 1905 the emperor deposited 200,000 talers in the Crédit
Lyonnais, designating the interest to go for the support of pilgrims
and monks in Jerusalem. A contract of six articles was drawn up,
witnessed by the Greek Patriarch, the Latin and Syrian bishops, and
signed in the presence of the entire Ethiopian community of
Jerusalem. The provisions of the contract forbade use of the money
for commerce, and in the event of a dispute between a pilgrim and
a resident monk, a tribunal was to be appointed. If the monk was
judged to be in the wrong he would be deprived of clothes and food
and expelled; nothing was said about what should happen if the
pilgrim were in the wrong. In the event that there should be a 15-year
period when no monks or pilgrims were in Jerusalem, the entire
amount with interest would revert to the Ethiopian government.[11]

It was the most responsible document yet drawn up by the
Ethiopian side for the regulation of affairs in Jerusalem. It was taken
to the holy city by Dejazmach Meshesha Werqe and French-speaking
Hayle Maryam Serabyon; the latter continued on to Constantinople
with a copy of the document. The large deposit in the Crédit
Lyonnais spoke loudly, and help appeared in the person of Baron
Nicholas de Chedèvre, a Russian colleague of the infamous Leontiev,
who, wishing to acquire merit in the eyes of Menilek with a view
to a concession for gold prospecting, lent himself energetically to
the Ethiopian cause. With the backing of a wealthy Greek banker
in Alexandria who had his eyes on commercial possibilities in
Ethiopia, Baron de Chedèvre went to Constantinople to ally himself
with Hayle Maryam Serabyon. Chedèvre was of enormous help. He
found a lawyer to get him into the Turkish archives where they found
a number of firmans* by the sultan attesting to ownership of Der-
es-Sultan by the Ethiopians. They bought these documents for 2,400
pounds sterling in gold, and with their Constantinople lawyer went
back to Jerusalem. There, between August and September 1905 the
Ethiopian mission took depositions from clerical representatives of
the Greek, Syrian, Maronite, Armenian and Armenian Catholic
churches, all of whom testified that Der-es-Sultan belonged to the

---

*They also found several letters from the khedive of Egypt to the sultan favoring
Coptic possession. This khedive was seeking good relations with Menilek of Ethiopia.
When told about his letters he wrote to the sultan to say that he had once believed
the lies of the Copts, but had changed his mind and would like his letters back.

Ethiopians. The lawyer and Baron de Chedèvre laid these documents before the court in Constantinople and received the prompt ruling: "Hand the keys of Der-es-Sultan to the Ethiopians."[12]

The Ethiopians celebrated with banker Zervoudakis at his home in Alexandria, but too soon. The ruling from Constantinople was ignored, a frequent occurrence in the waning years of the Ottoman empire. The Ethiopians returned to Addis Ababa. The emperor was presented with the firmans bought with the money of Zervoudakis, and they tried again the following year. Concentrating their efforts in Constantinople was probably a mistake considering how lightly the authority of the Turkish courts was felt in Jerusalem, but as it was the line of authority on paper, there was no alternative. Meshesha Werqe and his nine associates spent almost 10 months there, with side trips to Germany and to Rome, where the Ethiopian envoys were received by the Pope. Both Pope Pius X and the Kaiser were sympathetic to the Jerusalem problem, but neither could provide any concrete assistance.[13]

The question of the key became moot when the Ethiopians were permitted to knock down part of the wall that barred their access to Der-es-Sultan, and repairs to the dilapidated convent began. The chronicler wrote that a plaque was put up over the re-opened door which said, "The door of Der-es-Sultan was opened during the reign of Menilek II, beloved of God, and during the reign of Itege Taytu, the second Helena and light of Ethiopia, and during the rule of Sultan Abdul Hamid, king of Osmania." There are plaques commemorating the contributions of Yohannes IV, Menilek II, and Empress Taytu at Debre Gennet, but not at Der-es-Sultan.[14] This error in the chronicle can probably be attributed to the chronicler's ignorance of the precise location of Der-es-Sultan (within the Holy Sepulchre) and of Debre Gennet (outside the walls of the old city.)

After listing other real estate owned by Ethiopia in Jerusalem, the chronicler wrote, "Menilek and Taytu did more for the holy places in Jerusalem than any other kings [sic]" and gave a new "luster to the Ethiopian name in Jerusalem. People who did not know our country, when they saw all this said ... 'How happy we would be if we could see your country.' "

Awareness of outside opinion had been strong in the years after the military victory over Italy. Emperor Yohannes IV had concerned himself with the problem of ending the abject penury of the Ethiopians in Jerusalem, but he had also warned the monks against corrupting their minds with foreign ideas and urged them not to talk to white people.[15] Jerusalem had for centuries been the only place in the "other" world where Ethiopians had had consistent contact with other religions and nationalities. "Upgrading," as it were, its representation there was an intelligent foreign policy, though perhaps not consciously designed as such.

The church of Debre Gennet, surrounded by houses for pilgrims and monks, a residence for the *memher* and its gardens, was a source of great pride for Ethiopians. The complex inspired the chronicler, who had never seen it, to declare: "It was more beautiful than any church in Europe, Asia or Africa." He paraphrased the song of Solomon (I: 5-6) in having the church speak as a woman, "I am black, but I am the most beautiful of the monasteries of Jerusalem."

Though today priests, nuns, pilgrims and Ethiopians living in the new or old city of Jerusalem move easily between the church of Debre Gennet and the convent of Der-es-Sultan, ownership of the convent is still unresolved. The Copts presented a writ of complaint to the Israeli High Court of Justice in 1970 because the Ethiopians had changed the locks on the chapel doors of St. Mikael and the Four Living Creatures while the Copts were holding Easter services. The court ruled that the Copts should have the keys to those chapels, but in respect to the question of the ownership of Der-es-Sultan, the Israeli cabinet set up a committee which has yet to make a recommendation.[16]

15

"People from various nations ... began to come and go"

The presence of an Ethiopian delegation and a small display of artifacts at the Paris Exposition of 1900 caused something of a stir. The French government named a ship after Menilek, a "Marche Ethiopienne" was composed, and various commercial products blossomed with Ethiopian names. The visit of Abune Matewos to St. Petersburg, Constantinople and Jerusalem from 1901 to 1902 was of limited interest to the public, but the delegation headed by Ras Mekonnen to the coronation of Edward VII in 1902 received considerable press attention.[1]

On arrival in London, Ras Mekonnen learned that Edward's coronation was postponed because of illness. Mekonnen took advantage of the delay to go to Paris, where he inspected the offices of the Franco-Ethiopian railway company, and then went on to Zurich to visit Alfred Ilg. He was back in Westminster Abbey for the August ceremonies, toured the Woolwich Arsenal and paid a call on Lady Meux who had financed the reproduction of rare Ethiopian manuscripts. The famous cartoonist "Spy" made a drawing of him for an issue of *Vanity Fair*, under the caption, "Men of the Day."[2]

The traffic in the other direction was much heavier. "Discovering" Ethiopia, apart from the diplomats, traders, concessionaires, missionaries, surveyors and railroad, telegraph and telephone workers, were game hunters, explorers, writers, scholars, tourists and entrepreneurs. One of the hunters was in pursuit of the rare walia ibex, to be found only in Semen province. He wrote a book about his trip and asked Empress Taytu if he might dedicate it to her "in grateful remembrance of a pleasant sojourn in the capital ... and of splendid sport among the snow-clad mountains of her native country, Semen." She responded graciously with a letter which he reprinted in his book. Powell-Cotton noted a perceptive remark by Emperor Menilek when he visited the British camp where they had built some elegant stalls for the horses they had brought with them: "The English are a curious people ... they build houses for their horses before they have a roof over their own heads." The "quick" book author, Herbert Vivian, after wondering whether it would be of any advantage to Britain to take over Ethiopia, admitted, "It is no doubt reasonable that a nation of niggers possessing three-hundred-thousand rifles should take a tone different from that of niggers who are not permitted to possess arms, but they go too far when they presume to arrogate to themselves a superiority over civilized countries against which they could not possibly stand up." Vivian had one original observation in his text: since women carry all the wood it is sold by the "woman-load."[3]

Among those discovering Ethiopia was one woman, Nellie Pease, who accompanied her husband, A.E. Pease, liberal member of the British parliament, on a sporting trip in 1901. Hers is the sole published eye-witness description of this Ethiopian court* through the eyes of a woman.[4]

She described Entotto Maryam church† built and endowed by the empress:

Owing to the special favour of Queen Taitou, it is wonderfully decorated with gaudy, bloody pictures of the Saints. Some of them have had a particularly bad time of it, the blood spurting out from all sides, and heads rolling off. I was particularly sorry for St. Mark, who was being trailed about by the neck with a rope. Some of the most venerated panels were of European work of a low order: a ridiculous caricature of Leonardo da Vinci's "Last Supper," three curious pictures of God in Heaven, with Menilek and Queen Taitou robed in great splendour with the Virgin, and Ras Mekonnen with our Lord. It is only fair to state that these were the work of one of the Italian prisoners. All the good people full-face according to tradition and the bad in profile. It shocked the country when the Menilek coin had him in profile and it was said to have affected distribution. I believe the French hold the first place in the Queen's opinion; this is natural, considering the material help they gave Abyssinia against Italy, but had Italy won, there can be little doubt, they meant to have Harar and they [the French] had everything to gain by keeping Italy out until their turn came. It is difficult to prove to Abyssinia that we do not want to encroach — we only want to keep France from a monopoly and driving us [the English] out.

When Nellie Pease's husband had his audience with Menilek they discussed English political parties, Abyssinian suspicion of foreigners, the bad faith that stained some European powers

---

*Paulina Flad's diary of her travails while Emperor Tewodros's prisoner are published in her husband's book, J.M. Flad's, *Ein Leben für Abessinien*. Rosalia Pianavia-Vivaldi wrote a book about her life in Eritrea from 1898 to 1901. She was described by Governor Martini as a "troublesome wife, arrogant, exacting, meddlesome."
†The muralists of Entotto Maryam depicted the first Menilek and his mother, the Queen of Sheba, in the image of Menilek II and Empress Taytu.

and Mr Pease's hope that Menilek should never find the English wanting in good faith. Her husband told her that at their meeting Menilek had worn yellow-topped shoes of patent leather with no laces.

Nellie Pease wrote:

January 19, 1901. Alfred and I went to breakfast with Menilek for the Feast of Timkat. January 21, 1901. Alfred was told, "You cannot leave tomorrow because the Queen wishes to see Mrs. Pease." At 10:30 the next morning ... I received the message, "The Queen invites you to breakfast with her, at once." I reached the ghibbie which is half-an-hour from our residence a little before 12, and was taken into a high, cool and pleasant, but dark hall and told, "That is the Queen in front of you."

I was rather taken aback. The picture I had seen in England of Queen Taitou represented her as being tall and stout; my eyes being dazzled from the bright light outside, I did not recognize the lady lying on a divan quite close to the ground in front of me. However, I bowed low and the Queen gave me her hand and told me to be seated. The Queen is said to have been very handsome, but I could not judge this for while I was there she kept herself very much veiled, I rarely saw more than her dark eyes. The Queen has long thin fingers and a remarkably long thumb. [She] asked me why I was late. The interpreter replied that His Majesty had only invited me at 10 o'clock and so ... I added my own excuse.

"Please tell the Queen I regret this mistake. As the King said yesterday she would see me today I ought to have ordered my mule to be kept in, but I had never thought she would do me the honour to invite me to breakfast, and so, when the message came, all the mules were out. They are hard to catch, and the men, not being able to catch my mule, brought another, which nobody knew anything about. So, my husband, fearing some harm would come to me — for having done no work for several months, the mules are skittish — sent it back, and said I was to wait till my own mule came, which I did." This answer pleased the Queen. She said it was nice that my husband took so much trouble for me. After one or two more questions, a small table was brought in front of the Queen, and about four yards from the divan, and breakfast was served.

M. Ilg and his wife had been sitting opposite me on two high back chairs without showing any sign of life, but when breakfast was served they took their places at the table and spoke to me. Ilg sat facing the Queen and Mme. Ilg and I sat on his left and right, facing each other. During the meal, M. Ilg talked a good deal to the Queen in Amharic. She also talked to Mr. Beru, Colonel Harrington's interpreter, who had come with me and occasionally laughed a merry laugh which was nice to hear. But Mme. Ilg and I did not share in much that was going on, though every now and then [Mr. Ilg] translated something to her in the Zurich patois which I could not understand. They seemed pleasant, friendly people, but I don't think he realized that I was left out in the cold. Where so many languages are spoken, it is most confusing to remember who can understand and who cannot. The

Queen occasionally talked to me.

She asked how I liked the second course and I truthfully replied that I thought it was excellent. She said, "I will tell you how it is made. When the hotly spiced and peppered bread that you have been eating with your soup has doubled, and before it is baked, half-boiled eggs are put in the dough; it is then baked as bread loaves. Before the meal the loaves are cut open, the eggs are taken out with the spice that clings to them. They are served to you on your plate and the bread is handed around so you can eat it at the same time." I said, "I shall try to do this when I get home. I shall not say anything to my husband beforehand ... and then say it is an Abyssinian dish and I know he will be pleased."

The Queen thought a great deal about this and was amused and pleased. Presently, she said, "But you won't have the spices." I said, "No, but I think I can get them. If not I will take them from Abyssinia." The Queen said to Mr. Beru, "But she won't have the right cooking dish." I said I thought I could manage that too, and that I was sorry my house was such a long way off, because I should like to send some to Her Majesty to see how it succeeded. This interested her, as she was sure it would be a failure.

I said I would be very pleased if I might send her a wedding cake, and explained how we eat it at weddings and send it about. I thought she would like the almond icing and enjoy giving the cake to her friends.

She said "no" to this very decidedly and said her cook could make cakes, and she had already had cakes from Europe. I can imagine how stale and disagreeable these would be before they reached Addis Ababa. The Queen seemed to me to be too proud to show, and very likely to feel, interest or curiosity in any country outside her own. For instance, her first question was, "Had I seen the Queen of England?" When I said, "Yes," she turned the conversation at once as if to say, "We won't talk anymore about that."

I have been told she does not show any particular interest in our Queen,* but is extremely interested in the career of the Empress of China, and often asks, "Is there any news from China?"† Towards the end of dinner she said, "Your way of marrying is better than ours. You are allowed to see one another before you marry, and even when you are engaged you may meet. That is unheard of in our country."

---

*If Nellie Pease had been told this by Harrington of the British legation, he must have forgotten the keen interest shown by the empress in the cylinder recording of Victoria's greeting in 1899. The conversation might have been pursued had Nellie Pease known that on the very day (22 January 1901) she was talking to Empress Taytu, Queen Victoria died.

†The empress's interest in the 64-year-old Dowager Empress Tz'u-hsi must have been based on the reputation of the Chinese empress for hating foreigners. Tz'u-hsi had committed herself both to the fanatics (called Boxers) who would stop at nothing to expel foreigners from their soil, and the moderates who also wanted them to leave but feared that terrorism would lead to revenge by European nations, and America. Tz'u-hsi was obliged to abandon Peking in August 1900 as the foreign armies approached Peking to relieve the Boxer siege of the legations. As Mrs. Pease and Empress Taytu conversed, the Russians were occupying Manchuria.

After coffee was served, Mrs. Pease and the Ilgs left by separate doors. Mrs. Pease related that the fact that Ilg spent from daybreak to sunset with the emperor explained the abrupt ending to the party, and she regretted not having had a chance to talk to the Swiss couple. She thought Mme. Ilg dressed impressively: "She wears a white straw bonnet with feathers." Mrs. Pease had worn her ordinary blue cloth dress which was troublesome enough and said it was the first time she had gone anywhere without her pith helmet. "How does Mrs. Ilg get home without sunstroke?" She learned later that Mme. Ilg always used a sedan chair.

Reflecting on her visit, Nellie Pease remembered that the room in which they sat had a large panel reaching from ceiling to floor decorated with Swiss scenes, "in poor style." One picture was of William Tell; another showed skaters on a Swiss lake. She said to Mr. Beru, the interpreter, as she left, "I haven't any money. Should I give something to the attendants?" He answered, "Certainly not. No one who waited on you was less then a colonel in the King's army."

Col. Harrington had spent a great deal of time puzzling over what Mrs. Pease should take as a gift for Empress Taytu, and had finally decided she should take nothing but ask Her Majesty what she would like. Nellie Pease's reaction was:

I should have gone quite happily with this, if it had not been that just before getting to the palace gate, Mr. Beru asked me what present I was taking and seemed astonished, when I said, "nothing." I did as I was told and asked what I might have the honor of sending her from England. It was evidently not the right thing to say. Mr. Beru translated reluctantly, and the Queen said "When I want anything I will tell you."

Mrs. Pease missed meeting a fellow Englishwoman, who had also dined at the palace, but who left no such cozy account of two women exchanging recipes. Emily Vlassov had died in January 1900 and Menilek had done her and the Russian mission the honor of attending her funeral.

Her grief-stricken husband, the Russian minister, P.M. Vlassov, reported on Empress Taytu before he left the country with a strikingly different appraisal from his fellow diplomats:

She refrained from participation in affairs of internal politics, perhaps out of fear of taking upon herself responsibility for them, but in external affairs ... whenever she intervened, Taytu attained what she wanted. Thanks to her great bravery and persistence she was able to establish not only a large circle of partisans among highly placed people ... but rallied them to herself without reservation.

Vlassov's evaluation then veered into agreement with others: "There are increasing quarrels and arguments between the spouses — she insisting that Europeans are not only alien to Ethiopia, but dangerous, and that the *negus* instead of encouraging their influx should oppose it and should not agree to allow permanent representatives of Europe in the country." Vlassov and his wife and several members of his staff in their private tête-à-tête with the empress were treated to "extreme expansiveness." The empress greeted the party with these words: "Yesterday, the first day of our New Year, I gave prayers and received no one; today I wish to begin the New Year with a serious conversation and a meal with you — our only friends and brothers. I am certain that your presence here will bring to me and my country, happiness and peace in the coming year." Vlassov said that the usually silent empress talked with him and his wife, asking them about Russia and their life there. As they left her apartments she said:

Ethiopia does not have and cannot have friends other than the Russians; only they want good for my country — all other Europeans crave our destruction. I ask you not to believe the slanders of our enemies and believe only the words of the emperor, who, in return, will tell you the feelings and wishes of our people. Believe also that first and last our clergy sees in you Russians not only brothers in religion, but also magnanimous protectors and on you rest their hopes. Please tell this to His Majesty the Czar and his government.

To this, Vlassov responded that he hoped she would counteract the slanderers of Russia.* "Always, always, be assured of that," she answered.[5]

The activities of the "other" Russian, Nicholas Leontiev, were obviously not held against Vlassov. The emperor had learned that Leontiev, to whom he had granted unspecified lands to govern in June 1897 as recompense for his services to Ethiopia, had parlayed Menilek's letter of understanding into the "governorship of the Equatorial Province" and had gathered investors into societies in London, Paris and Brussels with promises of great returns from his

---

*Whether he was referring to the slanders by the new Social Democratic party in Russia (Lenin had been exiled to Siberia by this time) or the suspicions voiced by English leaders about Russian ambitions in the Far East is not known.

exploitation of this province.

In a letter to Leontiev, dated 1 April 1898, the emperor had said, "The rumor has reached me that you are bringing many Europeans with you to help organize the country I will give to you. If true, this does not please me."

The phrase, "many Europeans," has been interpreted as a sign of Menilek's acquiescence in the anti-European sentiments of Empress Taytu and her partisans, who accused him of selling their country to Europeans, though it was also true that Menilek himself was weary of the problems attendant on some of the concessions he had granted. Menilek's letter was a stern warning to Nicholas Leontiev who returned to Ethiopia two months after receiving it. He got only as far as Harar where he had a self-inflicted shooting accident. Vlassov so detested him that he refused to send one of the Russian doctors from Addis Ababa to care for him. Leontiev, inexplicably, was back in the emperor's favor and Menilek dispatched a doctor to him and said he would grant him the province northeast of Lake Rudolf. Called everything from a "thorough knave," "notorious scoundrel," "clown," "brazen ill-famed adventurer," to "a most charming type," and "adventurer of plausible address," Leontiev had a true friend in Alfred Ilg, who is presumed to have been the one who placated the emperor, and arranged for the doctor and the commission of the province. Leontiev had to return to Europe to recover from his wound. He went to see his shareholders and returned to Ethiopia the following year with a small army of assorted French, Russian and Senegalese. These were joined by a detachment of Menilek's soldiers and two Croatians, the Seljan brothers.* From June to October 1899, Leontiev's expeditionary force did what all of Menilek's colonizing armies had done: sack, kill and take booty.

Leontiev's expedition stepped on the toes of the British by removing their flag from Lake Rudolf† and angered both Ras Welde Giyorgis and Ras Tessema by trespassing on their lands. Though Leontiev

---

*Mirko and Stepan Seljan pretended to be Russian doctors crossing the desert between Zeyla and Harar and won instant respect from threatening Somalis. They reached Addis Ababa on 9 June 1899 and gave a concert on violin and flute for Menilek and Taytu. On learning that the Seljan brothers were trained in modern weaponry (both had been to military school), Menilek assigned them 300 soldiers, and they went with Leontiev to the southwest. When Leontiev left, the Seljans stayed as "governor," with Menilek's permission, until late 1901.
†The flags were replaced with Menilek's concurrence in 1900 by the J.J. Harrison party.

delivered a large booty to Addis Ababa, and though his violations of territory were partly Menilek's fault, the emperor was glad to see him go. Leontiev returned to Europe and produced a book in which he described the "Equatorial Province" as a terrestrial paradise teeming with game and luxurious vegetation and inhabited by a tranquil and hardworking population producing coffee, tobacco, cereals, corn, dura, honey, wax and olives. It had a perfect climate and deposits of iron, zinc, antimony, copper, gold and salt. Leontiev was exaggerating again, and he was soon being questioned by his "societies" who wanted to know where their money was going. Not satisfied with his answers, these investors appealed directly to Emperor Menilek.

Menilek's answer was to notify the legations that Leontiev had been relieved of all previous titles, credits and land grants:

I have learned [that he boasts] of having my permission to exploit the gold of Ethiopia ... and that he showed the Belgian society a letter which I gave him [to prove this.] I never gave such permission. The letter held by the Belgian society names this land 'Equatoria.' I have said nothing until now because I thought it might be a rumor. I did not believe that Leontiev could depart so far from my wishes. Send these words to your government so that in future he can do these things no more that create disputes between people.

Leontiev never recovered his reputation, such as it was. He disappeared from the diplomatic records of England, Italy and France, though he turned up in Rome in 1907, a pathetic derelict, to petition King Vittorio Emmanuel for reimbursement of expenses incurred 11 years earlier when he had escorted 50 Italian prisoners from Addis Ababa to the coast. Cesare Nerazzini, who had received that consignment of POWs, was asked to evaluate Leontiev's request. After delivering an indictment of Leontiev's theatricality and lust for personal acclaim, he recommended that without bothering to investigate his claim, the House of Savoy should grant him 20,000 or 30,000 lire, an approximation of the value of the mules used by the POWs on the trek. The Italian ambassador in Paris did not hand Leontiev the 30,000 lire until 1910, a few months before Leontiev died.[6]

The internal "coming and going" of high importance between Tigray and Shewa was the trip to Addis Ababa in May 1903 of Dejazmach Gebre Selasse to claim his bride, Amaretch Walelu,*

---

*Amaretch was the daughter of an unnamed sister of Welde Giyorgis, thus also the cousin of Ras Mekonnen and the emperor. Her father was Kenyazmach Walelu.

the niece of Ras Welde Giyorgis. Amaretch was a truly beautiful young woman much admired and photographed by foreigners. Dr. Annaratone, who visited her many times in Adwa where he was the company doctor for a mining syndicate, said that, in order to marry Gebre Selasse she had been required by the emperor to divorce her husband and leave behind her seven-year-old daughter.[7]

The marriage of Amaretch to the Tigrayan climaxed the emperor's preference for the 42-year-old Gebre Selasse over the two other governors who had shared the administration of Tigray since 1902. Gebre Selasse had cooperated in ending the rebellion of Rases Mengesha Yohannes and Sebhat from 1899 to 1900. He had also accepted the brief tenure of Ras Wele, and had faithfully and with pleasure executed orders from Addis Ababa to keep the peace with Eritrea. Gebre Selasse had long been a friend to Italy, having served as a *jus-basha* (native officer) under Italian command, "faithful to us to the end," according to Governor Martini. However, Martini was unaware that he had faithfully informed Menilek of everything that was going on in the Italian arena.[8]

During the seven months that Gebre Selasse was away from Tigray for his marriage and talks with the emperor, there was considerable unrest. Governor Martini spurned repeated requests from the insurgents (Gugsa Araya and Seyum Mengesha Yohannes) to help them, and even-handedly refused military aid to the "imperials." Martini's use of the phrase "imperial troops" reflects a shift in his way of looking at Menilek's rule of Ethiopia. Previously, whenever he referred to Menilek's soldiers they were the "Shewans."

As soon as Gebre Selasse returned to Tigray with his bride and wedding gifts — 150 slaves, 1,500 guns, 20 horses and 20,000 talers — he notified Martini that he would like to call on him. It was an acknowledgment of Martini's correct behavior regarding the insurgents.

Martini fretted about what it would cost him, but nevertheless produced a suitably lavish program for the visit from 21 to 26 January 1904. He was well aware that this was the first Ethiopian "diplomatic" recognition of the colony, and that Gebre Selasse was authorized to deal with him on border delineation, extradition, road building, commercial agencies and the extension of the telegraph lines. Martini was quite patronizing in his description of Gebre Selasse:

His eyes are alert — speaks Italian quite well — is very intelligent. He eats dextrously with a fork and sits at table as though he were used to it. He is sober — at least on this occasion — leaving untouched his second glass of champagne. He was delighted with my European furniture. He stopped immobile before a mirror and while taking a good look at himself, exclaimed, "So this is the man who would do much to please Weyzero Amaretch."

Martini had prepared a pretty carved box filled with soaps and perfumes as a gift for the bride and decided to add a mirror after seeing how much the *dejazmach* had enjoyed his own image. He noted how Gebre Selasse always referred to the lovely Amaretch as "my lady" and never as "my wife." Later he had occasion to ask Abreha Araya* why this was so. Abreha explained that it was because she outranked him, while he (Abreha) and his wife (Yetemegnu Wele) were equal in status, so he called her "my wife."

The visit was a great success and the Tigrayan lord confided in Martini, "Above all, I love the emperor, but after him comes Italy." While in Addis Ababa, he said, invitations had come from both the Russians and the English but he had accepted only those from Ciccodicola. Some Englishmen, he claimed, had tried to persuade him that the English colonial rule was more benign than the Italian, to which he had replied, "Oh no, no one is greater than Rome." Martini enjoyed this for he had great distrust of the British.[9]

In Addis Ababa the diplomatic war between Lagarde of France, Harrington of Britain and Ciccodicola of Italy was in full swing. These three men spent almost 10 years vying with each other for influence on the emperor, and Menilek successfully played one off against the other in his own interests.

The railroad from Djibouti to Addis Ababa was their main bone of contention. Financial difficulties had forced the French firm under contract to build the line to seek other investors, and British money had a controlling interest by the middle of 1901. French investors appealed to their government to thwart this reliance on British capital and had a favorable answer. Harrington made sure that Menilek understood the implications, namely, that the French government would own his railroad, and Menilek was gratifyingly furious. The line had been completed only as far as Dire Dawa, 110 kilometers

---

*Abreha Araya also spoke and wrote Italian, having been educated at the International Institute of Turin for two years; he thought himself superior to Gebre Selasse though in fact their genealogies were similar: Abreha was the nephew of Emperor Yohannes IV through a brother, and Gebre Selasse was related only through his mother.

from Djibouti. The emperor's refusal to attend the inauguration there in December 1902 must have been a true deprivation for one who so loved technology. Léon Chefneux, one of the original concessionaires, patiently renegotiated an agreement that was more to the emperor's liking, but construction was stalemated for six years.[10]

Though Italian expertise and money dominated the development of roads, telephone and telegraph, Ciccodicola was under constant pressure to gain customs advantages for goods carried on the railroad. Ciccodicola had a senior man, Ferdinando Martini, keeping an eye on him from Eritrea, while Harrington and Lagarde could run their duchies in Addis Ababa with almost no interference by their home offices.

Martini did not spare Ciccodicola in his diaries, but at the same time defended him in Rome and opposed his recall, averring that whatever his faults, he was high in Menilek's regard, an opinion affirmed by Harrington and the French writer, Hugues Le Roux. Ciccodicola constantly overspent his budget, but as Martini said in his defense, not a cent went into his own pocket. He had unwisely expended 100,000 lire on a new legation at Addis Alem, and then Menilek had decided not to move his capital there. "He has a perforated hand and merits censure," Martini told King Vittorio, but "thinks it necessary for our prestige." Lagarde and Harrington had twice the funds allotted to the Italian legation, admitted Martini.

Although he saved Ciccodicola from recall, Martini never stopped complaining about him. In August 1903 he learned from one of the telegraph technicians that "not only does the representative of the king of Italy have a *madama* but she sits at the same table with him and is served by his two white servants! Outrageous!"[11]

The Italians and the English were forced to cooperate in the campaign to trap Muhammad Abd-Allah Hassan (derogated as the "Mad Mullah") who criss-crossed boundary lines between their Somali colonies. Harrington and Ciccodicola joined to gain Menilek's cooperation and Harrington met the emperor's demand that two British doctors go with the Ethiopian forces.*[12]

With the arrival of an American mission in November 1903, there was a brief diversion for the quarreling diplomats and Menilek. American cotton sheeting, called *amerikani*, far exceeded any other

---

*This campaign against an early Somali nationalist movement was not successful. The Italians were able to arrange a truce in 1905 with Muhammad Abd-Allah Hassan that lasted until 1909.

nation's textile imports into Ethiopia. This especially annoyed the British who wanted to sell the Manchester product. In return, the United States bought Ethiopian skins, coffee and hides, but outside of trade, had no other interests on the east coast of Africa, and so posed no threat to European political aims.

The 28-member American group, consisting of 17 marines and five sailors, rode the train to Dire Dawa, where it had to compete with Ras Mekonnen for mules as he was requisitioning them for the Somali campaign.

Robert Skinner, head of the mission, was the American consul in Marseilles, and took the advice of Menilek's agent at Djibouti, Ato Yosef, to "speak simply, speak plainly and be sincere ... we would like better to see you as you are than to see you trying to seem like ourselves." They took a side trip from the train terminus to Harar to see Ras Mekonnen who gave them a male and a female zebra for the zoo in Washington, D.C.*

At one stage of the journey, Menilek's agent, Ato Paulos, told them that on the whole the emperor favored progress. The emperor complained, however, that strangers were becoming too numerous, and that they corrupted the people who were simple in character and easily deluded. Skinner presented Paulos with an American flag after explaining the meaning of its stars and stripes. Ato Paulos telephoned the emperor for permission to accept it. Skinner also used the telephone to announce their imminent arrival to Léon Chefneux, who was acting minister of Foreign Affairs as Alfred Ilg was in Europe.

On Friday, 18 December, the entire mission bathed and changed from their khakis into uniforms, Skinner being in a plain black suit and top hat. Once in the audience hall, Skinner stepped forward to shake hands with the emperor:

He looked at my commission with indifference and replied in Amharic, which was translated into French. I presented an invitation from President Theodore Roosevelt to participate in the Louisiana Purchase Exposition [in St. Louis]. Chairs were provided and 40 minutes passed quickly. The cannon roared out 21 guns and the band played "Hail Columbia" and the "Marseillaise." Our marines and sailors put up tents in the compound of Ras Welde Giyorgis and called it "Camp Roosevelt."

---

*Menilek gave them two lions. The records of the Zoo in Washington show that in 1904 one male lion was received from the "King of Abyssinia" and a spotted hyena from Mr. Skinner. In 1905 from the "King of Abyssinia" came one zebra, one lion, two gelada baboons, one north African ostrich and one Somali ostrich.

The following day Skinner got down to the business of a treaty of Commerce and Friendship. The draft made quite an impression because it was the first ever presented to Menilek already written in Amharic; it was the work of Professor Littmann of Princeton University. They presented Menilek with Littmann's edition of the Amharic chronicle of Emperor Tewodros. The treaty signed was unexceptional except for one clause that angered the other legations. Crimes committed in Ethiopia by Americans were to be judged according to the laws of Ethiopia and vice versa in the United States. The other nations fought hard in their treaties for bi-national commissions to judge crimes committed by Europeans.

Skinner gave Menilek a photograph of President Roosevelt and a book by him on north American game, some much-appreciated garden seeds, and a typewriter. When Menilek asked if a machine could be made to type Amharic, the difficulties of making a typewriter with 251 letters were explained. A late model rifle as usual pleased the emperor. "Without changing his posture on the throne he aimed it through an open doorway. There was a wild stampede for cover."

Menilek visited "Camp Roosevelt" and saw a demonstration of firing with blanks. He expressed an interest in having some. "I shall be able to teach some of my officers how to show courage under fire." "Everyone says he loves to joke," commented Skinner.

The Americans called on all the foreign legations. "We ate caviar and drank vodka with Lischine,* macaroni and Asti Spumanti with Ciccodicola, *foie gras* and champagne with Le Roux, and roast beef and port with Mr. Clerk [both Lagarde and Harrington were on home leave]. It filled us with a new respect for diplomacy as a profession and fine art ... to surround themselves with luxuries in this far-off spot." Skinner found the Russian installation the most interesting: "With no apparent stake in Ethiopia, no trade and no frontiers — yet this mission with its excellent medical services is presided over by the accomplished Lischine. The real purpose of the Russian diplomatic effort is a never-ending source of conversation."

Ciccodicola was busy managing the construction of the telegraph line from Addis Ababa north to connect with Massawa. Skinner had seen enormous camel trains from the train window *en route*, carrying pre-fabricated steel materials from Milan. Ciccodicola told him that

*Until the appointment of Konstantine Lischine in 1903, the Russians had considered their representation in Addis Ababa "temporary." The decision to make a "permanent" legation followed Abune Matewos' visit to St. Petersburg.

he had tried to replace American cotton with Italian, but "since you people grow nearly all the world's cotton, how can we expect to force you out!"

Skinner made the acquaintance of "Commandant Bénito Sylvain, envoy of His Excellency, the President of the Republic of Haiti to His Imperial Majesty the Emperor of Ethiopia,"* who was making his second visit. This highly educated, French-speaking scion of a wealthy Haitian family wore an elaborate uniform: Wellington boots, spurs, white breeches, sword, and on his chest the Cross of Solomon that Menilek had given him in 1897. Sylvain wanted "the greatest black man in the world" to become honorary president of the Society for the Uplift of Negroes. Skinner reported Menilek's reaction: "Yours is an excellent idea; the negro should be uplifted, but I am not a negro." In 1905 Menilek's name was listed along with 14 other monarchs and heads of state as "protectors" of the Society for the Uplift of Blacks.

The English interest in Ethiopia was obvious, said Skinner: "Two-thirds of the Ethiopian frontiers border upon British or Egyptian territory." He noted that the Englishmen used the word "nigger" but that "it was bereft of the half-affectionate swing it acquires in America." This absurdity, typical of American racial attitudes of the time, led to a footnote in American-Ethiopian relations completely ignored by Robert Skinner in his book.[13]

One month before his official trip, another American, a black Hispanic gentleman born in Texas and master of three languages, had been introduced to Menilek by Sylvain. His name was William H. Ellis. He had conceived a passionate interest in Ethiopia and thought of it as a place that would be receptive to immigrant American blacks who would aid in the development of the country. He had met Ras Mekonnen in London during the coronation of Edward VII, and Mekonnen had invited him to visit Ethiopia. When Robert Skinner was selected to negotiate the commercial treaty, Ellis was extremely disappointed that he had not been chosen. He was

*Since his previous visit Bénito Sylvain had acquired a Doctor of Laws in Paris, had written his thesis, "Etude historique sur le sort des indigènes dans les colonies d'exploitation," and had attended the first session of the Pan-African Association in London. He had also been promoted from honorary ensign in the Haitian navy to "Commandant" for the purpose of enhancing his status to carry a letter to the Ethiopian emperor urging that the freedom of African peoples be safeguarded and inviting his cooperation for the uplift of the "African race."

well off and lived on Central Park West in New York City with his English wife, Maud Sherwood. He had made his money working for Henry M. Hotchkiss, inventor of the machine gun, and was active on Wall Street where he was called "the Moor."

When Ellis saw Menilek, he described the work of Andrew Carnegie in helping the education of American blacks. Ellis then returned to the United States with two letters: a friendly letter to himself and one to Andrew Carnegie, both dated 17 November 1903.

Had Ellis not made so many bizarre statements to the press both before he left and on his return, history might have been a little kinder to him. Ellis had said:

Menilek wept when he heard how Lincoln freed the slaves.
Abyssinia is the richest country on earth in gold, silver, copper, iron, rubies ... and diamonds.
He [Ellis] will receive a concession to establish a bank and help systematize their laws, and obtain land as a colony for American negroes.
The emperor wears European clothes and a felt hat of American shape.
The empress and court ladies are dressed in Paris models.

Only the statement about the felt hat was true.[14]

Skinner brought back the commercial treaty, signed by Menilek on 27 December 1903.[15] It was ratified by the U.S. Senate on 12 March 1904. William Ellis went to Washington and asked for the privilege of taking the ratified treaty back to Ethiopia. The State Department chose for the mission the brother of the Assistant Secretary of State, Kent J. Loomis, who had offered to travel at his own expense to Ethiopia because he wanted to hunt lions. However, Ellis's knowledge of the country was valued and he was asked to go with Loomis. The two men shared a cabin on the ship which carried them across the Atlantic.

When the ship reached Plymouth in June 1904, Loomis was missing. His body was washed ashore near Cherbourg a week later. An autopsy showed contusions on the head which had occurred before death, but which could have been caused by a fall. Loomis, the other passengers testified, had imbibed freely of intoxicants during the voyage. William Ellis was permitted to continue with the mission and delivered the ratified treaty to Menilek in August 1904. On his return, Ellis's reports and statements were even more exaggerated than those made after his first trip. He had obtained mining concessions, three million acres of land to experiment with cotton growing, and he would establish the Royal Bank of Abyssinia. None of this was true.

When the subject of the mysterious death of Kent Loomis was raised again, Ellis fought back in the press. "The papers said I was a 'damned nigger.' Yes, I have African blood in my veins ... and Cuban and Mexican." He instituted a libel suit for defamation of character which was dropped when the State Department announced that no blame attached to Mr. Ellis for the death of Loomis.

Ellis's sensational claims generated a certain awareness of the existence of a sovereign power on the partitioned African continent. Skinner made an impression on Menilek as well. The emperor told an English caller that he found Skinner charming and that his austere black suit was a novelty after the blaze of color and decorations worn by European representatives. He commented that Skinner was a man who knew what he wanted and represented a country that knew what it wanted, namely, non-interference with trade, adding that he was glad that a large expanse of ocean separated his country from America.[16]

By the time Menilek made these remarks, he had been told just how wide that ocean was by Sarkis Terzian, whom he had authorized to buy "machinery" in America. The *Washington Times* of 23 November 1905 carried a feature story on Sarkis Terzian, "the Bismarck of Abyssinia," and Haji Abdulahi Sadiq, "prince, and governor of Harar." Haji Abdulahi Sadiq gave President Roosevelt a letter from the emperor, two ivory tusks and a lion, but he was neither a prince nor the governor of Harar.* Terzian

*The *New York Herald*, 23 October 1905, carried an interview with "Menilek's envoy." Haji Abdulahi Sadiq was amazed at the crowds of women on street cars, and was asked, "What do you think of them?" "I have had no chance to see them, so busy am I counting the stories on buildings," he answered. Told that one building had 32 stories, he asked to be taken there so he could say his prayers on the roof. "Sadik Pasha" explained the absence of credentials by saying he had lost his suitcase, but had sent two people to London to get them. These credentials did not exist. He was a trader and business associate of Terzian. After leaving New York he made his way to India and Afghanistan as a "respresentative of the emperor of Ethiopia." The British picked him up and returned him to Ethiopia where he was imprisoned for embezzlement, but released in 1907. In July 1908 Piazza, a correspondent for *La Tribuna*, met him in Harar where he did seem to be the "head of the Muslims," and had just come back from an attempted negotiation with the "Mullah" on Menilek's order. He told Piazza that he had gone from Constantinople on his gyrations of 1905 and 1906 to Vienna, Berlin, Paris, London, New York, Tokyo, Peking and India. He admitted trying to incite the Muslims in India against the English, but had been arrested for swindling a Bombay jeweler out of thousands of rupees. Returned to Ethiopia, Menilek kept him as head of the Harar Muslims, so that he could earn enough money to repay the emperor and pay his debts in Bombay — or so he said. In 1911 both he and Terzian were suddenly accused of having forged the emperor's seal six years before. For Terzian's denial of this charge and the account of his trip to America, see Eadie's *Amharic Reader*.

was not a "Bismarck," though he had helped Menilek conquer Harar in 1886, been rewarded with a district to govern, and shopped many times for the emperor's guns in Europe. The design of this trip may have originated in the heads of Terzian and Haji Abdulahi, though Alfred Ilg had telegraphed Vienna on Menilek's behalf to announce their arrival. Both of them had met the imaginative Ellis in Ethiopia and they saw him again in New York on their way to Washington, D.C. The Armenian and the Muslim were the only Ethiopians* to visit the United States during the reign of Menilek.[17]

While the appearance of the Americans in Ethiopia did not worry European interests — an American consul was not appointed until 1906 — the arrival of a German diplomatic mission in 1905 did alarm the French, English and Italians.

As early as 1901 Menilek had invited Kaiser Wilhelm to make a treaty of amity and commerce with Ethiopia. Dr. Friedrich Rosen headed a delegation of 20 members with a Prussian escort and 100 liveried servants dressed in the German national colors, which rode into the Ethiopian capital on 12 February 1905. A treaty was signed by Menilek on 7 March. Hans Vollbrecht, the doctor with the mission, had the most intimate contacts with the court.[18]

He described the excellent health of the emperor, and was impressed by his agility at the age of 60 in jumping from his horse when he visited the German camp on his way to Entotto with Empress Taytu. When the emperor caught a cold, Vollbrecht was called on the recommendation of the lady Yeshemabet, whom Vollbrecht had dosed with good results. During his consultation with Menilek, Vollbrecht praised the hot springs of Filwuha as therapeutically valuable and suggested that people be taught to drink the water for their health instead of just bathing in it. His next summons came from Empress Taytu.

"From this day [6 March 1905] I entered and left the palace

---

*The concept of citizenship of a foreign-born person such as Terzian had not yet developed. Having lived in Ethiopia since 1883 he may be considered a *de facto* Ethiopian. In May 1912 there was an edict: "He who wishes to make himself an Abyssinian subject will buy a paper to make his allegiance to government three months from today or leave Abyssinian dominions." (Eadie, *Amharic Reader*)

Menilek, about 1903

whenever I wanted." Kentiba Gebru* acted as translator. "The Empress removed her veil and Dejazmach Abate held up a *shamma* to screen her and myself from view." Dr. Vollbrecht was surprised at how different she was from the photograph he had seen:

God knows who made the picture for it has nothing to do with reality. She is in her forties, is of average size and has only a tendency to stoutness without being fat. She even has quite a nice waist though not with the perfection that European women effect with corsets. She wears only a silk sash around her hips. Under the dark eyebrows and long lashes her light brown eyes are reflective and melancholy. This lady has suffered much in her life, but her greatest sorrow is not having any children, and she has just received news that her mother is dead.

Indeed Yewub-dar had died at Debre Mewi in Gojam in her

---

*The German and English-speaking ex-mayor of Gondar whose petition for restoration of property had been taken up by Dr. Martin in 1901. The Rosen mission had brought to Ethiopia Gebre Heywet Baykedagn, who had spent the last few years studying in Berlin and in Vienna. After assisting the mission and Kentiba Gebru, whom he much admired, Gebre Heywet went to Ankober at the emperor's request to improve his rusty Amharic. He eventually returned to court as a scribe.

Taytu as she might have looked in   Taytu with her sister Desta and a
1903; the woman beside her is possibly   court eunuch, c. 1903
her sister Desta and the child may be   Institute of Ethiopian Studies,
Desta's grandchild, son of Gesesse   Addis Ababa

80s. Taytu had asked a doctor with a 1902 expedition to attend
her.* Dr. Goffin spent several months with Yewub-dar and her sister
Askala, "two excellent women full of heart and humor." He amused
them with tales of "Tom Thumb" and "Bluebeard" but had been
unable to cure Yewub-dar's paralysis which he treated with electric
massage.

Her funeral song had a verse that went, "She gave birth to a
daughter destined for a king and a son called to be a ras." The
empress did not go into seclusion or engage in hair-tearing or put
on the filthy clothes associated with mourning customs. Her secretary
wrote, on her behalf, her gracious thanks to the German mission
for the religious picture that they donated for her mother's grave.[19]

Vollbrecht found the empress absolutely charming. He observed
the wonderful relationship she had with her "sisters," nieces and

*There is only one reference to an encounter between mother and daughter after
Taytu's marriage to Menilek. It is in a song that conveys the idea that her mother,
to show respect for Taytu's rank, wanted to come to the border of her fief to
meet her, but Taytu, to show respect for her mother, insisted that they meet
half-way.

Menilek

young people of the court, and her relationship with Menilek:

Within the palace barriers between empress and emperor fall. After his strenuous duties he comes to the cozy, quiet room of his wife to find rest and diversion. They call each other "mother" and "father" exchanging news of the day ... often there was a party for the children, which the emperor liked to attend, loving these children as if they were his own. Once he remarked, "Mother, why hasn't God given us children?" Whereupon she consoled him, "Father, why are you sad? We have 14 million children for whose welfare we must care."

This paternal-maternal expression of the monarchy correlates with the actions of this royal pair. Considering what Kentiba Gebru, Vollbrecht's translator, had suffered by royal decree (disgrace and loss of property) he was charitable in what he conveyed to Vollbrecht:

Through the vicissitudes of life she has kept her heart full of love, kindness and solicitude for others. She is the most faithful comrade of the *negus* and has ... an unbelievable influence on politics.

They say she doesn't like foreigners and distrusts Europeans. The first is not true. She knows the worth of European culture and is the one who helps to introduce it into the country. True, she does mistrust Europeans.

Photograph of Taytu, taken about 1906 or 1907, showing the swelling of her tissues and her increased weight

Portrait of Taytu painted in 1907 by E. Senigov, a Russian whose sister worked at the palace for the empress. It is the only picture that shows the defect in her jaw described by Pietro Antonelli.

"Why do they come here? To help us unselfishly? No. They all want something ... do not keep their word — neither the important ones, nor the small fry." She loves her country. Her philosophy is "a free, independent Abyssinia for free Abyssinian people."

The medical consultation, Vollbrecht said, was conducted without false modesty. She agreed immediately when he said he must examine her and called a woman servant. "They went into the next room and she lay down." The *kentiba* and *dejazmach* were astonished and said that she had never been touched by a European. Vollbrecht reported:

I examined her thoroughly, not once but several times in succeeding days. I gave her massage and admired her beautiful arms and hands, especially her small feet not ruined by fashionable shoes. The only jewel she wore was a ribbon on her left ankle with five golden rings and a diamond on the clasp. She liked my treatment and felt much better in a few days and full of hope for a complete cure.*

*Vollbrecht did not specify what he was "curing." A non-medical source, Bénito Sylvain, said she suffered from "hydropsy." A photograph taken about 1907 or 1908 bears out this diagnosis: her features are badly distorted from edema that could be ascribed to water retention. Sylvain alleged that she refused an operation for her ailment though it was recommended by French, German and Russian doctors.

I started a great change in the way of life for the empress and her ladies in their idle life of reclining on pillows all day long. I made them walk and do gymnastics. It was amusing one morning when I arrived carrying a lot of large and small balls. I showed the empress different ball games and explained how good for her health this exercise would be. Everyone laughed, and Dejazmach Abate said it was impossible for the empress to do and against all etiquette. I insisted to the point where the whole palace was in an uproar and the emperor was told. The next day when I saw Menilek, he smiled and said, "It seems to be fine what you have ordered and the ladies are having a very good time." The wives of Ras Tessema and Ras Welde Giyorgis also participated and the ladies' quarter was full of sounds of merriment.

One day, Vollbrecht found the women crying and moaning. The wife of the state treasurer, Bejirond Mulugeta, had delivered a son two weeks earlier and had childbed fever. Vollbrecht tended to her for two days and she was out of danger. The empress thanked him with tears in her eyes.* Vollbrecht describes how he treated the other women:

I always took presents — chocolate, marzipan and toys. They were delighted with dolls that could be dressed and undressed, whose eyes opened and closed, and who said "mama" and "papa." Every morning we did gymnastics and practiced dances which were not easy. What every little child can do in Germany, they spent days learning. These Abyssinian ladies could not jump on one leg. There were three husbands there every time I came and Kentiba Gebru whispered to me that they thought I might elope with one of their wives.

When the German mission left the country (by the northern route via Begemder, Tigray and Eritrea) Menilek asked Vollbrecht to see his daughter, Zewditu, who had been unable to have a child by Gugsa Wele. Gugsa Wele was ordered to bring Zewditu to a village on their route so that they would not have to make a detour, and, as Vollbrecht recounted:

he was very handsome, but prematurely aged from his Don Juan life.

I was alone with the princess when I examined her. She was about 26, slim, charming and looked like her father. The *kentiba* told me she was far too nice a woman for a fellow like Gugsa Wele. I examined her thoroughly which took a long time, since I had to answer a lot of her questions. Everything was written down and explained over and over. I could not leave before I had a man-to-man talk with Ras Gugsa. The *kentiba* must have translated exactly what I said about his style of life

---

*The young woman, Teruwerq Jale, was related to Taytu through her mother. Her marriage to Ato Waqe was dissolved at the wish of the empress, and she married Mulugeta who was the nephew of Ato Waqe. (Zewde Gabre-Sellassie)

as he was highly amused.*

The German mission made a striking contribution to convenience at the royal residence in Addis Ababa. They repaired and extended the electric lighting, which as Minister Rosen explained to Governor Martini, could not have been done without the help of the Italian telegraphist, Bertolani, who provided them with materials. Their other gift, the *pièce de résistance* as Rosen called it, was a lorry. They had shipped it at the suggestion of Arnold Holtz, a German worker in the Ethiopian capital. Rosen said sarcastically that Holtz's great idea had fizzled because they had been unable to transport the vehicle beyond Dire Dawa.[20]

One of the young princesses who played with the German dolls confirmed Vollbrecht's picture of family life in the palace:

It was a very happy world as Menilek and Taytu were so fond of children. She was a very firm disciplinarian. Yes, we played with the dolls, though one of our favorite games was galloping about like horses. The boys went to school and the girls were taught weaving and cooking. Empress Taytu would bend over to handle our piece of cloth and praise one or another for doing the finest weaving.[21]

Weaving! Could the empress have been making her own statement about the dignity of labor that Menilek also tried to instill by edict and example? Weaving was one of the occupations despised by the Amhara, and people were brought to Addis Ababa from the Gamu highlands to do this work. Weavers, even today, live in their own communities at the foot of Entotto mountain.[22]

It is possible that this noblewoman meant spinning and not weaving, as Dr. Mérab said that Taytu "enjoyed her reputation as a spinner and was proud of it ... princesses treated it as a pastime and took pleasure in clothing their husbands, brothers or sons with cotton they had spun."[23]

Sometime in late 1902 or early 1903, the empress took into her employ a Mrs. Katherine Hall, a German-Ethiopian woman, remembered by Princess Yesheshwerq Yilma as "head of the mamites" (nursemaids) whom they called Welette Iyesus.† The non-

---

*Vollbrecht underestimated the ages of both Taytu and Zewditu. In January 1906 Zewditu was delivered of a daughter who died soon after.
†She was the daughter of C. Zander, one of the artisans imprisoned at Meqdela by Emperor Tewodros, and his Ethiopian wife. Katherine married another prisoner, Moritz Hall. Her son, Jacob, had by this time taken American nationality. (Bairu Tafla) Mrs. Hall was therefore the sister of Teresa Naretti, though sources show no contact between them.

German legations expended many words and much time worrying
about the pro-German impact Mrs. Hall and her son Jacob, who
organized a school for boys, might have on Empress Taytu and
Menilek.[24] Mrs. Hall did become very fond of Lij Iyasu, who was
her particular charge (and he of her), but as for impact on foreign
policy the legations' anxieties were groundless. Mrs. Hall could not
even protect Lij Iyasu from Taytu's "firm discipline." Dr. Vitalien
noticed one day that Iyasu hobbled with his legs chained together,
although he tried to conceal it. Iyasu had called the empress "old
woman" when she had put a stop to one of his caprices. Dr. Vitalien
pleaded his case with the empress who told Vitalien not to listen to
his heart. The boy had "sinned" and had to be punished.[25]

Taytu's plaint to Dr. Vollbrecht, "What do they all want?", echoed
her husband's query to the Duc d'Orléans in 1897. It showed a
healthy skepticism during a period of determined colonialism in
Africa. Skepticism and suspicion would increase, though the emperor
continued to hand out concessions for everything from ostrich
feathers to gold mining. If, by the end of 1905, the empress was tired
of "being stared at like a monkey," and refused to be accessible to
every foreign visitor who wished to see her, her retreat was
understandable. "I have never yet seen Empress Taytu, nor have I
had any communication with her entourage," grumbled one diplomat
after two months in the capital.[26]

Taytu's curiosity about foreigners was sated long before the end
of 1905.[27] For the favor-and-privilege seekers, both foreign and
domestic, the urge to talk to the empress only intensified, especially
as the health of the emperor declined.

16

Should Menilek die ...

With Ethiopia's borders either settled or the subject of negotiation with England, France and Italy, with the relative stability in Tigray and with the quiescence of the conquered peoples of Awsa and the southwest, gossip in the legations focused on what would happen to all this "peace" should Menilek die. This stream of speculation swelled to a torrent after the death of Ras Mekonnen in March 1906 as many people considered him, if not the heir to the throne, at least the man most capable of maintaining order and honoring the agreements Menilek had made. For Governor Martini of Eritrea, Mekonnen's death meant yet another delay in the projected meeting between him and the emperor of Ethiopia.[1] Menilek was deeply afflicted by his cousin's death. "He spent three days and nights weeping under a tent put up not far from the palace, striking his chest and moaning, 'My son, my son ... I have lost my right arm.' All the others copied him, except the empress ... who did not like the influence of Ras Mekonnen."[2]

The meeting with Martini was to be held at Borumeda in Wello, the fertile plain on which Menilek had conferred several times with Emperor Yohannes. Martini had said many times as a pre-condition, "To Addis Ababa, I will not go," because it would look too much like a visit of petition or homage. Martini had to change his mind when Ras Mekonnen died. The good faith of the emperor had been proven for he had left for Borumeda, the empress having preceded him, when they were called back to Addis Ababa by the sad news.[3]

Though unhappy at this turn of events, the 62-year-old Martini, now in his eighth year of office and ready to retire, began preparations for the longer journey at Menilek's urgent request. The empress, whose advice was not heeded, wanted the conference postponed until after the heavy rains. In retrospect, Martini might have wished her views to prevail for once, as he was to suffer 40 days of continuous downpour in the Ethiopian capital.

Martini's contingent took 53 days to reach Addis Ababa. In addition to his own party of 26, including some dashing *bersaglieri* sent from Rome to provide éclat, there were at least 10,000 soldiers of Abreha Araya, Gebre Selasse and Seyum Mengesha Yohannes, escorting them. They were slowed down by the special arrangements required for the suites accompanying Amaretch Walelu and Yetemegnu Wele,* the wives of Gebre Selasse and Abreha Araya respectively, as well as by the need to stop for rest and ceremonial receptions *en route*.

With his usual acerbity, Martini commented on each chief who entertained him. Wagshum Kebede "put on airs," and Ras Wele "drinks a lot" and annoyed Martini because he could not remember his name despite all the correspondence that had passed between them when Wele was governor of Tigray. "He does not have much head ... but is good with the poor who love him very much," explained Abreha Araya.[4]

Abreha Araya, Martini decided during the long trip, was a person whose company he enjoyed more than that of Gebre Selasse, who never missed an opportunity to "boast about the high-level connections of his wife." Martini and Abreha had long, frank conversations as Abreha's Italian was excellent, and he thought Italy the most beautiful country on earth; he loved Italian buildings, Italian furniture, and Italian food. So jealous was he of Gebre Selasse that he falsified the facts about him: "He is the son of a servant of my father who was once the ruler of all Tigray, but should the emperor grant him all of Tigray, which he would like, there would be rebellion. Oh, in Italy, a man of low birth can, with study, rise to be great, but in Abyssinia, no. Our country must be governed by nobility."

Martini asked what would happen if Menilek died, to which Abreya replied, "The heir is Iyasu, the son of Mikael, and he is my relative."

At Desse, Martini met the grandfather-in-law of Abreha, the famous Ras Mikael, and found him handsome and intelligent. The reception committee of 30,000 men was splendidly garbed. Mikael and Ras Wele wore crowns, and Mikael had removed his mourning clothes as the emperor had requested his chiefs to do on meeting Governor Martini.† "Mourning clothes" were the filthiest rags that

---

*Daughter of Bidwoded Wele and Sehin Mikael. (Zewde Gabre-Sellassie) Martini described her as the daughter of a daughter of Ras Mikael, married at the age of nine in late 1905 to Abreha.

†By the time this meeting took place, the decreed mourning period of 40 days for Mekonnen was officially over. Menilek gave the order to resume mourning when the Tigrayans reached Addis Ababa. Martini could not comprehend how these men could suddenly start sobbing, lacerating their cheeks and putting on dirty clothes for a man over whose death they felt no emotion. The "reformer *dejazmach*" as Martini called Abreha Araya, told him that he also thought these customs ridiculous: "I am obliged to wear the same clothes for 40 days, sleep on the ground where I get covered with insects and stink for miles around." He had changed his clothes three times since leaving Meqelle and said, "Not much but it is something!"

could be found, and Martini kept asking himself, "Why, oh why, is dirt a symbol of mourning?"

At Were Ilu, the property of Menilek's daughter, Zewditu, Martini met her maternal uncle, Habte Maryam, who administered the area for her. He noted approvingly the presence of a telegraph and telephone station and observed that Were Ilu was like a large hotel which straddled the route to and from Addis Ababa. At Doba, one of Taytu's fiefs and a customs post from which she claimed some 4,000 talers a year, Martini complained that they were poorly provisioned as the empress had not sent the order. Martini and Abreha Araya were in agreement that the number of customs posts, all in all, between Adigrat and Addis Ababa was grossly unfair to traders.

Though Martini waxed ecstatic over the beauties of the land through which he traveled, he also wrote, "What I wouldn't give to be alone in a house and not see anyone for eight days ... driving me crazy is the cold of the evening, cold of the night, cold of the morning, the brightness of the sunlight when it does shine ... and the thousands of people."

When they reached Wuchale, Martini received a telegram from Ciccodicola, informing him that the emperor had fainted while supervising some construction work at Entotto* but had recovered quickly and was back in Addis Ababa. Menilek had called the Italian in to witness his good health and told him to keep the incident a secret. Keeping a secret in Addis Ababa was impossible. The six legations (Russian, Belgian, German, French, English and Italian) all knew within hours. Dr. Kohanowski of the Russian clinic was nearest to Entotto and was called first. Then Menilek's personal physician, Joseph Vitalien, was sent for.

Vitalien, born in Guadeloupe, was Paris-trained. He had been recruited by Ras Mekonnen for a hospital in Harar in 1902, but Mekonnen relinquished him to the emperor at the end of 1904. The French legation supplemented his salary from Menilek, confident that his dark skin would give him special rapport with the emperor, and that his French nationality would make him acceptable at the palace. In this surmise they were correct.

---

*Taytu had insisted on a special tax to rebuild Entotto Maryam church. There were many complaints about the cost and uselessness of the project, which the chronicler admitted. "She refused obstinately to listen to them and had it rebuilt." When Menilek became ill at the construction site, many said, "I told you so."

Vitalien's report on Menilek's state of health in December 1904 was the first of many to appear in the files of the Quai d'Orsay. At that time, Vitalien wrote, "J'accuse syphilis dans jeune age," which Menilek later confirmed. He deplored the effect on Menilek's digestive tract of the Ethiopian diet — large quantities of hot pepper stew or raw meat, followed by two or three liters of honey wine. Vitalien noted that the emperor partook immoderately of Fernet Branca, a liqueur of high alcoholic content flavored with aloes, which has a laxative effect. He predicted that the emperor would live many years longer if he kept a more reasonable pace at work, and cut down on eating and drinking.[5]

While Menilek was not seriously affected by this "fainting spell," which was surely a "stroke" characteristic of the latent infection of his nervous system, it had followed so closely upon Mekonnen's death that intense concern for their own safety in the event of Menilek's death extended from legation personnel to the trading community.

From 6 June 1906, when a legation staff member met Martini a few days out of Addis Ababa, until the day he left on 28 July, security for Europeans was the obsessive subject at every social occasion. The obsession was further intensified when two powerful rases, as well as the emperor himself, blandly concurred that indeed the position of Europeans would be precarious in the event of Menilek's death.[6]

Riding towards the capital, the attaché briefed Martini on Menilek's health, saying that he "drinks too much, is exhausted, and will die soon." In answer to Martini's question, "Wouldn't the empress protect Europeans?" the attaché said:

Good heavens, she will have other things on her mind. She may be the first victim as she is hated for her harshness and continuous intrigue. See how she forced Menilek to name Yilma Mekonnen to Harar, when Mekonnen's deathbed wish was that his other son, Teferi, succeed him — and she was against the Borumeda conference because in that ambience she feared Menilek would decide against her brother in a dispute he has with Ras Mikael.[7]

Martini's agenda with the emperor consisted of the following items: first, punishment of a man who had tried to poison the Italian telegraphist at Adwa; second, permission for Italian commercial agents to work in Gondar, Desse and Debre Tabor; third, indemnity for raids already perpetrated on the Eritrea border and assurances that they would be prevented in future; fourth, removal of Desta Sebhat as governor of Agame because he was a "terrible drunk" and not a "good neighbor;" and fifth, permission for a telegraph line from Borumeda to Assab. These issues overlapped with Ciccodicola's responsibility for getting a commercial treaty with Ethiopia similar to those Menilek had signed with other nations. Ciccodicola was also seeking permission for an Italian resident at Lugh (on the border with Italian Somaliland), and protection for Italian interests on the border with Anglo-Sudan.

Martini believed that Ciccodicola had become intoxicated with his own high status with the emperor at the expense of pressing the interests of Italy. "If I do not insist, he just won't take matters up." Diplomatic conventions dictated that all of Martini's business be presented by Ciccodicola as the on-site diplomat. Martini had to admit that Ciccodicola was well regarded by Rases Welde Giyorgis and Tessema, Fitawrari Habte Giyorgis, and the emperor "who calls him to the *gibbi* often." But, he thought their regard had been purchased by a childish reliance on giving presents, and by Ciccodicola's servile, sycophantic behavior.

The reception was splendid enough for the Eritrean governor, who had been through several on his way to Addis Ababa. The hour-and-a-half review of 70,000 men was "unforgettable," especially the contingent of Shanqila* in white tunics and red caps, and the number of elephant-killers with their cockades of asparagus fern. Léon Chefneux, standing next to Martini, whispered to him that when Ethiopians hunt elephant they do so in groups of 50; everyone fires at the elephant at once, therefore each man wins the insignia.

The emperor paid Martini the special honor of walking out to meet him.† "He is very ugly; one of the ugliest men I have ever seen, but his smile is so sweet it illumines his face." Martini thought his eyes showed the effects of his recent attack and concluded that "he could never have made it to Borumeda." Menilek offered him a whiskey and soda and drank one with him in the middle of the morning.

A week passed before they talked business. The obligatory banquet was held, with Léon Chefneux, instead of the absent Ilg, settling the protocol balance between Lagarde, doyen of the diplomatic corps,

---

*More properly called Berta people. They were captured by Ras Mekonnen in 1899 and then trained by a military adventurer, the Marquis de la Guiborgère.
†A story, related only in a French source, tells that when the Englishman, Harrington, presented his credentials to the emperor, the emperor did not rise to greet him. Harrington backed away a few steps and waited for him to do so. Menilek said, "I do not get up except before the cross."

and Martini, the guest of honor. Chefneux explained to Martini the increased hostility to foreigners: "They are always taking up the emperor's time, at the expense of domestic problems." Other reasons were provided by each of the diplomats he called upon.

A French worker, fighting with an Ethiopian, had accidentally shot a woman bystander. There was much disgraceful drunkenness among the Greek, Armenian and Italian workmen. The British minister Harrington threw his weight around, especially when the populace did not dismount when he rode by as they did for their Ethiopian betters.[8]

Martini was amazed when he called on Léonce Lagarde, and found his reputation for pretentiousness belied. Not only was his *tukul* seedy and run down, the interior dirty, its furniture broken, but even the map of France on the wall was also torn and soiled. Lagarde wore clothes that matched his surroundings but "the food was good and we had an interesting talk."

Lagarde obliquely praised Empress Taytu's concern for her husband's health: "We hope the witch's prophecy is borne out — that the Queen will die first, then Welde Giyorgis, then Menilek. The empress feeds this prophecy to Menilek to put his mind at rest as he is old and feeling his infirmities." Lagarde expressed the view that it was not only foreigners who were hated, but also overlords. He said that, should Menilek die, people would take the opportunity to kill all of them.

Lagarde and Martini discussed the accord which was about to be signed in London between France, Italy and England regarding spheres of interest in Ethiopia. Lagarde disclosed his great contempt for the judgment of Harrington, who "put in writing a proposal to various chiefs that the emperor have a council of European advisers. This makes the Ethiopians think the Europeans want to take over their country." The empress, Lagarde continued, refused audiences to Harrington for some time after she saw that memo, and then summoned him to say, "We are ancient, we are small, but to become great we do not need Europeans. If the emperor wants councillors he will choose them from among his own people."[9]

Mr. Coates, the German minister, was naïve enough to agree with Harrington's proposal for a council of European advisers, and "doesn't seem to realize the significance of the empress's stated opposition." Martini was happy to learn that Coates had just repatriated about 40 Germans who had come from Palestine to establish some kind of utopian settlement. One of those Germans was David Hall, another son of the German-Ethiopian lady who was "close to the empress." Hall remembered the day of his arrival in Addis Ababa when he had waved at a friend just as the emperor was passing by on a mule. The emperor had thought that he was waving at him and sent an aide to find out who he was. On learning he was Mrs. Hall's son he invited him to lunch that very day. For 20 of the 28 days he was in the city, David and his mother had a meal with Menilek and Taytu. "She asked me many questions about Jerusalem and the condition of the monks to whom she had given much money. Just as I was leaving, the monarchs sent me 27 grams of gold in the form of *orkit* [rings], six from Menilek and four from the empress."[10]

The Russian legation was staffed by a chargé-d'affaires as Minister Lischine had died a few months earlier. "De Likatscheff was pleasant enough," wrote Martini, "tends to the rose garden planted by Lischine and to his crypt which is on the Russian compound." Apart from the good work of Drs. Valishin and Kohanowski at the clinic, the Russians had no commercial or diplomatic interests, he concluded.

Martini witnessed that inevitable creation of a diplomatic island so natural to foreigners in an alien culture. They met Ethiopians only at the racecourse, occasions which even the emperor enjoyed. "He showed his displeasure when Harrington's horse won the 'Mrs. MacMillan' cup, but otherwise indulged in a loud display of cheering and clapping."[11] Martini attended dinners, a ball, and the social club soirée, where Mme. Roux played the piano, Signora Ciarrone sang out of tune, Forgeron mumbled a Neapolitan song in French, and an orchestra composed of pianoforte and four violins played themes from *Lucia di Lammermoor* so out of harmony that Martini called them the "independents."

Martini found Abune Matewos a "liberal, intelligent man very different from Abune Petros." Matewos spoke of his trip to Russia and censured the Czar "who governs with force when all other European sovereigns are trying to govern with the consent of the people." "Hmmm," mused Martini, "what does he think goes on here?"[12]

The houses of Welde Giyorgis and Tessema Nadew "deserve to be called homes," for they had windows, doors and attractive furnishings. Welde Giyorgis told Martini that he had learned something from "whites" about building. His audience with Empress Taytu was short but agreeable. It had been postponed once because

she and her step-daughter, Zewditu, had been mourning the death
of Zewditu's daughter six months before. Also present was Kefey
Wele, now divorced from the incarcerated Ras Mengesha Yohannes,
and remarried to her first husband, and Weyzero Yeshemabet, whose
portrait Martini had just seen at the house of her husband, Welde
Giyorgis. The empress's *shamma* allowed him to notice her "eyes,
her many chins and dark, uneven teeth." He, as have many others,
said her pictures did not do her justice, making her look fatter than
she was. "She was very affable with Ciccodicola and scolded him
for not introducing his sister to her."

Menilek's and Taytu's fondness of Major Ciccodicola was
ephemeral in Martini's opinion. He found evidence daily that the
representative of Italy should be removed from his post. The
catalogue of Ciccodicola's sins was compiled while Martini waited
for Emperor Menilek to sign the commercial treaty and act favorably
on the rest of his agenda.

"This legation is a hell-hole. Not one person in it gets along with
another, excepting Caetani, who is wise and prudent and knows how
to stay calm during one of Ciccodicola's outbursts." Dr. Lincoln de
Castro and his wife were scarcely speaking to him, first because "he
dishonors his country by flaunting his Ethiopian mistress, and second
because he refused Mrs. de Castro permission to send something in
the diplomatic pouch. She went to Mr. Harrington who instantly
gave her space in his mail bag." Alfredo Ciarrone refused legation
invitations, offended that he had not been included at the banquet
in Martini's honor. Ciarrone, conceded Martini, was a trial to
Ciccodicola because he was "supposed to be an interpreter, but his
Amharic was so bad he needed an interpreter himself."

Of Ciccodicola, Martini wrote:

Ciccodicola confesses to being 15,000 lire in debt and owes 10,000 lire in
the piazza. He has a mania for buying things — toiletries, watches, clocks,
bronze statuettes — his house is a bazaar. There were 62, I repeat 62, rubber
stamps saying "Legation of Italy," eight gongs, quite expensive furniture
from Rome, useless silver trinkets — it is a mania and everyone knows it.

I learned today, and it didn't surprise me, that he had been given eight
slaves by the emperor — and gave four of them to his *madama* ... the
infamous Desta.

Martini was appalled when Ciccodicola's sister complained to him
one day that one of these slaves had run away and she was going
to protest to the emperor.

"And now — the worst. I learned that ... the emperor gave him some gold bars as a gift — valued at 3,000 lire and he accepted! Nor could I convince him to take up the interests of the mining society with Menilek. He said he would not bother the emperor or ask any favors."

On 8 July a telegram arrived saying that a Tripartite Pact had been signed in London and that a copy was on its way. Lagarde, Harrington and Ciccodicola followed instructions to go to the *gibbi* together to interpret the pact to the emperor. On that occasion, Harrington, continuing his egregious rudeness to Menilek, said, "You are out of your mind if you don't approve it." Menilek managed a calm reply, "You have had four years to make this accord and you want me to approve it in a day!" Empress Taytu was more succinct: "These people are crazy."[13]

The Tripartite Pact of 4 July 1906 provided for the maintenance of the status quo based on previous agreements signed between any two of the three powers and non-intervention in Ethiopian internal affairs. *But*, should the status quo be disturbed (that is, by the death of Menilek), British interests in the Nile valley would be honored and the water supply of the Nile, one of whose sources arose at Lake Tana in Ethiopia,* would not be cut off. Eritrea, Italian Somaliland and their hinterlands (that is, Tigray) would be in the Italian sphere. The French colony on the Somali coast, its hinterlands, and the zone required for the railroad would be in the French sphere. The French, in turn, guaranteed equal treatment on the railroad for the other two powers and a vaguely worded intention to place Italian and English representatives on the railway board of governors. Similar guarantees were made to the French on any railways built by the other two.[14] It was a tidy division of Ethiopia.†

Martini had been against submitting the agreement to the emperor, fearing that it would upset Menilek and delay action on Italy's commercial treaty. Menilek did indeed take his time and stated his views in writing six months later. He thanked the three governments

*Fear that the Ethiopians could disrupt the flow out of Lake Tana of Egypt and Sudan's life-line went back to the 14th century. The chronicler stated (1: 29) that Dawit II (1380-1412) stopped the flow of the Nile until the Muslims ceased to persecute Christians, but this statement is not founded on truth.
†Ras Welde Giyorgis, after the Tripartite Pact, withdrew his objections to Lij Iyasu as heir (on the grounds that "a Mohammedan's son can never rule over Abyssinia") and said, "it is better to submit to a Shanqila than to be a European slave." (Gebre Heywet)

for their interest in his independence, but wanted it clearly understood that there was to be no infringement of Ethiopia's sovereign rights.

Some five weeks after Martini's arrival in Addis Ababa, the emperor settled almost everything to the satisfaction of the Italians, even passing the death sentence on the man who had attempted the murder of the telegrapher at Adwa. Martini promptly asked for commutation to imprisonment, which was granted. Menilek gave permission for Italian commercial agencies to work at Gondar, Borumeda, and Desse, but not in Tigray. "Frankly," Menilek told Ciccodicola, "Tigray people are bad ... and if tomorrow they killed one of your agents, I fear you would use it as an excuse to invade us." Empress Taytu was not blamed for the length of time it had taken to get the Italian treaty signed. "It was completely understandable," wrote Martini, "because the articles in the Italian press said falsely that we were asking Menilek to cede Tigray to Italy." "Fool," "knaves," and "liars" were Martini's names for the press in Italy.

When Martini left the capital on 28 July 1906, legation personnel were still in a swivet over their own safety. Subsequent events would show how their anxieties fed on each other in their isolated life. No accord signed in London could force the three veterans, Ciccodicola, Harrington and Lagarde, to cooperate with each other. The only things they agreed upon were that conditions in Ethiopia and the personality of Emperor Menilek had been so romanticized by journalists and travel writers that officialdom and public opinion had a complete misconception of this "harsh, backward country."

Harrington went on a year's leave in December 1906 and could look back on a number of accomplishments. He had prevented the French government from taking control of the railroad, had acquired Ethiopian cooperation in the efforts to trap the "Mad Mullah," had convinced Menilek that he should put his seal on frontier and commercial-station agreements and agree to a railroad from Addis Ababa to the Sudan frontier, and had assisted in the establishment of the Bank of Abyssinia.[15] However, the efforts to trap the "Mad Mullah" failed and the railway was never built.

Just before Harrington's return in January 1908 with a "rich American wife," the emperor told Mr. Hohler, chargé, that he would rather Harrington did not return as he did not pay due respect and reverence to the crown. Hohler refused to send this message unless the emperor put it in writing. So Menilek wrote, "In all words that

Sir John speaks to us, civility is lacking."* Harrington returned anyway, and said that Empress Taytu apologized to him and implied that the French minister had told lies about him to the emperor. Harrington remained civil for the balance of his duty in Ethiopia and left for good in September 1908.[16]

The ailing Léonce Lagarde retired in 1907 after 23 years of service in the Horn of Africa. Despite the fiasco of the Bonchamps-Bonvalot-Clochette expedition to the Nile, and the stalling on the railroad, he had negotiated the return of French missionaries and the necessary treaties for frontiers and trade.

Martini's antipathy notwithstanding, Ciccodicola did not leave until October 1907 after an embarrassing disclosure in *Il Secolo di Milano* of his life style and profligacy with government money. Ciccodicola defended himself to the Foreign Office, saying that it was not he who went about conspicuously uniformed, and that he was in fact the only one of the diplomats who wore simple, ordinary clothes in public. He justified his outlays of money as necessary to Italian status. Regarding the woman, he explained that when he arrived in 1897, as the only Italian, with an Ethiopian interpreter and an Eritrean askari escort, his only option was to live in a native hut and in native style. When the French minister came and lived like an Abyssinian lord, but without a *madama*, it only gave impetus to gossip about his virility among the Abyssinians. Living with a native woman was the only way to run an establishment. When Harrington came, he too found it convenient to have an Abyssinian woman. "It is what everyone does. I never forced anyone to know my woman. Harrington and others of the English legation were acquainted with her and brought her gifts. At the *gibbi* it was neither a joke nor a scandal, and even secured me the friendship of the empress. It is absolutely false that members of the diplomatic community would not set foot in my legation."[17]

In any event, it was time for Ciccodicola, in poor health, to leave after 10 years in Addis Ababa. He, too, could look back on achievements. Borders with Italian possessions had been regularized, and Menilek owed his telegraph and telephone links throughout the empire to Italy. Mines under concessions in Welega and Tigray were

---

*Harrington bragged to Governor Martini when he saw him in Rome in March 1907 that in his farewell call on the emperor he had said, "You are all thieves; not you, but all your rases and dejazmaches." He said that Menilek had told him not to talk to him like that, to which Harrington had replied, "It is my duty to say it."

in operation, there was an all-weather road between Addis Ababa and Addis Alem, and another road had been started to link Asmara to Gondar which would increase trade through the Italian colony.

Menilek suffered another cerebral incident in August 1907. At his 63rd birthday reception on 19 August, the guests noted that he did not look well. Anton Klobukowski, a special envoy from France to get the railroad unblocked, smugly reported to the Quai d'Orsay that he was not as shocked as his colleagues because Dr. Vitalien had informed him about Menilek's "stroke."

Dr. Vitalien had become much respected at court. The empress "begged" him to hasten to the palace compound in January 1907 to treat her brother, Ras Wele. "I found him striking his servants, babbling, crying ... he did not even recognize Menilek who was present. At one moment he seized a sword and a revolver and killed an imaginary enemy. They disarmed him with difficulty. He heard voices. The enemy he fought was Ras Mikael." Ras Wele's behavior was the talk of the town according to an Ethiopian diarist:

While at Azaj Zamanel's house Wele heard that Ras Mikael was at Filwuha baths and said, "I will not let that Moslem spend the night there." He was about to go out wearing only a tiger skin when his son Gugsa forced him back. When Menilek heard, he reprimanded Taytu saying, "Are you not the cause of all this [bitter hatred between Wele and Mikael]?" and she said, "Wele did these things because he has lost his senses from illness ... not as a healthy person."[18]

Dr. Vitalien treated Ras Wele by isolating him, giving him prolonged baths and hypnotic suggestion, and having him under close surveillance for six weeks. "Today [12 March 1907] he resumed his duties but as an inveterate alcoholic, he can expect a recurrence."

Menilek's curiosity about the cause of his own and Ras Wele's illness was satisfied by Dr. Vitalien, who, working with a sheep's kidney, simulated with chemicals the long-term effects of venereal disease and the ravages of alcohol, which Menilek could observe with a magnifying glass. Menilek was so impressed that he asked Vitalien to repeat the experiment before members of the court.

Klobukowski may have been the source of an anonymous report in *A Travers Le Monde* in which the emperor's way of doing business was described:

While conferring with the minister of France on the railroad, a servant may whisper in his ear, "Sire, the locksmith needs nails to fix the lock." Menilek gives him the keys to the storeroom and says, "Take five nails, and if that isn't enough come and tell me." He maneuvers, promises, withdraws, sets French and Germans back to back, smiles at Russia, swears eternal friendship to England. "Ah, here is the Italian minister." Suddenly two grooms enter, "Sire, the mules have gotten out ... can't find their tracks." Menilek jumps from his throne, dashes out, climbs to his observatory and scans the streets and hills of Addis Ababa with his telescope to find the runaways. Thus a few nails or two donkeys can break up talks on the railroad which will connect his capital to the civilized world.[19]

Despite his stroke and his unpredictable behavior, Menilek got through the secret negotiations with Klobukowski and appointed Dr. Vitalien as his representative on the railroad board, replacing Léon Chefneux. Klobukowski crowed about the victory of medical diplomacy, "While ministering to the emperor, Vitalien had saved France thousands of francs." The talks leaked out and irritated both of France's partners in the Tripartite Pact as well as Menilek's advisers, but not the empress, who was informed and did not block the agreement signed with the French envoy, though she persuaded Menilek to renege two years later.

Klobukowski said the empress was difficult. In the first of several meetings with her, she was vehement about the behavior of diplomats who "with sweet words and friendly protestations insinuate themselves in order to chase out the Ethiopians." Her rudeness, he said, was modulated by her depth of feeling. "To tell the truth her diatribe tickled me," and he reports one such conversation:

I kept smiling and started to defend myself. "However," I ventured, "His Majesty Menilek ..."

"Oh, the emperor — he is too good and believes everything they tell him." With a shrug of the shoulders she said, "He is always cheated but I know he listens to you and has spoken well of you."

I hastened to offer her a magnificent silver pitcher as a gift from the Republic of France. She, indicating the spout, and with a look that leveled me like a pistol shot, said, "This looks like the beak of a bird of prey." I changed the subject.

I pretended not to hear. "The train Your Majesty slanders will take her to Palestine to the Holy Places." Suddenly subdued, she answered, "That is what I wish for."

On taking his leave, Klobukowski told the empress that he found her opinions so interesting that with her permission he would like to transmit them to Paris:

"You would dare do that?"
"But yes, why not?"

"What I said to you — the French government will know?" And her eyes sparkled with joy.

"Yes, by Pichon and Clemenceau."

Klobukowski sent a copy of his report to the empress after having it translated into Amharic. She sent word back to him that she was delighted. " 'Her Majesty,' the interpreter told me, 'showed your words to the emperor and he is still laughing. She said that you have a quality that is rare in a diplomat — frankness.' "

Ras Welde Giyorgis, who also saw the report, told Klobukowski that he had exaggerated the empress's anti-foreign attitudes which had been brought about because both Antonelli and Alfred Ilg* had betrayed her trust.[20]

Klobukowski did not show the empress another dispatch he sent to Paris in which he said that after a quarrel with Menilek one evening, the empress had been found crouching in the gardens. Their argument was purported to be over the use of German advisers which the empress was alleged to favor because of the influence of Mrs. Katherine Hall. The "empress crouching in the garden" is difficult to believe. That Mrs. Hall may have said that Germans would be better than those tricky French or arrogant English is certainly possible, but Menilek would have made up his mind on more evidence than the remarks of a *femme de ménage*. He did in fact send a delegation to Germany weeks after Klobukowski wrote this odd story, and it carried a letter asking for German support of Ethiopian claims in Jerusalem and an invitation to increase trade links between their two countries.[21]

After his two cerebral hemorrhages in August 1907 and in May 1908, Emperor Menilek issued a number of important edicts. Responding to his own intimation of mortality, which he called "fatigue," to persistent pressure from the legations to tell him who was in charge of what, and to the advice of the empress who wanted him to lighten the burden he carried, the emperor announced the formation of a "European-style" cabinet in October 1907.[22]

In Ethiopia's first cabinet, old functions were represented and

---

*Alfred Ilg had never "betrayed" the empress. He and his wife had left Ethiopia in April 1906. Family matters and business kept him in Europe. He resigned in 1907, citing his father's death and his children's educational needs. He was aware of Menilek's poor health and saw no future in Ethiopia without his patronage. He declined Menilek's invitation to return in 1908. It was said that his potential for profiting from the railroad had been wiped out by the Klobukowski treaty.

refined by a list of duties. An example is the Minister of Justice. The office of Afenegus had existed since antiquity and the man appointed at this time had been acting in that capacity since the 1880s. Afenegus Nessibu confessed to the British minister that he had not the least idea of his new duties and could not understand what it all meant. He continued to be the "hardest-worked official in the kingdom, spending his days hearing and deciding cases, which he summed up for the emperor who hardly ever reversed his decisions."[23]

The real change in the judicial system came a few months later, in March 1908, when another edict divided the country into six judicial districts with two judges for each geographical area. Even more innovative was the assignment of scribes to record decisions. Record-keeping held the promise of cutting down on the endless testimony of conflicting witnesses in the most common "court" case in the country, settlement of a land dispute. To this day, however, the traditional method of legal redress, an informal meeting before an individual with a reputation for fairness, is preferred to government-sponsored adjudication.

Once the legations got the cabinet they had proposed, they were able to complain about the appointments. Hayle Giyorgis, Minister of Commerce and Foreign Affairs, was the man whom they hated most. They considered him avaricious and unprincipled. The British minister thought of protesting his appointment. "If the foreign representatives had presented a united front ... there would have been little difficulty in procuring his removal. Unfortunately my Italian colleague and myself have learned from experience that it is futile to look to the French minister for cooperation." The British diplomat was dreaming. No degree of cooperation between the legations would have altered Menilek's appointment of the invaluable Hayle Giyorgis, who was Menilek's right hand in economic control of the empire.[24] The cabinet did not actually convene until the building for their meetings was completed in July 1908. Dr. Vitalien was invited, or rather "ordered," to be present. He gave some advice about improving the lighting of the room, enjoyed the food and drink and told them they should keep their deliberations secret. A few days after this meeting, Dr. Vitalien was called to attend the Minister of Justice, Afenegus Nessibu, but it was too late. The *afenegus* had subjected himself to mercury fumigation, a common and in this case a lethal form of treatment for syphilis.[25]

The first decision of the cabinet, the chronicler tells us, was that people must stop making bets in which the loser would receive 10,000 blows; to bet a horse, a mule, some honey, or money not exceeding 20 talers was permitted. The second and third rulings were of greater significance. The custom of confiscation of land belonging to a convicted criminal was nullified; the criminal was to have his animals taken or to be given corporal punishment. These lesser punishments were received with much relief, as the convicted felon's family would not be forced into homelessness. The next ruling involved inheritance and gave the right to an individual who had no children to name another person as his heir. Under the *Fetha Nagast*, imperial authority often seized the land when there were no children, even though the descendant's parents or siblings might be alive. The ruling was a more precise definition of private property.

More important than the formation of a cabinet, which simply gave a European name to an existing institution, was Menilek's edict on education. The astonishing part of the proclamation of 6 October 1907 was the inclusion of girls. The influence of Taytu is evident, as she herself was highly literate and was said to have taught the emperor how to read and write both Amharic and Ge'ez.[26]

The staff for the new school was present in Addis Ababa before the edict, having arrived from Alexandria in 1906. Employing Copts from Egypt was the concession made to Abune Matewos who rejected European teachers with as firm a determination as that of the empress. The edict on education was a tiny step towards the admission that the church, which prepared men, and a few women, for various church-related functions, "was not adequate for a developing nation."[27]

No young girls actually attended the new school. Even by 1913, Dr. Mérab said there were no schools for girls in the capital and that educated women could be counted on one's fingers, if one "excepted the royal women."

A saying of the people assures that the husband of a woman who knows how to read will not live long, for the woman who can read would have recourse to maledictions and malefices at the least reprimand from her spouse. A lettered woman would not take care of the house. An Abyssinian of my acquaintance said, when I asked why he did not have his only daughter take instruction, "Where would I get money to pay the priest to teach her, and then how would I buy a eunuch to keep an eye on the priest?"[28]

The empress, the emperor, Abune Matewos and many others were unalterably opposed to Protestant and/or Catholic conversion of their young people, the frequent result of attending schools sponsored by these faiths.

The empress had a well-deserved reputation for being anti-Catholic. In front of a group of people at the palace she embarrassed the interpreter of the French legation, an Ethiopian, by asking him "Are you a Catholic?" Menilek turned to her and said, "Taytu, are you his father confessor? What kind of question is this?"[29] Father Jarosseau and two colleagues were forced to wait six months in the capital before Menilek, despite the objections of his clergy and the empress, finally issued them a passport to go to Keffa to re-establish the Catholic mission there. Even in Keffa their troubles were not over. "A letter arrived while we were dining with Dejazmach Gebre Egziabeher, from Empress Taytu, which said, 'I know that the Catholic priest, Jarosseau, is with you. I order you to bring him to me dead or alive.'" The *dejazmach* offered Jarosseau mules so the trio of priests could flee to another place and said he would write to the empress to say that he could not find them. They were caught, chained and forced to walk to Addis Ababa. Just outside the city, they managed to get a message to Stévenin who went to them immediately. "I saw three priests covered with ants and sores, and ran to get help from Savouré who obtained a hearing from the *negus*. Menilek swore he knew nothing about it and promptly had them freed."[30]

Father Jarosseau remained thereafter in Harar where the Catholics established a school, an orphanage, a hospital and a leprosarium, and launched a monthly newsletter which became *Le Semeur d'Ethiopie*. A well-orchestrated campaign to open Addis Ababa to Catholics* was mounted. The Pope wrote a letter to the emperor in July 1906 commending to him the good works of Catholic missions. Menilek responded with his own purpose in mind (support on the Jerusalem question) sending the Pope the "Star of Ethiopia." The Pope made an exception to his policy of not accepting decorations from governments. The Vatican arranged with the "Equestrian Order of the Holy Sepulchre" (dedicated to those who defended the Holy Sepulchre from the infidels) to make the emperor

---

*Father Basile, without clerical garb, conducted mass secretly in the house of Armand Savouré in Addis Ababa or at the French legation from 1903 to 1907, at which time Menilek allowed the Catholics to operate openly. Two Franciscan sisters of Calais were permitted to teach the daughters of foreigners from November 1904.

of Ethiopia a member and named Father Marie-Bernard as Apostolic
Delegate to the court of Ethiopia. *Le Semeur*, whose editor was well
aware that every issue was translated into Amharic by readers at
the palace, carried a picture and tribute to Empress Taytu before
Father Marie-Bernard arrived with the decorations and gifts from
the Pope.

After the emperor's sympathetic welcome, Father Marie-Bernard
had to wait 11 days before seeing the empress, a delay caused by
the fact that she had gone to Entotto to celebrate the fête of Maryam,
and had then felt unwell for several days. During his 15-minute
audience, Father Marie-Bernard gave her the Pope's letter and gifts,
a rendition in mosaic of the Virgin and Infant Jesus. "She could not
keep back a cry of admiration ... and bowing she respectfully kissed
its base. She could not believe until I explained the craft of mosaic
work that it was something other than a painting, and said she would
write to His Holiness herself to thank him." "I know," added Father
Marie-Bernard, "that all missionaries and friends of the mission will
be happy to share this information." It was a clear signal of tolerance
for the Catholics.[31]

Menilek permitted two French priests to open a school at the
end of 1907 but required that they not wear religious costume or
make religious propaganda. "Religion and teaching are two different
things and must not be mixed," he said, overlooking that the church
of Ethiopia held a monopoly on education. Missionaries were
restricted to working with Muslims or animists, such as the Oromo,
or among the Felasha (Ethiopian Jews), and only if they had a permit
to do so.

Pressure to do something about non-secular education may have
derived from the fact that the number of men and women in Ethiopia
who could read and write the Oromo language was greater than the
number of non-clerical readers and writers of Amharic, the language
of rulers. At the Swedish Evangelical Mission at Emkullo in Eritrea,
they had been teaching Oromo men and women since 1866. When
the time came for a young male convert to marry, there was an
equally educated young woman ready to partner him. The
Evangelicals could send an Ethiopian-born family, rather than
Swedes, to take their mission to the Oromo. Ready for them to take
along were their tools: the New Testament, a hymn book and a
reader, all printed in Orominya.[32]

Under the protection of the aforementioned Dejazmach Gebre

Egziabeher* and his uncle, Fitawrari Dibaba, the mission began its work in Welega in 1899. The Evangelical, Gebre Ewostateos and his wife, Gumesh, were for a while on good terms with the Orthodox clergy because he spoke his sermons in Amharic and they could be certain he was not purveying any heretical ideas. Gebre Ewostateos and his companions founded a number of village schools, where they set aside special days for farming and training in crafts. Both boys and girls were instructed in spinning and weaving so that those without land could earn a living. Gebre Ewostateos introduced after-church gatherings at his home where both women and men were welcome and where seating arrangements were not dictated by social status. He rescued a number of slaves, thereby earning the enmity of slave traders, and shocked lay people and clerics alike by baking bread and mixing the pepper sauce while his wife was busy teaching.

Dejazmach Gebre Egziabeher relished the company and teaching of these missionaries, and so did his uncle, Dibaba. Dibaba even put aside all but one of his six wives, Welette Giyorgis: "She reads her testament in Orominya, has broken with the evil customs of women and believes in Jesus Christ." Dibaba learned to read after his wife's example.

Trouble came when Gebre Ewostateos showed no respect for the time-consuming repetition of *teskar* for the dead, conducted by the Orthodox clergy. The clergy protested to the *dejazmach*, who knew that the missionary was right in maintaining that there was nothing in Amharic or Ge'ez scriptures to prove that *teskar* had anything to do with redemption. But fearful of a complaint going to Addis Ababa, the *dejazmach* decreed there was to be no further discussion of the matter. When Gebre Ewostateos lost his life in a courageous attempt to save another Evangelical family from a fire in 1905, the Orthodox clergy spread the word that the Virgin Mary had taken vengeance on her adversary by burning him alive.

Another Oromo, Onesimos Nessibu, educated at the Swedish Emkullo Mission, arrived in Addis Ababa in March 1904 with his wife and five other teachers, including Aster Ganno, the young woman who had helped Onesimos translate the Bible. Onesimos was

*Gebre Egziabeher was the Christian name of the Oromo ruler, Moroda, who had been taken to Menilek's court in 1882 at the time of Ras Gobena's conquest. He had learned to read the scriptures in an Amharic Bible that Menilek gave him. The Amharic Bible had been printed by the Church Mission Society in its entirety by 1840. Menilek was given many copies about 1873.

introduced to Abune Matewos by Kentiba Gebru who had endured
much abuse for his foreign education, but was currently deemed
acceptable at the palace.

He was tutoring Lij Iyasu, the heir to the throne, in German.
Abune Matewos and the emperor granted him and his party
permission to go to Welega as long as he abstained from disputes
with the clergy about the Virgin Mary and the Saints, and about
fasting. "If his teaching deviates from our faith, let me know," wrote
the bishop, "but if not, let him teach; and no man is to prevent him."

Onesimos was delighted to be back among his own people, from
whom he had been stolen by slave traders 35 years before. Believing
himself protected by the letter from Abune Matewos and by the
joviality of Dejazmach Gebre Egziabeher, Onesimos did not follow
his predecessor's example of sermonizing in Amharic to keep the
Orthodox clergy from being suspicious. Before long the priest, jealous
of his intimacy with Gebre Egziabeher, complained that he was
blaspheming the Virgin Mary.

Afraid for his own skin, Gebre Egziabeher did not speak up for
Onesimos at his hearing before Abune Matewos in Addis Ababa in
May 1906, and Onesimos was condemned to exile from the country.
The emperor ordered a review of his case and decided that Onesimos
could return to the mission but was forbidden to teach. Onesimos
continued to read aloud from the Oromo Bible in his own home.

Two other graduates of the Swedish mission school, Gebre Heywet
Baykedagn and Mengesha Biru, also helped create the climate for
the education proclamation. Mengesha Biru, who had learned about
printing at the Emkullo mission, was allowed to put into working
order an old press that he found in the imperial storeroom. In June
1907 he had printed on it an open letter to the emperor asking him
to publish books and newspapers to promote general education and
provide information about the world outside Ethiopia. Gebre
Heywet, employed as a scrivener at the palace, was an outspoken
proponent of education as the road to progress.[33] Probably the
most persuasive voice was that of Aleqa Tayye, a renowned Ge'ez
scholar who had been recommended by the emperor as best fitted
to fulfil a request from Germany for someone to teach at the Berlin
School of Oriental Studies. From Germany, Aleqa Tayye wrote to
Menilek in May 1907 a moving letter in which he said, "Why do
we Abyssinians not progress? It is because we are not educated and
have not heard the words of the gospel and because in our country

people with knowledge are insulted and badly treated." Aleqa Tayye asked Menilek to think about the problem and to put an end to such insults by edict.[34]

In January 1908, four months after Menilek's education proclamation, he issued his *awaj* (public edict) on the dignity of labor:

They [metalworkers, weavers, potters, etc.] are in fact more important to the crown [than anyone].* Those whom you call traders and insult — they exchange goods we need. The indolent insult the wise. Looking down on people is due to lack of education. In faraway countries ... they respect those called engineers. Workers prosper. They are not insulted for their profession. You who insult people who use farm tools, turn my country barren. Insults to these people insult me, and those who do it will be imprisoned one year."[35]

Two new words entered the urban vocabulary at the end of 1907: "hotel" and "motor car." The first hotel was built at the encouragement of, and financed by, the empress. She had leased property to a Frenchman who rented rooms, and, impressed by his success, the empress had an Armenian architect design a large structure of two floors with spacious rooms, a salon and a verandah, with her name on it. As Aleqa Kenfe wrote:

The word "hotel" was not known before ... a large house for strangers was built ... called "hotel" ... where they served the finest dishes of Europe and Ethiopia; the King of Kings gave a banquet there; chiefs, soldiers, merchants, foreigners and people who lived outside the city who wanted to eat went to this hotel and paid according to what they ordered. One could pass the whole day there eating and drinking.[36]

Two of the first paying guests were Bede Bentley and Reginald Wells who drove the first motor car into Addis Ababa on 31 December 1907. The car was a Siddeley, an 18-horsepower, four-cylinder, open five-seater touring car that could travel at 65 kilometers per hour. Doing things that had never been done before was the private passion of Bede Bentley. When the "mad Englishman" unloaded his vehicle on the docks at Djibouti, the French governor thought he was insane not to put it on the train going as far as Dire Dawa, and made him sign a paper absolving the French of any

---

*As a Tigrayan told Pollera, "I never did menial work, such as metalworking, cloth weaving, hide scraping, nor have my ancestors ... I would rather wed my daughter to one of my servants than to a man who employs his hands in such servile tasks."

responsibility for his safety. Bentley had some knowledge of the terrain as he had been an intelligence officer with the British forces fighting the "mad Mullah" in the Ogaden in 1903.

Bentley's obstinacy brought him five months of danger and near disaster, but his perseverance and the talents of his mechanic, Wells, got him to Addis Ababa. They employed Somalis to lay planks across the sandy desert over which they traveled about five kilometers in five hours; they were attacked by the Issa Somali for breaking a promise to pay them a transit fee through their lands; they pulled the car with mules; they carried it, dragged it out of a river, pushed it up mountains and constructed parts as they needed them. Not more than 80 kilometers from Addis Ababa they punished their cook, Jildad, for stealing swigs of whiskey by adding to the bottle a substance that made him double up with cramps. The angry Jildad retaliated by putting some of his own medicine into their coffee. Bentley, warned, first offered the cup to Jildad who dashed it out of his hand, but with help Bentley forced him to drink it. Before their eyes, Jildad began to swell until he "lost all semblance of a man and his body became a puffy heap of bloated, livid flesh." Their horror at what they had done to Jildad was mitigated by the knowledge that he had intended Bentley to die in the same way.

Not more than an hour after they had checked into the Imperial Hotel (later called the Itege) where they could see their filthy, cadaverous bodies reflected in its gilt-framed mirrors, Wells and Bentley were invited to the palace. On pleading fatigue and the need to polish up the vehicle, an appointment was made for the following morning.

The emperor told them that he had been warned by his courtiers that if he got into this contrivance he might be blown up or driven off a precipice. Bentley suggested that two of these scoffers be ordered to be test-driven from the palace to the market and back, a distance that would take half an hour by mule. The streets were cleared by the emperor's order. Wells let out the throttle, drove to the market, bought some fruit to prove it and was back in six minutes. "I see you have frightened my poor ministers," Menilek said, grinning, when he saw the numb faces of the two passengers.

Then the emperor climbed into the front seat with Wells, while Bede Bentley and Thomas Hohler of the British legation sat in the

back. They drove at top speed down the Addis Alem road for 16
kilometers, turned around and came back. Menilek's disappearance
from sight for half an hour stilled the crowd, and as he came into
view a tremendous wail went up from the people "as though he had
come back from the dead."

The emperor went to the hotel the following day and chatted
to Bentley and Wells about cars, traction engines, and railways.
There were more and longer rides in the car. Menilek learned to
drive and asked the two men to train a chauffeur. It became clear
to Bentley and Wells that their original plan to drive on to Khartoum
was not to be realized: Menilek would never let them leave with
the car.

When the empress refused to ride in the car, Bentley was relieved
because "she was so fat." She was very charming to him and
complimented him on "doing something without talking about it."
She watched from her window as Bentley signaled to Wells to drive
the car round and round the courtyard. Then she asked Bentley to
do her a favor. Could he repair the cinematograph? Bentley did so,
and then handed it over to the Armenian projectionist who ran a
couple of reels of film. She "painfully rose to her feet," and gave
two massive gold bracelets to Bentley with a smile.[37]

On 22 January 1908 another car, a Nacke, was driven into
Addis Ababa by Arnold Holtz. The German had tried to beat
the Englishmen to Addis Ababa, and correctly blamed some
"shenanigans" by the British consul for his failure to win the
"race." Holtz was another in that handful of foreigners who
believed that Empress Taytu was much maligned; in his view
she was

worthy of being a ruler and top adviser to Menilek. The reforms ... show
that, like her husband, she is concerned with the progress of her people;
she favored the cabinet and the reorganization of the court system, and has
granted permission for Catholics to construct their own church — even
contributed to it. The new hotel, said to have cost a million francs, she has
given to the city.

Holtz was somewhat naive. The truth is that the empress was shrewd
enough to see the business potential in a hotel.[38]

Despite a flare-up of his chronic nephritis, Menilek went with
Taytu up to Entotto by mule in May 1908, intending to continue
on to Salale for the dedication of a church. That trip was cancelled
as Dr. Vitalien had put Menilek on a course of mercury. While at

Entotto the emperor signed an agreement with Italy ratifying the border with Italian Somaliland for which Italy paid three million lire. On 18 May Menilek suffered a "stroke" which temporarily paralyzed his right side. He was unable to return to Addis Ababa for three weeks.

From the day of his return on 10 June 1908, the empress monitored visits to the emperor and the dominant question at the legations changed from "Should Menilek die ...?" to "What is the empress up to?" Though the legations and principal chiefs had been notified officially of what they had known for several years, that Lij Iyasu was the heir to the throne, the Ethiopians said, "It is the forehead of Taytu that is holding up the empire."[39]

17

Empress Taytu becomes de facto ruler of Ethiopia

The emperor returned to Addis Ababa from Entotto on 10 June 1908, propped up on the back of a mule, having refused a litter on the grounds that it would cause anxiety to the people. He held no audiences and conducted no business. The empress was with him constantly. Only personal servants and Dr. Vitalien were allowed into his presence. "It is for this privilege that the function of doctor to the emperor is so sought after," wrote Charles Brice, the new French minister.

Even though a framework of government had been established in the form of the cabinet and the six judicial districts, it was obvious to all the legations that medical personnel would have more access to the emperor than diplomats and that Empress Taytu was the supreme channel of communication. The French believed themselves secure because Dr. Vitalien would uphold their interests. Their complacency was shaken when it was learned that the Ethiopian mission to Germany had hired a new doctor during their stop-over in Constantinople. The French minister quickly informed Dr. Vitalien who confronted Menilek. Menilek replied:

I should not have but one doctor — you said so yourself — remember you were sick yourself last week. I urged you two months ago to find a colleague and even advanced money for his travel. No one has come. Therefore I asked for a doctor in Turkey where they want less money. But you will always be number one — the new doctor will serve under you.

The French legation sent a telegram to Paris urging them to send the doctor with dispatch so that France would not lose its privileged position with Menilek. Dr. l'Herminier, a friend of Vitalien, arrived in August 1908.[1]

Just before l'Herminier's appearance, Menilek, not so free from superstition as he gave the impression of being, was unnerved by a disgusting trick. A cat, with its eyes slit, hindquarters broken, tail cut, and a sachet of poison tied around its neck, was secreted under Menilek's throne. Culprits were named and, though severely flogged, refused to identify the malefactor behind them for fear the sorcerer would "get" them. They were set free, but Menilek commented, "Those miserable wretches — they want me to die and don't consider the disasters that would befall my people on my death."[2]

Menilek's speech, by this time, was slurred and he walked with two canes. He was prepared to try anything and anyone who could give him hope. Dr. Mousali Bey, "a Syrian or an Egyptian with a New York degree," was admitted to the palace carrying a black box containing a Faraday electric machine, the medical fad of the time. Menilek knew that such treatment had been given to Empress Taytu's mother in 1902 for her paralysis, and Dr. Mousali Bey assured the emperor that he would cure his paralysis in a few weeks.

Dr. Vitalien rushed to the French legation to tell Brice that this treatment carried certain risks for the emperor and asked him to inform the empress. On hearing this, Taytu tried to dissuade Menilek, but he was adamant. Dr. Mousali Bey applied electric current to Menilek's paralyzed side for the first time on 14 August 1908 and four times thereafter. Menilek invited the foreign diplomats to his private apartments once during these treatments and Brice and Harrington found Menilek changed. "He was very thin, his eyes were dull, but his presence of mind was intact and he asked cogent questions about the railroad," wrote Brice. Harrington whispered in Brice's ear, and the whisper went straight to Paris, "Notice his frightful color — a sign of exhaustion — and precursor of death among people of his race."

Dr. Mousali Bey continued Vitalien's mercury ointment massage but added belladonna to the mixture. Dr. Vitalien fumed in the palace pharmacy while the new doctor controlled the royal patient; he believed that the belladonna was harmful to Menilek's nephritic kidneys. Menilek collapsed after an application of electric current on 24 August. He was carried to his room where he remained incommunicado for three days, even to the doctors. On the evening of 28 August the empress summoned Drs. Vitalien, l'Herminier and Wakeman and asked them to confer with Mousali Bey. Vitalien turned in a complete report of this consultation and Brice reported happily to Paris, "The French medical corps has won the day. We owe this honor to science and the stubbornness of Drs. Vitalien and l'Herminier ... who have contributed greatly to keeping our influence strong."

Dr. Mousali Bey had been rigorously interrogated by the two French doctors while Dr. Wakeman had been sympathetic to him. He admitted that he did not know exactly how much current he had applied, nor had he "measured arterial tension with a sphygmomanometer," as he had no such equipment. Dr. Mousali Bey insisted that Menilek was better and that the emperor believed his improvement was due to the effects of the electric current.

All the doctors, except Wakeman who declined, then examined the patient. "Abandon electric treatment!" pronounced l'Herminier when they rejoined Wakeman waiting outside. Wakeman did not agree. He thought treatments could be useful as soon as Menilek's coughing spells abated. Wakeman also approved Mousali Bey's injections of strychnine for Menilek's heart. The two French doctors approved continuation of mercury wth iodide of potassium; Wakeman disagreed. He opposed all mercury treatment in the African climate, saying he had seen too many die from it. In the end Wakeman signed their joint report, though he declined firmly to have any part in the treatment. The diagnosis had not changed since Vitalien's of 1904: "Endartérité cérébrale oblitérant spécifique et syphilisme tertiaire avec rénale manifestation." They foresaw that they could "fight it courteously and retard it, but the emperor's condition was incurable."

The unhappy Mousali Bey persuaded Dejazmach Abate and Bejirond Mulugeta to hold another hearing the next day, with questions prompted by him. Dr. Wakeman declined to attend on the grounds of illness. Dr. Vitalien was so incensed by the questions asked by Abate that he demanded that the emperor make a choice: "Either me or Mousali Bey." The message came back from the emperor that he wanted Dr. Vitalien. Abate thanked Dr. Mousali Bey, said it was a pity that his system had not worked and invited him to leave the country. His Faraday machine was destroyed after Empress Taytu was given a demonstration of its sparking wires. "He must have wanted to kill him," she said.

Within the week Menilek was dependent on Dr. Vitalien seconded by Dr. l'Herminier. "Don't let me die ... I have so much to do." He showed himself to the people on 11 September 1908, the New Year's Day of the Ethiopian calendar, and held a diplomatic reception on 20 September. His improvement was marked.

At the reception, the French minister, preening himself on the success of "his" doctors, remarked to Harrington that Menilek's presence was testimony to the efficacy of English and French medicine. Since Dr. Wakeman had disagreed with the French doctors, Harrington, who was about to leave the country for good, considered the remark patronizing and did not reply. After this snub, Brice walked over to congratulate the two doctors. "Menilek will be doing the empire's business, full-time,.within six weeks," they predicted.

They were wrong. Menilek was gravely ill a week later. Again, the palace grounds swarmed with provincial governors, court officers and soldiers. Then another doctor arrived.

It was Dr. Paul Mérab, who had been hired in Constantinople. Vitalien was so upset when Menilek and Taytu received Dr. Mérab without his being present that he immediately asked to be relieved and allowed to return to France to work on railway business as Menilek's representative. Permission was granted.

Dr. Mérab saw enough of the empress during his first interview to say that she had a set of false teeth. Indeed, the empress had acquired a dentist, Caracatsanis, who had accompanied a Greek commercial mission in 1907 and accepted a contract from her to stay. She listened attentively to Dr. Mérab's conversation with Menilek, watching "like a cat waiting to pounce." During Mérab's examination of the patient the following day, she was also present, "obtruding on Menilek's rather debonair ways with her haughty manners. The old *negus* seemed like an infant with his mother or an older sister sitting next to him."[3]

It is not clear from Mérab's writings how often he saw the emperor. He was placed in charge of the pharmacy when Dr. Vitalien left for Paris and it was Dr. l'Herminier who accompanied the emperor to Debre Libanos in December. What was perfectly clear was that Dr. Mérab hated Vitalien (who returned the following year), Dr. l'Herminier, the entire staff of the French legation, and Empress Taytu, whom he called "Her Very Fat Majesty." Of Vitalien he wrote, "He has a soul as black as his skin, a black hand and a black tongue." Of Dr. l'Herminier he wrote, "He was so fancied up in fine clothes he looked like a jockey and as a surgeon he wielded a butcher's knife." Seven months after Mérab's arrival, Dr. l'Herminier challenged him to a duel for spreading the rumor that he was guilty of "unnatural offenses." The British and French legations were forced into a rare moment of collaboration and between them persuaded the two doctors that it was unseemly for two Europeans to engage in a public quarrel.

Dr. Mérab must have been contentious, but one cannot help feeling sorry for him. He had closed his practice in Constantinople, had had cards engraved, "Dr. Mérab, de la faculté de Paris, Médecin de Sa Majesté Impériale Le Negus Menelick," and was out of a job virtually on arrival. Charles Brice was full of animus for the independent Mérab and refused him a grant to study the medicinal effects of herbs in Ethiopia. Mérab, in turn, though a French citizen by adoption (he was born in Russian Georgia), called the French doctors* "termites of French influence ... more politicians and intriguers than diplomats, more diplomats than doctors — and patriots and egotists above all."

In November 1908 Dr. l'Herminier advised the emperor to take a trip in order to get him away from the importuners at court. The sojourn, however, turned into the opposite of what l'Herminier had in mind. It became a religious pilgrimage to Debre Libanos with a retinue of 8,000 persons, despite the opposition of the head of the church, Abune Matewos.[4] The arduous journey, partly by carriage, began on 2 December. The first night, the emperor sent back a message to the French legation: he was cold and would they please send gloves. The next night came a request for blankets, which Brice sent, along with cakes and champagne. All of Menilek's doctors advised him to abstain from alcohol, a behest to which he paid little attention.

On 19 January 1909, Dr. l'Herminier sent a message to the French legation from Debre Libanos, saying that something had happened as he had not been allowed to see his patient for the past five days. It transpired that the empress and priests had pressed Menilek to try the miraculous but frigid waters of the shrine. When l'Herminier was finally admitted to Menilek's tent, the emperor begged him to forbid the icy baths, "They are killing me ... if you don't take me out of their hands, I will die."

Dr. l'Herminier wrote the empress a note saying that her august husband must have medical care only, that the immersions must stop and that the emperor should return to Addis Ababa immediately. The ablutions ceased, but the emperor did not return to the capital.

Despite their mutual hostility, Dr. l'Herminier summoned Dr. Mérab to Debre Libanos to assist in an operation for gunshot wound on an Ethiopian officer. While he was there he saw the emperor once,

---

*One doctor, Dr. d'Antoine de Taillas, gave himself the title "Consultant to His Majesty the Emperor." Dr. d'Antoine wrote from Addis Ababa on 9 February 1909 an endorsement by Emperor Menilek II of Abyssinia of a tonic called "Vin Mariani" which appeared in a promotion pamphlet called *Album Mariani* in Paris and New York in 1910. From 1908, when Dr. d'Antoine arrived, until 1911, Dr. l'Herminier and then Dr. Martin were official physicians.

in the presence of Empress Taytu. Mérab added his support to
l'Herminier's warning, "His Majesty must be kept warm." The
empress was angry, but on repeating his remark, Mérab said, "Oh
do whatever you want!" "Since I could not slam a door I slammed
my solar topee under my arm." The empress stopped him in a calmer
voice, and with a baleful expression said, "We people are more
accustomed to the cold than you are." Mérab returned to Addis
Ababa, after watching the religious ceremonies for Timkat which
Menilek and Taytu attended.

Menilek carried out business at Debre Libanos, against his doctor's
orders. He asked for all the documents on the railroad to be sent from
the French legation. Both he and Taytu saw Tigrayan delegations
with their usual array of complaints against each other.[5] Then,

> seeing that at Debre Libanos, only the men had a monastery, and noting
> that the Holy Book says that women must stay apart from men during
> prayers she said to Menilek, "Let us build a cloister reserved for women."
> The emperor agreed, knowing that in the time of St. Tekle Haymanot (c.
> 1215-c. 1313), founder of Debre Libanos, there had been a woman's place;[*]
> then he named as mother-superior a nun called Itot Djemanesh.[6]

It was no longer possible to conceal from the general public the
fragile state of Menilek's health, though Aleqa Kenfe wrote in his
diary that the emperor only had a skin disease and the official
euphemism for his partial paralysis was an "illness of the feet acquired
from getting off his horse to walk barefoot in the dew of early
morning."[7]

Menilek and Taytu traveled part of the way back from Debre
Libanos by car, but from the Entotto heights Menilek descended on
mule back, so that the people could see him. Cheering crowds lined
the road and people wept "as a baby does when separated from its
mother ... such joy ... on every street there were pictures of Menilek
and Taytu surrounded by flowers, and a cannon was fired 19
times."[8]

Léon Chefneux wrote to his former colleague Alfred Ilg that the
emperor had come back in no better a condition than when he went.

---

*Monasteries would not permit any women to enter. When Mr. and Mrs. Theodore
Bent made the laborious climb up to Debre Bizen in 1893, they stopped to rest near
its precincts. The monks rushed down towards them horrified at having so unholy
a thing as a woman so near. The monks wept when Bent dared to ask if his wife
could just wait there while he went on up, and said, "Better for us to die." (*Illustrated
London News*, 8 April 1893)

Kentiba Welde Tsadiq told the French minister, "Menilek is no longer capable of forming a sane opinion ... he can no longer govern." Count Colli di Felizzano saw Menilek at the palace on 6 March 1909 and said he looked better but that his mental faculties were impaired.

Suddenly, on 10 March, no one was allowed to enter the palace grounds without the express authority of Empress Taytu. Ten days later Menilek's diminished capacity was recognized in a statement read to the assembled chiefs of Tigray and Gojam by Negadras Hayle Giyorgis. Menilek's health would no longer permit him to work for the progress of Ethiopia, but "He had empowered a cabinet like the Europeans have," and commended to them his heir, Lij Iyasu Mikael.

The same day, the palace gates opened for the new German ambassador. Menilek received him while sitting in a wheelchair; he was paralyzed from the waist down on the right side. But his mental faculties were sufficiently acute for him to recognize, a few days later, an Austrian ethnologist* whom he had last seen four years before. He granted him permission to visit the incarcerated ex-king of Keffa and they discussed the method of succession to the Austro-Hungarian throne.

Dr. Charles Martin, the Ethiopian doctor who had been unable to reach a satisfactory contract in 1901, had returned to his country just as the royal entourage was leaving for Debre Libanos. He was about to leave for Debre Libanos on call when the emperor returned. He made it clear to the imperial councillors, Fitawrari Habte Giyorgis and Dejazmach Abate, that he still wished to make an arrangement with the Ethiopian government and leave the British colonial service. They offered him a job with Dr. Vitalien in the new Menilek II Hospital. Martin had written to Empress Taytu, and after "a month and 18 days" he had an answer in which she too hoped he would work in the fine new hospital built by the *negus*. He answered that he would be pleased to do so providing suitable arrangements were made. She did not invite him to visit the royal patient, nor was he invited to the April diplomatic reception. He blamed this omission on a snub by Lord Hervey, the British representative.

Menilek was not in immediate need of Dr. Martin. Yet another physician had appeared: Dr. Steinkuhler from Germany. Menilek did not inform his attending doctor, l'Herminier, until Steinkuhler

*F.J. Bieber and his industrialist friend, Emil G. Pick, were received on 24 March 1909. They considered Menilek's illness had been exaggerated.

arrived and then assured the Frenchman that he would see both doctors together. The German doctor leapt enthusiastically into the medical-diplomatic fray, certain that he would be able to cure Menilek with "benefits accruing to German interests."[9]

To Dr. l'Herminier the German said, "We shall abstract ourselves from our respective nationalities ... each of us remaining a good Frenchman and a good German with the interests of our patient at heart." Dr. Steinkuhler lied to the principal attendant of the emperor, Bejirond Mulugeta, that he and Dr. l'Herminier were in complete agreement on treatment.

Steinkuhler cheered the emperor by telling him that his condition was less serious than he had thought at first. Then, despite strong warnings from l'Herminier, he insisted on the resumption of electric stimulus for Menilek's paralysis. Dr. l'Herminier threw up his hands in disgust, and they parted company.

One day, in the course of treatment, Steinkuhler discovered that the current of his machine had been altered to generate a dangerous 190 volts, instead of the usual 140-50. He was convinced that either Mulugeta or the other aide, Metaferia,* had maliciously tampered with the equipment. He said nothing, but after another treatment Steinkuhler noted that Menilek was depressed and more nervous than usual and was moving with great difficulty. All were symptoms of cerebral vascular thrombosis, but Steinkuhler decided that his patient had been poisoned! The doctor asked Mulugeta for a specimen of Menilek's urine and all the food left from his most recent meal. On being told that the food had already been thrown out, he became even more suspicious. He tested the urine sample and in 24 hours delivered his conclusion to the German legation: "The emperor is being systematically poisoned with cyanide of potassium."

Steinkuhler had failed not only in medical diplomacy but also in scientific method. He had not had his tests verified by another doctor immediately; he did not investigate the health of the imperial food taster,[10] and he had submitted his report to the German legation instead of to his employer, the Ethiopian government. Steinkuhler's other faults lay in his arrogance and lack of tact. He commanded

---

*Metaferia was named Minister of the Palace in January 1908. He was the state treasurer of whom the French minister commented, "Where else could you find the Minister of Finance acting also as first gentleman of the bed chamber. He helps Menilek rise and puts him to bed, dresses and undresses him and is also a favorite of the empress."

that special care be taken to see that the utensils used for Menilek's food were clean. This insult to the housekeeping of the empress was allowed to pass for the moment.

Had the Germans deliberately wished to embroil the court of Ethiopia in insinuations and recriminations, they could not have chosen a better way of doing so. Ethiopia was a country where no one ever seemed to die of natural causes; it was almost routine that after the death of a person of note, it was said that he or she "was poisoned."[11]

Two months later, Dr. Steinkuhler and another German, Alfred Zintgraff,* who had arrived after the incident, made the accusation public. They, as well as Lij Iyasu's German tutor, had been barred by the empress from entering the emperor's private apartments. A rumor that Menilek was dead had circulated and a crowd had surged on to the palace grounds. Zintgraff, in a manic display of bad judgment, addressed this crowd in his competent Amharic and told them that their sovereign was in danger from evil persons in the palace. Bejirond Mulugeta, one of these "evil" people, came out and dismissed the crowd "in the name of Emperor Menilek." The two Germans managed to secure an appointment to see Menilek with the empress present. They demanded that Bejirond Mulugeta and Azaj Metaferia be arrested, interrogated and punished for the crime of *lèse-majesté*. The empress "got very excited and spoke wildly," and Menilek could not conceal his shock at these imputations against two faithful retainers.

Dr. Martin was finally summoned by Empress Taytu after more than six months in the country. "She looked well for her age and was very affable." She inquired whether he had a family (he had a wife and son in England) and then asked his opinion of the poisoning business. He advised her to hold a formal inquiry to settle the matter once and for all in order to safeguard her own reputation.[12]

On 27 July 1909, the doctors in Addis Ababa assembled to question Mulugeta and Metaferia in the presence of Abune Matewos. Absent were the Italians, Negri, de Castro and Brielli, who had reviewed

---

*Zintgraff arrived with his wife on 16 May 1909, to be foreign affairs and contracts adviser, having pleased Menilek (but not Taytu) during a stint as attaché at the German legation from 1907 to 1908. The empress lifted her veto of Zintgraff as soon as she learned that the French would be happy if he did not come. Steinkuhler, Zintgraff and the tutor Pinnow were all on private contracts with the Ethiopian government.

the German laboratory report and found it unconvincing. The assembled doctors waited four hours for Zintgraff and Steinkuhler, but neither appeared. The latter's eventual explanation was that the inquiry was not a proper judicial procedure and it would appear as though the Germans were on trial.

The German minister sent a circular to all the legations giving Steinkuhler's version of the entire episode to date. Ras Tessema also circulated a memorandum around the legations. His memo emphasized the insulting and thoughtless behavior of the two Germans in demanding a judgment on Mulugeta and Metaferia, men who had given many years of loyal service to the crown, and in their defamation of Empress Taytu.

The empress found herself with an unexpected ally. Brice of the French legation, only too happy to find his German rivals in trouble, contacted her sympathetically. The empress asked him to draft a refutation of Dr. Steinkuhler's allegations. He did so, and "she didn't change a word, sending it to every legation, including ours." Brice also drafted a letter for her to send to the Kaiser, in which she hoped their cordial relations would continue. She also expressed how deeply offended she had been by the false accusations as "empress and spouse."[13]

The empress had been under attack for months. Both Ethiopians and the foreign community thought she was taking advantage of Menilek's weak condition by making political decisions in his name, and indeed she was. But the gross behavior of the Germans had caused even her enemies to close ranks against foreign meddlers. Besides, the empress had no reason to dispose of her husband; his continued existence was the sole guarantee of her power.

Empress Taytu played her cards cleverly. In a letter to Ras Tessema, chairman of the cabinet, she offered to entrust the care of Menilek to whomsoever the government chose, and if they wished she would leave the capital. She vehemently absolved Mulugeta and Metaferia of any responsibility since everything was done under her personal surveillance. Ras Tessema, in the name of all chiefs, professed continued devotion to her and begged her to continue her loving care of the emperor.

Could Dr. Steinkuhler have been right in his allegations? Experts who have examined the evidence think not.[14] Cyanide of potassium is a quick killer. It has the distinctive odor of almonds and an amount the size of a pea could produce agonizing death in a sturdy person in less than an hour. The symptoms that had alerted Steinkuhler had been typical of those suffered by Menilek after his "stroke." Had the German doctor discussed his findings with Dr. l'Herminier or Dr. Vitalien, he might not have been so precipitous. It could be argued that Dr. Steinkuhler chose to suspect poison rather than face the fact that his prescribed electric stimuli had resulted in no positive change in the emperor's health.

The German minister saw Menilek and Taytu on 21 September and made no apology. He still believed that Steinkuhler was right, though he confided to the Italian minister that he thought the aim of the empress had been not to kill Menilek, but to keep him in a manageable condition. He told the monarchs that it would be embarrassing to send Dr. Steinkuhler back to Germany. Menilek muttered something along the lines of "That's your problem," and the empress avowed she would send her own representative to tell the Kaiser how badly his people had behaved. There had been an unfortunate incident at the German legation, peripheral to the central issue, but which had further strengthened the empress's antipathy towards the Germans. A woman who had entered the legation grounds to steal wood was caught and struck brutally by an attaché of the legation; she was pregnant, and aborted during the night. The German minister had tried to hush up the matter with money, but she was the wife of one of Menilek's soldiers, and her husband complained to the empress. Both Alfred Zintgraff and Dr. Steinkuhler were forced to leave the country.[15]

The scandal of the "poisoned emperor" was officially concluded with the publication in November 1909 of a pamphlet, *Le Docteur Nouvellement Venu*, written in French and Amharic at the order of Empress Taytu and with the eager assistance of the French establishment and the Lazarist mission press at Dire Dawa. Copies were mailed to European newspapers,* and delivered to the legations, as well as to provincial governors throughout the empire, and may be considered Ethiopia's first essay into international public relations. Its tone was sarcastic: "The poison lay in misunderstandings over salary and housing between the accusers and the accused," and it

---

*There had been articles about the alleged poisoning attempt in *L'Echo de Paris, Le Temps, Le Journal, Berliner Tageblatt, Indépendance Belge*, to cite a few. The French minister sent Taytu copies of favorable write-ups of *Le Docteur Nouvellement Venu* in *L'Echo de Paris* and *Le Petit Journal* and she thanked him for his efforts in publishing these articles.

contrasted the "demanding and threatening" behavior of the German doctor to that of the Russians, "who were truly like brothers," and to the French, who "lived in perfect accord with us."

Menilek's condition remained stable under the care of Dr. Martin, who became the imperial physician officially on 7 August 1909. The British government had approved his assignment "in view of the state of His Majesty's health and for political reasons," though Lord Hervey, chargé at the legation, considered Martin very foolish to become involved in the byzantine ways of the Ethiopian court.

Dr. Martin did not become an arm of British diplomacy, however. On the contrary he was free with his advice to the monarchs on matters other than medical, his counsel slanting towards making Ethiopia self-sufficient and better governed. He had no fear of the empress, telling her that officers of the government should receive sufficient remuneration so that they need not take bribes, and that regular taxation would be fairer than the present extortion-as-you-go system. He pleased her with his opinion that there had been too little forethought in granting concessions and monopolies. Martin was not against them; he wanted one for himself. The empress had already been reviewing the concessions and there was considerable nervousness among those who held them.[16]

On several occasions, the empress made her views on the English quite clear to Dr. Martin. She would approve a concession granted to him so long as the company was not English, and when he advised her to send an Ethiopian officer to accompany a British border survey, "she could not see the reason and only talked nonsense about the British having taken Abyssinian territory." During a reception for the new American envoys* she seemed not to be kindly disposed towards Americans because they spoke English, and she asked Dr. Martin to find a European, "anyone but an Englishman," to run the rubber concession.

---

*Hoffman Phillip and Guy Love arrived in June 1909, and were received by both Menilek and Taytu. The gifts they presented were all for Menilek, and Phillip wrote that the "countenance of Queen Taitu registered nothing less than rage. She had seized upon the volume depicting the pride of our navy, the pages of which she was furiously thumbing upside down." Phillip immediately asked the interpreter to explain that he had not expected her to be present and would welcome the first opportunity to offer his gifts to her. He subsequently gave her striped silk stockings, handkerchiefs and perfumes that he had purchased at his own expense as the State Department had refused to allow money to be spent on gifts for the empress. Phillip stayed only seven months, and on his departure Taytu received him as Menilek was too ill. She dispatched him with a letter from herself, lion and leopard skins, two spears and a shield.

Martin had a number of rows with the empress over Menilek's diet. The preferred home remedy in Ethiopia was a mixture of honey and clarified butter, which Dr. Martin begged the emperor not to take from Empress Taytu because it caused catarrhal congestion. The emperor, however, was too weak to resist her. Martin had his dietary orders written out in Amharic, but the empress insisted that it was impossible for the emperor to abide by those rules. Despite this, there was a steady improvement in Menilek. He was able to go out for carriage drives, he felt strong enough to attend one banquet in the throne room on St. Tekle Haymanot's day, 30 August 1909, and he lasted through another long affair for the New Year on 10 September.

Despite their many arguments, the empress and Dr. Martin were on good terms, though he found her "a shifty customer, ... full of conceit and conservatism, ... and ... underhanded in her methods." She saw to it that his salary was paid, his temporary housing cleaned up and furnished at her expense, that he received unencumbered title to some land and was provided with a loan from Menilek's coffers to build a new house.

On 5 October 1909 Dr. Martin noted, "The Tigray trouble is telling on the emperor ... he is looking haggard and thin and complains of feeling weak." The "Tigray trouble" was the impending battle between Dejazmach Abate* and Dejazmach Abreha Araya.†

Some months earlier, shortly after Menilek and Taytu had returned from Debre Libanos, 10 government appointments had been made. There was no doubt at any of the legations, informed by "high" Ethiopian sources, that they were the work of Empress Taytu. As French envoy Brice wrote, "The return of Menilek has calmed things down a little ... the native markets are deserted, commercial transactions with Europeans lessened. The empress has taken the preponderance. It is she who governs. Her actions are felt everywhere, but primarily in the various changes of high administration. Never before have there been such reversals."

Two changes made in March 1909 had been particularly

---

*Abate Bwalu had handled the inquiry into Dr. Mousali Bey's treatment of the emperor and negotiated some problems with the Bank of Abyssinia in February 1909. At the British legation he was considered slow to grasp new ideas, but once convinced, was very steadfast.

†Abreya Araya was the Tigrayan mentioned so often and so sympathetically by Governor Martini.

controversial: Dejazmach Demissew Nessibu* and Ras-Bidwoded
Mengesha Atikem† were shifted to posts of lesser responsibility even
though both men had large and loyal followings, and the latter was
a man who had served Menilek loyally since 1865. A third
appointment, and the most disruptive, was that of Dejazmach Abate
as overlord of Tigray and governor of Wag.[17]

The Tigrayans were bound to be offended not only because
Dejazmach Abate was a Shewan, but to compound the insult, he
was given the title of Wagshum. This title had belonged from time
immemorial to the hereditary rulers of Wag. Gwangul, the
incumbent, notified the emperor that he would not submit to Abate,
and Abreha Araya, governor of Enderta district, announced that
he would fight if Abate set foot in Tigray.[18]

It took several proclamations to round up enough soldiers to
follow Abate to Tigray, and it was said that they were recruited from
the dregs of Addis Ababa. Though appointed in March, Abate did
not leave the capital until mid-July, and even then his forces were
not considered strong enough to confront Abreha Araya, who, it
was rumored falsely, had been joined in rebellion by Seyum
Mengesha Yohannes. The empress ordered her nephew, Gugsa Wele,
and her brother, Ras Wele, to support Abate.

Dr. Annaratone, the Italian commercial agent at Desse, said that
Abreha made a conciliatory offer in September when the two armies
were scarcely four kilometers apart. Dr. Annaratone read the
telegrams and heard the telephone calls passing through the Desse
station. He reported that the emperor stalled for time on Abreha's
offer. The emperor, whose health between July and October was
good enough for him to be aware of everything that was going on,
sent Abate a telegram telling him to be alert and not to let Abreha
get away.[19]

Abreha recognized the stalling for what it was and made a surprise

---

*Demissew Nessibu was the son of the *afenegus* who died on 12 July 1908. Welega
and three smaller districts were taken from him. His stepmother, Desta, appealed
to the empress and he was granted two other areas. However, his dislike of Taytu
was strengthened as he had already been insulted when she took his wife, Aselefetch,
from him in 1901 in order to marry her to Yilma Mekonnen.
†His title Bidwoded (Beloved) indicated the high regard that the emperor had for him.
He appealed this demotion to Menilek, who was too weak to overrule the empress.
At the same time, two of his sons, Kebede and Merid, were promoted. His fiefs were
given to Seyum Tekle Haymanot who had just married the famous Aselefetch.
Mengesha died in 1910.

attack on Abate at dawn on 9 October 1909 at Korem. Three hours later, Abate telegraphed the emperor, "I, your soldier, have had a battle this morning with Dejazmach Abreha and ... have punished him." Abreha had been slightly wounded and was captured. Dr. Martin was with the emperor when the telegram arrived and said that Menilek cried in his excitement and joy. He ordered guns to be fired to announce the victory and "no one spoke of anything else the whole day and night."

Dr. Annaratone was called from Desse to Korem to take care of the wounded. There were thousands from both sides. Annaratone's caravan of medicinal supplies reached Korem a little behind Ras Wele, who had sent 500 soldiers but did not appear himself until the battle was over. The "sullen hindrance of Ras Wele prevented the wounded Tigrayans from coming near me," said the doctor. "The dead followers of Abreha were denied burial and were abandoned to the vultures — a nauseating spectacle which polluted the air." For two weeks Dr. Annaratone coped alone with the heat, mosquitoes, poor water supply and the wounded until Dr. l'Herminier arrived from Addis Ababa, sent by the empress at the urging of Dr. Martin.

The euphoria over the success of Abate was short-lived. On 25 October Dr. Martin had a fierce argument with Empress Taytu when he discovered that Menilek had not been taking the egg-and-milk flip that he had prescribed as the first nourishment of the day. The empress told Martin that there was no use in eating eggs, milk and vegetables "like a European," and said that Menilek must eat like an Abyssinian. "We parted at loggerheads. She is very obstinate and trying." The following day Dr. Martin found the emperor hypertense. He had eaten peppery food and drunk strong wine, but said he felt very well. "The empress jeered at me over the milk and egg business. I feared another stroke."

When Dr. Martin called the following morning, he was not allowed into Menilek's room until after midday. He found the emperor paralyzed and able to speak only a few words. He gave him digitalis and strychnine and the empress had some "Abyssinian dry vegetable infusion supposed to be good for 'grifta' or stroke, rubbed on his ears and face." Dr. Martin spent the night at the palace and informed Ras Tessema that Menilek might die.

Though high chiefs and legations had already been informed that Lij Iyasu Mikael was the heir to the throne, on 15 May 1909 a shock wave ran through the informed chiefs and legation heads. At a huge public convocation held on Jan Hoy Meda, the polo and sports ground, a proclamation was read: "My *lij* [my child] will succeed me." No name was included. There were many who could fit the category of "my child."

Only a few days previously, Menilek had been carried into the reception hall where his principal officers were gathered and Taytu had called out "in a loud voice, 'Who do you name as your successor? Who? Who?' He mumbled 'Lij ... Lij ...' She bent close to him, paled ... then called out, 'He says Lij Iyasu.'"[20] Between that meeting and the public assembly a few days later, she and Fitawrari Habte Giyorgis arranged to omit the name. Abune Matewos was also involved, for in his pronouncement of the anathema that would fall on anyone who did not follow the emperor's choice, he did not use the name of Iyasu. However, only Empress Taytu was accused of wanting to keep the door open for another candidate, such as her nephew Gugsa Wele, who as the son-in-law of the emperor qualified within the definition "my child," or even Tayye Gulilate, in his 20s, a great-grandson of King Sahle Selasse, raised at the palace and married to the empress's great-niece, Almaz Mengesha. Tayye had been supported vocally by the governor of Ankober, Welde Tsadiq. "Shewans! Have you lost your mind to think of crowning Lij Iyasu. I will put him in chains — he and Ras Tessema. Our legitimate *negus* is Tayye."[21]

As the emperor appeared to be dying, all confusion had to be cleared up. The empress rationalized her reservations by arranging Lij Iyasu's marriage to her six-year-old great-niece, Aster Mengesha, just before the public announcement on 30 October 1909 that the "*lij*" was Iyasu Mikael. Empress Taytu and the governor of Ankober were not the only ones who had serious doubts about the suitability of Lij Iyasu.[22] The old fears of the entrenchment of that powerful, once Muslim, Wello clan personified in Ras Mikael, the boy's father, surfaced again. There was reasonable concern over the boy's vulnerability to control by others because of his tender age, his frivolity and his apparent lack of dedication.

Nevertheless Lij Iyasu was named. Thus it was a teenage boy with the regent, Ras Tessema, sitting beside him, who presided over the trial of his relative, Dejazmach Abreha, and 25 other Tigrayans on 10 November 1909. Abreha's defense, "Menilek is ill and the government is in the hands of incompetents," did not save him from the death sentence. An appeal went to the sickroom of the emperor and with either a shred of will, or a fortuitous involuntary spasm, he nodded his head for commutation to life imprisonment.[23]

The reign of Emperor Menilek II was effectively over by March 1909, though he sporadically exercised his imperial voice. He raised a tremendous fuss in July 1909 when he learned that the empress and Regent Tessema had, in his name, removed two large areas from the hegemony of Abba Jifar, whose complaisance in 1882 had enabled Amhara conquest of the southwest territories. Menilek reminded Tessema and Taytu that he still commanded, and Abba Jifar's lands were restored.[24]

The emperor acquiesced by default in the appointments, edicts and decisions made in his name until 27 October 1909, when his mind and spirit died. Empress Taytu was firmly in control, as much because Ras-Bidwoded Tessema was as inept and indecisive as she was forthright, determined and authoritative.

18

The downfall of Empress Taytu

In one of the *double-entendre* verses of this period, the power of
Lij Iyasu stops the sun from passing over the vault of heaven, the
sun being Taytu.[1] Nothing could have been further from the truth.
It took the combined efforts of Ras Tessema, Fitawrari Habte
Giyorgis, five of *dejazmach* rank (Gebre Selasse, Lul Seged,
Demissew Nessibu, Wesene Tirfe and Merid Habte Maryam),
Negadras Hayle Giyorgis, Abune Matewos, and many other
influential persons behind the scenes to stop the "sun" empress. Lij
Iyasu had nothing to do with the confrontation, except as the heir
designate they had sworn to uphold.

For almost 30 years Empress Taytu had been a potent influence
on the policies and actions of Menilek. It was no surprise that when
Menilek became ill, she acted in his stead, promoting and demoting
with his royal seal. There were rumors that she intended to change
her *de facto* rule into the anointment of herself as "queen of kings,"
an ambition confirmed, many believe, by the wistful remark she
made when Zewditu Menilek became empress in 1916. "So they have
crowned a woman and it isn't I — it isn't I."[2]

Certainly in the event of Menilek's death, which was expected daily
after November 1909, Taytu intended to remain wealthy and a
respected personage, perhaps as a dowager empress, ruling a small
territory such as the ancient city of Gondar, or a flourishing district,
as Menilek's great-grandmother had ruled Menz in the 1830s. But
Menilek did not die and the atmosphere around the sickroom was
noisome with intrigue. The emperor's continuing heartbeat meant
that Lij Iyasu could not be crowned, nor could Ras Tessema exercise
authority in the heir's name. Part of the trouble lay in the character
and poor health of the regent. Tessema called himself only a simple
soldier with a poor head for political matters.[3] Others agreed with
him:

He is a miser though rich, treats his servants worse than slaves, has ruined
his province [Ilu Babor], is ungenerous with his soldiers and never able to
get the truth from sub-officers who perpetually quarrel with each other but
join together to deceive him — is so unsure of himself he can never make
up his mind. His staff joked when Lij Iyasu was sent to live under his tutelage

[March 1909] that "Lij Iyasu has taken over the education of Ras Tessema."[4]

Tessema's wife, Beletshachew,* was the empress's god-daughter, and the respect that Tessma owed the empress through this relationship contributed to his inability to stand up to her.

Empress Taytu knew that her appointment of youngsters aged 16 and 17 to positions of high responsibility and the demotion of loyal old servants of the emperor between March and June 1909 had generated fierce resentment. She could hear the grumbling by soldiers after the ritual distribution of gifts at Easter, in her name and not in Menilek's because she had been partial to her own corps.[5] She inspired the establishment of the "Bank for Agricultural Development," which was inaugurated on 2 September 1909. The bank was intended to be a counter to the British-controlled "Bank of Abyssinia" but it was obvious that the empress herself and the emperor were the only two contributors. In the idea of the bank she had made a bid to gain control of the imperial treasury and fatten it by peremptorily calling in loans which the emperor had made to foreign tradesmen and Ethiopian dignitaries.[6] She knew everything that was going on and acted swiftly when she learned in July 1909 of a plot to depose her. Would they like her to go away? She would leave for Gondar, or go to Jerusalem and live as a nun. Her offer to depart was at the time of the *brouhaha* over Dr. Steinkuhler's accusations that Menilek had been poisoned, and Ras Tessema "refused resolutely" to accept her offer, or to take part in the conspiracy to drive her from the palace.[7]

Teferi Mekonnen, who was to become Emperor Hayle Selasse I in 1930, was one of the empress's young appointees; he was 17 years old. He wrote in his autobiography that he was invited to join the July plot to drive the empress from the palace, but declined. "The plotters were jealous of her for doing all the work of government." The empress learned that Teferi Mekonnen had refused to participate and complimented him on his discretion, both for his refusal to join in and for not running to her with the tale. Teferi Mekonnen was not invited to the March 1910 cabal and of this he wrote, "She was

---

*After some 15 years of marriage, Ras Tessema had dignified his union with Beletshachew, by taking communion with her in 1907. Part of the ritual was confession of his sins, which obliged him to acknowledge Welde Rafael as his son by a servant of his house. Henceforth Welde Rafael became known as Kebede Tessema.

a strong-willed and efficient administrator with little feminine weakness about her. I had great respect for her — moreover it was with her support that I was appointed governor of Harar,* so the nobles did not dare tell me explicitly about this business."[8]

Ras Tessema managed to assert himself in November 1909 in order to have his cousin, Lul Seged, appointed as Minister of the Palace. The incumbent, Metaferia, went to the empress and volunteered to be relieved of his other post as well, Minister of Public Works, rather than endure this insult. She urged him to stay calm which he refused to do, and Ras Tessema had him chained. The empress intervened tactfully and won his release. Metaferia returned to the palace to help her care for Menilek.[9]

In late December the empress decided to detach a part of Tigray, Sokota district, from the command of Wagshum Abate, whose appointment there, unwise though it was, had been pushed by her, and who had won a costly battle on behalf of the crown. This inexplicable decision might not have been so disastrous had she not appointed her nephew, Amede Wele, to govern the important Sokota district. Abate took umbrage and telegraphed Ras Tessema, "Since in all Tigray there is no one who has not lost a brother, an uncle, sometimes a wife [in the fighting at Korem] I do not wish to live amidst such enemies."

On being shown the message the empress telegraphed Dejazmach Seyum Mengesha, "Now just as Tigray is settling down, here is Abate asking to return and abandoning the government we have given him. What do you think of this conduct?" Seyum's answer to the empress was to the point, "We approved of Abate's decision. He is not strong enough."[10]

At the time the empress was undercutting Abate, she resumed her efforts to disgrace Negadras Hayle Giyorgis, who, as Minister of Commerce, was in effect the financial chief of the country. She not only suspected him of heading the July conspiracy against her, but resented his payment of about 3,000 talers to Dr. Steinkuhler for travel expenses, medicines and instruments. She had Hayle Giyorgis chained on the palace grounds, and ordered her niece, Yetemegnu Alula, to divorce him. Subjecting this very important person to the indignity of chains shocked everyone, and word spread quickly

---

*Ras Tessema notified Teferi Mekonnen on 3 March 1910, "Though you are only a boy, the empress has appointed you." Teferi had already fathered a daughter, Romanewerq, whom he did not claim for many years.

through the city. Though not necessarily loved for himself, Hayle Giyorgis was someone to whom many owed their livelihood, and thousands of people flocked to the palace to offer their support. He was released. There was an inquiry in which Hayle Giyorgis was found guilty of investing state funds without permission and he agreed to repay the treasury which he did in due course, with ease.* She named in his stead Yigazu Behabte as Minister of Commerce on 10 January 1910.

Abate was ordered to return to Shewa. When he was on his way, the empress, concerned that he would arrive in Addis Ababa with too many armed soldiers, ordered him to relinquish his machine guns and cannon to Ras Wele in Yejju. Abate refused, but in response to pleas from Ras Tessema and the Minister of War, Habte Giyorgis, he turned over the heavy equipment and continued towards the capital. Scarcely 80 kilometers from Addis Ababa Abate was arrested by Taytu's deputy, Azaj Zamanel.

Ras Wele was appointed governor of Tigray, but declined the honor. The rumor factory had already produced the news that Empress Taytu intended to create a rival kingdom in the north, of which she would become sovereign with her brother's help. If such was her plan, her brother was a weak link. He was close to 70, notorious for his drinking habits and quite incapable of commanding obedience except in his own province of Yejju.[11]

Another rumor came all the way from Cairo to the British legation, whose minister, Wilfred Thesiger, immediately relayed it to Ras Tessema. Taytu and her brother were going to put his son, Gugsa, on the throne, and move the capital to Gondar where the empress had already sent 40,000 talers and many guns from the royal arsenal. This particular rumor was published in *Corriere della Sera*, bearing the byline of its Eritrea correspondent, Arnaldo Cipolla, who was about to follow up his story in Addis Ababa. By the time Cipolla reached Addis Ababa, the empress knew about his article and asked the Italian legation to have him leave. He did.[12]

Ras Welde Giyorgis, though deemed by many to be in the palm of Empress Tatyu's hand, was offended by the choice of Ras Tessema as regent instead of himself, and had distanced himself from the intrigues of Addis Ababa and returned to his capital in Keffa in June

---

*French diplomatic notes gave the figure of 160,000 talers as what he had to pay back to the treasury. The foreign legations, excepting Germany, despised Hayle Giyorgis, considering him usurious to an intolerable degree.

1909. Informants told the French minister that Welde Giyorgis obeyed no orders, had distributed arms to his men, conferred appointments without informing the central government and was ready to proclaim himself independent king of Keffa in alliance with the English in the Sudan.[13]

Throughout January 1910 the empress tended to the emperor and busied herself with economic matters. One evening when Dr. Martin came to mix up a cough medicine for Menilek, she asked him to find a European (not an Englishman!) to run a rubber plantation, whose product Dr. Martin could export. Dr. Martin knew that a rubber export concession was already in the hands of the Syrian gentleman, Ydilibi, who was in high favor for the wheelchair and other useful gifts he had brought the patient. She also talked to Martin about repairing the gold-washing machine and purchasing a new cartridge-maker, and offered him the traction engine concession which he also knew to be held by someone else. She asked Martin to query the American envoy about buying silver alloy in the United States suitable for coinage, in exchange for Ethiopian gold. All of these offers were attempts to find a job for Dr. Martin since there was little he could do for the royal invalid.[14]

On 19 January 1910 the empress issued a regrettably harsh proclamation. All people of non-Orthodox leanings would be imprisoned and condemned to God's righteous judgment.[15] It was aimed at Ethiopian converts to either Catholicism or Protestantism. One convert, Gebre Heywet Baykedagn, had already fled to Khartoum with the help of Dejazmach Gebre Selasse. Gebre Heywet's sins were his open advocacy of education and "learning from the west." While employed at the palace as a translator, his rendering into Amharic of Dr. Martin's instructions to Taytu on Menilek's diet was criticized by Taytu as un-Ethiopian. She was furious with him for his apparent support of Dr. Steinkuhler's accusations of poisoning. Gebre Heywet went to work for Anglo-Sudan intelligence, and in his report on the empress indicated more than "apparent" support of Dr. Steinkuhler:

So ... we find this capricious woman, an obstacle to everything good ... as the cause of all the misery and arbitrary rule. Officers appointed in the morning were dismissed in the evening. We see a woman searching her kith and kin "with a lantern" to raise them from dust to power. Every chief placed by the emperor was liable to instant dismissal and even degradation unless he declared for her faction or married one of her female relations. The once powerful master lay in a chamber tortured by reprimands and insults, giving such counsel to his chiefs as he was ordered to say beforehand. He lay there helpless, wretched and without hope of deliverance ... since Taytu tried to stop any treatment ordered by physicians.[16]

Another Protestant convert, Kentiba Gebru, had also incurred the empress's wrath for his association with the German doctor and had taken refuge in the German legation. He was blamed for the dissemination of a satiric couplet, written by yet another convert, Aleqa Tayye, which implied that the empress was guilty of trying to poison Menilek. Aleqa Tayye was far from Addis Ababa, living on a fief granted him by the emperor so that he could work on a history of Ethiopia. Soon after Taytu's edict against foreign religions he found himself the object of hostile questioning by his former patron, Meshesha Werqe, who tested his veneration for the Virgin Mary by demanding that he kiss her image — something Protestants would not do. Aleqa Tayye was brought before Abune Matewos and sentenced to imprisonment.[17]

The empress became increasingly rude and sarcastic to Dr. Martin by saying such things as, "Do you think you can cure the emperor by staring at him?" and "It was your treatment that made him speechless," and "Your noisy boots disturb the emperor." He knew she was trying to provoke him into leaving the country in a huff so that he would not have to be paid. But Dr. Martin was not one to be pushed around. He had a contract for 600 talers a month for three years whether he doctored Menilek or not. She insisted that other projects he might undertake were not worth 600 talers a month and he should take a reduction in pay and make up the difference from some concession. There was no excuse for her ill-temper with Dr. Martin except that she was under a terrible strain, caring for a shell of a man and desperately anxious about her future, aware that clouds were gathering over her, but incapable of changing her strategy.

Ras Tessema and Fitawrari Habte Giyorgis warned the empress in February that by naming only "her creatures" to office and irritating the foreigners she was embarking on a dangerous course. In a violent temper she shouted at Ras Tessema, "Shut up! You are an imbecile and now that you have brought it up, I will tell you why you say this. You are choking with honors and money and fear death from the bullets of Europeans and tremble because you may not be able to profit from what the emperor

has given you." To Habte Giyorgis she said, "You are nothing
but an invalid [he was crippled with rheumatism] and good
for nothing, so why don't you just go to bed." This excessive
rudeness no doubt convinced Ras Tessema that the "right moment"
had come "to impose his will on women as well as men ... by force
if necessary."[18]

On 20 March 1910 Lij Bayene, Minister of Post and Telegraph,
who also acted as liaison between the palace and the legations, told
Dr. Martin that there was a conspiracy afoot to remove the empress
from power and send her away. Count Colli of the Italian legation
heard of the plot from Dejazmach Gebre Selasse and Dejazmach
Demissew.

The conspirators gathered at the house of Habte Giyorgis who
announced, "We are displeased with everything the empress is doing
— especially the appointments and dismissals. The only good one
she has made is Teferi Mekonnen to his father's government at Harar
— we confirm him and cancel the rest. In future she will not interfere
in state affairs." There were a few dissenting voices but they were
shouted down. The group proceeded *en masse* to the house of Abune
Matewos.

As they were very excited, Abune Matewos brought out the gospels
and made them swear with their hands on the book that they would not
shed any blood. The bishop agreed to go to the *gibbi* and confront the
empress.

She refused to see him ... while her women, like furies, poured out into
the courtyard shouting curses and throwing stones. "Go away son of
foreigners. Dog! Go back to Egypt!"

Standing behind them, the empress said, "He is not a minister of
God — he is a shopkeeper." The bishop returned home and sent back
the message, "If you persist in not receiving me, you will be turned
over to soldiers." This frightened Empress Taytu sufficiently for her
to invite him to return.

Abune Matewos counseled Taytu to renounce power for the good
of the country. She answered:

I abandon joyfully the cares of government. They are an insupportable
weight for an old woman. If I carried this burden in the past — was
it for myself? Certainly not. It was done for the young king [Lij
Iyasu] and for Ethiopia. Who, other than myself, has fought beside
Menilek and listened to all affairs of state? Was it the regent, Tessema?
That old peasant! He is good only for disputing with farmers and
reaping fields of grain and coffee. Was it that vulgar Galla, Habte

A travel pass issued by Taytu. Seal: "Itege Taytu, Light of Ethiopia."

Taytu's red-and-white letter seal made in France

Giyorgis?* I warn you. If they attack me, I shall know how to defend myself.[19]

The next day, 22 March 1910, Taytu appealed to the legation that had always considered her their most obdurate enemy: the Italian. She sent a message to Count Colli to say that her life was threatened. Would he represent her position to other European ministers and could she deposit with him for safekeeping her money and her documents? He sent his reply, verbally, expressing his belief that neither her life not her dignity as empress would be violated. He regretted that he could not intervene in internal political affairs and hoped that she would acquiesce in the will of the people. Of course he would be happy to accept her documents.

This routine diplomatic ploy was blatant hypocrisy as intervention in internal politics by the British, French and Italians was also routine. Colli quickly informed Ras Tessema of the empress's message, and then visited the British and French legations. The three powers

---

*Conspirators during the July 1909 aborted coup used the same insult about Habte Giyorgis, a man liked by the foreigners because he was a "phenomenon of incorruptibility." Taytu used patronising words about the "Galla" as did others of the elite. A 1905 travel pass from her read, "This is sent from Itege Taytu, Light of Ethiopia. The bearer is Sharew, accompanied by four civilized Galla. He is coming to Begemder. Let him pass. Do not stop him. Written on 10 *megabit* 1898 in the city of Addis Ababa." (Copy of original provided by Richard Caulk)

concurred that they would maintain strict neutrality, but, if necessary, would err on the side of getting rid of Empress Taytu.

Later the same day, Colli received a written communication from the empress:

If in the past we have had debates about the border and other things, they were done in the interests of my country, not to make you unhappy. Don't condemn me for wishing the best for my country. Through Abune Matewos, the people say that while the *negus* is sick, I must not interfere in government. I told them, "Very well, I will not," and asked them to escort me to my lands. This is what is done in European countries — when one leaves the government one returns to one's own province. If they do not send me, I beg you to inform your king and ask you to guarantee the safety of my person, my goods and my people.

Yet another letter came from Taytu the following day in which she appeared to have recovered from this uncharacteristic abjection. "I am a prisoner in a place where I have had a crown and have commanded. Please write to Ras Tessema and Fitawrari Habte Giyorgis what I have said to you, for they and my own servants have made me a prisoner. You cannot be silent." She sent almost identical letters to the legations of Britain, France, Germany and Russia. The legations answered this appeal with their "neutral" non-intervention policy, but Count Colli's reply contained the additional sentiment that if people in Italy heard that she had left the side of the dying emperor, it would not make a good impression.

The empress appealed to the churchmen and religious associations of Entotto to whom she had donated so much:

For five months I have been nursing our master and have not come to you. Now the army stands against me and does not let me participate in government. They want me to sit in an empty room. Abune Matewos would excommunicate all people who would visit me. Without doing any wrong, the people of Shewa have made a sinner out of me. Do not open the church. Let fasting hymns continue.

The conspiring nobles and Abune Matewos went to see Taytu on 24 March. There was a dead silence until finally Empress Taytu asked coolly, "What brought you all here today?" Dejazmach Gebre Selasse, flanked by several other men of equal rank, stepped forward and spoke. "We wish you to confine yourself to caring for our sovereign, your husband, and refrain from the daily duties of government which should be handled in accordance with the proclaimed wish of our emperor, by the regent, Ras Tessema, in the name of Lij Iyasu, the heir to the throne." She reacted furiously, telling Gebre Selasse that he was a coarse and disgusting person, lacking the refinement of those brought up at court, and she was not surprised by his conduct because he was nothing but a shepherd. "Who has not been a shepherd?" was the clever rejoinder of Gebre Selasse, slipping in a dig at her Semen origins, Semen being famous for its sheep. He continued with some elegance, "We might all be only shepherds, but thanks to Emperor Menilek, we no longer herd sheep but have become shepherds of people." The empress turned to the others and asked if they were in agreement and they all nodded affirmatively.

She turned suddenly on Ras Tessema:

You instigated all this. Why don't you have the courage to come forward? I am grieved at your deceit. As for state business, some time ago I told you I would look after the emperor and leave everything to you — but you sent Ras Mengesha Atikem to ask me to carry on. What action have I taken without consulting you? Come now. Tell me!

Not so quick on his feet as Gebre Selasse, Ras Tessema insisted lamely that the empress had done some things against his wishes and that he had been the target of much criticism for letting her have her own way. Dr. Martin, who was present, said that Ras Tessema's response was feeble and reported that Taytu then had a spokesman read a statement in which she first denied that she had ever gone over the head of Tessema and then asked permission to go to her own province with the sick emperor, to the monastery of Debre Libanos, or to her fief in Bulga.

Nor did she like Abune Matewos's explanation of his complaisance and got quite hot and excited. They both seem to hate each other heartily," wrote Dr. Martin. He said there was a scrap between Ras Mengesha Atikem and Dejazmach Demissew Nessibu during the meeting in which they came to blows and had to be separated. Both Dr. Martin and Teferi Mekonnen, who was not present, implied in their accounts that the empress won a tiny moral victory, as the meeting closed with pleas from the assemblage that she stay and nurse the emperor. "She said she would think it over until Monday."[20]

That evening when Dr. Martin visited Abune Matewos, the prelate was still fuming as he ruminated on the events of the day. He told Martin that the empress had said that she did not care if the whole country was deluged with blood. On 27 March the empress informed Ras Tessema that she was willing to stay on and care for the emperor but would like an oath from all the chiefs that when Menilek died, she would not be molested, but permitted to go to her own lands with all of her belongings. The nobles refused to swear anything. "Just tell her she will be fairly treated."

The once mighty empress was dethroned. She made one final conciliatory effort through her confessor on 31 March. Getting wind of it, both the French minister, Brice, and the minister of the British legation, Thesiger, engaged in unabashed meddling in Ethiopian affairs. Both of them urged Ras Tessema not to give an inch.[21]

Brice went to see Habte Giyorgis, who, ailing, received him stretched out on a divan. With a listless, expressionless voice, he agreed with Brice on the irresponsible way in which the empress had wielded power. Their conversation went like this:

Giyorgis: That woman abused her authority and mistreated us; imposed her incoherent choices on us, and her wild ideas. She made difficulties for everyone ... us as well as you.
Brice (*laughing*): I noticed that. I received letters from her with the emperor's seal, breaking promises he had made [on the railroad].
Giyorgis: She is involved no more, thanks be to God, but she continues to intrigue. It is in her blood. She has just sent emissaries to beg pardon ... and aims to retake little by little ...
Brice: I hope you do not listen. All men who discuss things with women are doomed in advance. You have seen — all of you — when she looked you in the eye — you didn't dare move — you became small boys ...
Giyorgis: What you say is true. I never want to see her again. My illness has served me in this case and I was able to absent myself and be deaf to her appeal.
Brice: It is marvelous to have things cleared up. I saw 15-20,000 men collect, guns on shoulder, cartridges full ... and now everything has ended peacefully ...
Giyorgis: Your government thought we behaved well?
Brice: Extremely well.

Brice then urged Habte Giyorgis to trust foreigners as well as his own people. He brought up the question of the disorder being caused by former soldiers of the emperor who had not been paid, and told the Minister of War he should honor their demands and defuse their protests.

Giyorgis: You are right, but they pressed us when we hardly had time to turn around.
Brice: True. Events were precipitous. As for Taytu, she must stay where she is. Don't try to fight delicately with her, for in that game you would lose. She asks to make peace with you. Tell her you have never declared war and that you will respect her as long as she remains giving the emperor the care he needs. Don't waver. Don't see her. She would somehow manage you.

Giyorgis (*drawing his hand across his throat*): She will not be allowed to leave.

The French minister continued advising the government without a qualm.* When Dejazmach Abate made his triumphal entry into Addis Ababa on 14 April, Brice suggested that the occasion be used to demonstrate that the differences between the government and foreigners had been ironed out, and as doyen of the diplomatic corps he sat to the left of Ras Tessema.

The dismantling of the "Taytu network" was undertaken by the same methods she had used to create it. The race to ally oneself with either the regent, Ras Tessema, or the heir, Lij Iyasu, was on. Abate, promoted to Ras, was married to Tessema's half-sister. Demissew Nessibu married another half-sister. Negadras Hayle Giyorgis married a natural daughter of Tessema's after repudiating Yetemegnu Alula, Taytu's niece, who in fact had already separated from him. The heir to the throne was immediately divorced from Taytu's great-niece and married to Seble Wengel, the daughter of Ras Haylu (Seyum Tekle Haymanot), ruler of Gojam. Ras Haylu immediately divorced the niece of Taytu, Aselefetch ("who has much of her aunt's temperament in her"), and Teferi Mekonnen married Menen Asfaw, the divorced daughter of Lij Iyasu's favorite older half-sister, Sehin.[22]

Ras Gugsa Wele and Tayye Gulilate were arrested; Gugsa was charged with murder, although he had been far from the scene of the assassination of an emissary, who had gone to Begemder to relay the news of the empress's downfall. Gugsa Wele suffered painful confinement; he was kept in chains for so long that his legs became swollen, the metal having cut into his flesh. His wife, Princess Zewditu, who had lived in the palace grounds since July 1909 helping to care for her father, begged Tessema to ease his chains, but in vain.[23]

Azaj Metaferia and Bejirond Mulugeta were brought to trial. Both had been loyal to Empress Taytu. Mulugeta was charged with misuse of funds in the imperial treasury and Metaferia was accused of telling the empress about meetings of the cabal. "We only followed orders," they both said, though Mulugeta added to his defense an able accounting of the monies entrusted to him. Ras Abate, who presided over this vengeful tribunal, toyed with the notion of calling the empress to the witness stand, since it was her orders that they had

---

*Brice was, however, rebuked by the Quai d'Orsay for his actions; he defended himself saying it was necessary for French interests.

followed, but decided not to risk an effective public appearance by her. Both of the accused were let off with fines.

Ras Welde Giyorgis, having waited out the whole crisis, came to Addis Ababa in May 1910 to make his personal obeisance to the regency and was rewarded with the governorship of all the northern provinces though he refused to pledge allegiance to the new powers.

The ever intrusive French minister cautioned Ras Tessema about the dangers inherent in any communication between Taytu and her brother. Tessema proceeded to withdraw all but 15 of her personal attendants, which resulted in a fracas at the palace on 30 April. Those servants left to her mocked the troops on guard duty and threw stones at them. Lul Seged, who was in charge of the guards, told his uncle, Ras Tessema, that he could not keep order unless the rest of her people were removed.[24]

Despite her tribulations the empress had not lost her sardonic tongue. When Ras Tessema notified her that she might choose a few acquaintances to help her care for the emperor, she responded, "Even when Menilek was well, no person except those with whom he was acquainted approached him. You ought to know this." She wanted to know if this deprivation of male attendants was because her ears were not supposed to hear men's voices and just why was he inflicting this hardship on her.[25]

Actually she was in communication with her brother at the request of Ras Tessema. She urged her brother to make peace with Ras Mikael and wrote to Mikael asking him to do the same with Wele. She assured them both that in spite of the evil done to her, she was content; she reminded them of her desire to go to Jerusalem even before Menilek became ill and avowed that the marriage of Mikael's son to Wele's grand-daughter (annulled at the time of writing) was intended to make them eternal friends. She told Ras Mikael that Lij Iyasu was like her own son, and as God was her witness she would never have harmed him. She urged her brother to stay calm about the fate of his son, Gugsa Wele, still in chains, and recalled to him, "Even I, a woman, was imprisoned in the hands of Emperor Tewodros, so do not be sad about Gugsa, who is a man."

The only suspicious part of her letter to her brother was, "Even if it takes time, a father's curses never fail to be fulfilled," and on her own behalf, "Only you and Ras Mikael are able to mediate with Ras Tessema and have me pardoned." Wele, when sober, had been heard to say that his sister's conduct was crazy, but when intoxicated he would rant, "They destitute my sister, they imprison my son, they seize my province. I will know how to die with a gun in my hand."[26]

Even after depriving the empress of her visitors* and reducing the number of her servants, Ras Tessema continued to urge her to help deal with Wele. As an incentive he dropped the murder charge against Gugsa Wele: "How could he possibly condemn the husband of Menilek's daughter to capital punishment." He invited Taytu to name one of her priests to join the delegation being sent to parley with Ras Wele: "It would be a shame if Wele and Mikael died fighting each other."

With justified contempt Taytu informed the regent that since she had nothing to do with Wele's resistance to the government, he could choose whomever he liked for his delegation. Regarding his so-called favor to Gugsa Wele she said, "How could you hold a person like him ... even if he had murdered someone?" This bland elucidation of the meaning of elite power was followed by an admonition:

> Remember when a friend of Menilek's was killed by the Tigrayans, he dropped the matter, because he knew it would create chaos. Menilek said a country was governed with sensitive and shrewd tactics, not cruelty. It would be nice if you were that clever. As for me, I have already died with Menilek. I am dead. But if Ras Wele died, and Ras Mikael died, you would be hurt.

Missing in the sequence of letters was one in which Taytu must have offered to go herself to talk to her brother, as there is a letter from Ras Tessema thanking her for the offer, but saying that he wants her to rest. The last thing the shaky regency wanted was any face-to-face session between brother and sister. Ras Tessema restored her telephone privileges and gave her a long list of complaints against Ras Wele, including one that Wele was harboring the criminals whom his son had been accused of abetting.[27]

After July 1910 there were no more letters from or to the empress. In August there was a persistent rumor circulating in Addis Ababa that Menilek had regained his health.[28] The regent summoned a panel of doctors to examine the emperor. The doctors were given hostile looks by the priests surrounding Menilek as well as by the empress. She spoke only to Dr. Martin: "I intend to ask for

---

*Weyzero Desta, the widow of Afenegus Nessibu, visited her until December 1910 before being told by the empress not to come anymore. Dr. Vitalien had visited her until he was ordered by the French legation in May to stop. Teferi Mekonnen was allowed to pay his respects to her in May before taking up his post in Harar.

cupping.* Do you think that would make him ill?" Martin said that he could not say without examining him. Annoyed by this, she said she would have it done anyway and he could sit and watch. An Arab *hakim* performed the cupping as the doctors watched. They assured Ras Tessema that the emperor was still incompetent both mentally and physically. In September Ras Tessema again had to prove that the emperor was still alive. The chiefs filed before his supine body and many had difficulty holding back their tears. He had become incontinent, and was difficult to dress and feed. Often his nurses could not manage him until the empress intervened: he would obey her like a child.

No matter how often Ras Tessema changed the people around the captive empress, Taytu always managed to become mistress of her tiny kingdom. "It is her alone his entourage obeys." Menilek passed his days sitting in an armchair in the shade, but "they believe he notes the empress† when she is present."

Ras Wele was persuaded to come to Addis Ababa in November 1910, escorted by Lul Seged, but Taytu was not permitted to see him. She was told he was ill. The aura of omnipotence clung to the empress despite the constant watch on her. When anything untoward happened, from the death of Ras Abate's horse to the death of Ras Tessema on 10 April 1911, she was accused of involvement by sorcery or poison.[29]

The death of the regent opened a new struggle for power, this time between Ras Abate and Ras Habte Giyorgis. There were also renewed fears that the empress would make a comeback. Ras Abate ordered 1,500 soldiers to surround the palace grounds after Ras Tessema's death. There was even an attempt to keep the death a secret. His body was taken during the night to Debre Libanos and no funeral celebration was held. With the restraining hand of the regent gone, Ras Wele and his son Gugsa were brought to trial on the year-old murder charges and, with 18 letters of Ras Wele placed in evidence, were convicted. And who was behind them both? Empress Taytu

---

*Cupping was a common practice in both Ethiopia and Europe. A vacuum was created by placing a cup on the skin to draw blood to the surface; when the skin was scratched first it was called "wet" cupping, otherwise "dry". It was a harmless and useless technique.

†In late December 1911 Menilek apparently became agitated because he was aware that the regent and the heir had left town with a large entourage for a religious celebration. Ras Tessema returned and sat with him for a while. Menilek was sufficiently aware of him and calmed down.

of course, but they did not dare to mention her name. The empress
is purported to have attempted an escape at this time and was caught,
it is said, already mounted on a mule. It is possible that she may
have tried, since with both her nephew and brother imprisoned, her
hopes for an independent domain and a pardon vanished, but the
evidence is lacking.

The empress may have derived some perverse satisfaction when
Ras Abate was unmasked as ambitious for supreme power either
through nullifying Lij Iyasu's nominations or by assuming control
of the heir by chairing the regency council. She witnessed Abate's
attempted seizure of authority when he tried, on 31 May 1911, to
take command of the soldiers guarding her. Shots were exchanged
and Abune Matewos was summoned in haste. He and Echege
Tewofilos negotiated a cease-fire and heard the complaints of Abate
against Lij Iyasu. The rambunctious heir agreed to reform and listen
to the advice of his elders. One part of the story was that Abate
planned to obtain possession of Princess Zewditu, marry her, and
make himself emperor. Count Colli believed this, and the companion
rumor that Empress Taytu would abet him. The firm resolve of Habte
Giyorgis to back Lij Iyasu ended the matter. Abate left town with
his soldiers for his new assignment, Kembatta, with the assurance
of Lij Iyasu and Habte Giyorgis that no retaliation would be taken
against him.

This promise was not kept. A pretext was found: "He is scheming,"
and he was summoned back to Addis Ababa. Abate declined the
order on account of illness, but his *neftegna* received orders from
the central government that they would have their lands confiscated
unless they brought Abate in, and so they obeyed. Abate was handed
over to Ras Mikael who imprisoned him at Meqdela.[30]

Ras Mikael, who had judiciously kept his distance from his son
so as not to inflame the simmering resentment against his own
Muslim origins, finally made an authoritative back-up of Lij Iyasu
in Addis Ababa from November 1911 to January 1912. He succeeded
in papering over the fissures in government — a government that
consisted of a council with Lij Iyasu as its chairman. Mikael had
seen to the release from house arrest of his hated enemy Ras Wele,
and visited the empress in her quarters to see if he could reconcile
her with the regime, an acknowledgment that there were still many
who followed her lead. When he was not able to satisfy her demand
for restoration of her lands, since they had already been re-granted,

she withheld whatever weak influence she had.[31]

Lij Iyasu was a bright and personable lad and many people had great hopes for him. "When he becomes emperor in his own right he will astonish everyone by his intelligence and system of government, which would be carried out according to some European criteria and with justice, especially for the Galla [Oromo] population." But he appeared incapable of sustained dignified behavior. His boon companion was an older man, Tilahun,* who had been a servant in his mother's household, and to whom he granted the title Fitawrari. Tilahun's wife was said to have initiated Lij Iyasu to the joys of sex. The heir was often somewhat the worse for drink, and spent more time with women, roistering in the streets of Addis Ababa and petrifying the new police force,† than in learning how to be an emperor.[32]

Growing a moustache was his foremost concern at one point. Some nostrum from an Arab *hakim* on his upper lip made him nauseous and gave him a headache. The *hakim* was whipped, while Lij Iyasu slept off the ill-effects, though Dr. Martin said he was only suffering from too much champagne.

Possible, though hard to believe, is the report that the two wealthy widows of Ras Tessema and Afenegus Nessibu, Beletshachew and Desta‡ respectively, were employing magic powders and amulets to attract the boy's sexual favors. A malodorous powder (which Dr. Martin identified as dental powder) was detected in Lij Iyasu's quarters. In a search for the culprit who had planted the powder, the servants were beaten, two of them so severely that they died. Before dying they said that Beletshachew had acquired the stuff from Desta, who had been given it by Empress Taytu! Desta denied everything, saying these accusations were extracted by torture.

Stories like these provided some spice to the tenor of the empress's days, which were not exciting. She had a garden, went to chapel,

---

*Not long after being made Fitawrari, Tilahun was appointed to the lofty office of Afenegus and married a descendant of King Sahle Selasse, Weyzero Sekamyelesh Seyfu. Lij Iyasu treated her like a mother and she permitted him to keep his concubines in her house. (Zewde Gabre-Sellassie)

†In groups of four, wearing special hats, a police force had begun patrolling Addis Ababa in May 1909.

‡Beletshachew, about 30 years old, was much talked about because she had not gone into mourning when her husband died. Her designs on Lij Iyasu were more credible than the accusations against Desta, who was soon to go to Jerusalem where she retired to a spiritual life.

and supervised the care of Menilek who was washed, dressed, fed, massaged and pushed around in a wheelchair. The empress took ill in March 1912 and Weyzero Tsehay Werq Darge* was called from Salale to help Zewditu take care of her father. Two European doctors were summoned for the empress, and after they had waited all day, were told she would see neither of them.[33]

The capital was quiet after 13 February 1912 as Lij Iyasu and his entourage went north to visit his father, Ras Mikael. His absence, the legations complained, meant that no work could be done because his seal had replaced the emperor's on official documents. He had left Addis Ababa, they said, because a sorcerer had predicted that he would perish from a spell devised by Empress Taytu. Probably he was bored. Commendably, after spending Easter with his father and meeting with Ras Welde Giyorgis, he held many informal talks with people of all faiths, showing "compassion and interest." "Endowed with great oratorical and demagogic abilities ... he won their liking and forgiveness for his personal foibles, which they attributed to his youth."[34]

Lij Iyasu could not, however, sustain this excellent behavior. One year later, he returned to "Byzantium" from his long ramble, impatient to be installed in style at the imperial palace and have Menilek moved elsewhere. An effort was made to satisfy the young prince, and his ministers presented his proposal to the empress with the argument that it would give the sick man a change of scene. Doctors were sent to the palace to certify his ability to travel. The empress prevented them from entering with the cooperation of Gebre Maryam, head of the palace guard, who took seriously his commission to guard the emperor. The soldiers of Lij Iyasu then cut off the water supply and allowed in only enough food to nourish the emperor. In the early morning hours of 8 February 1913 Gebre Maryam saw that his own people who were sneaking food in had just been fired on, and ordered fire returned. After two hours of indiscriminate shooting, 30 were dead and 60 badly wounded. Gebre Maryam surrendered with the intercession of Abune Matewos who kept his promise that he would be exiled to Gojam and not executed.

French legation personnel saw the empress behind the whole sorry

---

*The independent daughter of Darge referred to in Chapter 12. Dr. Martin, who saw her at the time she received the summons to Addis Ababa, wrote, "A good many people here are glad she is going away."

business. Certainly if her aim had been to prevent Lij Iyasu from taking up residence at the palace, she was successful. She even had the temerity to rebuke the boy for harassing the brave servants of the emperor, for wanting the death of his grandfather, and for being the cause of all the disturbance. She told him that Menilek had had to be carried to an underground passage to avoid the bullets which had shattered every single pane of glass in the windows of his room. The empress also seized this opportunity to complain of being kept as a prisoner.

Lij Iyasu told the empress that he had had nothing at all to do with the violence and that his people had misinterpreted his orders. He assured her of his filial respect and declared that she was free to go wherever she liked with a guard of honor that he would provide. She did not take up his offer.[35]

The restless heir vacated the capital for most of the following six months, making a brief return in April when he signed an agreement with the Compagnie du Chemin de Fer for continuation of the railroad into Addis Ababa, then left again for Desse to stay with his father. He returned a few days before the death of the emperor.

Menilek died in the early morning hours of 12 December 1913 and was buried quickly without announcement or ceremony. It was a week before the legations could confirm that Emperor Menilek II was dead. They were equally mystified about the whereabouts of Empress Taytu, as she had been moved with a small retinue* at night and in secret to the hills of Entotto above Addis Ababa. Princess Zewditu remained at the *gibbi* until 1915 when she was rusticated to Falle, where she was allowed to live with her husband, Ras Gugsa.[36]

Still, no crown was placed on the head of Lij Iyasu. Though there was no law or tradition regarding age, he himself and certainly Abune Matewos believed that he should wait until he was 18.[37] The sorcerer who helped the heir make this decision did not predict that in two years' time Lij Iyasu would be a hunted fugitive.

The old empress, dressed simply, spent her days in prayer and fasting at Entotto. Loyal friends and relations who visited her kept her informed on what was going on below her mountain perch.[38]

---

*Among them was a young page, Desta Damtew (son of Menilek's envoy to Russia in 1895) about whom the French legation had already transmitted to Paris the false smut that during Menilek's incapacity Desta was in charge of extinguishing the lamp beside the empress's bed adjacent to the sick emperor and that in the darkness she drew him to her arms to satisfy that passion not yet extinguished "even at her age.".

No new day had dawned in Ethiopia.

Taytu would have shed no tears over the double dealing to which Dejazmach Gebre Selasse was subjected in Tigray. When he had left Addis Ababa after his careful organization of her downfall, Gebre Selasse had been promised that Tigray would return to its triumvirate administration, made up of Seyum Mengesha Yohannes, Ras Sebhat Aregawi and himself. In early 1914 when these nobles learned that Ras Mikael would be promoted to *negus*, overlord of Wello and Tigray, they met and agreed to oppose it. The action would reduce Tigray to a second-class province whose people could not appeal directly to Addis Ababa. All judicial and administrative appointments were to be submitted to Mikael.

The telephone had come into its own as the expediter of political and military events. Gebre Selasse telephoned Lij Iyasu to ask permission to come to Addis Ababa to explain the Tigrayan case against the appointment of Mikael. He was the elected messenger because of his known rapport with the boy and because his oldest son, Yohannes, had recently married one of Lij Iyasu's relatives. Ras Mikael promptly used the telephone at Desse to order Ras Sebhat, with a mixture of threats and promises, to stop Gebre Selasse at all costs. It was very costly. Though surprised by the attack of Ras Sebhat, whom he had considered as a surrogate father, Gebre Selasse defeated him on 25 February 1914. Sebhat and three of his sons died in the battle. Furious, Lij Iyasu ordered his father to hunt down Gebre Selasse and ordered Ras Welde Giyorgis to march from Gondar to help. Before Mikael could take to the field, Gebre Selasse was engaged in a bloody six-hour battle with the other member of the Tigray triumvirate, Seyum Mengesha Yohannes. Realizing that his forces were outnumbered by those of Welde Giyorgis who had advanced as far as Aksum, Gebre Selasse fled into the Danakil desert where he remained* until Lij Iyasu was deposed.[39]

The crown of *negus* was placed on the head of Mikael by the second-ranking bishop, Abune Petros, on 31 May 1914. Mikael immediately rewarded Seyum Mengesha with the title of Ras, the governorship of Tigray, and his daughter Tewabech in marriage.

---

*He returned to a position of honor in the government of Tigray under the Zewditu-Teferi Mekonnen government; his wife Amaretch, having failed to give him a child, asked to go to Jerusalem to live as a nun in 1914 and he purchased a house for her there in 1924; he made his peace with Seyum Mengesha and married his daughter, Welette Israel. Their son, Zewde Gabre-Sellassie, is the source of this account.

Although Seyum's appointment partially appeased Tigrayan sensibilities, Tigrayans and many Shewans were unhappy about the elevation of Mikael to "king of Zion." The riddance of Lij Iyasu was a subject of open discussion. However, guns firing in Europe in August 1914 sealed the young man's doom.

At the present historical distance the question of whether Ethiopia sympathized with the Allies or with the German-Austrian-Turkish entente of 1914 appears of little consequence. Ethiopia controlled no supply routes and had no strategic materials. Of importance to the Allies was the fact that Ethiopia had borders with their colonies and a large Muslim population on those borders. The fear that the Germans, with their allies, the Turks, might incite uprisings among Muslims against their colonial masters whose resources were stretched to the breaking point in the European war, was the subject of grave concern in Cairo, Khartoum, Nairobi and Addis Ababa.* Disasters for the British in the Dardanelles, setbacks to the Russians in Mesopotamia, the Turkish attack on the Suez Canal and German success in eluding the British in Tanganyika — all these made the question of where Lij Iyasu's sympathies lay an urgent issue for the diplomats in Addis Ababa.

Lij Iyasu's actions were not reassuring. When he actually resided in the capital long enough to be observed, there were constant reports of drunkenness and carousing. He was seen frequently in the company of the representative of the Sultan of Turkey. Just when he indicated that he was prepared to discuss the subject of where his sympathy lay in the European conflict, he would suddenly disappear.[40]

In March 1916 Wilfred Thesiger of the British legation made the long trek to Gore in an effort to track down Lij Iyasu, who had been away almost a year, to talk business with him. Unable to make contact, Thesiger returned to Addis Ababa and wrote on 14 April 1916: "The prince makes no secret of his sympathies for Islam — lives solely in the houses of Muslims and has adopted Muslim dress and custom. He has taken the daughters of Muslim chiefs as wives."

Lij Iyasu returned to Addis Ababa in time to attend a party given

---

*The Germans tried some subversion through Leo Frobenius and Solomon (David) Hall. Frobenius was stopped in Eritrea but the Italians forwarded his message that Germany would see that its ally, Turkey, settled the Ethiopian claims in Jerusalem if Ethiopia cooperated; Hall was arrested at the frontier and spent four years in an Eritrean prison; F.W. von Syburg got through, and met with Mikael and Lij Iyasu at Desse, but they did not commit themselves.

by the Turkish representative to celebrate the birthday of the sultan on 27 April. At the party an Ethiopian flag embroidered with the slogan, "God is great and Muhammed is his prophet," was presented to the Turkish envoy. To the British minister Lij Iyasu later denied that he had done such a thing; one of his aides had done it and he had put the culprit in chains.

Though the Allied legations kept pressing the Council of Ministers with every scrap of information about Lij Iyasu's religious inclinations, the prince was now 18 and old enough to know that the state religion was Christianity and that he was stabbing at the heart of the Ethiopian monarchial-church tradition by his reckless disregard of the church, even though his intentions may have been towards a long overdue rapprochement with Ethiopian Muslims.[41]

Some awareness that he should demonstrate his Christian faith must have been in Lij Iyasu's mind when he went up to Entotto to see ex-Empress Taytu and pray in "her" church. She prepared food for him which she served on the *messob* that had belonged to his grandfather. He ate nothing, having been sated with dire warnings that she might poison him, bade her farewell and left the city that night. Teferi Mekonnen had come to Addis Ababa in May, but when he asked permission of Lij Iyasu to return to Harar because his wife had gone into labor, Iyasu refused and sent soldiers to make sure he did not leave the city. Having eluded his guards, Teferi Mekonnen reached Entotto just after Lij Iyasu had left. The empress greeted him warmly and offered him the food left untouched by Lij Iyasu. He demurred, saying he was not entitled to eat from the table that had belonged to Emperor Menilek, but she assured him he was. The narrator of this story considered this gesture prophetic and related that she also confided to him that the mantle of government should be returned to her own shoulders.[42]

Lij Iyasu's departure from Addis Ababa that night was fateful. His absence gave his opposition complete freedom to plan how to get rid of him. Teferi Mekonnen, cautious at first, was anxious about his wife, Menen Asfaw, and his newborn son in Harar, for which city Lij Iyasu was heading. From Dire Dawa, Lij Iyasu telephoned Addis Ababa and instructed that Teferi Mekonnen be notified of his new appointment as governor of Keffa; he himself would rule Harar. Once in Harar, Lij Iyasu ordered that Menen (who was his niece), her daughter and the infant son leave at once for Addis Ababa so that she could join her husband and go to Keffa with him. Teferi

Mekonnen's cousin, Imru, pleaded with Lij Iyasu to let them wait until the baby had been baptized. Two days after this ceremony, on 6 September 1916, Weyzero Menen, her children, Kenyazmach Imru, and a few followers left on muleback for Dire Dawa, where they caught the train for Addis Ababa.*[43]

Thesiger had telegraphed London on 30 August 1916: "Movement among Shewan chiefs to depose Lij Iyasu." The following day Thesiger reported, "Movement collapsed on account of rain." There had been a heavy downpour but it was Negadras Hayle Giyorgis, not rain, who had prevented the essential participants, Abune Matewos and Echege Welde Giyorgis, from attending. The *negadras* was not only running the country on behalf of the absent emperor-elect, but he had also just married Lij Iyasu's beloved half-sister, Sehin Mikael. The bride was trapped in one of those paradoxes consequent on political marriage: it was her daughter, Menen, who had just had the child in Harar and whose husband, Teferi Mekonnen, was an active conspirator. Abune Matewos, the man who should have been most exercised about the alleged weakening of the church, was a very reluctant guest in the cabal. He was frightened of what Ras Mikael's vaunted army, 30,000 strong, would do.

The envoys of Britain, Italy and France speeded up matters by jointly presenting a *démarche* to the Council of Ministers on 10 September, drawing their attention to the perils of being allies of Turkey and Germany. The Ethiopians were not swayed so much by that argument as they were by the increased power of Allah. Steps were taken immediately to neutralize Ras Mikael by alerting Ras Welde Giyorgis at Gondar and Ras Haylu of Gojam (whose daughter had been repudiated in favor of Muslim girls by Lij Iyasu) to mobilize for a fight.

The palace courtyard was filled with chiefs on the morning of 28 September 1916. Abune Matewos had declined the invitation and Negadras Hayle Giyorgis had not been invited. The *negadras* came anyway and was told he would be admitted as soon as he produced the head of the church, which he did.

---

*This account is at complete variance with the one based on British diplomatic sources told by Leonard Mosley in his biography of Hayle Selasse, in which he said Menen was disguised as a Harari woman and smuggled out of Harar, to avoid being restored to her former husband, Lul Seged who was with Lij Iyasu. For one thing, Lul Seged was not with Lij Iyasu and the less dramatic version above was told to Zewde Gabre-Sellassie by Kenyazmach Imru (later known as the "Red Ras" for his progressive views) who was with Menen the whole time.

The charges were read: in sum, they accused Lij Iyasu of having adopted Islam and included all the details in the *démarche* submitted by the legations. Everyone looked to Abune Matewos who stuttered and hesitated, "If ... these ... things be true ..." There was a murmur of disgust and the *echege* propelled the bishop to the center of the crowd with a firm hand on his shoulder. Slowly he spoke, "From this day forth you are freed from your oath to the apostate Lij Iyasu," and pronounced his excommunication.

Many people were surprised when, the following day, it was proclaimed that Zewditu, daughter of Menilek, would be "Queen of Kings," with Teferi Mekonnen as her regent and heir. It was an event of tremendous moment: not only was Zewditu the first female sovereign since the "Queen of Sheba," but it was also the first time in Ethiopian history that an heir was designated at the same time as a monarch. In 1909, when the omnipotence of Empress Taytu had worried the nobles, one of them had assured the diplomats, "Never will a woman rule," and another that "No woman, directly, or indirectly, will ever reign in Ethiopia."[44]

Being named "regent and heir" instead of emperor was the price Teferi Mekonnen had to pay for the support of the old guard who feared he was too inclined towards "modern" ways. The price for Zewditu was a divorce from Ras Gugsa Wele, whose otherwise role of consort was deemed an invitation to the recrudescence of the influence of his aunt, Taytu, still alive at Entotto. On Zewditu's behalf, there was a statement, "Since God has chosen me, a woman, and assigned me this great crown and throne, I shall make a vow to live alone and not with a husband."[45] Gugsa Wele returned to his governorship of Begemder.

In the throne speech read for Zewditu on 30 September 1916 she reminded the people that Lij Iyasu had denied his grandfather, Emperor Menilek, what was not even denied to a stranger murdered on the road — a proper burial. "Have you ever heard of a Christian dying in the country where he lived, when it was forbidden to say his name in church or celebrate his funeral?" Zewditu made the symbolic claim that she had held her father's body in her arms for two years, three months and two days, and then was chased from the palace before she could commit his body to the ground.

In the manifesto that detailed the apostasies of Lij Iyasu there was a small gesture to placate Ras Mikael: "Lij Iyasu's father tried to set him on the right path but he would not listen." It did not work and

Ras Mikael took up arms in defense of his son who had eluded capture. Before Ras Mikael's defeat at the end of October 1916, his effective tactics and the fierce fighting of his men had caused a greater loss of life than was suffered by the Ethiopians fighting the Italians from 1895 to 1896.[46]

Though Zewditu's coronation did not take place until 11 February 1917, she invited her stepmother, Taytu, to return to Addis Ababa to live with her immediately after she was named to the throne. Taytu declined, but both Zewditu and Teferi Mekonnen paid respectful visits to the former empress at Entotto, and in a modest way Taytu resumed her old role of advising, encouraging and warning, but it is doubtful, as one source claimed, that she gave any "orders" regarding the strategy to trap Ras Mikael. Her request in November 1917 to be allowed to go to Gondar to end her days was refused, Teferi Mekonnen agreeing with the British envoy that "she must not be let out."[47]

Three months later Taytu was dead. She died on 11 February 1918 after a short illness during which she refused the services of a European doctor. There was a grand three-day funeral with guns firing, drums rolling and the traditional funeral feast provided by Empress Zewditu. There was a row of representatives from all the legations, who had felt compelled to ask their respective home offices for permission to attend. Ironically, the most moving obituary was written 10 years after her death by one of her worst enemies, Afewerq Gebre Iyesus, who had not merely sworn never to return to Ethiopia until she was dead, but had been forbidden to do so.* He quoted

---

*Afewerq Gebre Iyesus was perhaps the finest master of Amharic writing. He had quarreled with the empress in 1894 for having worn shoes while painting murals in Entotto Raguel church and for being "too European." He professed ignorance of what he had done wrong, and when he asked her why she denied him entrance to her private chambers, she said, "May you be crucified." He left Ethiopia vowing never to return while she lived. In fact he was declared a traitor in 1895 and 1896 for his role in persuading Gugsa Darge and Kitaw Zamanel to defect to Italy from their school in Switzerland. He wrote, among other things, a biography of Menilek and Taytu, a paean of praise and flattery, which he hoped would insure his return. It did not. He and his Italian wife came to live in Eritrea in 1914 where he wrote poems in praise of Lij Iyasu. As soon as Iyasu was deposed he wrote poems insulting him and in praise of Zewditu and Teferi Mekonnen. Zewditu named him as head of a mission to the United States in 1918 and subsequently as head of customs at Dire Dawa. He became Ethiopian minister to Italy from 1931 to 1935 and returned to Ethiopia to collaborate as chief of the court system during the Italian occupation from 1936 to 1941. After the liberation he was imprisoned and then rusticated to Jimma, where he died in 1947. (Zewde Gabre-Sellassie)

two young nobles* who were with her when she died:

> The blood slowly withdrew from that face which was once a rose, and on those eyes which once looked like great, luminous diamonds, the lashes slowly fell. Our hearts trembled. That dear, revered, glorious empress, who, at the side of the second Menilek, had reigned, aggrandized and made Ethiopia prosper, was now wrapped in her winding sheet and enclosed in a box where she would remain for eternity inside a tomb where no light would ever shine. What to do? Death cannot be turned away with either a raised shield, a lance or an unsheathed sword. Death is strong, cruel and determined. What to do? Hearts overcome with sorrow, we saw we could do nothing. So we called everyone to weep.[48]

"Reigned, aggrandized and made Ethiopia prosper" was an accurate tribute to the woman at the side of Menilek II. Her critical error was in acting like a man. The religious orthodoxy and dynastic rule that she supported so passionately tolerated all the violence inherent in preserving autocratic rule over a varied ethnic population when authority was vested in a man. Even though Empress Zewditu held the supreme title for 14 years, decision making was in the hands of her male regent and ministers.

If, in Taytu's opposition to "new" ideas she delayed what is often called "progress" it raises the question, "Why is Ethiopia today, despite the telegraph, telephone, television, roads, airplanes, still rent with civil and border wars, famine and ethnic and religious intolerance?" She did not oppose schools or medical care. She had the failing of all autocrats, namely, fear of change, and each administrative division of the country had another oligarch with the same fear.

She was not paranoid about foreign encroachment. The reality was that Germany, Belgium, Italy, Great Britain and France were taking title to Africa. Because of her intransigence which led to the Battle of Adwa in 1896, Ethiopia remained independent until 1935 when Benito Mussolini launched his revenge and created "Africa Orientale Italiana" with the help of airplanes and poison gas.

Consider the trickery and duplicity of many of the diplomats, traders and adventurers. Was it any wonder that Empress Taytu looked on them with suspicion? She exerted needed restraint on Menilek who had a tendency to make agreements because he was easily won over by the pleasant personality and generosity of the

---

*They were Ayelu and Admasu, the high-ranking grandsons of her cousin Bayenetch Merso.

envoy. In the end, with her concurrence, Menilek signed all of the treaties that established the borders of Ethiopia and its trade and diplomatic relations. The "Menilek era" was filled with remarkable events, not the least of which was the emergence of Taytu as an important historical figure. This era, usually dated from Menilek's coronation in 1889 to his death in 1913, should be renamed the "Menilek and Taytu era" and revised to date from 1883 when they were married, to 1910, when Menilek's mental faculties ceased to function and Taytu was deposed.

Epilogue

Lij Iyasu's father, Ras Mikael, was marched through the streets of Addis Ababa in chains in November 1916; he died in prison in 1918. Lij Iyasu himself was captured in 1921 and died in prison in 1935. Taytu's brother, Ras Wele, died in prison in June 1918.

Empress Zewditu built a mausoleum for her father in Addis Ababa and had Taytu's body brought from Entotto and buried beside him. Zewditu herself was buried there after her death on 1 April 1930. She was not told of the death of her ex-husband, Ras Gugsa Wele, two days earlier. He died in a battle with Teferi Mekonnen who was crowned Emperor Hayle Sellase I on 2 November 1930.

Fifty years after her death, Empress Taytu was honored in an Ethiopian stamp series entitled "The Great Empresses."* The announcement said that she was "admired for her beauty, grace, exceptional intelligence and ability," and ended with the surprising tribute that "she made available her constant and full support to the introduction of modern civilization in the country."

In Italy the empress lives on in such popular expressions as "Who does she think she is? La regina Taytu?" and "She is like Principessa Taytu," the latter used to describe a woman who has too tight a grip on her husband. The Italian designer, Bergamin, has christened two boutiques and introduced a line of accessories for the international market with the brand-name "Taitù," using an alluring blurb that this was the name of the Ethiopian empress, "whose every whim for something beautiful was indulged by her husband." So the myth-making goes on.

Most of the Ethiopian people, some 30 million, still live with poverty, disease and illiteracy, conditions which they dignify with their exquisite manners, family loyalty and devotion to religion. There are few prettier sights than a cluster of men and women wrapped in their white shawls, bobbing graciously to each other on the road, kissing each other's cheeks repeatedly as the 20th century whizzes by in a motor car. There are few bleaker tragedies than the

---

*The others in the series were the Queen of Sheba, Elleni, Mentewab, Seble Wengel and Zewditu.

TAITU 1890 A.D. ጣይቱ

፹ ላ ኢትዮጵያ 80c
ETHIOPIA

Study for the stamp design of Empress Taytu
by Afewerq Tekle for the series, "The Great
Empresses," issued on 2 March 1964

spectacle of Ethiopians continuing to suffer from periodic starvation
and turning their guns on each other in regional conflicts.

Women's lot improves only as the nation prospers. Educational
and professional opportunities opened up for women under Hayle
Selasse though these tended to favor already privileged women.
There are women in the diplomatic service and in the civil service
as nurses, doctors, veterinary surgeons, teachers and broadcasters;
and of course there are women in the army as there have always
been, except that now they wear uniforms and have ranks. Women
obtained the right to vote at the same time as men did in 1957, though
there was very little to vote for, nor is there much more in the mid
1980s.

Until the beginning of the famine in 1982, rural women were keen participants in literacy programs; now they simply try to stay alive. All the bizarre contrasts in cities everywhere in the developing world pertain to Addis Ababa. Alert, chic, professional women walk down the same street as women bent double with a load of wood on their backs. The bright young women at the University of Addis Ababa today know the name of Empress Taytu and speak of her admiringly. "She was brave and she stood up to men."

Notes

1 Taytu's fifth husband: Menilek, King of Shewa

Menilek's birth and early life are related in the *Chronique*, 1: 70-192.

1. Harris, *Highlands*, 1: 362, 411; 2: 224-319.
2. Cecchi, *Da Zeila*, 1: 249-50; Atsme Giyorgis ("Ye-Galla Tariq," ms. IEA, AA) gives his birthdate as 11 August. When Menilek began celebrating birthdays, which may have been the idea of a foreign adviser, the day on which it was most often marked was 19 August.
3. Rochet d'Héricourt, *Second Voyage*, 159.
4. Mahteme-Selassie, "Portrait Retrospectif," 60-8; Schweinfurth, "Einige Mitteilungen," 332-60.
5. See Armstrong and Fisseha, Basset, Cerulli, Cohen, Eadie, Faïtlovich, Fusella, Guidi, Mondon-Vidailhet, Moreno, Walker.
6. Pankhurst, "Misoneism," 227-320.
7. Cecchi (op. cit., 1: 251-3) implies that the dowager queens were so over-hasty to collaborate that they even shocked Tewodros; Zeneb ("La Cronaca") only implies an absence of heroics and that the wife, sister(?) and sons of Seyfu were imprisoned.
8. Massaia, *Miei 35 Anni*, 9: 25-8; Zeneb, op. cit., 172-3; Rubenson, *Tewodros*, 76; Eadie, *Amharic Reader*, 214; Crummey, "Tewodros as Reformer," 457-69; Lejean, *Théodore*, 183-5; Welde Maryam, *Théodore*, 30.
9. One lady, Yetemegnu, was more than concubine as Tewodros addressed her as Itege. Haile Gabriel Dagne, "Letters," 115-17.
10. Waldmeier, *Autobiography*, 12; Stern, *Captive*, 219.
11. Bairu Tafla, "Gärmamé," 1-3.
12. Stern, *Captive*, 220; Avedis Terzian, interview, AA, 3 April 1967. The *Chronique* (1: 102-3) says that Werqitu would have exchanged Menilek for her son had not Tewodros been so hasty with his executions while Stern (op. cit., 218) alleges that Werqitu's wish to barter Menilek was vetoed by her advisers.
13. Massaia, op. cit., 9: 106-8; Crummey, "Violence," 107-25; Rubenson, op. cit., 55.
14. Bairu Tafla, op. cit.; Cecchi, op. cit., 262.
15. Crummey, *Priests*, 14-27; Darkwah, *Shewa*, 58; Massaia, op. cit., 8: 173-4.
16. Rassam, *Narrative*, 2: 251; Stern, *Captive*, 353-4; Caulk, "Firearms," 611-13.
17. Massaia, op. cit., 8: 173-4.
18. Rubenson, *Tewodros* and *Survival* are excellent accounts of the reasons for and conduct of the British military campaign of 1867-8; Moorehead, *The Blue Nile*, is a good popular version; Holland and Hozier, *Record*, is the official account. A military surgeon did an autopsy on Tewodros which led to the rumor that the British had cut off his head. See also Conti-Rossini, "La fine di Re Teodoro."
19. Stanley, *Coomassie*, 323.
20. Massaia, op. cit., 9: 31-3, 69-81; Lande, "Un Voyageur," 1: 880; Cecchi, op. cit., 1: 270-9; Welde Maryam, op. cit., 55; Zewde Gabre-Sellassie, New York, 12 October 1983.
21. Zewde Gabre-Sellassie, *Yohannes*, 53.
22. Marcus, *Menelik*, 38-42; Rubenson, *Survival*, 303; Zewde Gabre-Sellassie, op. cit., 55-83.
23. Rubenson, *Survival*, 345-6. I have paraphrased this letter dated 6 December 1876.

24. Lande, "Un voyageur," 1: 877-903.
25. Massaia, op. cit., 10: 63-72; Landini, *Due Anni*, 20-76.
26. Marcus, op. cit., 50-3; Massaia, op. cit., 10: 151-9; Cecchi, op. cit., 1: 271-7; *Chronique*, 1: 135-6 tells of the plot but does not refer to Bafena. The chronicler at this time was Bafena's secretary and he accompanied her to Gojam. Menilek's scribe died on this journey and Gebre Selasse succeeded him as royal chronicler.
27. Bairu Tafla (op. cit.) writes that Germame was suspected of being implicated in the plot because his son, Semu-negus, had escaped from prison at the same time as Meshesha Seyfu was brought to Bafena.
28. Massaia, op. cit., 11: 5. In a letter to General Gordon, August 1877, Emperor Yohannes declared that Menilek was a rebel and had fled from him and that he had been deserted by Bafena because he had taken another mistress (Hill, *Gordon*, 208).
29. Cecchi, op. cit., 1: 442-3; Zewde Gabre-Sellassie, op. cit., 91-4; Fusella, "Le lettere," 3: 20-30; Bartnicki and Mantel-Niecko, "Role ... religious conflicts," 5-39; Massaia, op. cit., 11: 18-20, 60; Gonzague de Lassere, "Mgr. Massaia," 4-5.
30. Franzoj, *Continente*, 92-123; Caulk ("Territorial Competition") revises the sequence and causes of events in this war.
31. Aleqa Lemlem chronicle, folio 30; Soleillet, *Voyages*, 114-21; Zewde Gabre-Sellassie (note, 17 May 1984) states that all sources err when they say that Yohannes ordered Menilek to marry specifically Taytu or Bafena (e.g., Marcus, op. cit., 71 and Giglio, *Mar Rosso*, 5: 241, Antonelli letter from Entotto, 19 September 1887).
32. Afewerq Gebre Iyesus, "Menilek," 1: 35-6; Mérab (*Impressions*, 2: 45) identifies the man as Wube Serahbezu; Heruy, *Ye-heywet*: "she died suddenly after Menilek took communion with Taytu;" Zervos, *L'Empire*, 59: "died in 1887;" *La Grande Encyclopédie* refers to Bafena as "empress" and says she died in 1890.
33. Zewde Gabre-Sellassie, 10 September 1977; Gonzague de Lassere ("En Pays Galla," 394-5, 405) talked to Menilek on 28 April 1883. His letter to Arnauld d'Abbadie from Haylu Amba (22 May 1883) has the earliest mention of the marriage in a foreign source (d'Abbadie, ms. NA 10222, BN).

2 The background of Taytu Betul Hayle Maryam

1. *Chronique*, 1: 193-204; Afewerq Gebre Iyesus, "Menilek," 1: 35-6; Hussein Ahmed, "Some Problems."
2. Berry, "Solomonic Monarchy," 126-31.
3. Rubenson, *Tewodros*, 16.
4. Booklet, *Menilek II Mausoleum*; dates are incorrect for Menilek's birth, coronation and marriage to Taytu. Rosa (*L'Impero*, 84) says that Taytu was born in 1856; Elets (*Emperor*, 58) says 1854; Mérab (*Impressions*, 2: 26) says 1852; Pétridès (*Le Héros*, 289) gives 1844. The most frequent expression of her age was "about 30 at the time of her marriage to Menilek [1883]" and about 64 at the time of her death in 1918.
5. Parkyns, *Life*, 1: 165; Guidi, "Proverbi," 114; Lejean, "Notes," 253.
6. Combes and Tamisier, *Voyage*, 4: 26.
7. Lefebvre, *Voyage*, 1: 186; 2: 86. Dr. Petit's notes survived; he was eaten by a crocodile.
8. D'Abbadie, ms. Vatican, Carton 4; Rosenfeld, "Eight Women," 72-7; Parkyns, *Life*, 1: 170-1; Plowden, *Travels*, 51, 209; Hoben, "Amharic verbal behavior."
9. Interview, mother and aunts of Almaz, wife of Teshager Woobe, AA, 29 April 1967; doubts that Yewub-dar was the mother of Wele in Martini, *Diario*, 2: 317 and Del Boca, *Gli Italiani*, 1: 549. Heruy (*Ye-heywet*) says Wele was the younger

brother of Taytu. Tsegaye (interview, 24 June 1985) said her birthplace was Aditi.

10. Pearce, *Life*, 2: 83; Conti-Rossini, "La Cronaca," 130; de Castro, *Nella Terra*, 1: 46; d'Abbadie, *Douze Ans*, 1: 162; Combes and Tamisier, *Voyage*, 2: 92; Mekonnen Endalkatchew (*Good Families*, Chap. 3) is the source for her youth in Were Sehin.

11. Massaia, *Miei 35 Anni*, 1: 133; de Castro, "L'Ostetricia;" Annaratone, *In Abissinia*, 59; Terrefe Ras-work, "Birth Customs;" *Fetha Nagast*, 133; Mikael Hailu, *L'Etiopia*; Guidi, "Proverbi," 93. UNICEF in 1982 reported: one child in six does not survive first year; one mother in 50 dies in childbirth; 60 per cent of children under four are underweight and one child in 15 is mentally or physically handicapped.

12. Hosken, *Genital Mutilation*. WINN is a private international group collecting data on female circumcision. Somali and Sudanese women have been taking action against the practice (see Raqiya Haji Dualeh, *Sisters in Affliction*). Walker, *Abyssinian*, 2; de Castro, *Nella Terra*, 1; Prorok, *Dead Men*, 70; Mérab, *Médecins*, 186-9; Cook, "Damage," 3; Verzin, "Sequelae," 163-9; and Ambrogetti, *La Vita Sessuale*. Mérab alleged that hemorrhage and infection from circumcision were rare as did Dr. Yohannes Martin (note to author, 5 November 1969).

13. Ephraim Isaac, *Ethiopian Church*, 32; Mikael Hailu, op. cit., 12.

14. Heughlin, "Bruchstuche," 813-14; interview, aunts of Almaz, AA, op. cit.

15. "Welde Gabriel" in Antonelli; "Welde Maryam" in Mekonnen Endalkatchew; "Welde Giyorgis" in Mérab; "Maru" in Ramzi Tawrus.

16. Griaule ("Mythes," 15-26) and Menghistu Lemma ("Snatch and Run") treated the aggressive factor in play form; Ezra Gebre-Medhin ("Wedding Customs") describes a children's game in which marriage is enacted as capture, as does Cohen ("Jeux Abyssins"); Cassiers ("Mercha," 62) shows persistence of custom; Kifle Widajo, "Wedding Customs," 2: "proof is symbolically given by presenting a rose and loaf of bread to the girl's parents.

17. Combes and Tamisier, op. cit., 2: 122; Pankhurst, "Saint Simonians," 169-223; Levine, *Wax*, 102.

18. Mérab, op. cit., 3: 389, 589; Annaratone, *In Abissinia*, 47-60; Graham, "Report on manners;" and Bernatz, *Scenes*, plate 21.

19. Griaule, op. cit.

20. Rassam, *Narrative*, 2: 149.

21. Leiris, "Le Culte des Zars," 130; Morton, "Aspects of Spiritual Power;" Torrey, "Zar Cult;" and Messing, "Group Therapy."

22. Mérab, op. cit., 2: 54; Mondon-Vidailhet, *Le Temps*, 2 April 1910. These sources said she could compose *qene*, but Zewde Gabre-Sellassie (note, 12 October 1983) believes she composed some form of poetry, but not *qene* which takes a student working assiduously nine years or more to master.

23. Gebre Heywet, "Empress Taitu," ASAK. The death and character of Dinqinesh in *Le Semeur*, October 1907.

24. Tsehai Berhane Selassie, "An Ethiopian medical textbook," 167.

25. Father Ferdinand's diary, ms., IES. Aleqa Kenfe's diary (ms. 342) says that Menilek went to Firkuta to ask Bafena to return to "our home," and that as late as February 1883 he asked her to take communion with him, which she refused to do, knowing he would not keep his vows.

26. Zewde Gabre-Sellassie (6 July 1977) said his name was "Wonde" which may account for Antonelli's confusion with "Wonde of Ambasel."

27. Gebre Heywet, op. cit.; Heruy (*Ye-heywet*) reported a saying that Ethiopia would achieve greatness under a woman named Taytu and emperors before Menilek had women named "Taytu" fetched for them; interview, Avedis Terzian, AA, 3 April 1967.

3 King Menilek and Queen Taytu, 1883-9

All references to the chronicler are from *Chronique*, 1: 209-57. Antonelli references are from "Rapporti sullo Scioa," 11-123, unless otherwise noted.

1. Ferdinand diary, August, 1883.
2. Audon, "Voyage," 469.
3. Zewde Gabre-Sellassie, *Yohannes*, 122-51.
4. Battaglia, *Prima Guerra*, 178-83, 208-9; Giglio, *L'Impresa di Massaua*, 79-169.
5. Giglio, *Etiopia-Mar Rosso*, 3: 245-6; Traversi, *Let-Marefià*, 268; Gebre Zadiq/d'Abbadie (25 May 1886), d'Abbadie ms. NA 10222.
6. Parisis, Borumeda, 28 February 1886, *Nea Ephemeris*.
7. Giglio, *Etiopia-Mar Rosso*, 6: 194.
8. Borelli, *Ethiopie*, 203-55; Audon, "Voyage," 113-16; Traversi, op. cit; Vanderheym (*Une Expédition*, 140) repeats the anecdote of Borelli.
9. Pankhurst, "Foundation ... Addis Ababa," 31-61 and "Menilek and ... Addis Ababa," 103-17; Mérab, *Impressions*, 2: 119-20: "Menilek permitted Taytu to name the city as compensation for not having a child to christen." Many women believed that the waters of Filwuha could cure sterility; Garretson, "History and Development," 1-12.
10. Zewde Gabre-Sellassie, *Yohannes*, 222-3.
11. Ibid., 218; Caulk, "Occupation of Harar;" Rubenson, *Survival*, 346; Anon., "Viaggio," 343.
12. Garretson, "History and Development," 8; Atsme Giyorgis, "Ye-galla Tarik" (notes from R. Caulk).
13. Borelli, op. cit., 179, 253.
14. Afewerq Gebre Iyesus, "Menilek," 1: 38; Eadie, *Amharic Reader*, 203; Aleqa Tekle Iyesus ms., IES, Chap. 17.
15. Antonelli, Entotto, 20 October 1887, Let-Marefià, 14 March 1888; Margarita/Taytu, Rome, c. 13 January 1888, *LV*, 15.
16. Zewde Gabre-Sellassie, op. cit., 237-49; Erlich, *Ethiopia*, 120; del Boca, *Gli Italiani*, 1: 277-96.
17. Zewde Gabre-Sellassie, ibid.; Cerulli, "Canti popolari," 574.
18. Marcus, *Menelik*, 104; Capucci, Akaki, 28 December 1888, *BSAI* (1889); Antonelli, Aden, 6 August 1888, *LV*, 14.
19. Rosetti, *Storia Diplomatica*, 55-6; Rubenson, *Survival*, 384; Caulk, "Yohannes IV," 32-42.
20. Zewde Gabre-Sellassie, op. cit., 285; Tubiana, "Quatre généalogies," 49; Fusella, "Abissinia e Metemma," 210-11.
21. Menilek/Umberto, AA, 26 March 1889, *LV*, 15.
22. Levine, *Wax*, 142.
23. In particular Carlo Giglio and Sven Rubenson. The latter summed up his convincing arguments in "Professor Giglio, Antonelli" and the former in "Article 17 of the Treaty."

4 A queen becomes empress

All references to the chronicler are from *Chronique*, 1: 264-86.

1. Pankhurst, "Great Ethiopian Famine," 1: 95-124.
2. Taddesse Tamrat, *Church and State*, 59; Bidder, *Lalibela*, 34-40.
3. Zaghi, *I Russi*, 1: 173-82; Rollins, "Russia," 148.
4. Martial de Salviac, "Mission," 44.
5. For history of this title see Rubenson, "The Lion," 75-85.
6. Menilek sent his letter regarding Matewos's elevation over Petros on 5 November

1889 (copy provided by R. Caulk). The argument between Petros and Matewos over precedence is in *Chronique*, 1: 303-4. Levine, *Wax*, 27; Chadwick, *Early Church*, 275.

7. Tekle Tsadik Mekouria, "Les noms," 170.
8. It was not the one-woman achievement implied by the chronicler as Taytu had the assistance of Welde Gabriel, Lul Seged, Dejazmach Ymer-Muhamed Qanqe and Kenyz. Berile.
9. Zaghi, *Crispi*, 58.
10. Del Boca, *Gli Italiani*, 1: 354-7.
11. Rubenson, *Wichale XVII*, 58; Zaghi, "La missione Maconnen," 366-76; Atsme Giyorgis, ms. 47; Zaghi, *I Russi*, 1: 182; interview, aunts of Weyzero Almaz, AA, 28 May 1967.
12. 20,000 died, according to Salimbeni (Zaghi, *Crispi*, 165); Ilg, who went to Tigray with Menilek, estimated that 15 per cent of the army died from smallpox, dysentery, typhus and bronchitis (Keller, *Ilg*, 43; Traversi, *Let-Marefià*, 332-3).
13. Zaghi, *Crispi*, XXXIII. Salimbeni said even worse things about Ragazzi: "his house was full of whores ... he had often been drunk at court." (ibid., 102).
14. Zaghi, ibid., 105, 125, 192, 255-6, 259, 267.

5 Taytu and the Treaty of Wuchale

1. Victoria/Menilek, Osborne, 20 February 1890; Rubenson, *Wichale XVII*, 18.
2. Traversi, *Let-Marefià*, 316.
3. Rubenson, *Wichale XVII*, 16-20
4. Fusella, "Le lettere," *c.* December 1869. Debtera Assaggakhan wrote that Meshesha Tewodros was living in fear in Shewa because the Shewans wanted to kill him [for being the son of his father?]. Obviously Menilek protected him, for in another letter in early 1871 Menilek had named him a *dejazmach*, and when Menilek became emperor he confirmed him as governor of Qwara.
5. "Missione Antonelli," *LV*, 17. The Antonelli quotes that follow are from this document.
6. Ibid.; Afewerq Gebre Iyesus, "Menilek," 1: 129.
7. It is very likely that they were brought back by Alfred Ilg who was in Rome about the time they were published in November and December 1891.
8. Pedrazzi ("Rievocazione," *La Settimane Modenese*, 14 December 1935) believed that Salimbeni died by misadventure and not by suicide.
9. Traversi, op. cit., 367-9, 371, 376-7.
10. Del Boca, *Gli Italiani*, 1: 470.
11. Traversi, op. cit., 373-9.
12. Ibid., 417. Traversi explained how he knew so much about what was said at court: "Simple. At the banquets, many chiefs tell me ... they are keeping their options open ... until late March 1894 I heard frequent protestations of friendship for Italy."

6 Four years of famine; Mengesha Yohannes of Tigray submits

All references to the chronicler are from *Chronique*, 1: 301-2, 311-13, 317-18, 322-64.
1. Pankhurst, "Great Ethiopian Famine," 1: 95-124; 2: 271-94.
2. Afewerq Gebre Iyesus, "Menilek," 2: 296-9; Traversi, "Lo Scioa," 224-31.
3. Caulk, "Armies as Predators," 467-9.
4. Afewerq, op. cit., 1: 122.
5. De Coppet, *Chronique*, 1: 313, note 5.
6. Traversi, *Let-Marefià*, 384; Le Roux, *Chez la Reine*, 54-61; Mérab (*Impressions*,

3: 65) says that Menilek's paternity was proved because the girl had registered the encounter with a scribe at a church.

7. Mérab, op. cit., 2: 44; Capucci (18 January 1895) referred to some bastards of Menilek's and other nobles, who had been "hidden away" in Semen and had just been brought to the capital by Gesesse, Taytu's nephew ("Alla Vigilia," 535); Jarosseau (MC) says she was an Oromo from Wello named "Desseta."

8. Heruy, *Ye-heywet*, entry on Wesen Seged; Zewde Gabre-Sellassie (note, 12 October 1983) provided the information about Ayeletch Abarasa. The doubtful paternity of his mother was used to oppose Lij Iyasu, her son by Ras Mikael, when he was titular head of state from 1913 to 1916; Mantegazza (*Menelik*, 204) confuses identity when he says that Shewa Regga was the daughter of Bafena.

9. Zaghi, *I Russi*, 1: 194-5; Mashcov, "Il secondo viaggio;" Rubenson (*Survival*, 396) has letters Menilek/Czar, 18 March 1892, and Mekonnen/Czar, 18 March 1892.

10. Mondon-Vidailhet, *Le Temps*, 12 June 1893 (Ankober, December 1892), and 18 July 1893 (AA, December 1892).

11. Traversi, op. cit., 404-5, 408.

12. Mérab, op. cit., 2: 75; Zaghi, *Crispi*, 60, 86, notes 10, 11, 27, 28; del Boca, *Gli Italiani*, 1: 464-7; Traversi, op. cit., 376; Zaghi, *I Russi*, 1: 294-5.

13. Mondon-Vidailhet, *Le Temps*, 28 July 1893 (AA, March 1893), and 30 August 1893 (Entotto, 15 July 1893); Heruy, *Ye-heywet*: "Long history of border fights between them [Wele and Mikael];" Annaratone, *In Abissinia*, 124; Martini, *Diario*, 4: 180; Melli, *La Colonia*, 89.

14. Mondon-Vidailhet, *Le Temps*, 17 August 1893.

15. Keller, *Ilg*, 110; Traversi (2 April 1886) describes previous attempt, *BSGI*, 23 (1886).

16. Pankhurst, "Menilek ... utilisation," 36.

17. Vanderheym, *Une Expédition*, 83-4.

18. Marcus (*Menelik*, 144) says that Tekle Haymanot was the chief dissident in a series of small rebellions in late 1892. R. Caulk (letter to author, 7 September 1982) disagrees.

19. Vanderheym, op. cit., 69-70; Rubenson, *Survival*, 161.

20. Erlich, *Ethiopia*, 186-7; and Pianavia-Vivaldi, *Tre Anni*, 221.

21. Monfreid, *Ménélik*, 186.

22. Corazzini, *Tribuna*, 7 June 1890.

23. Capucci (AA, 16 November 1894) in Zaghi, "Alla Vigilia," 530.

24. Ibid., 535; Vanderheym, op. cit., 147-91; and Pariset, *Al Tempo*, 35.

25. Duchesne-Fournet, *Mission*, 2: 389.

26. Zaghi, *I Russi*, 1: 322; Pianavia-Vivaldi, op. cit., 224-6; Baratieri, *Mémoires*, 143; Melli, op. cit., 91-3.

27. Martini, *Diario*, 2: 450-1. Salimbeni commented on Felter in 1891, "I never in my life met such an inveterate gossip," Zaghi, *Crispi*, 333. Pétridès (*Le Héros*) did not spare Empress Taytu in his biography of Mekonnen yet made no reference to any innuendo regarding Yeshemabet's death.

28. IFO, Ethiopia 42/1, Fasc. 2-8 contains the correspondence on Jerusalem. See also Pedersen, *Ethiopian Community*. Taytu/Traversi has the date 13 September 1893 at the top; at the bottom is "4 *teqempt*" which is equivalent to 13/14 October 1893.

29. Nerazzini, Rome, 26 January 1895, *LV*, 14; Traversi (*Let-Marefià*, 421-3) prints letter from Capucci, Rome, 11 April 1897, which says that Mekonnen asked the emperor if he could purchase the Italian geographical station and Menilek consented, thereby annoying the empress who wanted to add it to her holdings at "Dens and Mawanz."

30. Stamps were printed in Paris in 1893. Coins were engraved with Menilek's image at the Paris mint in February 1893. Pankhurst, "Ethiopian Monetary," 78-9;

Vanderheym, op. cit., 55.
31. Baratieri, *Mémoires*, 165-6; Zaghi, "Alla Vigilia," 535, and *I Russi*, 1: 316-18.
32. These views were shared by Traversi, Piano, Capucci, Felter and Baratieri. This quote is a shortened version from Zaghi, *I Russi*, 1: 316-18.
33. Zaghi, ibid., 1: 288.

7 The Russians are coming

1. The section on the Russians is drawn from Zaghi, *I Russi*, 1: 237-74; Guidi, "La chiesa Abissinia;" Efrem, *Journey*, 83-4; Mashcov, "Il secondo viaggio," 841-86; *Chronique*, 1: 370-81; Rollins, "Russia's Ethiopian Adventure;" Elets, *Emperor Menelik*, 60; Zaghi, "Alla Vigilia," 536-51.
2. Zaghi, "Alla Vigilia," 551; Pariset, *Al Tempo*, 46.
3. Ilg's activities in Capucci memo in Zaghi, "Alla Vigilia," 541; and French failure to press Italy in Marcus, *Menelik*, 160.
4. Erlich, *Ethiopia*, 189-91.
5. Elets, *Emperor*; Rossi, "La Incerta Politica," 344-56.
6. Del Boca, *Gli Italiani*, 1: 555; Zaghi, "Alla Vigilia," 530. The last empress to have her own army was Menen, the mother of Ras Ali, in the 1840s.
7. Pariset, *Al Tempo*, 35-9.
8. Keller, *Ilg*, 84; Conti-Rossini (*Italia ed Etiopia*, 175-6) has a slightly different version of the proclamation. The 1888 proclamation in Ragazzi, Entotto, 30 November 1888, *LV*, 15.
9. *EO*, 1: 12 (December 1957), 347.
10. Berkeley, *Campaign*, 126.
11. Del Boca, op. cit., 1: 556.
12. Ibid., 1: 560.

8 War with Italy: Amba Alage, Meqelle, Adwa

The events are covered in *Chronique*, 2: 389-454.
1. Zaghi, "Lo sbarco," 993-1002. The British foreign secretary answered a letter from the Italian ambassador to London of 24 December 1895 asking if Italian troops could debark at Zeyla as a show of force to scare Mekonnen and Menilek. Britain replied in the negative, citing an agreement with France on 2 February 1888.
2. Mondon-Vidailhet, *Le Temps*, 23 January 1896 (Entotto, 29 October 1895).
3. Hans, "L'armée," 886; Mondon-Vidailhet, *Le Temps*, 27 January and 2 April 1896; Elets, *Emperor*, 68-9.
4. Antonelli, *LV*, 15, 280-307; Ilg, "Die äthiopische;" Sambon, "Etiopia militare," 100-24.
5. Del Boca, *Gli Italiani*, 1: 587-90; Baratieri, *Mémoires*, 224-8, 233.
6. *Chronique*, 2: 409-10.
7. Grazioli, "Onoranze;" del Boca, op. cit., 1: 591-600. Italian sources said 3,000 dead and wounded on the Ethiopian side; Menilek's message to Mondon-Vidailhet said 277 dead and 349 wounded, *Le Temps*, 4 April 1896 (AA, 15 February 1896).
8. Del Boca, op. cit., 1: 599-603; Bellavita, *Adua*, 235.
9. Merid Welde Aregay ("Southern Ethiopia," 168-9) recounts the weakening impact of a fasting period on the soldiers of Emperor Galadewos in March 1559.
10. Antonelli, "Rapporti sullo Scioa," 68-98; Annaratone (*In Abissinia*, 23-30) described in the same way an expedition of 1910.
11. Zaghi, *I Russi*, 2: 204. The letter was intercepted by the Italians.
12. Del Boca, op. cit., 1: 617-34; Berkeley, *Campaign*, 195; Moltedo, *L'Assedio*,

127-88; Raimondo, *L'assedio*, 143-243; Riguzzi, *Macallè*, 25-50; Lemmi, *Lettere*; Partini, *I Nostri Ufficiali*; Mantegazza, *Menelik*, 154; Felter, "La relazione" and *La Vicenda*; de Lauribar, *Douze Ans*; Mondon-Vidailhet, *Le Temps*, 4 April 1896; Pétridès, *Le Héros*, 173-6; Battaglia, *La Prima Guerra*, 678-91.
13. Del Boca, *The Ethiopian War*, 9; Bassi, "Diario," 223.
14. *La Stampa*, 16 March 1896. The letter, dated 26 February 1896, was first published in the *Kronstadt Gazette*, from which it was translated into Italian.
15. The story of one of these mis-informers is in *EO*, 1: 11 (1957). *La Stampa* (4 March 1896) says Baratieri was fed information that Menilek would go to Aksum on 1 March to be re-crowned and that all the rases would attend; Wylde (*Modern Abyssinia*, 102) says that many of the women who had free run of the Italian camp were spies for Menilek.
16. Del Boca, *Gli Italiani*, 1: 637-8, 646-7.
17. Battaglia, *La Prima Guerra*, 733-76; del Boca, op. cit., 1: 649-90; Berkeley, *Campaign*, 257-344.
18. "La Bataille d'Adoua," 222-30.
19. Cerulli, "Canti popolari," 601.
20. Elets, *Emperor*, Chap. 16.
21. Tedone, *Angerà*, 29-31.
22. Jonquière, *Les Italiens*, 336: "300 reached Asmara carried on the backs of women and on litters;" Wylde (*Modern Abyssinia*, 131) reported that Queen Margarita sent doctors to fit prosthetic devices; Afewerq Gebre Iyesus ("Menilek," 143) says that it was Ras Mengesha Yohannes who insisted on the punishment while de Lauribar (*Douze Ans*, 624) says that Taytu demanded it.
23. Estimates of Ethiopian dead range between 4,000 and 8,000. On the Italian side, 6,000 Italians and askaris died.
24. *The New York Times*, 7 March 1896; *Le Petit Journal*, 29 March 1896; *Harpers Weekly*, 4 April 1896.
25. Katz, *Fall*, 113.
26. *La Guerra Italo-Abissinia* (Milan). Its editor, Eduardo Ximenes, went to Eritrea after the battle of 1 March, though it was first published on 1 February 1896 and ceased in August 1896. Fabio Coen and Guido Cantoni provided me with the doggerel they remembered from their childhood.
27. Gebre Heywet Baykedegn, "Empress Taitou," ASAK.
28. Mother and aunts of Almaz, wife of Teshager Woobe, AA, 29 April 1967.
29. Cerulli, op. cit., 602.
30. Del Boca, op. cit., 1: 668; Traversi (*L'Italia*, 89) went further and said that Taytu threatened to take command herself. Several historians have candidates for "architect of victory." Greenfield (*Ethiopia*, 123) names Ras Alula, and Pétridès (*Le Héros*) names Ras Mekonnen.

9 Peace negotiations; prisoners of war; the Russian Red Cross

1. Del Boca, *Gli Italiani*, 1: 711. It was two months before permission was given for a burial detail to come. *La Guerra*, 29 June 1896; *La Stampa*, 14 March 1896.
2. De Lauribar, *Douze Ans*, 538-68.
3. Giudici, "I preliminari," 92.
4. *Chronique*, 2: 451; Erlich, *Ethiopia*, 193.
5. Wylde, *Modern Abyssinia*, 175, 300. Zewde Gabre-Sellassie identified the discarded wife as Taffesech and said that she was part Egyptian.
6. Mondon-Vidailhet, *Le Temps*, 1 July and 2 November 1896, and 24 February 1897.
7. Pariset, *Al Tempo*, 61, 65-7; Yaltasamma, "Les Amis," 42.
8. Zaghi, *I Russi*, 2: 233. The myth of Clochette's active participation persisted in

Canevari, *Il Generale*, 97, written in 1936. *The Spectator*, 7 March 1896: "Italians explain their defeat by the presence of French and Russian officers ... we question this. Drill does not improve Oriental soldiers like the Abyssinians." The verse in Cerulli, "Canti popolari," 601.

9. Mondon-Vidailhet, *Le Temps*, 14 July 1896 (AA, 5 May 1896). The cook of Baratieri was among the captives assigned to the palace (Carry, "La Captivité," 517).
10. D'Amato, *Da Adua*, 67; Pàntano, *Ventitre anni*, 68.
11. Del Boca, op. cit., 1: 734-5.
12. Nicoletti-Altimari, *Fra gli Abissini*; Tedone, *Angerà*, 25-105, 145-82; d'Amato, *Da Adua*; and Frisina, *L'Italia*, 326.
13. Zaghi, op. cit., 2: 247-56; Rollins, "Russia's Ethiopian Adventure," 233-6; Shchusev, "To the Source," 201-2; Pankhurst, "Beginnings of modern medicine," 124-6; Amdur, *Bull. Int. Soc. Croix-Rouge*, 28 (1897); Right, "Russian Red Cross," 167-74.
14. Noailles, "Mgr. Macaire," 69-72; del Boca, op. cit., 1: 731-2.
15. Zaghi, op. cit., 2: 231-91.
16. Del Boca, op. cit., 1: 729-32; Giglio, "Il Trattato," 237-51.

10 Diplomacy: domestic failure and foreign success

1. *Chronique*, 2: 450.
2. Wylde, *Modern Abyssinia*, 168-493; Bairu Tafla, "Some Documents," 184-90.
3. *Chronique*, 2: 456-60.
4. The money was not transferred until March according to a letter from Ilg to Chefneux, 4 May 1897, and was only 6,200 at that time. IFO, Pos. 51/1, Fasc. 1.
5. D'Orléans, *Une Visite*, 69.
6. Vigneras, *Une Mission Française*, 111-95; Negussay Ayele, "Rhetoric and reality," 22-3; Pinon, "La résurrection," 840.
7. Mondon-Vidailhet, *Le Temps*, 17 April 1897 (dateline AA, 24 February 1897); Marcus, *Menelik*, 177-9; FFO, NS Eth., "Pol. Etrangère," July 1894-7, Chefneux, 5 March 1897.
8. Lagarde's craving for a title was stimulated by Leontiev's success at obtaining "Count" from Menilek. "What is Count and how much does it cost?" Menilek asked his adviser, Ilg. Ilg said it cost nothing (Michel, *Mission*, 90-2).
9. Bonchamps, "Une mission," 404-31; Mondon-Vidailhet, *Le Temps*, 16 June 1897 (AA, 15 April 1897); Ilg/Chefneux, AA, 6 April 1897, op. cit.
10. D'Orléans, op. cit., foreword; Ilg/Chefneux, AA, 14 June 1897, IFO, op. cit.; Poncins, "Voyage," 432-88, "Menilek myth," 424-33.
11. Amulree, "Prince Alamayou," 8-15; unpub. diary of Capt. Speedy through courtesy of his great-niece, Jean Southon.
12. Marcus, op. cit., 181-3; Brockett, "British Somaliland," 278.
13. D'Orléans, op. cit., 148, 153-4, 163.
14. The reproduction was financed by Lady Meux; Gleichen, *With the Mission*, 258; Rodd, *Social and Diplomatic Memories*.
15. Del Boca, *Gli Italiani*, 1: 428, 572-4, 746-7; Vannutelli and Citerni, "La Fine," 460-5.
16. Ilg/Chefneux, 15 July 1899, Chefneux papers (courtesy of Richard Caulk).
17. Mondon-Vidailhet, *Le Temps*, 31 May 1898 (AA, 18 April 1898); Lagarde, AA, 24 December 1897, FFO, "Pol. Etrangère," June 1897-December 1898.
18. Wurtz, "Hygiène publique," 498.
19. Zaghi, op. cit., 2: 248; Bulatovich, *With the Troops*, 195-235; Bulatovich was the subject of a novelized biography, *The Name of Hero*, by Richard Seltzer, 1981. It was based on Katznelson, "Alexander Bulatovich," 175-86.

20. Zewde Gabre-Sellassie, London, 8 August 1971.
21. Pankhurst, "Foundation of Addis Ababa," 51.
22. Mondon-Vidailhet, *Le Temps*, 25 October 1897 (AA, 22 September 1897).
23. Zaghi, *I Russi*, 2: 293, 300-3.
24. Bervin, *Bénito Sylvain*, 88, 143-4; d'Orléans, *Une Visite*, 118; Mondon-Vidailhet, *Le Temps*, 16 June 1897 (AA, 17 April 1897).
25. Ilg/Chefneux letters in IFO, op. cit. and also Chefneux papers (courtesy of Richard Caulk); Zaghi, *Crispi*, 198, 255-6; Keller, *Ilg*, 217; Pariset, *Al Tempo*, 132, 138; Pease, *Travel and Sport*, 3: 89; Yaltasamma, "Les Amis," 33; and Le Roux, *Ménélik*, 233.
26. *Chronique*, 2: 462-3; Lange, *Domination and Resistance*, 65, 71.
27. Michel, *Mission*, 162. Date of Menilek's letter, 27 *sene* (*c.* 3 July 1897).
28. Michel, op. cit., 241, 246, 394.
29. Rollins, "Russia's Ethiopian Adventure," 286.
30. Pariset, *Al Tempo*, 117-25; Emily, *Mission Marchand*.
31. Yaltasamma ("Les Amis," 22-6) was vitriolic, saying that Lagarde had done nothing to improve port facilities while in charge of Obok and Djibouti; and that his morals were suspect. Mondon-Vidailhet, Yaltasamma added (under a pseudonym), had done everything to prevent Lagarde's appointment to Addis Ababa; he then attacked Mondon-Vidailhet as a "puny little man, whose third-rate pen praised Menilek regardless of virtue or vice, and was as vain and jealous of Lagarde as Lagarde was of him."
32. Yaltasamma, "Les Amis," 41-4.
33. Mondon-Vidailhet, *Le Temps*, 25 March 1898 (no dateline); Bulatovich (op. cit., 123-30) describes the daily routine in much the same way.
34. In his column of 13 July 1896 printed in *Le Temps* (13 September 1896) Mondon-Vidailhet included a translation of one of the few letters in existence from Empress Taytu. In it she said that the manuscript she had sent him might contain mistakes, as the original had been destroyed by the dervishes when they plundered Gondar, but had been rewritten at her command by the priests at Gondar, from memory. This letter is in the Mondon-Vidailhet collection at the Bibliothèque Nationale, Paris. See also Mondon-Vidailhet, "Une tradition éthiopienne," 259.

11 The "end" of Ras Mengesha Yohannes

1. French envoy Lagarde alleged that Mengesha's rebellion was aimed solely at the empress, whose firm hand he particularly resented, since she had once been the subject of his father (15 November 1898, FFO).
2. *Chronique*, 2: 474-83. Money was not transferred until August 1898, and considering that Menilek had received 10 million lire from Italy in reparations, Mengesha Yohannes may well have considered the sum sent to him a pittance as Tigray had suffered the most from the war.
3. Martini, *Diario*, 1: 73-485.
4. De Lauribar, *Douze Ans*, 294-9; Ambrogetti, *La vita sessuale* and Martini's *Diario*. All four volumes of Martini have references to one scandal after another.
5. Martini, op. cit., 2: 18, 271, 288.
6. De Castro, *Nella Terra*, 2: 239, 529.
7. Martini, op. cit., 4: 342.
8. Ibid., 2: 196. These were the words of the Lazarist, Father Coulbeaux. Zewde Gabre-Sellassie (note, 12 October 1983) avows that Mekonnen's rule was much more acceptable than Wele's.
9. Arén, *Evangelical Pioneers*, 406.
10. Del Boca, *Gli Italiani*, 1: 754, 762. A subsequent adjustment of the border on

15 May 1902 included the desired Kunama area within Eritrea. The sum of money was calculated as the "capitalized value of the tribute from the provinces which have fallen under foreign rule [Italian]." Pankhurst, "Tribute, Taxation," 3: 106. Talers in the amount of 10,000 to Mekonnen and 50,000 to Wele are on record.

11. Zewde Gabre-Sellassie (12 October 1983) said his father was 15 years old when he was sent to the International Institute of Turin after serving a short jail term at Massawa for some unknown infraction. It was Ras Kassa Haylu, then a page at Menilek's court, who told him that he had logged in his father's messages from Eritrea.

12. Erlich, *Ethiopia*, 203.

12 Political marriage; religious law and customary behavior

1. Martini, *Diario*, 2: 196.
2. Gebre-Wold-Ingida Worq, "Ethiopia's Traditional System;" Mahteme Sellassie, "Land System;" Hoben, *Land Tenure*; Ambaye Zekarias, *Land Tenure*; Assefa Dula, "Land Tenure;" Guenet Guebre-Christos, "Position of women;" Pankhurst, *Economic History*.
3. D'Abbadie, *Douze Ans*, 128; Crummey, "Women and Landed Property," 444-65 and "Family and Property," 207-10.
4. Avedis Terzian, AA, 3 April 1967. Estimates of the size of Taytu's army vary from 3,000 to 18,000. The latter figure from Mérab (ms. 3370, CM). Only figures for 1902, 1903 and 1904 available for her private treasury in Pankhurst, "Ethiopian Monetary," 95-6.
5. Mondon-Vidailhet, *Le Temps*, 2 April 1910.
6. Bairu Tafla, "Marriage," 16. Gebre Heywet Baykedagn, Sudan Intelligence, 2/19/154.
7. Capucci (AA, 18 January 1895) in Zaghi, "Alla Vigilia," 535; Pease, *Travel and Sport*, 3: 210; Mérab, *Impressions*, 3: 47.
8. Mérab, op. cit., 1: 174; Klobukowski, AA, 19 March 1907, FFO ("Pol. Intérieure"); Gamerra, *Ricordi*, 37, 48; Lagarde (Djibouti, 29 May 1906) quoting Ato Yosef, "a violent brute who detests the French;" *Le Semeur*, October 1907, describes his childhood at court, favor with Menilek and his kindness to the missionaries.
9. Mérab, op. cit., 2: 251, 3: 50; Zaghi, *Crispi*, 267; Martini, op. cit., 4: 452; Montandon, *Au Pays*, 296; Bairu Tafla, op. cit., 18.
10. Bairu Tafla, "Gugsa Wale," *Encyclopaedia*, 1; Martini, op. cit., 2: 232-3.
11. Zewde Gabre-Sellassie, Washington, D.C., 6 July 1977.
12. Mekonnen Endalkatchew, *Good Families*, 39-41; Pariset, *Al Tempo*, 26; Bairu Tafla, "Some Aspects," 1-9 and "Darge" entry, *Encyclopaedia*, 1; Harbeson, "Afar," 24-68.
13. Heruy, *Ye-heywet*, has a short biography on each of Darge's children; Zaghi, *I Russi*, 2: 108; Zewde Gabre-Sellassie, op. cit., "Their [Askala and Damtew] relationship before marriage was an open secret;" d'Orléans (*Une Visite*, 193) was shown a letter from Tsehaye Werq in which she asked the palace to send her 16-caliber cartridges and noted her seal was similar to Taytu's — a star within a sun.
14. Bairu Tafla, "Two ... Provincial Kings," 29-40; Heruy in *Ye-heywet* said Belew disagreed with his father about everything; as Tekle Haymanot was only 51 when he died, the usual accusations of poisoning were made about his death (Martini, op. cit., 2: 338); Aleqa Kenfe diary (January 1901).
15. Cerulli, "Canti popolari," 596; Lemlem chronicle of Yohannes IV, Mondon-Vidailhet collection, BN.
16. Her sister, Desta, may have been married to some Gojam noble as her son Gesesse

went to visit her there in February 1895 (Zaghi, "Alla Vigilia;" Capucci, 3 March 1895); Avedis Terzian (op. cit.) said, "Not on good terms with her sister."

17. Le Roux, *Chez la Reine*, 246-541; Vollbrecht, *Im Reiche*, 3; Cerulli ("Canti," 638-9) credits two short poems to Bezebeh in which he tells of his love for her and his desire to take her virginity and how he marries despite opposition from Gojam and from her father, Ras Mikael; Mérab (op. cit., 3: 49) mentions a princess who died in childbirth at the age of 12.

18. Dr. Martin's diary, 4 October 1900. Dr. Martin's diary is in the hands of his family. I have used a copy made by Peter Garretson.

19. Cipolla, *Nell'Impero*, 69.

20. Mérab, op. cit., 3: 49.

21. Zewde Gabre-Sellassie, Oxford, 11 June 1967; and Garretson, "Näggädras," 418-23.

22. Trimmingham, *Islam*, 153, 227.

23. Taddesse Tamrat, *Church and State*, 61, 116-18; Alvarez, *Narrative*, 44-8; Perruchon, "Le Règne de Lebna Dengel," 274-6; Ludolf (*New History*, 173) was told by Abba Gregory that at the end of his days Lebna Dengel gave himself up to luxury and love of women.

24. *Fetha Nagast*, 76-81, 92, 96, 130-5; Pollera, *L'Abissinia*, 206-7.

25. Antonelli, "Rapporti," 23 November 1887; Mérab, op. cit., 3: 41, 44. Known marriages for Darge (4), Gesesse (3), Hayle Giyorgis (4), Habte Giyorgis (3), Lul Seged (3), Mengesha Yohannes (5), Mikael (6), Menilek (3), Tekle Haymanot (3), Seyum Mengesha (8), Wele Betul (4), Aselefetch (7), Kefey Wele (3), Taytu Betul (5) and Zewditu Menilek (4).

26. Eshete Tadesse, "Preparation of Täg," 105.

27. Le Roux, *Ménélik*, 206; Pollera, *La Donna*, 62-3; de Castro, *Nella Terra*, 1: 157-62; Mérab, op. cit., 3: 54-7.

28. Collat, *Abyssinie*, 20; Pollera, ibid.; Mérab, ibid.; Tedone, *Angerà*, 140; Stern, *Wanderings*, 289; Walker, *Abyssinian*, 42-8.

29. Annaratone (*In Abissinia*, 59) found procured abortions rare, but spontaneous abortion common; Mérab, *Médecin*, 69-72, 169-72; Wurtz, "Hygiène," 495; Strelcyn, "Les Médecines;" Cacciapuoti, "Medicina;" Tsehai Berhane Selassie, "Ethiopian medical;" Griaule, *Le Livre de Recettes*.

30. Sumner ("Ethiopian Philosophy," 114), but on 128 says "wisdom is the characteristic that marks [a good woman] from other women."

31. Perini, *Di qua*, 425; Mérab, *Impressions*, 3: 230; Annaratone, op. cit., 58; Walker, op. cit., 165; Beckstrom, "Divorce," 295; and Cassièrs, "Mercha," 71.

32. Levine, *Greater Ethiopia*, Table 2, 62-3 and "Concept of Masculinity," 17-23.

33. See Abdhurahman, Armstrong and Fisseha, Borello, Cohen, Faïtlovich, Guidi, Fusella, Leslau, Mondon-Vidailhet, Offeio, and Hailu Gabre-Hiot.

34. Soleillet, *Voyages*, 297.

35. Messing, "Ethiopian Folktales," 69-72.

36. Cerulli, "Folk Literature," 76-7.

37. Annaratone, op. cit., 446; Leslau and Leslau, *African Poems*; Offeio, "Proverbi," 295-7.

38. Cohen, "Couplets amhariques," 65-80. The poem was commissioned by Ligaba Welde Gabriel and recited at the home of Hayle Giyorgis in 1910. The sentiments expressed about certain individuals date it after the fall of the empress in March 1910.

39. Littmann, *Publications*, 2: 271-83; Cerulli, "Canti," 574; Plowden (*Travels*, 145) says that any man who sang was called "woman."

40. Perruchon, "Le règne de Iyasu I;" *Fetha Nagast* has a rule that men are not to dress like women and vice versa, 127; Pankhurst, "History of Prostitution," 159-78.

41. Pankhurst, op. cit.; Cecchi, *Da Zeila*, 1: 315; Vigoni, *Abissinia*, 154.
42. De Lauribar, *Douze Ans*, 294-9.
43. Mérab, op. cit., 3: 60; Dr. Wakeman alleged that in 99 per cent of divorce cases it was at the woman's initiative (Jennings and Addison, *With the Abyssinians*, 89).
44. Laketch Dirasse ("Survival techniques") prefers the term "public wifehood" to prostitute.
45. Mérab, op. cit., 2: 54 and 3: 51; Pease, *Travel and Sport*, 3: 200-15; Armbruster, Annual Report 1908, PRO/FO 371/396/298.
46. Mérab, op. cit., 3: 33, 96; Bairu Tafla ("Marriage") gives date of edict as 6 March 1908, his source being Mahteme Sellassie, *Zeker Neger*. Because of extensive comment in reports by diplomatic representatives in Addis Ababa in March 1909, and the entry in Dr. Martin's diary on 6 March 1909, I believe it is a misprint.
47. Guenet Guebre-Christos, "Position of women;" Daniel Haile, *Law and the Status of Women*; Mondon-Vidailhet, *Le Temps*, 2 April 1910; Kane, *Ethiopian Literature*; Gerard, "Amharic Creative Literature."

13 *"In Ethiopia they begin to speak by wire"*

All references to the chronicler are from *Chronique*, 2: 483-6, 497-507.
1. Gleichen, *With the Mission*, 176; Pankhurst, "Misoneism," 290-303 and "Firearms," 135-80.
2. Pariset, *Al Tempo*, 153-4; Ilg had previously brought a telephone in 1890 (Zaghi, *Crispi*, 125).
3. Garretson, "The telephone," 3.
4. Harris, *Highlands*, 2: 389; Lejean, *Théodore*, 10; Douin, *Histoire*, 3: 313.
5. Capucci, 5 January 1888; Zaghi, "Alla Vigilia," 527-8.
6. Pariset, op. cit., 127-30; Pankhurst ("Menilek and ... utilisation") tells how Serpouhi Ebeyan made shirts and capes for the emperor as well as umbrellas for the church. She washed the emperor's clothes in imported soap and also baked bread for him. The latter activity was said to have provoked the jealousy of Taytu who hid the bread.
7. Abraham Demoz, "Emperor Menelik's Phonograph Message," 351-3; Ullendorff, "Queen Victoria's," 622-3; d'Orléans (*Une Visite*, 167, 193, 200) said he recorded the voice of Menilek but no trace of it has been reported.
8. Michel, *Mission*, 101; Pariset, op. cit., 155-6
9. Comboul, the mining engineer, made a brief visit to Ethiopia in 1889 and returned in 1896 when he found these deposits. He died in 1902. Michel, op. cit., 527-8; Duchesne-Fournet, *Mission*, 1: 202.
10. Dr. Martin's diary, 26 December 1899, 23 January, and 1 February 1900.
11. Buckle (ed.), *Letters*, 3: 560-1; Powell-Cotton (*Sporting Trip*, 138) says Taytu was so concerned when her dog was sick that she sent the animal over to the British compound to Dr. Wakeman with an escort of 60 men.
12. Harrington, AA, 2 January 1900, PRO/FO 403.
13. Dr. Martin's diary, 26 November 1899 to 29 February 1901; background of Martin in Pankhurst, "Beginnings of Modern Medicine," 132-3.
14. Harrington, op. cit., 4 January and 13 May 1901.
15. Pankhurst, "Foundation ... Addis Ababa," 51.
16. Martini, *Diario*, 3: 22, 25, 34.
17. Aleqa Kenfe diary, 30 October 1902, 14 January 1904, IES; and de Castro, *Nella Terra*, 1: 159-60.
18. Garretson, "History and Development," citing Colli, AA, 15 June 1903.
19. Le Roux, *Chez la Reine*, 45; Weertz, interview, AA, 30 March 1967; Rosa, *L'impero*, 84-5.

20. Antoine(?), interview, AA, 3 March 1967. He was the son of one of the Greek workmen.
21. Aleqa Kenfe diary, 9 December 1901: "He went to his own country, Egypt, for reasons known only to God and Menilek" and returned 22 *yekatit* (1 March 1903); Rollins, "Russia's Ethiopian Adventure," 307.
22. Taddesse Tamrat, *Church and State*, 60.
23. Philippos, *Know Jerusalem*, part 3.
24. Adugna Amahu, "Ethiopian Orthodox Church;" Zaghi, "Alla Vigilia;" Capucci, letter, 8 August 1892: "There is feeling against Matewos. *Sotto voce* they wish he would go back where he came from as things have been bad ever since he arrived." Imputations against Matewos are found in Mérab, *Impressions*, 1: 249 and a sympathetic view of the bishop in Hentze, *Am Hofe*.

14 Jerusalem and Ethiopia

In the *Chronique*, Jerusalem is mentioned repeatedly. The principal references for this chapter are 2: 489-90 and 512-19.
1. Bruce, *Travels*, 5: 60-1; 7: 225.
2. All historical references unless otherwise noted are from Tedeschi, "Profilo storico;" Cerulli, *Etiopi in Palestina*; Philippos, *Know Jerusalem*; Pedersen, *History*.
3. Bairu Tafla (ed. and trans.), *Chronicle of Yohannes*. There were 25 letters between January 1869 and January 1887.
4. Philippos, op. cit., 161; Pedersen, op. cit., 42-3.
5. Italian consul, Jerusalem, 18 May 1894, IFO, Etiopia/Jerusalem.
6. Ibid.; protests by a few Shewan monks were reported by the Italian consul on 30 April, 10 May and 29 July 1895, and by Tigrayan monks on 28 June 1896.
7. Ibid., n.d., January 1899. On 12 August 1899 the consul said, "On 19 July he left in disgrace and was required to go to Ethiopia;" Philippos (op. cit.) says "he is owed much;" Heruy, *Ye-heywet*, "Taytu quarreled with him and exiled him;" Pedersen, op. cit., 51-2. In letter to author from Jerusalem, 6 February 1983, Pedersen provided information on the end of Welde Semayat's life.
8. Vlassov, AA, 12 August 1898, SU-R (provided by the Soviet Academy of Sciences, Moscow).
9. Financial transactions in IFO, Etiopia/Jerusalem.
10. Martini, *Diario*, 3: 419, 426.
11. The contract is in the *Chronique*, 2: 512-14. Details on the deposit Menilek made in the Crédit Lyonnais in 1905 and its disposition in 1941 are described by Pedersen, op. cit., 120-1.
12. Pedersen, op. cit., 58-60.
13. *Le Semeur* (October 1907) records reception by the Pope; Bairu Tafla (*Ethiopia and Germany*, 114) the visit to Germany.
14. Tedeschi, op. cit., 149; Pedersen, op. cit., 53; Zewde Gabre-Sellassie, 27 October 1983.
15. Bairu Tafla, *Chronicle*, letter of 28 December 1886.
16. Pedersen, op. cit., 137-8.

15 "People from various nations ... began to come and go"

Chronique, 2: 539-40.
1. Morié, *Les civilisations*, 2: 407; Rollins, "Russia's Ethiopian Adventure," 305, 323-6.
2. Pankhurst, "Ras Makonnen visit," 295, 297; Pétridès, *Le Héros*, 243-50.

366 Taytu and Menilek

3. Rosenfeld, A Chronology, 197-222; Vivian, Abyssinia, 248; Powell-Cotton, Sporting Trip, 135.

4. Pease, Travel and Sport, 3: 18, 85-90, 122, 200-21.

5. Vlassov, AA, 12 August, 10 September 1898, SU-R (provided by I.S. Katznelson of Soviet Academy of Sciences); Rollins, op. cit., 294; Morié (op. cit., 2: 470) claims that Emily Vlassov was buried at Menilek's order in the cemetery for emperors of Ethiopia, but there was no such place.

6. Zaghi, I Russi, 2: 300-12; Gamba ("L'Azione Russa," 63-83) says that d'Orléans took Leontiev to a surgeon at Djibouti; Martini (Diario, 1: 102) has a report from Ciccodicola of 28 February 1898 that Menilek was aware of Leontiev's claims; Lazarevich, "Researches ... Seljan," 1-6; Leontiev's book, Provinces Equatoriales, does not have his name as author.

7. Annaratone, In Abissinia, 60, 72; Littmann, Publications, 1: 7; Faïtlovich, Notes d'un voyage, 36-9; and Martini, op. cit., 4: 318, 402.

8. Martini, op. cit., 3: 346; Zewde Gabre-Sellassie, 13 October 1983.

9. Martini, op. cit., 3: 265-8, 278, 346, 356, 369, 470 and 4: 397; del Boca, Gli Italiani, 1: 762-3.

10. Marcus, Menelik, 201-4; Morié, op. cit., 2: 498-505.

11. Martini, op. cit., 3: 88, 254.

12. Jennings and Addison, With the Abyssinians, 87. Dr. Wakeman, who spoke Amharic, was sent from Addis Ababa to join Dr. Dunn.

13. Skinner, Abyssinia; Marcus, "A Note," 165-8; Shinn, "A Survey," 297-311.

14. Pankhurst, "William H. Ellis," 89-121.

15. Morié (op. cit.) alleges that the American draft was revised, unbeknownst to Skinner, by Ciccodicola and Clerk of the British legation.

16. Hallé, To Menelik, 284-6.

17. Pankhurst, "History ... Armenian Relations," 3: 366-78; Love, AA, 18 February 1911, U.S.A.; Piazza, Alla Corte, 133-6; Bairu Tafla (letter to author, 15 May 1984) gave information about Ilg's telegram.

18. Scholler, "Letters," 506; Vollbrecht, Im Reiche, 113-21; and Rosen, Eine Deutsche.

19. Fassika Bellete, "Death customs," 17-27; Debebew Zellele, "Taskar," 29-33; Parkyns, Life, 2: 53-60; Ullendorff ("Some early Amharic letters") has Agafari Tezazu's letter of thanks of 6 April 1905; Duchesne-Fournet, Mission, 2: 110, 320 on Dr. Goffin; Cerulli ("Canti popolari," 603) interprets the song about Yewub-dar.

20. Martini, op. cit., 3: 551, 554.

21. Yesheshwerq Yilma, interview, AA, 5 January 1967. She was brought to the palace to live after her father, Yilma Mekonnen, died in 1907. Mérab, Impressions, 3: 405-7.

22. Olmstead, "Ethiopia's Artful Weavers;" Burley, "The despised weavers of Addis Ababa," 145-50.

23. Mérab, op. cit., 3: 404.

24. Bairu Tafla (Ethiopia and Germany, 102) is positive about when she arrived despite Lagarde (AA, 5 June 1906, FFO): "She came several months ago and if she exerts any influence it is not in favor of Germans;" Le Temps, 7 June 1906: "Since death of Mekonnen, Taytu all-powerful. She trusts a woman of Tigray married to a German and the increase in Germans is in great part her work;" Brice (AA, 22 June 1908, FFO): "Last year when Coptic school opened, all princes and sons of chiefs sent there, except Lij Iyasu ... Mrs. Hall has the child cornered, has spoiled him and opposed his going to school with others on pretext he should not mix with them, but have special teacher. I used all my influence and [Menilek] ordered his grandson to go to [Coptic] school; Klobukowski (AA, 27 March 1907, FFO): "Jacob Hall is tutoring the heir in the grandeur and strength of Germany;"

Mekonnen Endalkatchew (*Abyssinian Refugee*, 70): "Taytu chose a German governess for [Lij Iyasu] ... revolutional ideas disturbed the brain of the young prince."
25. Brice, AA, 13 September 1908, FFO.
26. Mantegazza, *Menelik*, 204; Hohler, AA, 18 December 1907, PRO/FO; Le Roux, *Ménélik*, 189, 200.
27. In an interview with *Neue Zuercher Zeitung* (10 September 1903) Ilg said, "They wrong the empress, accusing her of hostility to Europeans. True, she ... does not feel compelled to respond to all demands for audiences and people take that as antipathy."

16 Should Menilek die ...

1. Martini, *Diario*, 4: 138-378. There had already been delays due to a cholera epidemic in Yejju, mourning for the wife of Ras Weldiye, and the usual paranoia about France and England; Hamilton, "Schedule ... Agreements."
2. Mérab, *Impressions*, 1: 187-8; Pétridès (*Le Héros*, 119, 216-17, 228, 238, 278) stresses Taytu's hatred of Mekonnen.
3. Martini, op. cit., 4: 287. The chronicle does not mention the Martini meeting and says only that Menilek left on 12 *megabit* (21 March 1906) for Wello but that the rains were so terrible he decided not to impose the march through the mud on his soldiers and returned to Addis Ababa (2: 521). De Castro (*Nella Terra*, 2: 512-13) confirms unusual rains.
4. Martini, op. cit., 4: 369, 376-81.
5. Rosenfeld, *Medical History*, 15-16.
6. Harrington, AA, May 1906-November 1907, PRO/FO.
7. Martini, op. cit., 4: 418-19; Haile Sellassie (*My Life*, 25): "She pestered Emperor Menilek saying, 'Give it to [Yilma] for my sake.' "
8. Europeans constantly protested insults to them. Pariset, *Al Tempo*, 128; Harrington, AA, September 1905, PRO/FO; Martini (op. cit., 4: 447, 481) was told by Chefneux that "hatred of foreigners was their own fault" and observed himself that "whites here discredit the race." Aleqa Kenfe diary for 1906 cites many incidents of violence between foreigners.
9. Martini, op. cit., 4: 444.
10. David Hall, interview, AA, 22 July 1966. Mr. Hall returned to Ethiopia eventually to spend the rest of his life. At the age of 90, when this interview took place, his speech and memory were clear and sharp. His wife who was present and as discreet as he, was nonetheless not averse to saying softly that Taytu had many people poisoned.
11. Aleqa Kenfe diary (IES, 19 December 1904, 23 January 1905, 19 January 1908 and January 1909) refers to the popularity of the race track.
12. Martini had stopped off to call on Abune Petros en route (4: 310-12); Giglio (*Mar Rosso*, 2: 244) reports that Emperor Yohannes was disgusted with Petros and wrote to Menilek, "When dogs and priests are rabid there is no cure;" allegation that Petros took over an ex-mistress of Ras Mengesha Yohannes in IFO, 1900 (Fasc. 54/1).
13. Martini, op. cit., 4: 503.
14. Work, *Ethiopia, A Pawn*, 317-22.
15. Bank chartered on 10 March 1905 as an affiliate of the National Bank of Egypt.
16. Hohler, AA, 29 November 1907 and Harrington, AA, 31 January and 6 December 1908, PRO/FO; the "rich" American wife was Amy MacMillan, daughter of Senator J. MacMillan from Grosse Pointe, Michigan; uncivil remark Harrington/Menilek in Martini, op. cit., 4: 604.

17. Ciccodicola, AA, 8 April 1907, IFO.
18. Aleqa Kenfe diary, IES, January 1907; Le Roux, AA, 21 September 1907, FFO.
19. "Les occupations," TVM.
20. Klobukowski, "La question," 286-93; Klobukowski, AA, 5 September 1907, FFO. No information has come to light on why Taytu thought that Ilg had betrayed her, except the impression that Ilg had not been careful enough about Ethiopian interest on the railroad. Keller (*Ilg*, 218, 227) denies that the empress forced him to resign; Bertin ("Les Européans") says that Ilg was disgraced by Taytu.
21. Klobukowski, AA, 15 July 1907, FFO; Scholler, "Letters," 507.
22. *Chronique*, 2: 527-8. In July 1906 Chefneux told Martini (ibid., 4: 506) that "Taytu being more intelligent than the emperor, sees the need to decentralize power and lighten his burden."
23. Selamu Bekele and Vanderlinden, "Introducing the Ethiopian Law Archives;" Bairu Tafla, "Civil Titles;" Hohler, AA, 27 October 1907.
24. Clerk, AA, 10 April 1907 and Hohler, AA, 28 October 1907, PRO/FO; Garretson, "The Näggädras," 418-22.
25. Brice (AA, 12 July 1908, FFO) encloses Vitalien's report.
26. *Chronique*, 2: 529-30; Klobukowski, AA, 8 October 1907, FFO; Arèn, *Evangelical Pioneers*, 432; Mérab, *Impressions*, 2: 54.
27. Teshome Wagaw, *Education*, 14; Paulos Milkias, "Traditional Institutions."
28. Mérab, op. cit., 3: 347.
29. Avedis Terzian, interview, AA, 21 March 1967.
30. Pariset, *Al Tempo*, 74-5, 88.
31. *Le Semeur*, April, July, August and October 1907.
32. Arèn (*Evangelical Pioneers*) provides all information on the education mission.
33. Caulk, "Dependency," 569-82.
34. Alemé Esheté, "Alaqa Taye," 14-30.
35. Mahteme Sellassie, *Zeker Neger*, 431.
36. *Chronique*, 2: 530; Aleqa Kenfe diary, 8 *hedar* (*c.* 18 November 1907); Briscese, "L'unico Catasto," 69; de Castro, *Nella Terra*, 2: 232.
37. Hallé, *To Menelik*; Nicholson, *A Toy*.
38. Holtz, *Im Auto*, 58; Hohler (*Diplomatic Petrel*, 143) admits: "German car arrived first but I persuaded Menilek not to look at [it] until he had been in the Siddeley."
39. Rosenfeld, *Medical History*, 19; Brice, AA, 20 June 1908, FFO; Martini (op. cit., 4: 62) notes Lij Iyasu as the heir in December 1905.

17   Empress Taytu becomes de facto ruler of Ethiopia

1. Rosenfeld, *Medical History*, is the source for all references to Menilek's health unless otherwise specified.
2. Mérab (*Impressions*, 3: 260) has the "cat" story incorrectly dated as 1907, and says that the same form of sorcery was used against Abune Matewos.
3. Mérab, ibid., 2: 55. Caracatsanis came with the Zervoudakis commercial mission in September 1907 (letter from George Caracatsanis, 19 July 1979). Dr. Martin said, 22 September 1909, that the dentist had asked him to speak to Menilek and Taytu about his unpaid salary. Martin did and the empress answered that the dentist had already made a lot of money from other patients and activities.
4. Dr. Martin, ibid., 22 December 1908. Henceforth, quotes from this diary will not be footnoted, unless specific date is relevant.
5. Brice, AA, 8 February, 9 April 1909 and 3 January 1910, FFO.
6. *Chronique*, 2: 537. Zewde Gabre-Sellassie checked the Amharic original of the chronicle and found the correct spelling of the name, not as in the French translation.

7. Aleqa Kenfe, 21 *hedar* (30 November 1908), IES; and *Chronique*, 2: 535.
8. Aleqa Kenfe, 6 *yekatit* (13 February 1909).
9. Menilek requested a doctor, a tutor for the heir, and a foreign policy adviser from Germany. Scholler, "Letters exchanged," 508.
10. Powell-Cotton (*Sporting Trip*, 128) mentions food tasters, and Dr. Martin said the empress had someone take a laxative he had prescribed before permitting the emperor to take it; Mérab, op. cit. 3: 522.
11. For example, Afenegus Nessibu, Ras Tessema Nadew, Zikargatchu, Negus Tekle Haymanot, Yeshimabet Ali and Wesen Seged. None had a factual basis. Avedis Terzian (interview, 3 April 1967) maintained that poison was given in food, and not in coffee as alleged in the Zikargatchu report (Borelli). Terzian added that women were often used by the state to destroy a man because a woman's loyalty was not deep. During the monthly dosage of *kosso* for worms, people were especially wary of poison. The Armenian pharmacy was a popular place where they would take their *kosso* "from a good hand." Women might use cactus milk, a slow acting corrosive, in cooking, and the man died gradually; Lejean ("Voyage," 270) learned from the botanist, Schimper, of a tree called *djibera* whose sap was used as poison.
12. Dr. Martin's wife died after he returned to Ethiopia in late 1908. He married Qetsela Werq Tullu in 1911. Information about the English wife came to light in Hervey (AA, 13 February, 23 September and 4 November 1909, PRO/FO), because a Mr. Gould of Bath made a complaint about non-payment of bills. Martin cleared up the misunderstanding. He had sent money to his wife, who had died in the meantime so the money had not reached the landlord.
13. Taytu/Emperor of Germany, AA, 13 August 1909, enclosed in Brice (AA, 23 August 1909, FFO); also in Bairu Tafla, *Ethiopia*, 279-81.
14. Dr. Henry L. Verhulst, Poison Control, Public Health Service, Bethesda, Maryland, 3 March 1968; and Marion Kelly, B. Pharm., London, 20 April 1973.
15. Colli, AA, 25 August 1909, IFO; and Brice, AA, 27 September 1909, FFO.
16. British, French and Italian diplomatic notes from 13 March to December 1909 have numerous references to concession review or cancellation.
17. Brice, AA, 1 May 1909, FFO; Colli, AA, February 1910, IFO; Dr. Martin's diary, March-July, 1909.
18. Bairu Tafla, "Civil Titles;" Brice, AA, 20 July 1909; Colli, AA, 28 May, 30 September, 2, 8 October, 9 November, IFO.
19. Annaratone, *In Abissinia*, 102-4. Commenting on what he learned, the doctor wrote, "Curious this openness ... as if no wish for secrecy. For communications that are not urgent or private they use a cypher;" Brice (AA, 22 October 1909, FFO) makes it clear that the French legation also has access to the telegraph messages.
20. Pétridès, *Le Héros*, 296.
21. Brice, AA, 10 November 1909, FFO; de Coppet, *Chronique*, appendix, 2: 540; Colli, AA, 22 July 1909, IFO; Doughty-Wylie, AA, 14 November 1911, PRO, brought up his name again when people were unhappy about Lij Iyasu, and on 2 May 1914 reported that Tayye "onetime hope of Shewa" had been imprisoned.
22. Mérab (op. cit., 3: 563): "He has a penchant for debauchery."
23. Dr. Martin, 10 November 1909.
24. Brice, AA, 18 July 1909, FFO.

18   The downfall of Empress Taytu

1. Moreno, *Raccoltà*, 31.
2. Avedis Terzian, AA, 21 March 1967; Brice, AA, 30 April 1909, FFO; as early

as 1903 a wire service, Agence Fournier, printed the rumor that she wished to
be empress in her own right.

3. Clerk, AA, 10 April 1907, PRO/FO.
4. Gebre Heywet Baykedagn, "Ras Tessema," ASAK, 12 April 1910.
5. Brice, AA, 3 March, 9, 30 April, 1 May 1909, FFO.
6. Garretson, "History and Development," on monopolies; Colli, AA, 9 March,
   8 April 1909, IFO.
7. Colli, op. cit., 3 July, 25 August 1909.
8. Haile Sellassie, *My Life*, 30.
9. Brice, AA, 1 November 1909, FFO.
10. Brice, AA, 2, 3, 6 January 1910; Colli (AA, 22 April 1910) considered the treatment
    of Abate the final straw, but also said that it was the emperor's decision and
    not Taytu's to appoint Abate; Dr. Martin's diary, 24, 26 December 1909; Zewde
    Gabre-Sellassie, 27 October 1983.
11. Brice (AA, 3 January 1910) said that Wele was appointed on 26 December 1909
    and refused the nomination on 3 February 1910; Clerk (AA, 10 April 1907,
    PRO/FO) sketched Wele as "old, imbecilic, syphilitic and alcoholic."
12. Colli (AA, 8 February 1910) believed that Cipolla had attributed ideas to Wele
    without evidence.
13. Brice, AA, 28 February 1910.
14. Dr. Martin's diary, January 1910.
15. Cederqvist, AA, 24 March 1910, in Arén, *Evangelical*, 433, n. 324.
16. Gebre Heywet Baykedagn, "Taitu", ASAK, op. cit.
17. Persecution of Aleqa Tayye was carried on by Abune Matewos after Taytu's
    downfall, Arén, *Evangelical*, 433; Ullendorff, "Early letters," 267; Dr. Martin
    reported on 21 May 1910 that Matewos made a speech at the Coptic school in
    which he urged Tessema to drive all Catholics from Ethiopia; Mérab (ms. 3370,
    120): "She was not alone in religious persecution, there was also Abune Matewos
    and Afenegus Estifanos."
18. Brice, AA, 3 January, 18 February 1910, FFO.
19. Colli (AA, 21 March 1910) believed that the empress knew what was going on
    for she had called 5,000 troops of her own army into the city on 6 March and
    given them arms.
20. All accounts agree in every essential way. In addition to the diplomatic notes
    of France, Britain and Italy the story is told in Mérab, *Impressions*, 2; Annaratone,
    In Abyssinia; Cohen, *Le Petit Temps*, 27 January 1911; Remond, *La Route*; Zewde
    Gabre-Sellassie (27 October 1983) told the story about his father.
21. Thesiger, AA, 3 April 1930, PRO/FO; Brice, AA, 13 April 1910, FFO.
22. Bairu Tafla, "Marriage," 20-1; Doughty-Wylie, AA, 7 July 1911, PRO/FO.
23. Brice, AA, 21 May 1910, FFO.
24. Dr. Martin's diary, 30 April, 4 May and 4 June 1910; Love, AA, 27 June 1910,
    U.S.A.; Brice, AA, 4 May 1910.
25. Taytu/Tessema, 22 *miazia* (30-31 April 1910), Letter Book, NL, AA.
26. Taytu/Wele and Taytu/Mikael, op. cit., undated, but contents determine a date
    between 22 and 29 April 1910; Mérab, op. cit., 2: 238.
27. Tessema/Taytu, 27 *sene* 1902 (4 July 1910); Taytu/Tessema, 28 *sene* (5 July 1910);
    Tessema/Taytu, 3 *hamle* (c. 11 July 1910) are all in Letter Book, op. cit.
28. Dr. Martin, 4 August and 4 September 1910; Brice, AA, 4, 18 August 1910; a similar
    rumor went about in 1912 and had to be denied by an official statement from
    the Council of Ministers, 21 December 1912, in Eadie, *Amharic Reader*, 170-2.
29. Love, AA, 1 June 1911, U.S.A.
30. Colli, AA, 15 June 1911; de Coppet, "L'Ethiopie," 624-5; Zewde Gabre-Sellassie,
    note, 4 September 1983, on the *neftegna*; Dr. Martin, 13-31 May 1911; Doughty-

Wylie, AA, 1-16 June 1911, PRO/FO; Montandon (*Au Pays*, 385) alleged that Abate was a former lover of Taytu.

31. Marcus, *Menelik*, 256-7.

32. Doughty-Wylie was marginally less hard on Lij Iyasu than his superior, Thesiger. On 2 June 1911, PRO/FO, Doughty-Wylie wrote, "He is followed by a mixture of Armenians, Turks, Greeks and Abyssinians who encourage him to silly orgies. He beat Menilek's soldiers with a stick and struck a minister at the polo grounds ... but ... he is not a bad boy, just requires firm treatment;" Mérab, op. cit., 2: 242: "he is sweet, modest, and has a noble air."

33. Dr. Martin (19 July 1911) said Desta had been Iyasu's mistress, but that the poisoning accusations were ridiculous; Martin (29 March 1912) on her illness; Maugin, AA, 18 April 1912, FFO.

34. Brice, AA, 23 February 1912; de Coppet, "L'Ethiopie," 625-7.

35. Brice, AA, 18 March, 5 December 1912, 10 February 1913; Mérab, op. cit. 2: 263-4; Dr. Martin, 8 February 1913. However, Marcus (*Menelik*, 260) and Avedis Terzian (interview, 3 April 1967) said Taytu left the palace in February 1912; I believe they are both wrong. Colli said she left on 4 April 1913 (IFO); Yesheshwerq Yilma (interview, 5 January 1967) said, "after Menilek died." British note (29 December 1916, PRO/FO) says, "She has been at Entotto only during the last year;" Heruy (*Ye-heywet*) wrote, "she was ordered out by Lij Iyasu after Menilek's death." Mérab (op. cit., 2: 240, 272) insists that Menilek died in 1909 and that Taytu died at the palace in December 1913 despite all evidence to the contrary.

36. *Documents rélatifs*. In her throne speech Zewditu specified that she "cared for her father's body two years, three months and two days" before being forced from the palace; Zewde Gabre-Sellassie (27 October 1983) said she lived at Falle with Gugsa; local people at Entotto Raguel say Menilek's remains were in a room carved out of the hill just north of the church until he was moved to the mausoleum built by Zewditu (*Welcome to Ethiopia*, 29). In November 1985 the guardians of this cave at Raguel would not let anyone enter without paying them money.

37. Dr. Martin, 5 May 1911.

38. Yesheshwerq Yilma (interview, 28 November 1966) said that she and her mother visited Taytu. Desta Damtew, "who started as a page at her court and voluntarily accompanied her into exile." Southard, 9 February 1929, U.S.A.

39. Marcus, *Menelik*, 262-4; Dodds, AA, 1 March 1914 and Doughty-Wylie, AA, 2 May 1914, PRO; Zewde Gabre-Sellassie, 4 December 1983.

40. Thesiger, AA, 25 February 1914; Dodds, AA, 13 March 1914; and Thesiger, AA, 14 April 1916, PRO/FO; Colli, AA, 30 April 1916, IFO.

41. Marcus, *Menelik*, 270 and "The Embargo," 214. In the latter Marcus writes, "victory of the Central Powers would facilitate his plan for turning Ethiopia into a more egalitarian community." Historians John Markakis, Donald Levine and Richard Greenfield all use the word "alleged" regarding Lij Iyasu's apostasy.

42. "The reasons for Abeto Iyasu's leaving the throne," de Castro, *Nella Terra*, Vol. 2.

43. Thesiger, AA, 21 August 1916, PRO/FO; *Documents rélatifs*; de Coppet, "L'Ethiopie," 627-30; Haile Sellassie, *My Life*, 46-56.

44. Colli, AA, 20 May 1909, IFO, quoting Habte Giyorgis; Mantegazza (*Menelik*, 209) gives no source.

45. Haile Sellassie, op. cit., 157.

46. Thesiger (AA, 1 November 1916, op. cit.) estimated casualties for both sides at 20,000; loss at Adwa was estimated at 7,000.

47. Interview, Yesheshwerq Yilma, AA, 28 November 1966; Greenfield, *Ethiopia*, 141; Campbell, AA, 30 November 1917, PRO/FO.

48. Afewerq's account was first published in *Aemro*, 3 March, 1927, and then reprinted in *Oriente Moderno* in Italian.

Bibliography

DIPLOMATIC ARCHIVES

For those who wish a more detailed description than the one below, see either Marcus's *Life and Times of Menelik II* or Zewde Gabre-Sellassie's *Yohannes IV.*

Abbreviated as:

French foreign office archives, Quai d'Orsay,   FFO
     d'Orsay, Paris: "Nouvelle Série, Ethiopie,
     1897-1918," is divided into bound volumes,
     "Politique Etrangère," "Politique Intérieure" and
     "Dossier Général."

Italian foreign office archives, Farnesina, Rome: IFO
     much material published in *Libro Verde*, 10, 15,   LV
     18; *Documenti Diplomatici* and *L'Italia in Africa*,   DD
     Etiopia-Mar Rosso, cited Giglio.

British diplomatic notes in Public Records Office,   PRO/FO
     Kew, Richmond, Surrey: FO 401-403-407; 371/396.

U.S. diplomatic records in National Archives,   USA
     Pennsylvania Ave, Washington, D.C.

Anglo-Sudan Archives, Khartoum, Sudan: notes   ASAK
     provided by Peter Garretson.

Soviet Union (Russia): notes provided by   SU-R
     I.S. Katznelson, Soviet Academy of Sciences.

German foreign office archives, Bonn: provided   GFO
     requested documents.

National Library, Addis Ababa, Ethiopia, has   NL
     what is available as government records and those
     used were provided by Peter Garretson and
     Richard Caulk.

NON-GOVERNMENTAL ARCHIVE COLLECTIONS

Institute of Ethiopian Studies, Addis Ababa, has   IES
     the original or a copy of:
     Atsme Giyorgis, "Ye-galla Tarik" ms. 138;
         copy of ms. 302, BN, Paris.
     Ferdinand, Father, diary copy; original at Capucin
         mission, Nazareth, Ethiopia.
     Kenfe, Aleqa, diary; original with Aleme Eshete,

copy is ms. 342.

Tekle Iyesus, Aleqa, "Tarike negest," ms. 254.

Capucin mission, 32 Rue Boissonade, Paris: CM
  Dr. Paul Mérab, 3 vols. of typescript, ms. 3370
  and "Quinze pièces concernant le Dr. P. Mérab,"
  ms. 3373.

Bibliothèque Nationale, Paris   BN
  Manuscrits Ethiopiens:
    D'Abbadie collection: NA 10166, 10222
      (1871-91); 10221 (1861-78); 21200; 22430-1;
      23848-52. Contains letters from Taurin de
      Cahagne, Gonzague de Lassere, Gebre Sadiq
      and Gugliemo Massaia. Griaule collection: 4
      mss.
    Mondon-Vidailhet collection: ms. E. 260 was
      given to him by Empress Taytu; Aleqa
      Lemlem mss. (diary); portions of Aleqa
      Kenfe diary.

Vatican Library, Rome: VL
  D'Abbadie, Arnauld papers; 2 volumes have been
  published, in 1980 and in 1983.

IN PRIVATE HANDS

Diary of Dr. Charles Werqneh-Martin. My references based on copy made
  by Peter Garretson.

INTERVIEWS AND LETTERS TO AUTHOR

Cantoni, Guido, Dr., interview, Washington, D.C., November 1969.

Caracatsanis, George, letter, Bulawayo, Rhodesia, 10 July 1979.

Coen, Fabio, interview, 12 April 1972, Mystic, Conn., U.S.A.

Endalkatchew Mekonnen, letter, New York, 8 August 1966.

Gebez Wondemagnu, Qes, interview, Entotto, 12 April 1967.

Hall, David, interview, AA, 22 July 1966.

Imru Zelleke, interview, Washington, D.C., 15 April 1984.

Kelly, Marion, B. Pharm., letter, London, 20 April 1971.

Loepfe, Willi, letters, Zurich, 11 May 1975 and 20 June 1982.

Mahsente Habte Maryam, interview, AA, 30 January 1967.

Menghistu Lemma, interview, AA, 10 June 1966.

Terzian, Avedis, interviews, AA, 21 March and 3 April 1967.

Teshager Woobe; interview, aunts and mother of his wife, Almaz, AA, 26
  May 1967.

Tsegaye Gebre Medhin, interview, Washington, D.C., March 1985.

Verhulst, Henry, Dr., letter, National Institutes of Health, Bethesda, Md., U.S.A., 15 March 1968.

Weertz, Maurice, interview, AA, 2 March 1967.

Yemane Berhan, Elizabeth, interview, AA, 22 November 1966.

Yesheshwerq Yilma, interviews, AA, 26 November 1966 and 5 January 1967.

Yohannes Martin, Dr., letter, AA, 5 November 1969.

Zewde Gabre-Sellassie, interviews, letters and notes from 11 June 1967 to September 1984.

UNPUBLISHED THESES AND PAPERS

Adugna Amahu, "The Ethiopian Orthodox Church becomes Autocephalic," HSIU, AA, 1969 (notes provided by R. Caulk).

Andromeda Tafara, "The role and status of Ethiopian women," Howard U., Washington, D.C., 1968.

Beletu Mengistu, "A short biography of *Abune* Matewos," paper, AAU, 1982 (notes provided by R. Caulk).

Berry, La Verle, "The Solomonic Monarchy at Gondar 1630-1755," Boston U., Boston, Mass., April 1976.

Brockett, A.M., "The British Somaliland Protectorate to 1905," Lincoln College, Oxford, England, 1969.

Caulk, R.A., "The Origins and Development of the Foreign Policy of Menilek II, 1865-1896," London U., England, August 1966.

Cook, R., Dr., "Damage to Physical Health from Pharaonic Circumcision (Infibulation) of Females," WHO, Eastern Mediterranean, 1975.

Garretson, Peter, "History and Development of Addis Ababa," London U., England, 1974.

"The telephone and telegraph system in Ethiopia, 1897-1935," paper, African Studies Conference, Los Angeles, California, 19 November 1979.

Guenet Guebre-Christos, "Position of women in communities of different levels of societal development," U. of Chicago, 1980.

Hussein Ahmed, "Some problems of the Gebre Sellase Chronicle," AAU, 1977 (provided by Richard Caulk).

Laketch Dirasse, "Survival techniques of female migrants in Ethiopian urban centers," paper, 3rd Int'l Congress of Africanists, AA, 1973.

Lazarevich, A-S, "Researches of the Seljan brothers in Ethiopia," paper, 3rd Int'l Congress of Africanists, AA, 1973.

Merid Welde Aregay, "Southern Ethiopia and the Christian Kingdom," London U., England, 1971.

Morton, Alice, "Aspects of Spiritual Power in Ethiopia," London U., England, 1973.

Rollins, R.J., "Russia's Ethiopian Adventure, 1888-1905," Syracuse U., 1967. University Microfilms #6712077.

Tekle Tsadik Mekouria, "Les noms de baptême et l'étude généalogique des rois d'Ethiopie (XII-XX siècles) à travers leurs noms patronymiques," cyclostyle, Belgrade, Yugoslavia, September 1966 (courtesy of Donald Levine).

PUBLISHED SOURCES

Abbreviations

AA	Addis Ababa
AAf	*African Affairs*
AAU	Addis Ababa University
ACISE	*Atti di Congresso Internazionale di Studi Etiopici* (1959-72)
AION	*Annuario dell'Istituto Orientale di Napoli*
AL	*Anthropological Linguistics*
ANL	Accademia Nazionale dei Lincei, Rome
ASC, MSU	African Studies Center, Michigan State University, East Lansing, Michigan 48824
ASR	*African Studies Review*
ATCSC	*Atti di terzo congresso di studi etiopici coloniale* (Rome, 1937)
BAV	Biblioteca Apostolica Vaticana
BESAA	*Bulletin Ethnological Society*, Addis Ababa
BSAI	*Bolletino della Società Africana d'Italia*
BSG	*Bulletin de la Société de Géographie*, Paris
BSGI	*Bolletino della Società Geografica Italiana*
BSGL	*Bulletin de la Société de Géographie*, Lille
BSGLyons	*Bulletin de la Société de Géographie*, Lyons
BSKG	*Bulletin Société Khédiviale Géographie*, Egypt
BSOAS	*Bulletin, School of Oriental and African Studies*, University of London
CEA	*Cahiers d'Etudes Africaines*
CSCO	*Corpus Scriptorum Christianorum Orientalium*
EA	*Encyclopaedia Africana, Dictionary of African Biography*, 1, Ethiopia-Ghana
EC	*Esploratore Commerciale*
E.C.	Ethiopian calendar
ECA	Economic Commission for Africa, U.N., Addis Ababa
EN	*Ethiopianist Notes*; became *Northeast African Studies*, 1979
EO	*Ethiopia Observer*
GAAI	*Gli Annali Africa Italiana*
GG	*Gazette Géographie*

GIA	La Guerra Italo-Abissina, Milan, 1895-6
GSAI	*Giornale della Società Asiatica Italiana*
GSA	*Giornale Società Africana*
HSIU	Haile Sellassie I. University, now Addis Ababa University
IES	Institute of Ethiopian Studies, Addis Ababa
IJSP	*International Journal of Social Psychiatry*
IJAHS	*International Journal of African Historical Studies*
JA	*Journal Asiatique*
JAH	*Journal of African History*
JAL	*Journal of African Law*
JAS	*Journal of African Studies*, UCLA
JEL	*Journal of Ethiopian Law*
JES	*Journal of Ethiopian Studies*
JHM	*Journal of History of Medicine and Allied Sciences*
JRAS	*Journal of Royal African Society*
JSS	*Journal of Semitic Studies*
MAL	Munger Africana Library, California Institute of Technology
MC	*Les Missions Catholiques*
MKKGGW	*Mitteilungen der Kaiserliche und Köngliche Geographischen Gesellschaft in Wien*
NA	*Nuova Antologia*
NAS	*Northeast African Studies*
NG	*National Geographic*
NUP	Negro Universities Press/Greenwood; Westport, Connecticut
OM	*Oriente Moderno*
OUP	Oxford University Press
P. 1st USICES	*Proceedings of First United States Conference on Ethiopian Studies*, East Lansing, Michigan, 1975
P. 3rd ICES	*Proceedings of Third International Conference on Ethiopian Studies*, 3 vols. (HSIU, 1969-70)
P. 4th ICES	*Proceedings of Fourth International Conference on Ethiopian Studies*, Rome, 1973
P. 5th ICES	*Proceedings of Fifth International Conference on Ethiopian Studies*, U. of Illinois, 1979. Nice, France, section of this conference is entitled *Modern Ethiopia*
RAL	Reale Accademie dei Lincei, Rome
RCI	*Rivista delle Colonie Italiane*

RDM   Revue des Deux Mondes
RGC   Revue de Géographie Commerciale
RHR   Revue de l'Histoire des Religions
RMI   Rivista Militare Italiane
RPL   Rivista Politica e Litteraria
RRAL   Rendiconti dei Reale Accademie dei Lincei
RS   Revue Semitique
RSE   Rassegna di Studi Etiopici
RSO   Rivista Studi Orientali
TJAH   TransAfrican Journal of African History
TM   Le Tour du Monde
TVM   A Travers le Monde
U.N.   United Nations
VGEB   *Verhandlungen der Gesellschaft für Erdkunde zu Berlin*
WHO   World Health Organization
WINN   *Women's International Network News,* Lexington, Mass., U.S.A.

Abbadie, Antoine d', *L'Abyssinie et le roi Théodore* (Paris, 1868); English translation in *The Catholic World*, 7 (1868).
"La procédure en Ethiopie," Extr. de la *Nouvelle Revue Histoire de Droit Français et Etranger* (1888).
Abbadie, Arnauld d', *Douze Ans de Séjour dans la Haute-Ethiopie*, 1 (Paris, 1868); 2 and 3 (BAV, Rome, 1980, 1983).
Abdalla, Raqiya Haji Dualeh, *Sisters in Affliction* (Zed, London, 1982).
Abdurahman Mohamed Korram, "Oromo Proverbs," *JES*, 7: 1 (1969); 10: 2 (1972).
Abir, Mordechai, *Ethiopia, the era of the Princes* (Praeger, New York, 1968).
Abraham Demoz, "Emperor Menelik's Phonograph Message to Queen Victoria," *BSOAS*, 32: 2 (1969), 251-3.
Aescoly, A.Z., "La colonie éthiopienne à Jerusalem," *Aetheopica* (1935), 20-6, 44-9, 88-95.
Afewerq Gebre Iyesus, *Il Dagmawi Menilek* (The second Menilek) (Rome, 1901); Italian translation by Fusella in *RSE*, 17 (1961'), 19 (1963).
(Death of Empress Taitu), Italian translation in *OM*, 7: 5 (1927).
Ityopya, guide du voyageur en Abyssinie (Rome, 1908).
Album Mariani, 1910 (Cabinet des Estampes, BN, Paris).
Alemé Esheté, "Alaqa Taye Gabra Mariam (1861-1924)," *RSE*, 25 (1971-2).
Alvarez, Francisco, *Narrative of the Portuguese Embassy to Abyssinia (1520-1527)* (Hakluyt Society, 1881).
Amato, Nicola d', *Da Adua ad Addis Ababa* (Salerno, 1898).
Ambaye Zekarias, *Land Tenure in Eritrea (Ethiopia)* (AA, 1966).

Ambrogetti, P., *La vita sessuale nell'Eritrea* (Biblioteca del Pervertimenti Sessuale, Rome, 1900).

Amdur, M.K. and Cleckley, H.M., "Observations of a Russian Neuropsychiatrist in Ethiopia during the War with Italy in 1896," *Medical Bulletin of Veterans Administration*, 12 (April 1936).

Amulree, Lord, "Prince Alamayou of Ethiopia," *EO*, 13: 1 (1970).

Annaratone, Carlo, *In Abissinia* (Rome, 1914).

Annual Report of Smithsonian Institution (Washington, D.C., 1904, 1905).

Antonelli, Pietro, *Menilek, imperatore d'Etiopia* (Rome, 1891).

    Taitu, imperatrice d'Etiopia (Rome, 1891).

    "Nell'Africa Italiana," Extr. *NA* (July 1891).

    "Il primo viaggio di un Europeo attraverso l'Aussa," *BSGI*, 26 (1889).

    Letters from Ethiopia, 6 November 1879, 29 March and 8 May 1880, 3 June 1883, 11 December 1886, *BSGI*, 17 (1880), 20 (1883), 24 (1887); other letters in *BSAI*, 1 (1882), 2 (1883) and *EC*, 2 (1887), 4 (1889).

    "Scioa e Scioani," *BSGI*, 19 (1882).

    "Il mio viaggio da Assab allo Scioa," *BSGI*, 20 (1883).

    "Il mio ritorno dalla Scioa," *NA*, 32 (1882).

    "Usi e costumi abissini," *Piccola Rivista di Scienze, Lettere* (Rome, 1892).

    "Rapporti sullo Scioa del Conte Pietro Antonelli," *DD* (1890).

Area Handbook for Ethiopia (Amer. U., Washington, D.C., 2nd ed., 1971).

Arèn, Gustav, *Evangelical Pioneers in Ethiopia* (Stockholm, 1978).

Armstrong, W.H. and Fisseha Demoz Gebre Egzi, "Amharic Proverbs," *EO*, 12: 1 (1968).

Arnoux, Pierre (see Lande).

Assaggakhan, Debtera (see Fusella).

Assefa Dula, "Land Tenure in Chercher Province," *EO*, 12: 2 (1969).

Aubry, Alphonse, "Une mission au Choa," Extr. *BSG* (Paris, 1887).

Audon, Henri, "Voyage au Choa (1884-1888)," *TM*, 58 (1889).

Baeteman, J., "Au Pays de Menelik," *BSGL*, 60 (December 1913).

    "Croquis blancs au pays Abyssins," *MC* (1913).

Bairu Tafla, "Civil Titles and Offices in the Reign of Emperor Menelik II, 1889-1913," *P. 4th ICES* (Rome, 1973).

    Chronicle of Yohannes IV (Wiesbaden, 1977).

    Ethiopia and Germany; cultural, political and economic relations, 1871-1936 (Wiesbaden, 1981).

    "Four Ethiopian biographies: Dajjazmac Gärmamé, Gäbrä-Egzi'abeher Moroda, Balca and Kantiba Gäbru Dästa," *JES*, 7: 2 (1969).

    "Marriage as a political device, an appraisal of a socio-political aspect of the Menilek period 1889-1916," *JES*, 10: 1 (1972).

    "Ras Dargé Sahlä-Sellasé c. 1827-1900," *JES*, 13: 2 (1975).

    "Three portraits: Ato Asmä Giyorgis, Ras Gobäna Daci and Sähafé Tezaz

Gäbrä Selassé," *JES*, 5: 2 (1967).

"Some aspects of land tenure and taxation in Salale under Ras Dargé, 1871-1900," *JES*, 12: 2 (1974).

"Two Ethiopian biographies: Wahni Azaj Wäldä Sadeq Abba Menzir, 1838-1909; Fitawrari Habte Giyorgis Abba Mechal, 1853-1926," *JES*, 6: 1 (1968).

"Two of the last provincial kings of Ethiopia: Negus Täklä Haymanot Abba Tanna of Gojjam, 1850-1901 and his sons; Negus Wäldä Giyorgis Abboyyé Abba Säggäd c. 1859-1918," *JES*, 11: 1 (1973).

"Some documents on nineteenth century Ethiopia from the Nachlass of Gerhard Rohlfs," *RSE*, 29 (1982-3).

"Gugsa Wale," *EA*, 77.

"Kassa Haylu," *EA*, 93.

Baratieri, Oreste, *Mémoires d'Afrique (1892-1896)* (Paris, 1899). Translation of Italian issued in 1898.

Bardi, P., *Pioniere e soldati d'Abissinia* (Milan, 1936).

Bartnicki, A., and Mantel-Niecko, Joanna, "The Role and Significance of the Religious Conflicts and People's Movements in the political life of Ethiopia in the 17th and 18th centuries," *RSE*, 24 (1969-70).

Basset, René, *Mélanges Africains et Orientaux* (Paris, 1915).

Bassi, M., "Diario," *GIA*, 218.

"La Bataille d'Adoua," *GG*, 21: 215 (November 1896).

Battaglia, Roberto, *La Prima Guerra d'Africa* (Turin, 1958).

Baxter, P.T.W., "Ethiopia's unacknowledged problem: the Oromo," *AAf*, 77: 308 (July 1978).

Beckstrom, J.H., "Divorce in Urban Ethiopia ten years after the Civil Code," *JEL*, 6: 2 (December 1972).

Bellavita, E., *Adua, i precedenti, la battaglia, le consequenze (1881-1931)* (Genoa, 1931).

Bent, J.T., "In the north of Abyssinia" (photos by Mrs. Bent), *Illustrated London News*, 8, 29 April and 6 May 1893.

The Sacred City of the Ethiopians (London, 1893).

Berkeley, G.F.H., *The Campaign of Adowa and the Rise of Menelik* (London, 1902).

Bernatz, J.M. *Scenes in Aethiopia*, 2 vols. (Munich and London, 1852).

Bertin, G., "Les Européens en Abyssinie," *TVM*, 14 (22 February 1908).

Bervin, Antoine, *Bénito Sylvain, apôtre du relèvement social des noirs* (Haiti, 1969).

Bianchi, Gustavo, *Alla Terra dei Galli* (Milan, new ed., 1886).

Bidder, Irmgard, *Lalibela* (New York, 1960).

Bieber, F.J., "Reise durch Äthiopien und den Sudan," *MKKGGW*, 53 (1910).

Bonchamps, C. de, "Une Mission vers le Nil Blanc," *BSG*, 19 (1898).

Borelli, Jules, *Ethiopie Méridionale* (Paris, 1890).

Borello, P.M., "Proverbi Galla," *RSE*, 5 (1946), 7: 1 (1948), 24 (1971).

Bottego, V., *Il Giuba Esplorato* (Rome, 1895).

Boulatovich (see Bulatovich).

Briscese, Anselmo, "L'unico catasto in Etiopia istituito da Menelik II nel 1909," *ATCSC*, 1 (Rome, 1937).

Bruce, James, *Travels to Discover the Source of the Nile, 1768-1773*, 5 vols. (Edinburgh, 1790).

Buckle, G.E. (ed.), *The Letters of Queen Victoria*, 3 (1896-1901) (London, 1928).

Budge, E.A.W., *A History of Ethiopia, Nubia and Abyssinia*, 2 vols. (London, 1928).

(See *Kebra Negest*).

Bulatovich, A.K., *With the Troops of Menelick II*, E.S. Katznelson (ed.) (Academy of Science, Institute of Eastern Authority, Moscow, 1971).

"Une expédition au lac Rudolphe. Les campagnes de Ménélik," *Journal des voyages et des aventures de terre et de mer*, 297 (10 August 1902).

Burley, Dexter, "The despised weavers of Addis Ababa," *P. 5th ICES*.

Cacciapuoti, R., "Medicina e farmacologia indigena in Etiopia," *RSE*, 1 (1941).

Campbell, G., "Labour and the Transport Problem in Imperial Madagascar," *JAH*, 21 (1980).

Canevari, E., *Il generale Tommaso Salsa e le sue campagne coloniale* (Milan, 1935).

Canton, W. (ed.), *History of the British and Foreign Bible Society*, 4 vols. (London, 1904-10).

Capucci, Luigi, Letters in *BSAI*, 5 (1886), 6 (1887), 7 (1888), 8 (1889).

and Cicognani, L., "In viaggio per lo Scioa," *BSAI*, 4 (1885), 5 (1886).

(See Zaghi for other letters.)

Carry, F., "La Captivité des Italiens en Abyssinie," *Le Correspondant*, 188 (July-September 1897).

Cassièrs, Anne, "Mercha: an Ethiopian woman speaks of her life," *NAS*, 5: 2 (1983).

Castelletto, A., "La figlia di Ras Alula" (Milan, 1888). English translation, *EO*, 15: 3 (1972).

Castro, Lincoln de, "De Zeila au Harar," *BSKG*, 5 (1898).

"L'ostetricia in Abissinia," Estr. *Atti Società Italiano di Ostetricia e Ginecologia*, 12 (1907).

Nella Terra dei Negus, 2 vols. (Milan, 1915).

"Un escursione al monte Zuquala al lago Zuai e nei Soddo," *BSGI*, 45 (1908).

"Il primo caso di ginecologia forense in Abissinia," *Ginecologia Moderna*, 3: 8 (August 1910).

"L'arte di Esculapio tra gli Abissini," and "Medicina vecchia e nuova in Abissinia," *BSGI*, 45 (1908).

"La città e il clima di Addis Abeba," and "Criminali, giudici e tribunali etiopici," *BSGI*, 48 (1911).

Etiopia: terra, uomini e cose (Milan, 1936).

Caulk, Richard, "Dependency, Gebre Heywet Baykedagn, and the birth of Ethiopian Reformism," *P. 5th ICES*.

"Firearms and princely power in Ethiopia in the Nineteenth Century," *JAH*, 13: 4 (1972).

"Armies as predators: soldiers and peasants in Ethiopia, c. 1850-1935," *IJAHS*, 11: 3 (1978).

"The occupation of Harar: January 1887," *JES*, 9: 2 (1971).

"Harar Town and its Neighbors in the Nineteenth Century," *JAH*, 18: 3 (1977).

"The army and society in Ethiopia," *EN*, 3 (Spring 1978).

"Religion and State in Nineteenth Century Ethiopia," *JES*, 10: 1 (1972).

"Territorial competition and the battle of Embabo, 1882," *JES*, 13: 1 (1975).

"Yohannes IV, the Mahdists, and the Colonial Partition of Northeast Africa," *TJAH*, 1: 2 (1971).

"Minilik II and the diplomacy of commerce: prelude to an imperial foreign policy," *JES*, 17 (1984).

Cecchi, Antonio, *Da Zeila alle frontiere del Caffa*, 3 vols. (Rome, 1886-7).

Cerulli, E., *Etiopi in Palestina*, 2 vols. (Rome 1958, 1960).

"The Folk Literature of the Galla of Southern Abyssinia," *Harvard African Series*, 3 (varia Africana) (Boston, 1922).

"Canti popolari amarici," *RRAL*, 25: 3 and 4 (1916).

"Una raccolta amarici di canti funebri," *RSO*, 10 (1924).

Chadwick, Henry, *The Early Church* (Penguin, 1967).

Chojnacki, S., "Some notes on the history of the Ethiopian national flag," *JES*, 1: 2 (1963); "A second note ..." *P. 3rd ICES*; "Third Note ..." *RSE*, 28 (1980-1).

"Christmas at the Capital of Menelik," *Blackwoods Magazine*, 190 (September 1911).

Cicognani (see Capucci).

Cipolla, Arnaldo, *Nell'impero di Menelik* (Milan, 1911).

Cohen, Marcel, "Couplets amhariques du Choa," *JA*, 205 (1924).

"Jeux abyssins," *JA*, 18 (1911).

Le Petit Temps (news from AA), 21 January 1911.

"Cérémonies et croyances abyssines," *RHR* (September-October 1912).

Collat, O., *Abyssinie actuelle* (Paris, 1906).

Combes, E. and Tamisier, M., *Voyage en Abyssinie, 1835-1837*, 4 vols. (Paris, 1838).

Conti-Rossini, Carlo, *Italia ed Etiopia dal trattato d'Uccialli alla battaglia di Adua* (Rome, 1935).
"La fine di Re Teodoro in un documento abissino," *NA* (16 October 1936).
"La cronaca reale Abissinia dall'anno 1800 all'anno 1840," *RRAL* (1917).
"Canti popolari Tigrai," *Zeitschrift für Assyriologie*, 17, 18, 19 (1903-6).
"La cronaca abbreviata dei re d'Abissinia," *GAAI*, 1: 1 (10 May 1938).
"Nuovi documenti per la storia d'Abissinia nel secolo XIX," *RRAL* 8: 2 (1947).
"Vicende dell'Etiopia e delle missioni cattoliche ai tempi di Ras Ali, Deggiac Ubie e Re Teodoro," *RRAL*, 5: 25 (1916).
Conzelman, W.E., *Chronique de Galawdewos* (Paris, 1895).
Coppet, Maurice de, "L'Ethiopie de 1909 à 1916," Appendix 13, *Chronique* (see Guébrè Sellassié).
Corazzini, N., *La Tribuna*, 7 June 1890.
Coulbeaux, J.B., *Histoire Politique et Religieuse d'Abyssinie depuis les temps les plus reculés jusqu'à l'avènement de Ménélik II*, 3 vols. (Paris, 1929).
"Au pays de Ménélik," *MC* (Paris, 1898).
Crabites, Pierre, *Americans in the Egyptian Army* (London, 1935).
"Croix-Rouge, Ethiopie," *Bull. Internationale des Sociétés de la Croix-Rouge*, 28 (1897).
Crosby, Oscar, "Abyssinia, the country and people," *NG*, 12 (1901).
"Personal Impressions of Menelik," *Century*, 63 (April, 1902).
Crummey, Donald, *Priests and Politicians* (Oxford, Clarendon, 1972).
"The Violence of Tewodros," *JES*, 9: 2 (1971).
"Tewodros as Reformer and Modernizer," *JAH*, 10: 3 (1969).
"Women and Landed Property in Gondarine Ethiopia," *IJAHS*, 14: 3 (1981).
"Family and Landed Property Amongst the Amhara Nobility," *JAH*, 24 (1983).

Daniel Haile, *Law and the Status of Women in Ethiopia* (ECA, AA, 1980).
Darkwah, R.H.K., *Shewa, Menilek and the Ethiopian Empire* (Praeger, 1975).
Debebew Zellele, "Taskar or Kurban," *BESAA*, 1 (December 1957).
Decaud, H., "L'Abyssinie," *RGC*, 54 (1904).
Del Boca, Angelo, *The Ethiopian War, 1935-1941* (U. of Chicago, 1969).
Gli Italiani in Africa Orientale, 2 vols. (Lateri; Rome-Bari; 1976, 1979).
Demographic Year Book (United Nations, 1974).
Dictionary of Ethiopian Biography, 1 (IES, AA, 1975).
Diehl, C., *Byzantium* (Rutgers U., 1957).
Le Docteur Nouvellement Venu (Dire-Daoua, Imprimerie St. Lazare, 1909).
Documents relatifs au coup d'état d'Addis Abeba du 27 Sept. 1916 (Dire-Daoua, Imprimerie St. Lazare, 1916).

Douin, G., *Histoire du règne du Khedive Ismail*, 3 vols. (Cairo, 1936-41).
Duchesne-Fournet, J., *Mission en Ethiopie, 1901-1903*, 2 vols. (Paris, 1908-9).
Dye, William, *Moslem Egypt and Christian Abyssinia* (New York, 1880).

E.B., "La battaglia di Adua dal campo Abissino e da fonti russe," *RMI* (1897).
Eadie, J.I., *An Amharic Reader* (Cambridge, 1924).
Efrem, Archimandrite, *Journey to Abyssinia* (trans. of Russian title) (Moscow U., 1901).
Elets, Yu. (pseud. for Leontiev), *Emperor Menelik and his war with Italy* (trans. of Russian title) (St. Petersburg, 1898).
Emily, Dr., *Mission Marchand* (Paris, 1912). Reissued 1935 as *Fachoda, mission Marchand (1896-1899)*.
Encyclopaedia Africana, Dictionary of African Biography, 1 (Ethiopia-Ghana) (Reference Pub., New York, 1977).
Ephraim Isaac, *The Ethiopian Church* (Sawyer, Boston, 1968).
"Social Structure of the Ethiopian Church," *EO*, 14: 4 (1971).
Erlich, H., *Ethiopia and Eritrea during the scramble for Africa: a political biography of Ras Alula 1875-1897* (ASC, MSU and African Studies, Tel-Aviv U., 1982).
Eshete Tadesse, "Preparation of Täg among the Amhara of Säwa," *BESAA*, 8 (1958).
Ezra Gebre-Medhin, "Wedding Customs Practiced in Shoa," *BESAA*, 2 (December 1953).

Faïtlovich, J., *Proverbes Abyssins* (Paris, 1907).
"Nouveaux proverbes abyssins traduits et expliqués," *RSO*, 2 (1908).
"Versi abissini," *GSAI*, 23 (1910).
Notes d'un voyage chez les Falashas; rapport présenté à M. le Baron Edmond de Rothschild (Paris, 1905).
Fassika Bellete, "The death customs among the Amharas of Säwa," *BESAA* (December 1957).
Felter, Pietro, "La relazione di Pietro Felter sullo sgombero di Macalè," *RSE*, 3: 3 (1943).
La Vicenda Africana (Brescia, 1935).
The Fetha Nagast (trans. by Abba Paulos Tzadua, ed. Peter Strauss) (Faculty of Law, HSIU, 1968).
Flad, J.M., *Ein Leben für Abessinien* (Basel, 1936). Contains Paulina Flad's diary.
Franzoj, Augusto, *Continente Nero* (Novara, 1961). 1st edn. in 1885.
"Letter from Shoa, 26 March 1883," *BSGI*, ser. 2: 8 (1883).
Frisina, F., *L'Italia in Abissinia e nel Sudan* (Alexandria, 1919).
Fusella, L., "Abissinia e Metemma in uno scritto del *Belatta* Heruy," *RSE*, 3: 3 (1943).

"Menilek e l'Etiopia in un testo amarico del Bāykadān," *AION*, 4 (1952).
"Le lettere del *Dabtara* Assaggākhañ," *RSE*, 12 (1953), 13 (1954).
"Proverbi amarici," *RSE*, 3 (1942).

Gamba, P., "L'Azione Russa in Etiopia," *GAAI*, 1: 1 (1938).
Gamerra, G., *Ricordi di un prigionero di guerra nello Scioa* (Florence, 1897).
    Fra gli Ascari d'Italia a ricordi di Mohammed Idris (Bologna, 1899).
Garretson, Peter, "The Näggädras, Trade and Selected Towns in Nineteenth
    and Early Twentieth Century Ethiopia," *IJAHS*, 12: 3 (1979).
Gazetta dell'Emilia, 25-26 November 1935.
Gebre Heywet Baykedagn, *Atse Menelek-na Ityopya* (Asmara, 1912). See
    Fusella for translation.
    (Analyses of Empress Taytu and Ras Tessema in ASAK, Khartoum.)
Gebre Selassie, *Tsehafi Tezaz* (see Guébrè Sellassié).
Gebre-Wold-Ingida Worq, "Ethiopia's Traditional System of Land Tenure
    and Taxation," *EO*, 5: 4 (1962).
Gerard, Albert G., "Amharic Creative Literature: the early phase," *JES*, 6:
    2 (July 1968).
Giel, R. and van Luijk, J.N., "Patterns of marriage in a roadside town in
    South-western Ethiopia," *JES*, 6: 2 (1968).
Giglio, Carlo, *L'Impresa di Massaua, 1884-1885* (Rome, 1955).
    "Article 17 of the Treaty of Uccialli," *JAH*, 6: 2 (1965).
    "Il Trattato di Pace Italo-Ethiopico del 26 Ottobre 1896," *P. 3rd ICES*,
    1 (1966).
    (ed.), *L'Italia in Africa: Etiopia-Mar Rosso*, 6 vols. (Poligrafico dello stato,
    Rome, 1958-66).
Girma-Selassie Asfaw, David L. Appleyard, with Edward Ullendorff, *The
    Amharic Letters of Emperor Theodore of Ethiopia to Queen Victoria
    and her Special Envoy* (OUP/British Academy, 1979).
Giudice, Barbaro lo, "I Preliminari di pace di Faras-Mai del 1896," *RSE*,
    2: 1 (1942).
Gleichen, A.E., *With the Mission to Menelik, 1897* (London, 1898).
Golani, V.Y., "A.V. Yeliseyev, writer and traveler," *Russia and Africa*
    (Africa Institute, Moscow, 1966).
Gonzague de Lassere, Father, "De Zeila a Farre, voyages en pays Galla,"
    MC, 14 (1883), 551-2, 561-2, 585-7, 598-600, 609-11, 618-21.
    "Mgr. Massaia et l'empereur Yoannes," *L'Exploration*, 10 (1880).
    (See also Non-governmental Archive Collections.)
Gordon, Charles (see Hill, G.B.).
Graham, D., "Report on manners, customs and superstitions of people of
    Shoa," *Journal of Asiatic Society of Bengal*, 12 (1843).
    Glimpses of Abyssinia, Lady Erskine (ed.) (London, 1867).
La Grande Encylopédie, 1896-1902 (Paris, 1903). See entry on Menilek.

Grazioli, F., "Onoranze abissine alla salma di Toselli," *L'Avvenire*, 30 August 1897.

Greenfield, R., *Ethiopia* (Pall Mall, London, 1965).

Griaule, M., *Le livre de recettes d'un dabtara abyssin* (Paris, 1930).

"Mythes, croyances et coutumes du Begamder (Abyssinie)," *JA*, 35 (1928).

Guébrè Sellassié, *Chronique du règne de Ménélik II*, 2 vols. (Paris, 1930, 1931). Trans. into French by Tesfa Sellassie, published and annotated by Maurice de Coppet.

Guida dell'Africa Orientale Italiana (Milan, 1938).

Guidi, Ignazio, "La chiesa Abissinia e la chiesa russa," *NA*, 26: 3 (16 April 1890).

"La chiesa Abissinia," *OM*, 2 (1922-3).

Proverbi, strofe e racconti abissini (RAL, Rome, 1894).

"Proverbi abissini," *OM* (April 1894).

"Proverbi, strofe e favole abissine," *GSA*, 5 (1891).

"Leggende storiche di Abissinia," *RSO*, 1 (1907).

La Guerra Italo-Abissinia Illustrata (1 February-August 1896, Milan).

Haile Gabriel Dagne, "The letters of Emperor Teodros to Itege Yetemegnu," *EO*, 10: 1 (1972).

"The Gebzenna Charter, 1894," *JES*, 10: 1 (1972).

Haile-Michael Misginna, "Betrothal and marriage customs in Endärta," *BESAA*, 8 (July 1958).

Haile Selassie, *My Life and Ethiopia's Progress, 1892-1937*. Trans. and annotated by E. Ullendorff from the Amharic published in AA, 1973-4 (London, New York, OUP, 1976).

Hailu Gabre-Hiot, "Omens in Ethiopia," *BESAA*, 8 (July 1956).

Hallé, Clifford, *To Menelik in a Motor Car* (London, 1913).

Hamilton, David, "Schedule of International Agreements relating to the Boundaries of Ethiopia," *EO*, 16: 2 (1973).

Hans, A., "L'armée de Ménélik," *RDM* (15 June 1896).

Harbeson, J., "Afar Pastoralists in Transition and the Ethiopian Revolution," *JAS* (UCLA) 2 (1978).

Harris, W.C., *The Highlands of Ethiopia*, 3 vols. (London, 1844), reprinted (Gregg, Farnborough, 1968).

Hartmann, R., *Abyssinien und die übrigen gebiete der Ostküste Afrikas* (Leipzig, 1883).

Hentze, Willy, *Am Hofe des Kaisers Menelik von Abessinien* (Leipzig, 1908).

Heruy Welde Selasse, novellas trans. by J.L. Moreno in *OM* (1932 and 1933).

Ye-heywet Tarik (A history for posterity — biographies) (AA, 1922-3).

Notes courtesy of Peter Garretson.

(See Fusella.)

Hesseltine, W.B. and Wolf, Hazel C., *The Blue and the Gray on the Nile*

(U. of Chicago, 1961).

Heughlin, T. von, "Bruchstuche aus einer Reise in Abyssinien," *Ausland*, 26 (1853).

Hill, G.B. (ed.), *Colonel Gordon in Central Africa, 1874-1879* (London, 1881).

Hoben, Susan J., "Amhara verbal behavior: a commentary," *AL*, 18: 8 (November 1976).

Hoben, Allan, *Land Tenure Among the Amhara of Ethiopia* (U. of Chicago, 1973).

Hohler, Thomas, *Diplomatic Petrel* (London, 1942).

Holland, T.J. and Hozier, H.M., *Record of Expedition to Abyssinia*, 2 vols. (War Office, London, 1870).

Holtz, Arnold, *Im Auto zu Kaiser Menelik* (Berlin, 1908).

Hosken, Fran P., *Genital Mutilation of Women in Africa* (MAL, Caltech, 1976).

The Hosken Report: genital/sexual mutilation of females (WINN, 1979).

Huntingford, G.W.B., *The Land Charters of Northern Ethiopia* (IES, AA, 1965).

Ilg, Alfred, "Die äthiopische Heeresorganisazion," *Schweizerische Monatschrift für offiziere aller Waffen*, 8: 4 (1896).

L'Afrique Explorée et Civilisée, 13: 3 (March 1893), note on Ilg. (See Keller and Loepfe.)

"The Italians at Kassala," *Saturday Review*, 78 (28 July 1894).

Jarosseau, A., (letter), *MC* (1 July 1910).

Jennings, J.W. and Addison, C., *With the Abyssinians in Somaliland* (London, 1905).

Jesman, C., *The Russians in Ethiopia* (London, 1958).

"The Tragedy of Meqdela," *EO*, 10: 2 (1966).

Jonquière, C. de la, *Les Italiens en Erythrée* (Paris, 1897).

Jonveaux, Emile, *Two Years in East Africa* (London, 1875).

Jousseaume, F., "Sur l'infibulation ou mutilation des organs génitaux de la femme chez les peuples de la Mer Rouge et du Golfe d'Aden," *Revue d'Anthropologie*, 4 (1889).

Impressions de voyages en Apharras, 2 vols. (Paris, 1914).

Kane, T.L., *Ethiopian Literature in Amharic* (Wiesbaden, 1975).

Katz, R., *Fall of the House of Savoy* (Macmillan, New York, 1971).

Katznelson, I.S., "Alexander Bulatovich: man of unusual destiny," *Russia and Africa*, 175-86 (Africa Institute, Moscow, 1966).

Kebede Tessema, *Ye-tarik Mastawesha* (historical memoir) (AA, 1969-70).

Kebre Negest (trans. by E.A.W. Budge as *The Queen of Sheba and her only* son Menylek, London, 1922).

Keller, Conrad, *Alfred Ilg; sein Leben und sein Wirken* (Leipzig, 1918).

Kifle Widajo, "Wedding Customs among the Amhara," *BESAA*, 2 (December 1953).

Klobukowski, A., "La Question de l'Abyssinie," *La Revue de Paris*, 18 (15 September 1926).

Kolmodin, J., *Traditions di Tsazzega et Hazzega* (Upsala, 1912, 1913, 1916).

Krapf, J.L., *Travels, Researches and Missionary Labours* (London, 1860).

Krezeczunowicz, G., "The Nature of Marriage under the Ethiopian Civil Code," *JAL*, 11 (1967).

Kulmer, K.M., *Im Reiche Kaiser Meneliks* (Leipzig, 1910).

Lande, L.L., "Un voyageur français dans l'Ethiopie méridionale" (papers of Pierre Arnoux), *RDM* (15 December 1878 and 15 January 1879).

Landini, L., *Due anni col Marchese Antinori* (Città di Castello, 1884).

Lange, Werner, *Domination and Resistance; narrative songs of the Kafa Highlands*, monograph 8 (ASC, MSU, 1979).

Langer, William, *Encyclopedia of World History* (Houghton-Mifflin, Boston, 1968).

Lauribar, Paul de (pseud.), *Douze ans en Abyssinie* (Paris, 1898).

Lefebvre, M. Th., *Voyage en Abyssinie*, 6 vols. (Paris, 1845-9).

Leiris, Michael, "Le Culte des Zars à Gondar," *Aethiopica* (1933).

Lejean, G., *Voyage en Abyssinie exécuté de 1862 à 1864* (Paris, 1872), based on articles in *TM* 1864-7.

   Théodore II, le nouvel empire d'Abyssinie et les intérêts français dans le sud de la Mer Rouge (Paris, 1865).

Lemmi, F., *Lettere e diari d'Africa* (Rome, 1937).

Leontiev, N., *Provinces Equatoriales d'Abyssinie: expédition du dédjaz comte N. de Léontieff* (Paris, 1900).

   (See Elets.)

Le Roux, Hugues, "Voyage au Ouallega — itinéraire d'Addis Ababa au Nil Bleu," *Géographie*, 4 (1901).

   Ménélik et Nous (Paris, 1904).

   Chez la Reine de Saba (Paris, 1914).

Leslau, Wolf, "Ethiopic proverbs in Chaha," *Word*, 5 (August 1949).

   and C. Leslau, *African Poems and Love Songs* (Peter Pauper, 1970).

Levine, Donald, *Wax and Gold* (U. of Chicago, 1974).

   Greater Ethiopia (U. of Chicago, 1974).

   "Concept of Masculinity in Ethiopian Culture," *IJSP*, 12 (1966).

Libro Verde, XV, Etiopia (Ministero degli Affari Esteri, 1890).

Littmann, Enno, *Publications of the Princeton Expedition to Abyssinia*, 4 vols. (Leyden, 1910-15).

Loepfe, W., *Alfred Ilg und die Äthiopische Eisenbahn* (Atlantis Verlag,

Zurich, 1975).

Loring, W.W., *A Confederate Soldier in Egypt* (New York, 1884).

Ludolf, J., *A New History of Ethiopia* (London, 1862; new edn. Sasor, London, 1982).

Macaire, Mgr., "Mon voyage en Abyssinie," *BSKG*, 4 (1897).

Mahteme Sellassie Wolde Maskal, "The Land System of Ethiopia," *EO*, 1: 9 (1957).

Zeker Neger (Past Things) (AA, 2nd edn., 1970).

"A study of the Ethiopian culture of horse-names" (trans. Bairu Tafla), *JES*, 7: 2 (1960).

"Portrait rétrospectif d'un gentilhomme éthiopien," *P. 3rd ICES*, 3 (AA, 1970).

Maindron, M., "Ménélik et son empire," *La Revue de Paris* (15 June 1896).

Mantegazza, Vico, *La Guerra in Africa* (Florence, 1896). 3rd edn. 1906.

"Dopo la morte di Makonnen: l'imperatrice Taitu e rivalità Anglo-Tedesca," *Corriere delle Sera*, 12 June 1906.

Menelik, l'Italia e l'Etiopia (Milan, 1910).

Gli Italiani in Africa — l'Assedio di Macallè (Florence, 1896).

Marcus, H., *The Life and Times of Menelik II* (Oxford, Clarendon, 1975).

"The first U.S. Mission to Ethiopia," *EO*, 2: 3 (February 1957).

The Modern History of Ethiopia and the Horn of Africa: a select annotated bibliography (Hoover, Stanford, 1972).

Marein, Nathan, *The Ethiopian Empire; Federation and Laws* (Rotterdam, 1954), excerpt "Laws Affecting Women," *EO*, 3 (1957).

Martial de Salviac, Father, *Une Peuple Antique ou une colonie gauloise au pays de Ménélik* (2nd edn., Paris, 1902).

"Mission des Galla," *MC*, 2 (1901).

Martini, F., *Il Diario Eritreo, 1897-1906*, 4 vols. (Florence, 1946).

Martini, Sebastiano, *Ricordi ed escursioni in Africa dal 1878-1881* (Florence, 1886).

Marshall, H. and Stock, M., *Ira Aldridge, the Negro Tragedian* (S. Illinois U. Press, 1968).

Mashcov, V., "Il secondo viaggio in Abissinia del Mashcov, 1891-92," *BSGI*, ser. 3, 7 (1894). Trans. from *Novoe Vremia*.

Massaia, Gugliemo, Father, *I Miei Trenta-cinque anni di missione nell'alta Etiopia*, 12 vols. (Rome, 1885-95). 2nd edn., 1921, in 2 vols.

Mekonnen Endalkatchew, *Taitu Bitoul*, in Amharic (private printing, 1957).

Abyssinian Refugee: why was the Lion of Judah defeated? (Jerusalem, 1939).

Melkam Bet Seboch (Good Families) (AA, 1957).

Melli, B., *La colonia Eritrea* (Parma, 1899).

Menelik II Memorial Mausoleum, pamphlet (AA, 12 December 1962).

Menghistu Lemma, "Snatch and Run, or marriage by abduction," *EO*, 7: 4 (part 2) (1964).

and Pankhurst, Sylvia, "On the eve of the battle," *EO*, 1: 11 (1957).

Mérab, Paul, Dr., *Impressions d'Ethiopie*, 3 vols. (Paris, 1921, 1922, 1929).

Médecins et Médecine en Ethiopie (Paris, 1912).

(See Non-governmental Archive Collections.)

Messing, Simon, "Group Therapy and Social Status in the Zar Cult," *Culture and Mental Health* (New York, 1949).

"The non-verbal language of the Ethiopian toga," *Anthropos*, 55 (1960).

"Ethiopian folktales ascribed to the late 19th century Amhara wit, Aleka Gabre Hanna," *J. American Folklore*, 70 (1957).

Metodio da Nembro, Father, *La Missione dei minori Cappuccini in Eritrea, 1894-1952* (Rome, 1953).

Michel, Charles, *Mission de Bonchamps, vers Fachoda* (Paris, 1900).

Mikael Hailu, *L'Ethiopia descritta da un Etiope: usi natalize nell'Amara* (Topological Tracts, Naples, 1890).

"The Mission to Menelek," *The Spectator*, 27 February 1897.

Moltedo, G., *L'Assedio di Maccalè* (Rome, 1901).

Mondon-Vidailhet, Casimir, *Le Temps*, 1 May 1892-2 April 1910.

"La rhétorique éthiopienne," *JA*, 9-10 (1907).

"Proverbes abyssins," *JA*, 3-4 (1904).

"Une tradition éthiopienne," *RS*, 12 (1904).

(See Welde Maryam.)

Monfreid, H., *Ménélik tel qu'il fut* (Paris, 1954).

Montandon, G., *Au Pays Ghimmira* (Paris, 1913).

Moorehead, Alan, *The Blue Nile* (New York, 1962).

Moreno, M.M., "La cronaca al dabtera 'Zaneb,'" *RSE*, 2 (1942).

Raccoltà di Qéné (Rome, 1935).

Cent fables amhariques mises en écrit par le dabtara Kenfe (Paris, 1948).

Morié, L.J., *Histoire de l'Ethiopie*, 2 vols. (Paris, 1904).

Les civilisations africaines (Paris, 1904).

Mosley, Leonard, *Haile Selassie, the Conquering Lion* (London, 1964).

Nabokov, Vladimir, *Eugene Onegin*, 4 vols. (New York, 1964).

Negussay Ayele, "Rhetoric and reality in the making of boundaries on the Horn of Africa in 1897," *EO*, 13: 1 (1970).

Neue Zuercher Zeitung, 10 September 1903.

New York Times, 22 March, 4 May 1896.

New York Herald, 23 October 1905.

Nicholson, E.R., *A Toy for the Emperor* (London, 1965).

Nicoletti-Altimari, A., *Fra gli Abissini* (Rome, 1897).

"Tradizione e leggende abissini," *Rivista d'Italia*, 1 (1903).

"Da Assab a Cassala" and "Da Cassala a Adua," *RMI* (1895).

Noailles, Vicomte de, "Mgr. Macaire: création du partiarcat copte, ambassade auprès de Ménélik en 1896," *Le Correspondant*, 188 (July-September 1897).

"Les occupations de Ménélik," *TVM*, 15 (1909).

Offeio, Father, *Dall'Eritrea; lettere sul costumi abissini* (Rome, 1904).

"Proverbi Abissini in lingua tigray," *Anthropos*, 1 (1906), 3 (1908).

Olmstead, Judith, "Ethiopia's Artful Weavers,"*NG*, 143: 1 (1973).

Orléans, Duc Henri d', *Une Visite à l'Empereur Ménélik* (Paris, 1898).

Pankhurst, Richard, *Economic History of Ethiopia, 1899-1935* (HSIU, 1968).

"Special Issue on the battle of Adowa," *EO*, 1: 11 (1957).

"The Beginnings of Modern Medicine in Ethiopia," *EO*, 9: 2 (1965).

"Ethiopian monetary and banking innovations in the nineteenth and early twentieth centuries," *JES*, 1: 2 (1963).

(ed.), *The Ethiopian Royal Chronicles* (OUP, AA, Nairobi, Lusaka, London, 1967).

"Firearms in Ethiopian history, 1800-1935," *EO*, 6: 2 (1962).

"Foundation of Addis Ababa," *EO*, 6: 1 (1962).

"Menilek and Addis Ababa," *JAH*, 2: 1 (1969).

"The Great Ethiopian Famine of 1888-1892," *JHM*, 21 (April, July 1966).

"An Historical Examination of Traditional Ethiopian Medicine and Surgery," *Ethiopian Medical Journal*, 3: 4 (July 1965).

"History of Ethiopian-Armenian Relations, *Revue d'Etudes Arméniennes*, 12 (1977), 13 (1978-9).

"Ras Makonnen visit to Europe, 1902," *EO*, 14: 4 (1971).

"Menilek and the utilisation of foreign skills," *JES*, 5: 1 (1967).

"Misoneism and innovation in Ethiopian history," *EO*, 7: 4 (1964).

"Introduction to Pushkin's Ethiopian Ancestry," *EO*, 1: 8 (1957).

"The Saint Simonians and Ethiopia," *P. 3rd ICES*, 1 (AA, 1969).

"Tribute, taxation and government revenue in 19th and early 20th century Ethiopia," *JES*, 5: 2 (1967), 6: 1 (1968), 7: 2 (1969).

"William H. Ellis," *EO*, 15: 2 (1972).

Pàntano, G., *Ventitre anni di vita Africana* (Florence, 1932).

Pariset, Dante, *Al Tempo di Menilek* (Milan, 1937). Memoirs of Stévenin.

Parisis, N., letter to *Nea Ephemeris* (Athens, 28 February 1886).

L'Abissinia (trans. from Greek) (Milan, 1888).

Parkyns, Mansfield, *Life in Abyssinia*, 2 vols. (London, 1851).

Partini, F., *I Nostri Ufficiali d'Africa* (Rome, 1905).

Paulos Milkias, "Traditional Institutions and Traditional Elites: the role of education in the Ethiopian body politic," *ASR*, 19: 3 (1976).

Pearce, Nathaniel, *The Life and Adventures of Nathaniel Pearce*, 2 vols. (London, 1831).

Pease, A.E., *Travel and Sport in Africa*, 3 vols. (London, 1902).
"An Audience with Menilek," *Evening Standard*, 7 May 1901.
Pedersen, Kirsten, *The History of the Ethiopian Community in the Holy Land from the time of Emperor Tewodros II till 1974* (Ecumenical Institute for Theological Research, Tantur, 1983).
Pedrazzi, A., "Rievocazione sulla tragica fine del Conte Augusto Salimbeni," *La Settimane Modenese*, 14 December 1935.
Perini, Ruffilo, *Di qua dal Marèb* (Florence, 1905).
Perruchon, J., "Légendes et le Règne de Lebna Dengel," *RS*, 1 (1893), 5 (1898).
"Le règne de Galâwdêwos," *RS*, 2 (1894).
"Le règne de Iyasu I," *RS* (1901).
· *Le Petit Journal*, 9 February and 29 March 1896.
Pétridès, Pierre, *Le Héros d'Adoua* (Plon, Paris, 1963).
Philippos, Abuna, *Know Jerusalem* (Berhanena Selam, AA, 1972).
Phillips, Hoffman, *Abyssinian Memories* (privately printed, Santa Barbara, California, 1948).
Pianavia-Vivaldi, Rosalia, *Tre Anni in Eritrea* (Milan, 1901).
Piazza, G., *Alla Corte di Menelik; lettere dall'Etiopia* (Ancona, 1912).
Pinon, René, "La résurrection d'un état africain," *RDM*, 2 (1 and 15 April 1901).
Plowden, Walter, *Travels in Abyssinia* (London, 1868).
Pollera, Alberto, *L'Abissinia di ieri; osservazioni e ricordi* (Rome, 1940).
La Battaglia di Adua del 1 Marzo 1896 narrata nei luoghi ove ful combattuta (Florence, 1928).
La Donna in Etiopia (Monografie e rapporti coloniali, Rome, 1922).
Poncins, Edmond de, "The Menilek Myth," *Nineteenth Century*, 265 (March 1899).
"Voyage au Choa," *BSG*, 19 (1898).
Portal, Gerald, *My Mission to Abyssinia* (London, 1892). Reissue of private printing, 1889.
Powell-Cotton, P.H.G., *A Sporting Trip Through Abyssinia* (London, 1902).
Prorok, Khun de, *Dead Men Do Tell Tales* (New York, 1942).
Prouty, Chris, and Rosenfeld, Eugene, *The Historical Dictionary of Ethiopia* (Scarecrow Press, 1981).
Puglisi, G., *Chi e? dell'Eritrea* (Asmara, 1952).

Ragazzi, V., letters in *BSGI*, 22 (1885); 23 (1886); 24 (1887); 25 (1888).
"Relazione sul viaggio dallo Scioa ad Harar," *BSGI*, 1 (1888).
Raimondo, G.B., *L'assedio di Macallè* (Finalborgo, 1901).
Rassam, Hormuzd, *Narrative of the British mission to Theodore*, 2 vols. (London, 1869).
Remond, G., *La route de l'Abbai noir* (Paris, 1924).
Ricci, Lanfranco, "Vita di Waletta Petros," *CSCO* (Louvain, 1970).

Right, M.V., "Russian Red Cross Expedition to Ethiopia," *Russia and Africa*, 167-74 (Africa Institute, Moscow, 1966).

Riguzzi, Alfonso, *Macallè, diario; Quarantacinque giorni di assedio* (Palermo, 1901).

Rochet d'Héricourt, *Second voyage sur les deux rives de la Mer Rouge, dans le pays des Adels et le royaume de Choa* (Paris, 1846).

Rodd, James (Baron Rennell), *Social and Diplomatic Memories, 1894-1901* (London, 1923).

Rodinson, M., *Magie, Médecine et Possession à Gondar* (Paris, 1967).

Rosa, Ottorino, *L'impero del leone di Guida* (Brescia, 1913).

Rosen, Felix, *Eine Deutsche Gesandtschaft in Abessinien* (Leipzig, 1907).

Rosenfeld, Chris Prouty, "Eight Ethiopian women of the *Zemene Mesafint*, 1769-1855," *NAS*, 1: 2 (1979).

   The Medical History of Menilek II, 1844-1913 (MAL, October 1978).

   The Chronology of Menilek II of Ethiopia (ASC, MSU, 1976).

Rossetti, Carlo, *Storia Diplomatica dell'Etiopia durante il regno di Menelik* (Turin, 1910)..

Rossi, Adolfo, "La Incerta Politica Africana," *NA*, 156 (16 November 1897).

Rubenson, Sven, *The Survival of Ethiopian Independence* (Heinemann Educational Books, London, 1976).

   King of Kings, Tewodros of Ethiopia (HSIU/OUP, 1966).

   Wichale XVII; the attempt to establish a protectorate over Ethiopia (HSIU, 1964).

   "Professor Giglio, Antonelli and Article XVII of the Treaty of Wichale," *JAH*, 7: 3 (1966).

   "The Lion of the Tribe of Judah," *JES*, 3: 2 (1965).

   "The Adwa Peace Treaty of 1884," *P. 3rd ICES*, 1 (AA, 1969).

Salbucci, Settimio, *Taitu* (Vantage Press, New York, 1961).

Salimbeni, Augusto, "Tre Anni di Lavoro nel Gojjam," Extr. *BSGI*, 11 (1886).

   "Diario d'un pioniere africano," *NA*, 384 (16 March, 1 and 16 April 1936). (See Zaghi.)

Sambon, Luigi, "Etiopia militare," *BSAI*, 9 (1890).

Sangiorgi, G.M., "Un problema da evitare: il Meticciato," *ATCSC*, 2 (Rome, 1937).

Sapelli, A., "Ricordi di un vecchio soldato d'Africa: 1887-1896," *NA* (March-April 1935, May-June 1935).

Savoia, S., "Proverbi Tigrini," *RSE*, 3 (1943).

Schneider, R., and Vanderlinden, J., "A propos d'un manuscrit de Casimir Mondon-Vidailhet addressé à Ménélik II," *JES*, 7: 2 (1969).

Scholler, H., "Letters Exchanged between Ethiopian and German Emperors," *P. 5th ICES* (Chicago, 1979).

Schweinfurth, G., "Einige Mitteilungen über seinen dreijährigen Besuch in der Colonia Eritrea," *VGEB*, 19 (1892).

Selamu Bekele and Vanderlinden, J., "Introducing the Ethiopian Law Archives: some documents on the first Ethiopian cabinet," *JEL*, 4: 2 (1967).

Seltzer, R., *The Name of Hero* (Houghton-Mifflin, Boston, 1981).

Le Semeur d'Ethiopie (A Nos Chers Bienfaiteurs) (newsletter of Lazarist Mission in Ethiopia). 1897-1910 on microfilm at MSU.

Shchusev, P.V., "To the Source of the Blue Nile" (trans. of Russian title), *Geog. Izviestiva*, 36 (1900).

Shinn, David, "A Survey of American-Ethiopian Relations prior to the Italian Occupation," *EO*, 14:4 (1971).

Silberman, Leo, "Why the Haud was Ceded," *CEA*, 2 (1961).

Singer, Norman, "The dissolution of religious marriage in Ethiopia," *JEL*, 4 (1967).

Skinner, Robert, *Abyssinia of today* (London, New York, 1906).

Soleillet, Paul, *Obok, le Choa, le Kaffa* (Paris, 1886).

Voyages en Ethiopie (January 1882-October 1884) (Rouen, 1886).

The Spectator, London, January-June 1896.

La Stampa, Turin, 1895-8.

Stanley, Henry M., *Coomassie and Magdala* (London, 1874).

Steffanson, B.G. and Starrett, R.K. (eds.), *Documents on Ethiopian Politics*, v. 1 (Documentary Publications, Salisbury, N.C., 1976-7).

Stern, Henry A., *Wanderings Among the Falashas in Abyssinia* (London, 1862).

The Captive Missionary (London, c. 1870).

Stévenin memoirs (see Pariset).

Strelcyn, Stefan, "Les Médecines du Begamder et du Tchelgas (Ethiopie) d'Abbabä Garrad," *Africana Bulletin* (Warsaw, 1966).

"Un traité éthiopien d'hygiène et de diététique," *Africana Bulletin* (Warsaw, 1964).

"Les traités médicaux éthiopiens," *CEA*, 2 (1961).

Médecines et plantes d'Ethiopie (Warsaw, 1968).

"Les écrits médicaux éthiopiens," *JES*, 3: 2 (1965).

Sumner, Claude, "Ethiopian Philosophy, 'The Book of the Wise Philosophers,'" *Abba Salama*, 2 (1971), 6 (1975).

Sylvain, Bénito, "L'accord nécessaire entre des blancs et des noirs en Afrique," *BSGL*, 45 (March 1906).

Taddesse Tamrat, *Church and State in Ethiopia, 1270-1527* (Oxford, Clarendon, 1972).

Taddesse Tewolde, *Ye-Itege Taytu Betul* (Kuraz, AA, 1974 E.C.).

"Taitou, the Abyssinian Empress," *Harpers Weekly*, 40: 318 (4 April 1896).

Taurin de Cahagne, Father, letters of 1866-77 published in *Le Semeur d'Ethiopie* (March 1908; January, July, August and November 1909; February and May 1911).

Tawrus, Ramzi, *Kitab Hadir al-habasa wa mustaqbiliha* (Cairo, c. 1906) (notes of Peter Garretson).

Tedeschi, S., "Profilo storico di Dayr es Sultan," *JES*, 2: 2 (1954).

Tedone, G., *Angerà: i ricordi di un prigionero di Menelik dopo il disastro di Adua* (Rome, 1915; reprint Giordano, Milan, 1964).

Le Temps, Paris, 1890-1911.

Terrefe Ras-work, "Birth Customs of the Amharas of Sawa," *BESAA* (December 1957).

Teshome Wagaw, *Education in Ethiopia: prospect and retrospect* (U. Mich., Ann Arbor, 1979).

Torrey, E. Fuller, "The Zar Cult in Ethiopia," *IJSP*, 13: 3 (1967).

Traversi, Leopoldo, *Let-Marefià* (Milan, 1931).

    L'Italia e l'Etiopia, da Assab a Ualual (Bologna, 1935).

    "Lo Scioa ed i paesi limitrofi," *BSGI*, 26 (1889).

    Letters from Ethiopia in *BSGI* 23 (1886); 24 (1887); 25 (1888); 26 (1889); 30 (1893); 31 (1894) and *BSAI*, 6 (1887).

    "Gli eredi di Menelik," *RPL*, 6 (15 March 1902).

    "Il conte Pietro Antonelli," *RCI*, 9: 1 (1935).

    "Il dottore Raffaele Alfieri," *RCI*, 9: 2 (1935).

    "Un pionieri Pietro Felter," *RCI*, 10: 2 (1936).

Trimingham, J.S., *Islam in Ethiopia* (2nd edn. Cass, London, 1965).

Tsehai Berhane Selassie, "An Ethiopian Medical Textbook," *JES*, 9: 1 (1971).

    "The life and career of Däjazmač Balča Aba Näfso," *JES*, 9: 2 (1971).

Tubiana, Joseph, "Quatre généalogies royales éthiopiennes," *CEA*, 2 (1962).

Ullendorff, Edward, *The Ethiopians* (OUP, 1960).

    "Queen Victoria's Phonograph message to the Emperor Menelik of Ethiopia," *BSOAS*, 32 (1969).

    "Some early Amharic letters," *BSOAS*, 35: 2 (1972).

Van Luijk (see Giel).

Vanderheym, J., *Une Expédition avec le négous Ménélik* (Paris, 1897).

Vannutelli, L. and Citerni, C., "La fine della spedizione Bottego," *Rivista Geografica Italiana*, 4 (1897).

    L'Omo (Milan, 1899).

Veitz, Sophie, *Views in Central Abyssinia* (London, 1868).

Verzin, J.A., "Sequelae of Female Circumcision," *Tropical Medicine*, 5 (October 1975).

"Viaggio d'esplorazione d'un abissino tra l'Aussa e le Scioa," *BSGI*, 24 (1887).

    Unattributed, it is by Yosef of Let-Marefià.

Vigneras, Sylvain, *Une Mission Française en Abyssinie* (Paris, 1897).

Vigoni, Pippo, *Abissinia* (Milan, 1881).

Vitalien, Joseph, *Pour l'indépendence de l'Ethiopie* (Paris, 1919).

Vivian, Herbert, *Abyssinia* (London, 1901).

Vollbrecht, Hans, *Im Reiche des Negus Negeste, Menelik II* (Stuttgart, Berlin, Leipzig, 1906).

Waldmeier, T., *Autobiography of Theophilus Waldmeier* (London, 1887).

Walker, C.H., *The Abyssinian At Home* (London, 1933).

Welcome to Ethiopia, Joel Rasmussen (ed.) (AA, n.d., c. 1966).

Welde Maryam, Aleqa, *Chronique de Théodros II, roi des rois d'Ethiopie* (Paris, 1905). Trans. C. Mondon-Vidailhet. English trans. by Weld-Blundell in *JRAS,* 6 (1906-7).

Wellby, M.A., *Twixt Sirdar and Menelik* (London, New York, 1901).

Work, Ernest, *Ethiopia, A Pawn in European Diplomacy* (New York, 1936).

Wurtz, R., "Hygiène publique et privée en Abyssinie," *La Semaine Médicale* (7 December 1898).

Wylde, A., *Modern Abyssinia* (London, 1901).

'83-87 in the Soudan (London, 1888, reprinted NUP, 1969).

Yaltasamma (pseud. for Antonin Goguyer), "Les Amis de Menilek II," *Dépêche Coloniale,* 33:4 (1899).

Young, E.H., "Female circumcision," *Nursing Mirror* (12 March 1949).

Zaghi, C., *Crispi e Menelich nel diario inedito del Conte Augusto Salimbeni* (Turin, 1956).

I Russi in Etiopia, 2 vols. (Guida, Naples, 1972).

"I fratelli Naretti," *RCI,* 9 (1935).

"La missione del Maggiore Salsa al campo sciona prima di Adua," *RCI,* 10 (1936).

"La conquista di Cassala," *NA* (September-October 1934).

"L'Italia e l'Etiopia alla vigilia di Adua nei dispacci segreti di Luigi Capucci," *GAAI,* 4: 2 (1941).

"Lo sbarco italiano a Zeila e l'atteggiamento inglese durante la campagna del 1895-96," *RCI,* 9: 2 (1935).

"La missione Maconnen in Italia," *RCI,* 10: 1 (1935).

Zeneb, Aleqa (see Moreno).

Zervos, Adrien, *L'Empire d'Ethiopie, le miroir de l'Ethiopie moderne 1906-1936* (Alexandria, Egypt, 1936).

Zewde Gabre-Sellassie, *Yohannes IV of Ethiopia* (Oxford, Clarendon, 1975).

Zintgraff, A., *Der Tod des Löwen von Juda* (Berlin, 1932).

Index